DE 63018-5

Social Capital in Europe: Similarity of Countries and Diversity of People?

International Comparative Social Studies

Editor-in-Chief
Dr. Mehdi P. Amineh
Amsterdam School for Social Sciences Research (ASSR),
University of Amsterdam and International Institute for
Asian Studies (IIAS), University of Leiden

Editorial Board
Dr. Sjoerd Beugelsdijk, Radboud University, Nijmegen,
the Netherlands
Dr. Simon Bromley, Open University, UK
Prof. dr. Harald Fuhr, University of Potsdam, Germany
Prof. dr. Gerd Junne, University of Amsterdam, the Netherlands
Dr. Tak-Wing Ngo, University of Leiden, the Netherlands
Prof. dr. Mario Rutten, University of Amsterdam, the Netherlands

Advisory board
W.A. Arts, University College Utrecht, the Nertherlands
Chan Kwok-bun, Hong Kong Baptist University, Hong Kong
S.N. Eisenstadt, Jerusalem, Israel
L. Hantrais, Loughborough University, UK
G.C.M. Lieten, University of Amsterdam, the Netherlands
L. Visano, York University, Canada

VOLUME 16

Social Capital in Europe: Similarity of Countries and Diversity of People?

Multi-level analyses of the European Social Survey 2002

Edited by

Heiner Meulemann

BRILL

LEIDEN · BOSTON
2008

This book is printed on acid-free paper.

Library of Congress Cataloging-in-Publication Data

A C.I.P. record for this book is available from the Library of Congress

ISSN 1568-4474
ISBN 978 90 04 16362 1

Copyright 2008 by Koninklijke Brill NV, Leiden, The Netherlands.
Koninklijke Brill NV incorporates the imprints Brill, Hotei Publishing,
IDC Publishers, Martinus Nijhoff Publishers and VSP.

All rights reserved. No part of this publication may be reproduced, translated,
stored in a retrieval system, or transmitted in any form or by any means, electronic,
mechanical, photocopying, recording or otherwise, without prior written permission
from the publisher.

Authorization to photocopy items for internal or personal use is granted by
Koninklijke Brill NV provided that the appropriate fees are paid directly to
The Copyright Clearance Center, 222 Rosewood Drive, Suite 910,
Danvers, MA 01923, USA.
Fees are subject to change.

PRINTED IN THE NETHERLANDS

CONTENTS

Chapter One   Introduction 1
Heiner Meulemann

PART ONE
CAUSES OF SOCIAL CAPITAL

Chapter Two   Does the State Affect the Informal Connections between its Citizens? New Institutionalist Explanations of Social Participation in Everyday Life 41
Tom Van der Meer, Peer Scheepers and Manfred te Grotenhuis

Chapter Three   Is Altruism More Effective Where it is Required More? Collectivity-Orientation and Involvement in Interest, Issue and Religious Associations 73
Heiner Meulemann

Chapter Four   What Makes People Trust in Their Fellow Citizens? 103
Katja Neller

Chapter Five   What Determines Citizens' Normative Conception of Their Civic Duties 135
Bas Denters and Henk van der Kolk

Chapter Six   Why Television Does Erode Social Capital and Why Newspaper Reading Does Not 159
Rüdiger Schmitt-Beck

PART TWO
CONSEQUENCES OF SOCIAL CAPITAL

Chapter Seven   Social Capital and Political Involvement 191
Jan W. Van Deth

Chapter Eight   Social Capital and Political Trust 219
  Oscar W. Gabriel and Melanie Walter-Rogg

Chapter Nine   Explaining Level and Equality of Political
  Participation. The Role of Social Capital, Socioeconomic
  Modernity, and Political Institutions 251
  Edeltraud Roller and Tatjana Rudi

Chapter Ten   Social Capital and Empowerment at the
  Work Place 285
  Heiner Meulemann

CONCLUSION

Chapter Eleven   Retrospect and Prospect 313
  Max Kaase

Index 321

CHAPTER ONE

INTRODUCTION[1]

Heiner Meulemann

European history is a history of nations. The great caesuras of European history—1648, 1815, 1919, 1945 and 1989—have settled hot and cold wars, realigned borders between nations, and created new nations. Each nation has its distinct history, its own constitution, political tradition, dominant Christian denomination, folklore, and—mostly—language. Moreover, this nation specific heritage still strongly forms the ways people think and act. As of today, cross-national survey research has revealed an enormous diversity of attitudes and behaviors between European countries.

This volume is devoted to cross-national survey research and focuses on a single concept, *social capital*—which appears as the *first* part of the book's title. Social capital comprises a person's social relations in the sphere between private life and organizations, which is called the civil society. It is held by persons, but made out of relations between persons, within societies small and large. It may be distributed unevenly amongst persons so that uneven levels between countries result as well. It may be caused by attributes of persons, such as education or media use, and by characteristics of societies, such as affluence or inequality. In addition, it may have consequences for persons as well as for countries.

Different levels, causes, and consequences of social capital between countries reflect the differences of their constitutions. Constitutions govern the social life in political, economic and cultural organizations and are not directly concerned with the daily life of people. Even if a constitution is not a blueprint for organizational life, it draws the boundaries and provides the opportunities, which create the differences between countries. If a political party needs at least five percent of the

---

[1] Jaclyn Verghis has very much improved the English in all chapters. Jan Malguth and Johannes Bannwitz have helped me in the editing process. I am very grateful to them. Also, I am grateful to Hans-Jürgen Andreß, Tilo Beckers, Katja Neller, Peer Scheepers, Manfred te Grotenhuis, Tom van der Meer and Jan van Deth for helpful comments to the introduction.

vote in order to get its first seat in the Parliament, it is more difficult to establish a new party than if the hurdles are lower. If a law entitles the establishment of workers' councils in firms or grants unions a seat in the boards of firms, unions can become more influential than if there is no such law. If a law grants churches state support in collecting taxes, churches are better off financially than if state and church constitute independent social spheres.

Yet a country's constitution rarely regulates the intermediate sphere of the civil society—just because of its informality.[2] This sphere can develop its own mores and rules, and the diversity of people can be expressed through attitudes and behaviors alike in every country. Therefore, the causes and consequences of social capital may be similar within European countries. To give some examples for similar causes, education may stimulate work in associations, well-being may similarly breed social trust, and reading newspapers may foster political involvement while viewing television may hedge political apathy. To give some examples for similar consequences, good relations with other people may ease political involvement, and being engaged in associations or in unions might help to attain empowerment at the work place. In short, differences between *civil societies* may reflect differences between *societies*—rather than between constitutions.

Thus, social capital is a particularly adequate premise to investigate the question whether a *similarity of countries* is intertwined with a *diversity of people*—which forms the *second* part of the book's title. There are two further reasons to expect this combination. Firstly, the similarity of countries is enhanced because only European countries are analyzed in this volume. European nations share many historical roots: Roman law and Christian churches, the Protestant reformation and the Enlightenment, industrialization and urbanization, bureaucratization and nation building, nationalism and imperialism, secularization and institutional differentiation. Presently, moreover, they share the goal of European unification. These commonalities of the past and the present may form people's characteristics just as strongly as nation specific histories.

---

[2] This does not preclude that governments try to foster the civil society of their countries as the case studies in chapter 8–11 in Hooghe / Stolle (2003), and Stolle (2003: 30–34) in particular show, but throws doubts on the feasibility of such an endeavour. For more references to, and an analysis of, this question see van der Meer et al. (chapter 2).

Secondly, even if no such communalities were at work, the diversity of European countries so readily visible at face value may, at least partly, become spurious when differences between the populations constituting their societies are taken account of. If people from Northern European countries trust each other more in everyday life than people from Southern European countries, is this due to "Northern" and "Southern" traditions or to the facts that mean education is higher in Northern Europe and that education breeds trust? It may be so or it may be not. Yet if the European countries share a history and unite at present, and if some part of the differences reflects population compositions rather than national traditions, one may suspect that European countries in fact engender similar ways of thinking and acting while within each country the people are divided in similar ways.

Whether the similarity of countries and the diversity of people are intertwined, cannot be ascertained by looking at either "level" only. Rather both must be considered in two steps. Country differences must pass the test of different populations. Moreover, if they do, it must be examined how far they can be explained by some cause characterizing the countries. These two steps describe the so-called *multi-level analysis* in a nutshell. It is applied in all the contributions of the book—hence the *subtitle of the book*.

Social capital has become increasingly popular in cross-national survey research at least since the 1990s (van Deth et al. 1999, Dekker / Uslaner 2001, Gabriel et al. 2002, Dekker / van den Broek 2006, Torcal / Montero 2006). To position the present volume within this research, our stance to three questions will be presented in this introduction. What do we understand as social capital? Which kinds of effects on social capital do we investigate? Which methods do we use to investigate it? Finally, the data source and the study design will be introduced.

1. Defining Social Capital: Social Relations as Resources of Actors in Contexts

1.1 *Social Capital: Criteria*

Social capital means many things to many people. Some attribute it to persons, others to groups, organizations, networks, even to societies. For some it comprises capabilities such as "social skills" (Bovenberg 2003: 405, Muffels 2003: 439), attitudes such as trust, and norms or values such as civic morality (Newton 1999); for others it comprises social relations used as resources in purposive action (Lin 2001a, b).[3] Typically, it is defined by its positive functions for a group, as in Putnam's (1993: 167)—almost canonical—definition: social capital "refers to features of social organization, such as trust, norms and networks that can improve the efficiency of society by facilitating coordinated action." I see two ambiguities in this definition, which I will try to disentangle.

Positive and negative functions
Firstly, if the relative clause "that can improve" is taken as an analytical criterion, "features of social organization" are the *genus proximum*, and "improve" is the *differentia specifica* of the definition. Social capital is some *good* feature of organization. Bad, even morally or functionally neutral features cannot become social capital. Thus, the density of a social network is a social capital not per se, but only if it improves cooperation. A climate of trust and the validity of norms in a group are its social capital, but a hostile climate and a high crime rate are not.

However, the same feature of organization may produce goods and evils (Portes 1998: 15–18, Newton 1999: 9, Paldam 2000: 634, Paxton 2002: 269–272, Field 2003: 71–90, Torcal / Montero 2006: 11, van Deth 2006: 103–105). There are virtuous and vicious cycles of interaction in a group. The bureaucratization of a party or a firm may enhance its power, but also its immobility on a political or economic market. The density of a clique may breed trust, but also gossip, resentment, and distrust, depending on who is located at the central "nodes". Therefore, it seems advisable to strip the *differentia specifica* of moral or eu-functional connotations and reduce it to whatever the output is from the interactions in a group. Social capital is a feature of social organization, which facilitates the production of group products, rather than of good products alone. Social capital is "productive", but the product need not be a good one.[4]

---

[3] Problems of the definition and measurement are discussed in Portes (1998), Paldam (2000), Fine (2001), Lin (2001a), Adam / Roncevis (2003), Field (2003), and Halpern (2005). A thematically structured bibliography is found in www.socialcapitalgateway.org/eng-readinglist.htm.

[4] The reference to positive functions more often appears in the political science literature, which looks for the foundations of democracy (van Deth et al. 1999, Newton 2006, van Deth 2006) than in the sociological literature, which is interested in the life chances of actors. Thus, Lin (2001b: 12) defines social capital as "resources embedded in a social structure which are accessed and/or mobilized in purposive action".

Groups and persons
Secondly, "features of social organization" are understood as the collective good of organizations. Organizations can be distinguished by their social capital—just as by their constitution, their function, their structure, or their size. According to this understanding, the grammatical singular "organization" is accidental. Yet it has its own meaning: "organization" is a process sustained by persons. Members of a group establish relations in which they interact, "organize themselves", so that some collective product results.

Thus, the productivity of a network, a climate of trust, and the validity of a norm will result from the interactions between persons. The *productivity* of a network will result from the flow of exchanges between persons with more or less a central position and more or less a benevolent intention. A *climate* of trust in a group is created, if a sufficient number of members reciprocate benevolent actions, keep promises, provide support for others, and are honest; if this number goes down, trust will become increasingly costly and risky, creating a vicious circle which will lead eventually to a climate of distrust. The *validity* of a norm in a group is established when a sufficient number of members adhere to the norm and a sufficient number of members sanction violations of other members; if this number goes down, a vicious circle of deviance and tolerance will be set into motion and the norm will break down (Weber 1980: 16; Axelrod 1984). In brief, the *productivity* of networks will develop from the behavior of its members, the *climate* of trust from trustworthy actions of its members, the *validity* of a norm in a group from the endorsement of the norm among its members. Features of organization are established bottom up from the social positions, the actions and attitudes of its members. Therefore, the *genus proximum* of the definition are not the organizations, but the persons.

In sum, social capital is any property of a group member, which contributes to group outputs—good or bad. However, this definition goes too far in the opposite direction and looses the "social" aspect by including every personal qualification that contributes to group outputs. If inventive or assiduous members contribute more than unimaginative or lethargic ones, one would attribute this surplus to their human or cultural, instead to their social capital. Therefore, the definition should

---

This definition—as the one given here—locates social capital as a means of the actor stemming from its social relations.

be restricted to include only those outputs, which result from group membership. A group is defined by a common interest (Olson 1965). In pursuing this common interest, that is, in producing a group output, members form social relations with each other so that interactions are more densely knit amongst members than with non-members. Thus, not any attribute of a group member develops their social capital, but rather the features, which derive from group membership. The social capital of a group member, then, is the sum of their social relations *in the group*. A group member "possesses" a position and some relations in the group, and the characteristics of this position and these relations—the centrality and the prestige of the position, the directness and length of the relations, in brief: every dimension which a formal analysis of networks can attribute to positions and which "generators" of an ego-centered network may reveal as relations (Burt 2001)—are their social capital.

Intimate and non-intimate relations
However, this definition still seems too broad. For, it refers to any group, including to those formed from intimate relationships, which are commonly[5] not regarded as social capital. Intimate relationships are sexual

---

[5] The exclusion of intimate relationship is explicitly justified on theoretical grounds in Warren (2001: 56–59) and implicitly made in most empirical investigations of social capital, which refer to "trust, norms and networks" (Putnam 1993: 167). *Trust* refers to "people" (see the phrasing of question A8–A10 in the European Social Survey www.europeansocialsurvey.org), and is a problem only *beyond* the family (e.g. Uslaner 2002: 29). *Norms* of reciprocity (e.g. not cheating on taxes) proscribe not to exploit others beyond the family. Moreover, the family is—as already stated by Weber (1980: 214, household communism)—the social domain where reciprocation is stretched for a much longer time span than in everyday relations and in the society at large (if not totally suspended). *Networks* are mostly operationalized by memberships in associations. Even the "informal connections" investigated by van der Meer et al. (chapter 2) refer to "social meetings" which take place outside the nuclear family (or its substitute forms) (C2)—otherwise one need not "meet"—and to helping relations "not counting anything you do for your family, in your work, or within voluntary associations" (E20). Even more interestingly, the only question, which includes relations within the nuclear family "Do you have anyone with whom you can discuss intimate and personal matters", produces a uniform response rate of about 90–95% in every country. Obviously, as nearly everybody can resort to the family (of origin or destination) for this purpose, there are no differences between countries—and most probably between persons as well.—Although Halpern (2005: 13–28) contends that "almost all researchers would agree that non-familial social networks...are clear examples of social capital", he considers the family as a level of analysis for social capital. On the other hand, he analyzes the family as one of the main causes of social capital (248–250)—which it indeed is (for trust see Uslaner 2002: 76-83). The fact that the family is one of the most important causes of social capital is

and generational relations. As they rest on biologically defined qualities, there are only a few of them; moreover, everybody can, and most will enter into them. They are practiced in the nuclear family and its more recent substitute forms, as partnerships or patchwork families—in what has been termed "private living arrangements". "Private" is what Parsons (Parsons / Shils 1951) has called "particularistic": the person is essential for the relation. There are many mothers in the world, but only my mother is "my mother"; I cannot choose amongst mothers for the one who suits me the best. Social capital, however, consists of "universalistic" relations in "public" realms, that is, of relations, which persist with interchangeable persons. Each member of my tennis club is, in principle, equally welcome as a partner on the tennis court or in the club bar, and even beyond the club. Therefore, I can choose amongst them those, which suit me the best.

In brief, as social capital characterizes the departure of persons from their private living arrangements, it seems reasonable to exclude intimate relationships from the definition and to introduce a new *differentia specifica* with reference to kinds of groups. *Social capital, then, is the sum of social relations a person holds beyond intimate living arrangements.*[6] Yet social capital does not "capitalize" by itself. In order to not decay, it must be, as every sort of capital, utilized by its owner. What can actors gain from their relations when they pursue goals within their group?

1.2 *Relational capital and system capital: Concept and measurement*

Due to its relational nature, the possession of social capital becomes more useful when there are more relations in the group within which they are established. Therefore, the "relational capital" of persons has been distinguished from the "system capital" of their group (Esser

---

also a strong argument to exclude family relations from its definition.—The distinction between intimate and non-intimate relations is implicitly made also in economics when "marriage specific" capital is seen as a form of its own—neither human nor social capital (Becker 1976: 242–4). It is furthermore explicitly made in Becker's distinction between the fixed "fundamental" relations a person is embedded in as a member of an intimate group and the variable investments a person puts into building up social relations beyond these fundamental relations (Esser 200: 243–246).

[6] The definition refers to relations while other definitions (Esser 2000: 236, 243, 260; Lin (2001a: 25, 2001b: 17; Yang 2007) refer to resources available through or features of relations. Alter may be accessible to Ego, yet refuse to share resources with Ego (Lin 2001b: 21). Although to use the resources is the ultimate goal of social capital, therefore, it seems appropriate not to include the accessibility of resources in the definition. How well partners provide access to resources is an empirical question.

2000: 235–268, Gabriel et al. 2002: 27). This distinction, however, makes sense only if the system capital is *conceived* of independently of persons as the sum of their relations. While a person may aim to manipulate and to improve their relational capital, the system capital of a group, although created by the members, exists independently of each member's will. This emerging quality is visible in at least two ways. Firstly, relations between all group members are regarded. Then the system capital is the *network* of the relations knitted between members in pursuance of the group goal; it is the social structure of the group. Thus, the sum of ownership relations between firms of an economy is the system capital of that economy. Secondly, some of the relations are bundled in *civic associations*. Then the system capital is the sum of civic associations acting within the group. Thus, the sum of civic associations in a society at large, often designated as its "third" or "voluntary sector" (Anheier / Salamon 2001), constitutes its system capital. If one wants to measure these two kinds of system capital in population surveys, two problems arise.

Firstly, system capital is the aggregation of the many decisions made by persons to establish their relational capital. In this process, there inevitably is some *interdependency*; some are eager to and some detest emulating other people. In the measurement procedure, this interdependency should be, in principle, followed up over time until a system capital is established. Yet the measurement practice in population surveys is to neglect interdependency and time and to compute means within groups at a single point in time. This abbreviation of the measurement procedure cannot be justified by its practicability alone (van Deth 2002: 87). Fortunately, there are substantive reasons as well. Often people make decisions, without looking at others, according to their interests and values. For example, one joins a tennis club because one wants to play tennis, and one supports Amnesty International because one is a convinced liberal—irrespective of what others like and believe. If the interdependency in the aggregation process can be neglected for substantive reasons, the formation need not be followed up over time and can be measured as the result of the formation at a single point in time. The most straightforward, though theoretically demanding, way to measure the system capital of a group, then, is to compute the mean relational capital of its members.

Yet, secondly, this bears the danger of circularity, namely identifying system capital with relational capital. The sum of the relations of all persons does not necessarily amount to the system capital of the group.

If two persons are related to each other, there is only one relation and it is, strictly speaking, not correct to total the relation each one has to become two relations. Yet in population surveys with *random sampling* it is highly improbable that two persons are drawn which hold a direct relation such that there will not be much wrong with totaling the relations. Similarly, if two persons join the same association it is strictly not correct to count a system capital of two associations. Yet again, random sampling seems to keep the problem within limits. More importantly, multiple memberships reflect the size of the association so that the addition of all personal memberships can be regarded as the system capital of the associations of a society, weighted by its importance.

In sum, social capital consists of the relations of persons, it basically is *relational capital*. Yet relations may add up within a group to create a *system capital*, which either consists of the network or the civic associations in that group. Although the system capital is conceived of as independent of the relational capital, the measurement of system capital through mean values of relational capital can be theoretically—if there is little interdependency—and empirically—if there is random sampling—justified. Thus, the mean values of relational capital can be taken as *indicators* of properties of the system capital. Which properties of the system capital can become fruitful for a group member in pursuance of their goals?

1.3 *System capital: From social relations to a climate of social trust and the validity of norms*

Density of social relations
The first property of system capital, which might become useful for an actor, is the density of the relations from which it is built up. A person with relations in a network of high mean personal relationships is more able to move from their position to any other person in the network than is possible for a person holding the same number of relations in a network with low mean personal relationships. For, each partner in the denser network is likely to have a greater number of relations than each partner in the less dense one, thereby increasing the ways to attain a goal aimed at. The value of relational capital increases with the system capital.

While the sheer quantity of relations within a group increases the number of ways an actor can attain a goal aimed at, the quality of the relations affects the probability of the attainment on each of these ways. In particular, the "niceness" of relations eases the goal attainment process of both partners.[7] "Nice" people at first sight accept each other. They approach others openly and optimistically and treat others friendly unless taught otherwise—they even try to teach friendliness to the unfriendly. They start interactions with a cooperative move, and they end up with a higher common product than for people starting with a non-cooperative move (Axelrod 1984: 33–54). "Nice" relations form between people when each partner is prepared to start with a cooperative move. More specifically, "nice" relations result from two "nice" tendencies of the partners: to trust each other and to endorse norms of cooperation.

"Niceness" of social relations: climate of social trust

Social trust is the "excess propensity to cooperate" which overrides the suspicion that a purely egoistic partner will not give back (Paldam 2002, see also Halpern 2005: 246–250, Kiyonari et al. 2006). It is a general world-view, which does not reflect, but moulds experience; it is "moralistic" rather than "strategic" (Uslaner 2002: 15–26). I will give you an advance of whatever currency—money, advice, or help—without expecting an immediate return from you. Yet I hope to get something in return eventually from someone else, and I am even prepared to get nothing back at all. The more members of the group think likewise, the longer the chain of reciprocation can be, and the stronger is the climate[8] of trust in the group. Thus, social trust can be generalized from the present interaction partner to the anonymous group member.

Social trust is learned in relations where the probability of disappointment is low, in the "particularistic" relations of the family (Uslaner 2002: 76–77). Yet it is reinforced reciprocally in "universalistic" interactions beyond the family. I trust in others who have repeatedly not disappointed me, and others trust in me if I have repeatedly not disappointed them. My trust in others, therefore, indicates the trust others have in me. Trust eases cooperation and reduces transaction costs (Paldam 2000: 635–6). Someone who trusts in others will most probably be embedded in a climate of trust. Social trust, therefore, must not be seen as

---

[7] A formal classification of the features of social relation, which possibly build up social capital is given in Yang (2007).

[8] The metaphor of a "climate" captures the fact that relations are aggregated; therefore, I prefer it to the term often used term "culture of trust" which suggests a global quality (e.g. Bornschier / Volken 2005: 5).

a personal attitude alone, but as an indicator of trustful relations.[9] In brief, if social trust is understood as an indicator of the "niceness" of relations, a climate of social trust can be seen—just as the density of social relations—as a system capital useful for persons. A climate of trust helps each group member to pursue his or her goals.

"Niceness" of social relations: validity of norms of cooperation
Just as social trust, the endorsement of norms of cooperation can be more or less strongly reciprocated in everyday interaction. Norms of cooperation, such as the proscription not to steal or not to claim benefits one is not entitled to, are justified by the norm of reciprocity[10] alone which ultimately appeals to personal interest—in contrast to norms of institutions, such as marital fidelity or the obligation to care for one's children, which are additionally justified by values the person beliefs in, such as "the family" or "life" (Knack / Keefer 1997: 1265, Meulemann 1998: 412–415, Portes 1998: 7–9). If enough people follow norms of cooperation and enough people sanction their violation, the norm becomes valid. Translated from behavior to attitudes governing the behavior, this argument runs as follows: if enough people endorse a norm, it becomes valid. Consequently, the more a norm is held among someone's interaction partners, the more one can uphold this norm oneself. Just as social trust, then, the endorsement of norms of cooperation may be seen as an indicator of a positive attitude among the person and their partners. In brief, if the endorsement of norms is understood as an indicator of "nice" relations, the validity of norms

---

[9] Social trust is distinguishable from trust in political institutions by the possibility of reciprocation on the same level of interactions partners. My trust in others is confirmed by the trust others have in me and vice versa so that my trust in others can be taken as an indicator of *my* social capital. However, my trust in political institutions is, due to the fact that there is no everyday interaction between citizen and institutions, as a rule not responded to by the institutions. It is not an indicator of *my* social capital, but, if anything, an indicator of the social capital of the *institutions*. The argument to justify trust as an indicator of the social capital of the trusting person holds for interpersonal relations, but not for the relation of citizens to their political institutions. Nevertheless, trust in institutions is often considered as a dimension of social capital beyond social trust—as e.g. in Paxton (1999: 105) and in the contribution of Gabriel / Walter-Rogg in this volume.—Empirically, social trust is not related to trust in government (Uslaner 2002: 148–154, 190–216, Halpern 2005: 180).

[10] For that reason, norms of cooperation are sometimes termed "norms of reciprocity" (e.g. Hooghe / Stolle 2003:2). In my opinion, the plural is inappropriate here. "The norm of reciprocity" (Gouldner 1960) is a meta-norm which justifies many norms most of which regulate the cooperation among citizens.

of cooperation can be—just as the density of social relations—seen as a system capital useful for persons. The validity of norms helps each group member to pursue their goals.

In sum, the distinction between the density and the "niceness" of social relation allows to classify system capital into the triad of dimensions which in Putnam's—and other writers' (e.g. Newton 1999. Paxton 1999, 2002: 256, Paldam 2000, Esser 2000: 257, van Deth 2002: 82–84)—definition is not more than an enumeration: "such as trust, norms and networks".[11] Yet if the definition of social capital as a person's possession of social relations is taken seriously, only the density of networks can be justified directly as a dimension of system capital, while a further argument is required in order to classify a climate of social trust and the validity of norms of cooperation as dimensions of system capital—namely in how far they stand for the "niceness" of social relations. A climate of social trust and the validity of norms of cooperation are indicators of a benevolent aspect of social relations prevailing in a group, which has not been measured directly with reference to relations, but indirectly as a mean value of attitudes. This difference becomes evident if one switches back from system capital to relational capital. Just as the density of the relations in a group constitutes its system capital, so are the relations of a person its "relational" capital. However, whereas a climate of trust and the validity of a norm of cooperation in a group are easily understood as system capital, it makes no sense to regard trust or norm endorsement as the social capital of a person. While pursuing my goals, I do not profit from my trust or from my norm endorsement, but from the climate of trust or the validity of norms in my group.

---

[11] Often trust and norms are termed the "cultural" (van Deth 2002: 80) or "attitudinal aspects of social capital"—in contrast to the "structural (networks)" aspect (e.g. Hooghe / Stolle 2003: 2). If this triad really would refer to a single concept, the correlations should be at least moderately high. In fact, they are low to nil (Whitely 1999: 41, Newton 2006, Stolle 2003: 30–34, Halman / Pettersson 2001: 76, Halman / Luijkx 2006: 77). Given their different distances to the core of the concept, namely social relations, this is not surprising.—Halpern (2005: 9–13, 32–35, 71) distinguishes "three basic components of social capital": networks, norms and sanctions, but takes trust as in indicator, or even as a part, of norms. Yet trust is an attitude, so that Halpern's triad is the same as the common one.

1.4 Context: Social order and opportunity structure of countries

In this volume, the group considered as the bearer of system capital will be countries. Countries are a context more remote to persons than communities are. When in need, one addresses relatives, neighbors, mayors, or parsons before state agencies. Nevertheless, countries serve as contexts to utilize relational capital in two ways. On the one hand, countries are identified by a name and a border, a constitution and laws, a folklore and customs. Thus, contexts eventually become "social facts" governing the citizens' actions (Durkheim 1895). This kind of context will be called the *social order*. On the other hand, countries develop resources of action such as money, educational degrees and bureaucratic power which circulate among its citizens and make up different "life chances" (Weber 1980: 531). This kind of context will be called the *opportunity structure*.

The social order consists of *norms directly* guiding a person's actions. These, in turn, are valid because most people endorse them and because, in large parts, they are written down in the legal form of a constitution. Thus, a concept of equality is defined in the constitution of many countries while achievement—equality's twin value—remains a representation in the minds of the population of a country from which many different concepts may be derived and formulated. Typical variables of the country's social order are an index for federal or unitary constitution (Denters / van der Kolk, chapter 5) or the percentage of Protestants, which indicates the strength of a tradition of self-determination in religious matters (Meulemann, chapter 3). The *social order* guides actions in just the same way a person's endorsement of a norm does—the only difference being that it binds every citizen alike while the *endorsement* varies between citizens.

The opportunity structure sets *de facto* a range of options for every citizen over and above the citizen's personal resources and thus *indirectly* affects a person's actions. It results from the actions of all citizens and all organizations within a country. Thus, the interactions between people of different capabilities, efforts and qualifications result in social inequality which restricts social trust (Neller, chapter 4) or the disposition to social change (Bornschier / Volken 2005). Or, a long established democracy facilitates the establishment of associations. Typical variables of the opportunity structure are the Gini index of income inequality or the age of democracy. The *opportunity structure* of a country provides options and sets restrictions in just the same way as the *opportunity profile* of a person, the combination of their resources, does—the only difference being that it is given for every citizen alike while the opportunity profile varies between citizens.

2. Hypotheses for Country Effects on Social Capital: Causes and Consequences

If social capital is a person's resource within a group context and if the groups considered are countries, it should be analyzed on both levels. How the contributions of the volume see causes and consequences of social capital on both levels is shown in figure 1 and will be reviewed in the following section.

On the level of persons, that is, the lower line, it is investigated which resources and attitudes *cause* social capital and which *consequences* flow from social capital. Accordingly, the volume is divided into two parts: in the first part, causes are examined and social capital is the dependent variable, in the second part, consequences are examined and social capital is the independent variable. The production of the resource "social capital" is at stake in the first part, its "capitalization" in the second part. On the level of countries, that is, the upper line, the context is analyzed either as affecting the *mean* of the dependent variables, indicated by the arrow *a*, or as affecting the *effect* of some independent on the dependent variable, indicated by the arrow *b*. As will be explained

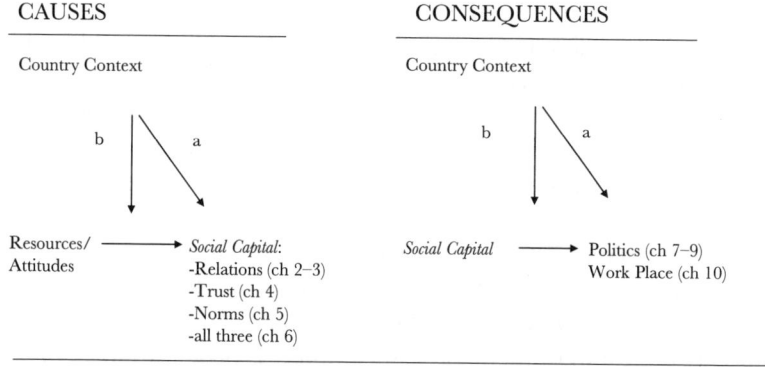

a = effect on mean, b = effect on relation (also effects on parameters of a regression equation)

Figure 1: Causes and Consequences of Social Capital, in the present volume

in section 3, *a* and *b* also designate effects on the respective parameters of a regression at the person level.

2.1 *Causes*

Country effects on social capital
Country effects on social capital must be explained through some specific process at the country level. This is obvious when the context variable is a global quality, which cannot be derived from lower level variables. Yet it holds as well when the context variable is the aggregation of a person variable within countries. Three examples will be discussed now.

Firstly, rich people more often engage in voluntary associations than poor people—no matter whether "people" signifies persons or countries. On the level of persons, having a high income is a resource which facilitates engagement in voluntary associations; therefore, the higher a person's income, the higher the engagement in voluntary associations. On the level of countries, the higher the Gross Domestic Product per capita (GDPpc) of a country is, the higher the mean engagement in voluntary associations. But why? The fact that the average citizen is richer in richer countries and therefore has more resources can no longer explain the country differences once the income of persons has been taken account of.[12] The "average citizen" cannot serve as a theoretical explanation of country differences. Rather, such an explanation must identify mechanisms at the country level. Such a mechanism could be as follows: economic progress leads to societal and occupational differentiation, which increasingly requires the organization of interests in associations; that is, it enlarges the supply and, consequently, the demand of, associations (Meulemann, chapter 3).

Secondly, television use is detrimental for social capital. On the level of persons, looking at television makes people passive such that the motivation to socialize and to accumulate social capital is reduced; it occupies time so that the opportunity is reduced. On the level of countries, living amongst many heavy television users means that one cannot socialize and accumulate social capital. The opportunity structure

---

[12] For example, Bornschier / Volken (2005: 13) use the same argument of availability of resources to justify hypotheses on the impact of income and of GDPpc on the disposition to change.

is unfavorable, no matter how strong the motivation and how favorable the opportunity profile are; even if my viewing habits leave me time for socializing with others I cannot socialize when most others watch television (Schmitt-Beck, chapter 6). At face value, this seems to be an "average citizen" argument: greater mean television time is greater mean passivity and less mean time to socialize, and therefore less mean social capital. However, looked at more closely, it refers to a country level mechanism. Mean television time indicates negative interdependencies, or vicious circles, within the group which suffocate a conceivable social capital production.

Thirdly, there are no differences in the teachings of the Catholic and Protestant church as to engagement in associations. On the person level, therefore, one cannot expect a difference of engagement between members of the two churches. However, the social order of the two churches is different. Catholicism is organized "top down" in a hierarchical, centralized, and authoritarian bureaucracy; Protestantism organizes itself "bottom up" in egalitarian communities (Meulemann, chapter 3). On the country level, therefore, a Protestant tradition will produce a higher level of engagement than a Catholic tradition; moreover, this tradition can be measured by the percentage of denominational membership. On the person level, there is an independent variable, but no corresponding explanatory argument. On the aggregate level, therefore, hypotheses cannot be founded on "average citizen" arguments, but on country-specific traditions, which may or may not be measured by the averages of person variables. Thus, it can be examined whether different *social orders* lead to different organizations, which more or less foster a person's engagement.

Social differentiation and choices of collective actors
These hypotheses on country effects rest on either one of two arguments. The first argument is *developmental*. It refers—in accord with the sociological tradition from Durkheim (1893) onwards—to *social differentiation*, which functions as a basic process from which further developments result. It constructs a chain of incremental societal processes, which are not under the direct control of politics and, therefore, cannot be easily stopped or reverted. Three such intermediating developments will be mentioned. Firstly, social differentiation establishes *social subsystems*, functionally specified to serve needs formerly served unnoticed in everyday life (Luhmann 1968). In particular, systems of social security substitute

informal networks and exonerate them so that they can more easily serve for less basic needs, such as enjoying social gatherings for their own sake (van der Meer et al., chapter 2). Secondly, social differentiation leads to *pluralization* of social cleavages. A greater number of social positions means more diversity of interests, so that more associations are founded. This increasing supply of associations in turn increases the participation of people in associations (Meulemann, chapter 3). Thirdly, social differentiation increases *social inequality*, which in turn reduces social trust (Neller, chapter 4).

As the examples show, social differentiation is the driving force behind the development of the *opportunity structure* of a country. Yet its offspring developments can, but need not be beneficial for the accumulation of social capital. Just as social differentiation proceeds slowly, the opportunity structure of a country has a strong gravity or path dependency and cannot be changed overnight. One may generalize that social differentiation affects the opportunity structure rather than the social order of a country.

The second argument refers to *choices of collective actors*—parliaments and governments, churches and unions, firms and associations—at branching points in the history of a country, which could have been made otherwise and can be revised later on. They produce *events* critical for a country's development. Thus, the present "corporatist" social-political regime in Germany still reflects the social policy of Bismarck during the 1870s; and Great Britain has switched only recently, through Thatcher's reforms in the 1980s, from a "corporatist" to a "liberal" regime. Similarly, European countries have become "Catholic", "Protestant" or "Mixed" since the Thirty-Years-War and the resulting territorial re-alignments, and West Germany has been transformed from a "Catholic" to a "Mixed" country through the influx of refugees after the Second World War. Recently, East European countries have switched from a state socialist to a capitalist social order. In these examples, the choices of collective actors have changed the *social order* of a country almost overnight. They have re-set the normative frame within which social differentiation and its offspring developments continue to proceed with their inherent gravity. They may affect some of these offspring developments sooner, some later, and some not at all. One may generalize that choices of collective actors affect the social order, but not the opportunity structure—at least not directly and immediately.

Contributions in this volume

As shown in figure 1, the first group of contributions investigates the impact of the country context on the social capital of persons, controlling for the relevant person level variables; most of them test several country contexts so that only the most important ones will be reviewed here. All contributions analyze the impact of countries on *means* of social capital (arrow a), and some of them additionally analyze the impact of countries on some *effect* on social capital (arrow b).

Van der Meer et al. (chapter 2) investigate how *mean* participation in informal networks is affected, among others, by the social security system—a feature of the social order—and by the Gross National Product per capita—a feature of the opportunity structure. Moreover, they also test whether the *effect* of income on participation decreases with GNPpc, in other words whether national income functions as a substitute (see section 2.3) for personal income as a means to establish informal networks. Meulemann (chapter 3) asks whether the *means* of the belonging to and the engagement in voluntary associations are affected by religious tradition—a feature of the social order—and by religious heterogeneity—a feature of the opportunity structure. He does not test hypotheses on *effects* of person level variables on person level variables. Neller (chapter 4) examines whether *mean* social trust depends on good governance—a feature of the social order—and on social inequality—a feature of the opportunity structure. Moreover, she finds that social inequality decreases the *effect* of well-being on social trust. Denters and van der Kolk (chapter 5) examine whether the *mean* endorsement of civic norms depends on the type of democracy—a feature of the social order—and on the age of democracy—a feature of the opportunity structure. In addition, they extensively test whether these country characteristics determine the *effects* of person level variables on endorsement, yet cannot find evidence for that. Schmitt-Beck (chapter 6) throws a fresh view on the popular thesis that social capital is undermined by television: if many country fellowmen are occupied by television viewing, few are available for socializing. Thus, average viewing time constitutes an opportunity structure, which restricts building up social capital, in the same way as the personal habit of heavy viewing—yet on the higher level of country *means* and through different mechanisms. He does not examine whether person level *effects* depend on country variables.

2.2 Consequences

If social capital is seen as a person's possession of social relations, which possibly crystallize on the group level, as shown in section 1.3, a general hypothesis on the consequences of social relations follows which I will call the *reinforcement hypothesis*. A person's relations have the more—valuable or detrimental—consequences the more densely knit the network is they are a part of, the relational capital "capitalizes" the more the higher the system capital. The reinforcement hypothesis contends a *cross-level interaction effect* between system capital and relational capital, between a context and a person level variable. Yet an interaction effect presupposes main effects. In particular, interactions effects have two consequences for the corresponding *main effect of the country context variable* in multi-level analyses.

Cross-level interaction effects and main effects of country context variables
Firstly, although an interaction effect can be at work without the corresponding main effects, interaction effects should not be tested without the main effect of the country variable (the main effect of the person level variable is no more at stake because it has been the reason to start a multi-level analysis). For example, social capital is the more fruitful in order to attain personal prestige the more it is in line with values of the social order, so that one should expect that being a member of a Communist party was fruitful in the German Democratic Republic (GDR) and harmful in the old Federal Republic of Germany (FRG). Assume that party members had a mean prestige of 70 and non-members of 30 in the GDR and party members had a mean prestige of 30 and non-members of 70 in the old FRG, that the four groups had the same size, that membership is coded 1 and non-membership −1, and that living in the GDR is coded 1 and living in the FRG −1; then, state and social capital have zero main effects but a strong cross-level interaction effect (of: ((70−30)−(30−70))/4 = 20, to be added according to the coding to the general mean of 50). Yet the artificiality of the example shows that this combination will rarely be found empirically. Therefore, the main effect of the country context should be examined as well. However then, it must be theoretically justified. Moreover, there must be two independent justifications for the cross-level interaction and the country context main effect.

Secondly, although an interaction effect of variables A and B on Y can be expressed both ways logically—A conditions the impact of B on Y, and B conditions the impact of A on Y, as can be verified in the example—one of these ways is often preferable in multi-level analysis: countries condition the person level effect. For persons are "nested" in countries; and higher level collective actors which control the social order are able to condition the impact of the lower level person characteristic on some dependent variable. In the example, countries condition the effect of membership on prestige; members and non-members live in either state. However, it is difficult to imagine how membership conditions the effect of countries on prestige; members and non-members do not choose where to live. This, of course, is a rule of thumb—not more. All but one of the contributions of this volume, which test interaction effects, regards countries as the conditioning factor on person level effects. Yet one contribution (van der Meer et al. Chapter 2) presents good arguments to look at persons as conditioning country level effects as well and compares both ways.

Two specific forms of cross-level interaction can be distinguished. We discuss how both relate to the main effect of the country context drawing on two contributions of the volume.

Reinforcement and compensation

As argued in section 1.3, a climate of social trust can be considered as the system capital of a country and be measured by the mean attitudes of its citizens. It constitutes an *opportunity structure*, which conditions the person level effect of social trust on political involvement. On the one hand, if mean social trust is high, trustful people can act, as they feel inclined to; express opinions, discuss politics, and participate in decisions without fear of resentment, revenge or derision. The effect of social trust on political involvement can be strong. On the other hand, if mean social trust is low, trust is unlikely to be reciprocated so that it cannot become a forceful motivation to get involved politically. The effect of social trust on political involvement should be weak (van Deth, chapter 7). Thus, there is a cross-level *interaction* effect of the climate of trust and the social trust of persons on their involvement. Moreover, both effects go in the same direction; the reinforcement and the interaction effect are *positive*.

However, a *main* effect of mean social trust on mean political involvement has not been justified by this argument and is not easily derived with arguments concerning social differentiation or decisions of collective actors. Social differentiation means more social interaction, which, depending on its quality, may decrease as well as increase trust, and consequently involvement. Moreover, collective actors can decide over tax rates, public health insurances and many other parameters of social systems, but not over mean social trust. Therefore, one should examine cross-level interaction effects without the main effect of the corresponding country context, as van Deth does. Nevertheless, social differentiation may affect mean political involvement through other paths, of which two are examined by Deth. Firstly, social differentiation leads to politicization. On this path, it increasingly requires capacities of the state to govern the society, so that politics gain relevance among the societal sub-sectors and in the life of people and ultimately people get more involved in politics. Therefore, government consumption and state intervention should increase mean political involvement. Secondly, social differentiation goes hand in hand with economic growth, which facilitates political involvement. On this path, the GNPpc should increase mean political involvement. In brief, one country context determines *effects* of person variables on political involvement, but *not the mean* of political involvement; another country context determines *the mean*, but *not the effects*.

While the context variable has increased a positive person level effect in the last example, it decreases a positive person level effect in the following. Country and person level effects go in the opposite direction, and the cross-level interaction effect becomes negative. This negative case of reinforcement will be called *compensation*.[13] The example is as follows. Workers use their personal union membership—some of their social capital—to attain greater empowerment at the work place. Yet, trade unions seek to improve work place conditions collectively. The more legal means unions have to co-determine work conditions or the more bargaining power unions have relative to employers, the less a worker needs to resort to the personal social strategy to attain empowerment. Thus, a feature of the *social order* or a feature of the *opportunity structure* will compensate for an effect on the person level. There is a negative cross-level *interaction* effect of the position of unions in the country and the union membership of persons on their empowerment at the work place.

However, there are also reasons to expect a *main* effect of the position of unions in the country on mean empowerment. The more co-determination is granted to unions and the more bargaining power

---

[13] Further examples of compensations (as well as reinforcements): Wellman / Frank (2001: 249–253), Freitag / Bühlmann (2005: 592–595).

they have obtained, in brief, the more the balance between collective actors favors unions, the more they can improve the mean empowerment of their clientele. Arguments about the cross-level interaction effects are justified independently from arguments about the main effect of the respective country context, so that both can be examined simultaneously. Moreover, both kinds of arguments refer to the same country context variable: the position of the unions in the country (Meulemann, chapter 10).

Contributions in this volume
As shown in figure 1, the second group of contributions investigates the impact of country context characteristics—among them the *system* capital within a country—on attitudes or behaviors in the arena of politics and of work relations, controlling for the *relational* capital. As all of them examine reinforcements of some form, main *and* cross level-interaction effects of country context variables are tested—that is, the impact of the country context on *means* of (arrow a) *and* on some *effect* of social capital (arrow b) on attitudes and behaviors.

Van Deth (chapter 7) examines the consequences of social capital on political involvement. He analyzes the effect of state intervention—a feature of the social order—and of economic development—a feature of the opportunity structure—on *mean* political involvement, controlling for person level variables, in particular, for relational capital. In addition, he analyzes how the person level *effect* of the relational capital on political involvement is conditioned by the system capital; this is done for each of the three aspects of social capital. Gabriel and Walter-Rogg (chapter 8) examine the consequences of social capital on political trust. They examine the effect of mean civic norms—a feature of the social order and a sort of system capital—and of the age of democracy—a feature of the opportunity structure—on *mean* political trust, controlling for person level variables, in particular, for social trust as an aspect of relational capital. As well, they test whether the *effect* of interpersonal trust on political trust is conditioned by the country context, with negative results. Roller and Rudi (chapter 9) examine the consequences of social capital on political participation. They investigate whether the political institutions—a feature of the social order—or socioeconomic modernization and system capital—features of the opportunity structure—affect *mean* political participation. Although they do not test whether the person level effect of social capital is conditioned by system capital, they do test whether the political institutions, in particular, the electoral system, condition the *effect* of education. Meulemann (chapter 10) examines the consequences of social capital on empowerment at the work place. He examines the effect of mean union membership—a feature of the opportunity structure and a sort of system capital—on *mean* empowerment, controlling for person level variables, in particular for relational capital. Also, he analyzes how the *effect* of relational capital—the number of people supervised in the firm and the number of exit options outside the firm—is determined by the system capital of mean union membership.

As it happens, all contributions of this section assume that social capital is benign for its bearer and undergo a search for positive consequences. This is due to the kind of questions they choose to pose—which refer to kinds of social capital geared to produce positive consequences.

3. Investigating Country Effects on Social Capital: Systematic Comparison

All contributions of the volume use the methodological perspective of a systematic comparison. It goes beyond a comparison of cases[14] in four respects: the *explanation of country differences by variables of the country context*, as against a description using proper names; the *control of explanatory person characteristics*, as against a mere analysis on the level of countries; the examination of *two series of general questions*, as against the use of ad hoc questions; and the treatment of these questions in statistically adequate hierarchical models, so called *multi-level analyses*, as against the application of simple regression analyses.

3.1 *Explanation by variables of the country context*

All contributions start with a comparison of means between countries. However, they go on to explain the differences between countries using variables, which characterize the country context. In accord with "the logic of comparative inquiry" (Przeworski / Teune 1970), they substitute proper names with country context variables and develop hypotheses about their effect on country means.

---

[14] Examples of a comparative study as a series of case studies are Dekker / Uslaner (2001), Hooghe / Stolle (2003), and Putnam (2002).

To give an example, social trust is much higher in Denmark, Norway, Finland and Sweden than in Portugal, Italy, Slovenia, Hungary, Poland and Greece, and the United Kingdom, Austria, Germany, Luxembourg, Belgium, Spain, and France are somewhere in between. This ranking (see Neller, chapter 4) partly overlaps and partly disagrees with the rankings of other sets of countries in other analyses. Without an explanatory context variable one sticks to the description of the differences in the sets of selected countries. With an explanatory variable, such as social inequality, one can compare and validate different analyses in spite of the differing country selections.

In this manner, it is possible to advance from singular descriptions to general laws. Proper names are substituted by explanatory concepts on the level of countries—which has been common practice since long on the level of persons. Just as we are not satisfied with the result that Miller has more friends than Smith and want to know why this is the case, we should not be content with the result that social trust is higher in Denmark than in Greece but investigate why this is the case. Just as we need more than two persons to settle the first question, we need more than two countries to settle the second. However, in contrast to the difference between Miller and Smith, the difference between Denmark and Greece may be due to the differences in the population compositions of these countries.

3.2 *Control of explanatory person characteristics*

Countries largely differ in their composition according to independent person variables. If their effect is not controlled for, these differences in the population compositions are wrongly attributed to the country context. Correlations between country variables are interesting from a descriptive point of view, yet the explanation of some mean attitude or behavior in countries through the country context is possible only if the effect of person variables on this attitude or behavior has been controlled for.[15]

To illustrate, the example will be further explored. If the social trust of a person depends on subjective well-being and if, furthermore, mean well-being is higher in the very countries where mean social trust is

---

[15] For example, many contributions in Arts et al. (2006) and in Ester et al. (2006) report impressive differences between country means, but do not control for person level determinants.

high, a more or less big part of the country differences in social trust is due to the different population compositions of the countries according to well-being rather than to differences of the social order. The same argument as for subjective well-being can be made for the educational success, the membership in associations, or the denominational affiliation of a person.[16] Therefore, the determinants of social trust at the level of the person have to be examined comprehensively before the effects of the social order of a country on mean levels of social trust can be meaningfully examined.[17]

3.3 Two series of general questions

Once the country contexts and the person characteristics have been identified, the influence of the country context on some attitude or behavior must be examined. As figure 1 shows, the country context can influence (a) the *country mean* of some attitude or behavior and (b) the effect of some explanatory person characteristic on the attitude or behavior, that is, the *country slope* of person level regressions. Then, two series of questions must be examined.

The first series refers to the *country mean* of the dependent person variable. (1) Are differences of mean person level variables between countries large enough to justify further examination? (2) If so, do mean differences remain even if person characteristics have been controlled for which are differently distributed within countries and affect the dependent variable? (3) If so, can these remaining mean differences be explained by the country context? The second series refers to the *country slope* of some independent person variable on the dependent

---

[16] For this reason, a country level relation is disconfirmed if the corresponding individual level relations cannot be found. It must be spurious and does not retain some theoretical information in itself—as Newton (2006) contends for the relation between social trust and political confidence. Similarly, social trust correlates strongly with the disposition to change between countries, but the individual level impact of social trust on the disposition to change is nil in a multilevel analysis including mean social trust as a predictor; the positive effect of mean social trust on the disposition to change, although statistically significant, is small according to the ICC (.10) (Bornschier / Volken 2005: 16–17, 21).

[17] One may see a danger of *over*-controlling here. The mean difference of well-being etc. can be, in turn, caused by other country contexts. Yet the effect of well-being on social trust must be controlled on the person level before a country level effect can be meaningfully explored. I see only one criterion to exclude a person level control variable, namely when its effect is spurious because of country contexts. Yet this is difficult to imagine as persons are nested in countries (see section 2.2).

person variable. (4) Are differences of slopes of some explanatory person characteristics big enough to justify further examination? (5) If so, can the slope differences be explained by the country context?

Question (2) differs from question (1) only insofar as independent person level variables are considered. In both questions, means of person variables are compared between countries, but in question (1) the *raw* mean, and in question (2) the *net* (of some person level influence) mean is at stake. Both questions examine whether the variance of the means is large enough to be analyzed further. Both questions, therefore, correspond to question (4) which examines whether the variance of the slopes is large enough to be analyzed further. Question (1), (2), and (4) do not describe countries by context variable, but treat them as cases designated by proper names. Statistically, question (1) requires an analysis of variance, and questions (2) and (4) require an analysis of covariance; both analyses see countries as "treatments" rather than as bearers of some context variable. Nevertheless, question (1), (2), and (4) are by no means superfluous. If they are answered negatively, something positive is detected; countries, in spite of their seeming differences, have a similar mean of, and similar effects on, the dependent variables. So far, there are general laws at work and one need not care for country contexts. However if they are answered positively, one should go on to questions (3) and (5), which no longer describe countries by their proper names but explain differences between them by context variables.

3.4 *Multi-level analysis*

Questions and equations

In order to answer the two series of questions, person level variables must be analyzed as dependent on person and country variables *simultaneously*. That is, so-called multi-level analyses must be applied. Statistically, this is a special, namely hierarchical, regression technique (HLM, hierarchical linear model) which is required if the *individuals* of a sample are embedded in *aggregates*, as in our case *persons* within *countries*.[18] HLM-regression, first, regresses an individual level characteristic on individual level characteristics and, second, regresses the intercept and

---

[18] Individuals and aggregates can be many other things besides citizens and countries, e.g.: pupils and schools, workers and firms etc. Therefore, we use the terms "individuals" and "aggregates" to refer to multi-level analysis as a general perspective, and the terms "persons" (or "citizens") and "countries" to refer to its specific application here.

the slope of the first regression on aggregate level characteristics. How questions (1) to (3) are treated in regression equations of the intercept, and questions (4) to (5) in regression equations of the slope is shown in table 1, in the simple case of one explanatory variable on the individual as well as on the aggregate level (Hox 2002: 50–54, 63). For the following, it is assumed, that the individual level variable X is "grand mean centered", that is, expressed as deviations from the overall mean, so that the intercept of the individual level regression can be interpreted as the mean individual, in our case, the "mean European". Also it is assumed, that the aggregate level variable Z is centered so that the intercept of the aggregate level regression can be interpreted as the mean of the aggregates, in our case European countries.

Table 1: Analysis of variance, analysis of covariance, and multilevel analysis: Questions and equations; one individual and one aggregate level predictor

Analysis	Individual	Aggregate: intercept (=mean)	Aggregate: slope
Variance	$y_{ij} = \beta_0 + \varepsilon_{ij}$	(1) $\beta_0 = \gamma_{00} + u_{0j}$	
Covariance	$y_{ij} = \beta_0 + \beta_1 x_{ij} + \varepsilon_{ij}$	(2) $\beta_0 = \gamma_{00} + u_{0j}$	(4) $\beta_1 = \gamma_{10} + u_{1j}$
Multi-level	$y_{ij} = \beta_0 + \beta_1 x_{ij} + \varepsilon_{ij}$	(3) $\beta_0 = \gamma_{00} + \gamma_{01} Z_j + u_{0j}$	(5) $\beta_1 = \gamma_{10} + \gamma_{11} Z_j + u_{1j}$
Questions		(1)(2) $V(u_{0j})$ significant? (3) γ_{01} and $V(u_{0j})$ significant?	(4) $V(u_{1j})$ significant? (5) γ_{11} and $V(u_{1j})$ significant?

In the first line, the analysis of variance, question (1) is treated. On the individual level, there is no independent but a dependent variable with varying means in the aggregates. If the intercept equation is inserted into the individual level equation, the individual level dependent variable is decomposed into the grand mean γ_{00}, an effect u_o for each aggregate j, u_{oj}, and an error for each individual i in each aggregate j, e_{ij}. In our case, u_{oj} is the value country j deviates from the social capital of the "mean European", and e_{ij} the value individual i deviates from the mean social capital in country j. Statistically, it is tested whether the variance of u_{oj}, that is the variance of the country means, is significant and, furthermore, whether it is large enough relative to the total variance. As a rule of thumb, the percentage of between country variance of the total variance, the so called intra-class correlation coefficient (ICC), should not fall below. 10.

In the second line, the analysis of covariance, questions (2) and (4) are treated. *As for question (2),* the intercept equation is of the same kind as in question (1). But the intercept stems from a regression of Y on X; γ_{00} now is the grand mean, net of the effect of X. That is, different distributions of X in the aggregates have been taken account of, so that the intercept no longer reflects the composition, but only the context. Statistically, the same kind of test as for question (1) is carried through for the means net of the effect of X. Also one additional test whether γ_{00} significantly deviates from zero is executed but is not substantively interesting so that it will not be considered for this and the following questions.

As for question (4), the equation for the slope has the same form as the equation for the intercept in question (1): γ_{10} is the mean slope which holds for all individuals in all aggregates, and u_{1j} is the value added to the slope for aggregate j. If the slope equation is inserted into the individual level equation, then, X affects Y on two ways: the mean slope and the addition to it for each aggregate. Statistically, it is tested if the variance of the slopes u_{1j} is significant such that an explanation of slope differences by the aggregate context is worth the effort. Furthermore, it is also tested whether the mean slope γ_{10} deviates from zero. Yet as this test refers to the mean individual level effect it is left out of consideration in the following examination of the aggregate level effects.

In the third line, the multi-level analysis proper, question (3) and (5) are treated. On the individual level, nothing has been changed in comparison to the second line. On the aggregate level, a context variable Z explains the intercepts or slopes. *As for question (3),* γ_{00} is now the mean, net of the effect of X and Z. Statistically, it is tested whether the effect of Z on the means, γ_{01}, is significant and whether there remains a significant variance of u_{oj} after Z has explained some of the variance of the intercepts so that one should search for further explanatory aggregate variables. *As for question (5),* γ_{10} is now the mean slope, net of the effect of X and Z. It is tested whether the effect of Z on the slopes, γ_{11}, is significant and whether there remains a significant variance of u_{1j} after Z has explained some of the variance of the slopes so that one should again search for further explanatory aggregate variables.

Comparison with country specific regressions
The advantages of such a multi-level analysis become visible if it is compared with a set of single level analyses within each higher level aggregate. Suppose social capital is regressed on 10 person level variables

in 20 countries, so that the intercepts, the ten slopes and the error variances—that is, altogether 240 parameters in a 12*20 table—must be compared between countries.[19] Obviously, such a table is not easy to overlook. However, more importantly, it is not efficient. It describes each country separately so that they are compared ex post and expectations are not justified. In contrast, a multilevel analysis explicitly tests differences and requires ex ante a justification of what is expected.

To test country differences in a multi-level analysis, a single regression of social capital on its 10 predictors in the total sample of 20 countries is computed, that is, the individual level equation of the second or third line of table 1 with 10 instead of only 1 X-variable. Then it is tested whether the intercept, the 10 slopes, and the error variances vary significantly over countries. Instead of 12*20 person level parameters, only 12 person level parameters are estimated plus—depending on the question asked—a few country level parameters. If question (2) is examined, only one additional parameter for the error variance of the intercept u_{0j} is tested. If question (4) is examined for a single one of the ten predictors, one additional parameter for the error variance of its slope—termed from u_{1j} to u_{10j}—is tested. Thus, it is investigated *step by step* whether intercept, first to tenth slope, and error variance vary between countries. If the tests for the variation of means and slopes over countries are all negative, one need not continue further and knows that the level of social capital and its causal mechanisms are the same in each country. However, if the intercept variance u_{0j} is significant, one proceeds to question (3); and if one of the variances of the slopes u_{1j} to u_{10j} is significant, one proceeds to question (5). That is, one examines country variables Z, which can predict some of the intercept or slope variation. In terms of the 12*20 table, one examines how strongly the values of the first 11 rows depend on one or more additional country characteristic.

This combination of a person level regression with a step-by-step test of the country variance of its parameters compresses and extends the information of the cumbersome 12*20 table at the same time. Where countries are alike, one needs only one parameter; where countries are different, one can search for variables and parameters, which explain the difference. Thus, it is explicitly tested what has been implicitly assessed

---

[19] Recent examples fort his analytical strategy can be found in Whiteley (1999: 41), Dekker / Ester / Vinken (2003: 236–237). Lima / Novo (2006: 23).

through the inspection of the 12*20 table: namely a test of means, of 10 interaction effects and a comparison of explained variances. Thus, multi-level analyses produce a smaller number of parameters and a simpler structure of results than a set of simple person level analyses.

Yet the number of parameters can be inflated also in a multi-level analysis. For, if the *step by step* tests are replaced by a *simultaneous* test of the equations, first, for means and slopes and, second, for several individual level predictors in a single analysis, the number of country level parameters increases. First, if *means and slopes* are considered *simultaneously*, that is, if questions (2) and (4) or questions (3) and (5) are examined simultaneously, a third parameter for the *covariance* of the error of the intercept and the error of, say, slope u_{01} is tested in addition to the error variance of the intercept u_{0j}, and of the first slope u_{1j}. Second, the number of error variances increases with each *additional* person predictor considered because the new slope has its own error variance, a covariance with the error of the intercept, and furthermore covariances with the errors of the former slopes. If both intercept and slope and all 10 person level predictors are considered simultaneously, the number of country level parameters increases to 11 error variances plus 10 intercept and slope error covariances plus (10*9)/2 slope error covariances which equals 66 parameters.[20] Of these, only the 11 error variances are of substantive interest while the remaining 55 covariances indicate only in how far the estimates of the 11 parameters of substantive interest do overlap. In a simultaneous test of the aggregate equations, therefore, the advantage of a smaller number of parameters and a simpler structure of results may be lost.

Yet this danger can be avoided if the tests are restricted in advance on *theoretical* grounds. As for the test of means, the context variables to be examined in step (3) must be specified. As for the tests of slopes, assumptions on the generality or specificity of laws must be justified for each person level predictor. The researcher is forced either to justify the hypothesis that general laws hold in each country *or* to specify which slopes vary according to which context conditions. As for the first alternative, the step-by-step procedure for question (4) is adequate and the expectation is that the variances of u_{1j} to u_{10j} are all insignificant. As for the second alternative, one must justify which context variables

---

[20] The rule is: if there are p predictors (including the intercept), there are p(p+1)/2 (co)-variances, that is 11(12)/2=66.

can affect a person level slope and test this effect according to question (5). Moreover, one must be aware that one implicitly assumes general laws for the remaining person level predictors (e.g. in chapter 2 van der Meer et al. restrict themselves to context effects on the effect of income on participation).

In sum, a multi-level analysis is preferable to a set of single level analyses not only because it eases the presentation of results, but above all because it subjugates the comparisons under explicit tests and requires theoretical justifications for them. It forces the researcher to make three decisions: first, for which individual level predictors hold general laws and for which is a variation of the effect on the dependent variable expected; if variation is expected, second, which aggregate variables are expected to explain it; third, are these expected aggregate effects tested step by step or simultaneously. None of these decisions has to be made when one looks at single regressions within contexts.

Comparison with regressions on country dummies
Yet why not attribute country variables to each person and compute an Ordinary Least Squares regression (OLS) on the person level only?[21] True, this also reduces the confusion of 220 coefficients. It even allows explicit tests of mean and slope differences between countries (Langer 2004: chapter 3) and therefore forces the researcher to make the theoretical decisions on relevant country contexts explicit in the same way as a multi-level analysis. Nevertheless, OLS is less straightforward and flexible than HLM in testing the two series of questions. The two levels are not treated in different equations so that ways how context variables may affect individual level variables are not made explicit.

Apart from this strategic weakness, OLS has two statistical deficiencies. Firstly, significance tests of the OLS-coefficients ignore the fact that persons are sampled within countries and wrongly assume that each person is drawn independently from the same population.[22] Therefore, the variance of the sample and, consequently, the standard errors of the coefficients are underestimated so that effects are more likely to become significant. This is the more so the stronger the country effects are. When persons are nested in countries, OLS-regression is adequate

---

[21] Examples for this procedure are found in Arts et al. (2003: 298) where 15 countries are considered and up to 8 country predictors are used.
[22] Apart from that, the degrees of freedom are far too high: they depend on the number of persons instead of the number of countries.

only if countries have no effect at all on the dependent variable—a case that is not interesting from a substantive viewpoint (Snijders / Bosker 1999: 39–41). As sample sizes are very large in comparative survey research, the statistical inadequacies often do often not affect the tests of person variables, but it can affect the test of country variables, particularly, if the number of countries is small and the number of country level predictors is comparatively high such that a high multi-collinearity of country predictors becomes probable. In contrast to OLS-, HLM-regression furnishes the appropriate "conservative" tests where context effects do not become all too easily significant. Secondly, OLS-regression does not allow estimating the explained variances on the different levels independently while HLM-regression does.

4. Data Source and Study Design

The European Social Survey 2002: A "most similar design"
Over and beyond the common methodology of a systematic comparison, a common data source is shared by the contributions of this volume: the European Social Survey 2002. It has been carried through in 22 European countries with about 45 000 respondents. It has been meticulously planned and administered applying the same rules in each country. In comparison to previous research looking at only a handful of countries, 22 countries make up a large sample. In comparison to survey research of thousands of people within countries, 22 is a very small sample. More importantly, in comparison to the requirement of every regression that the units should outnumber the independent variables by at least 1, this is a satisfactorily large sample. Moreover, according to the rules of thumb of statistical test theory for minimal sample size, which vary between 20 and 30, it is just sufficient.[23]

Yet our sample is drawn from an already small statistical universe, namely European countries. Europe consists—depending on where one draws the border, whether one includes tiny countries (San Marino), and how one treats former countries (Yugoslavia)—of some 40 countries. Thus, the sample consists of more than half of the universe. This is good but could, of course, be better. More important than the question how "representative" the sample is, however, is the fact that

---

[23] For questionnaires, sampling procedures, and data sets see the website: www.europeansocialsurvey.org.

the universe itself is a meaningful entity so that the range of possible dimensions of internal differentiation is restricted. In contrast to many other comparative survey series which cover all continents and follow a "most different design", the restriction of the ESS to Europe amounts to a "most similar design" (Przeworski / Teune 1970) of a country comparison.

In a "most similar design", as in an experiment, many causes are controlled so that a few can be tested. To give two examples: firstly, whether a country has experienced colonialism passively is irrelevant for the classification of European countries (there is only Ireland and, if you wish, Malta and Cyprus), but relevant for the countries of all other continents. Secondly, social orders in Europe differ according to whether they have a Catholic, Protestant or Mixed tradition and how strongly the churches are fostered by the state, while social orders on the globe differ according to whether they are Christian or affiliated to other world religions and whether they have cast religion into the institutional mould of churches or not. There is less variation of country context within Europe than within the globe, but there are more opportunities to pin down the crucial differences of the social order within a common historical frame. Consequently, there are lesser chances to detect differences between countries and a greater risk to find no difference at all. A "most similar design" allows a more rigorous test but favors similar results across countries.

Similar results across countries: homogeneity of means and generality of laws
As the "similarity" is defined by the common past and present of Europe, even the failure of the test of differences has a positive message. If differences of *means* between countries cannot be detected according to questions (1) to (3), one may talk of a homogeneous European people. If differences of the *effect* of person variables on person variables between countries according to questions (4) and (5) cannot be detected, one may talk of general laws on the person level, which at least hold in Europe.

Differences of *means* between European countries, which look impressive according to question (1), may shrink drastically if one goes on to question (2). They must not be taken at face value. The more they can be attributed to the composition of the country populations, the less important are the differences of the country context. People matter, not countries. Differences are phenotypic, not genotypic. If *all* differences were explained by country specific population compositions, there would be only one population of Europeans—homogeneous across country borders and similarly heterogeneous within the borders of each country.

Differences of *effects* of person variables on person variables should be examined, of course, if cross-level interactions—reinforcements or compensations—are to be expected beforehand. However, there is a good reason to test effect differences even without a specific theoretical justification. If the test of different effects turns out negative, the respective relation may be regarded to be a general law—as long as a "most different design" does not show otherwise. Either one has a specific suspicion that a person level mechanism works differently in different countries. Then one should test this suspicion thoroughly, that is, treat questions (4) and (5). Or one has no such specific suspicion. Then one should nevertheless conduct an exploratory test of effect differences in order to establish the person level effect as a (provisionally) general law; that is, one should treat question (4) only (Snijders / Bosker 1999: 74).

In sum, within the "most similar design" of European countries, a multi-level analysis is suitable to test the question in the title of our volume: similarity of countries and diversity of countries?

5. Conclusion: Similarity of Countries and Diversity of Countries in Europe—and Elsewhere?

To sum up, although this volume treats a popular topic in social science, it has some characteristics, which have commonly not been combined in the literature. The contributions are bound together by four characteristics: as for *substance*, social capital is defined through social relations and measured on the person and country level; as for *theory*, hypotheses on how the country context affects causes and consequences of social capital are developed; as for *method*, country differences are tested by a series of general questions which weigh country effects against person effects; and as for *data and design*, the same data source of European countries is used and a "most similar design" is applied.

As it seems, the "most similar design" has indeed favored similarity. Quite a few results of the contributions suggest that neither mean nor effect differences between European countries are as impressive as they seemed at first sight. Many *mean differences* reflect in large parts population differences (Neller, van Deth, Gabriel / Walter-Rogg; chapter 4,

7 and 8);[24] yet this is not always the case (van der Meer et al., Roller / Rudi; chapter 2 and 9). Of the many *effect differences* examined (Neller, Denters / van der Kolk, van Deth; chapter 4, 5, and 7) only a few pass the test (van der Meer et al., Meulemann; chapter 2 and 10). Yet in all contributions, person qualities explain at least some of the social capital of persons or of some of its consequences. This may have reasons with regard to substance and to method. With regard to substance, the civil society may be indeed—as suggested at the beginning of this introduction—relatively unaffected by the different constitutions of countries. With regard to method, the systematic comparison on two levels may have enabled the contributions of this volume to uncover a lot of homogeneity across the European countries, but similar diversities within most of the European peoples. Hence, the question mark of the subtitle of the volume becomes itself questionable. Regarding the causes and consequences of social capital, Europe seems to be a single, yet internally diversified unity. It remains to be seen whether the person level relations remain similarly important, once a "most different design" is applied and Europe as well as non-European countries are examined.

References

Adam, Franc / Roncevis, Borut (2003): Social capital: recent debates and research trends. *Social Science Information* 42: 155–183.
Anheier, Helmut K. / Salamon, Lester M. (2001): Volunteering in cross-national perspective: Initial comparisons. *Civil society Working Paper 10. Available from the Center for Civil Society Studies at the Institute for Policy Studies at the Johns Hopkins University.*
Arts, Will / Hagenaars, Jacques / Halman, Loek (2003): The Cultural Diversity of European Unity. Findings, Explanations and Reflections form The European Values Study. Leiden—Boston: Brill.
Arts, Will / Halman, Loek / van Oorschot (2003): The welfare state: Villain or hero of the piece? 275–310 in: Arts et al. (eds.), loc. cit.
Axelrod, Robert (1984): The evolution of cooperation. New York: Basic Books.
Becker, Gary S. (1976): The Economic Approach to Human Behaviour. Chicago and London: The University of Chicago Press.
Bornschier, Volker / Volker, Thomas (2005): Trust and the Disposition to Change in Cross-Nation Perspective: A Research Note. *Electronic Journal of Sociology*, download of November 2006.

---

[24] That much of the country differences are compositional is also the result of the following other multi-level analysis: Gelissen (2003) on public consent to divorce in 32 European countries; Poortinga (2005) on the effect of personal social capital on subjective health in 22 ESS countries 2002; Halman / Luijkx (2006) on personal and country level effects on social capital in 22 ESS countries 2002.

Bovenberg, Lans (2002): Unity produces diversity: The economics of Europe's social capital. 403–419 in: Arts et al. (eds.), loc. cit.
Burt, Ronald S. (2001): Structural Holes versus Network Closure as Social Capital. 31–56 in: Lin et al. (eds.).
Dekker, Paul / Ester, Peter / Vinken, Henk (2003): Civil Society, social trust and democratic involvement. 217–254 in: Arts et al. (eds.), loc. cit.
Dekker, Paul / Uslaner, Eric M. (eds.) (2001): Social Capital and Participation in Everyday Life. London / New York: Routledge.
Dekker, Paul / van den Broek, Andries (2006): Is volunteering going down? 179–206 in: Ester et al. (eds.), loc. cit.
Durkheim, Emile (1893): De la division du travail social. Paris: Presses Universitaires de France (1960).
Durkheim, Emile (1895): Les règles de la méthode sociologique. Paris: Presses Universitaires de France (1960).
Esser, Hartmut (2000): Soziologie—spezielle Grundlagen. Band 4: Opportunitäten und Restriktionen. Frankfurt: Campus.
Ester, Peter / Braun, Michael / Mohler, Peter (eds.) (2006): Globalization, Value Change, and Generations. A Cross-National and Intergenerational Perspective. Leiden—Boston: Brill.
Field, John (2003): Social Capital. Key Ideas. London: Routledge.
Fine, Ben (2001): Social Capital versus Social Theory. Political economy and social science at the turn of the millennium. London: Routledge.
Gelissen, John (2003): Cross-national differences in public consent to divorce: Effects of cultural, structural and compositional factors. 339–370 in: Arts et al. (eds.), loc. cit.
Gouldner (1960): The norm of reciprocity. A preliminary statement. *American Sociological Review* 25: 161–178.
Halman, Loek / Luijkx, Ruud (2006): Social capital in contemporary Europe: evidence from the European Social Survey. *Portuguese Journal of Social Science* 5: 65–90.
Halman, Loek / Pettersson, Thorleif (2001): Religions and social capital in contemporary Europe: results from the 1999/2000 European Values Study. 66–94 in: Moberg, D.O. / Piedmont, R.L. (eds.). Research in the Social Scientific Study of Religion. Volume 12. Leiden: Brill.
Halpern, David (2005): Social Capital. Cambridge: polity.
Hooghe, Marc / Stolle, Dietlind (eds.) (2003): Generating Social Capital. Civil society and Institutions in comparative Perspective. New York: Palgrave Macmillan.
Hox, Joop (2002): Multilevel Analysis. Techniques and Applications. Mahwah, NJ—London: Erlbaum.
Kalmijn, Matthies (2003): Country differences in sex-role attitudes: Cultural and Economic explanation. 311–335 in: Arts et al. (eds.), loc. cit.
Kiyonari, Toko et al. (2006): Does Trust Beget Trustworthiness? Trust and Trustworthiness in Two Games and Two Cultures. *Social Psychology Quarterly* 69: 270–283.
Knack. Steven / Keefer, Philip (1997): Does social capital have an economic payoff? *The Quarterly Journal of Economics* 62: 1251–88.
Langer, Wolfgang (2004): Mehrebenenanalyse. Eine Einführung für Forschung und Praxis. Wiesbaden: VS Verlag.
Lima, Maria Luisa / Novo, Rosa (2006): So far so good? Subjective and social well-being in Portugal and Europe. *Portuguese Journal for Social Science* 5: 5–33.
Lin, Nan (2001a): Social Capital. A theory of Social Structure an Action. Cambridge: Cambridge University Press.
——— (2001b): Building a Network Theory of Social Capital. 3–30 in: Lin et al. (eds.).
Lin, Nan / Cook, Karen / Burt, Ronald S. (eds.) (2001): Social Capital. Theory and Research. New York: Aldine de Gruyter.

Luhmann, Niklas (1968): Soziologie des politischen Systems. *Kölner Zeitschrift für Soziologie und Sozialpsychologie* 20: 705–733.
Muffels, Ruud (2003): One European World of welfare of many: The role of values, behaviour and institutions. 433–448 in: Arts et al. (eds.), loc. cit.
Newton, Kenneth (1999): Social capital and democracy in modern Europe. 3–24 in: van Deth et al. (eds.).
——— (2006): Institutional confidence and social trust: aggregate and individual relation. 81–100 in: Torcal / Montero (eds.).
Meulemann, Heiner (1998): Die Implosion einer staatlich verordneten Moral. *Kölner Zeitschrift für Soziologie und Sozialpsychologie* 50: 411–441.
Olson, Mancur (1965): The logic of collective Action. Cambridge: Harvard University Press.
Paldam, Martin (2000): Social Capital: One or Many? Definition and Measurement. *Journal of Economic Surveys* 14: 629–653.
Paxton, Pamela (1999): Is Social Capital Declining in the United States? *American Journal of Sociology* 105: 88–127.
——— (2002): Social Capital and Democracy: An interdependent Relationship. *American Sociological Review* 67: 254–277.
Poortinga, Wouter (2005): Social Capital: An individual or collective resource for health? *Social Science & Medicine* 62: 292–202.
Portes, Alexandro (1998): Social Capital: Its Origins and Applications in Modern Sociology. *Annual Review of Sociology* 24: 1–24.
Przeworski, Adam / Teune, Henri (1970): The Logic of comparative social inquiry. New York: Basic Books.
Putnam, Robert D. (1993): Making Democracy Work. Princeton, NJ: Princeton University Press.
——— (ed.) (2002): Democracies in Flux. Oxford: Oxford University Press.
Snijders, Tom / Bosker, Roel (1999): Multilevel Analysis. London etc.: Sage.
Stolle, Dietlind (2003): The sources of Social Capital. 19–42 in: Hooghe / Stolle (eds.).
Torcal, Mariano / Montero, Jose Ramon (eds.) (2006): Political Disaffection in contemporary Democracies. London / New York 2006.
——— (2006): Introduction. 3–21 in: Torcal / Montero (eds.).
Uslaner, Eric M. (2002): The moral foundations of Trust. Cambridge: Cambridge University Press.
Van Deth, Jan W. (2002): Measuring social capital: orthodoxies and continuing controversies. *International Journal of Social Research Methodology* 6: 79–92.
——— (2006): Benevolent aspects of social participation. 101–12 in: Torcal / Montero (eds.).
Van Deth, Jan W. / Maraffi, Marco / Newton, Ken / Whiteley, Paul F. (eds.) (1999): Social Capital and European Democracy. London / New York: Routledge.
Warren, Mark E. (2001): Democracy and Association. Princeton University Press: Princeton and Oxford.
Weber, Max (1980): Wirtschaft und Gesellschaft. Grundriß der verstehenden Soziologie. Fünfte revidierte Auflage, besorgt von Johannes Winckelmann. Tübingen: Mohr.
Wellman, Barry / Frank, Kenneth (2001): Network Capital in a Multilevel World: Getting Support from Personal Communities. 233–274 in: Lin et al. (eds.).
Whiteley, Paul F. (1999): The origins of social capital. 25–44 in: van Deth et al. (eds.).
Yang, Keming (2007): Individual Social Capital and Its Measurement in Social Surveys. *Survey Research Methods* 1: 19–27.

PART ONE

CAUSES OF SOCIAL CAPITAL

CHAPTER TWO

DOES THE STATE AFFECT THE INFORMAL
CONNECTIONS BETWEEN ITS CITIZENS?
NEW INSTITUTIONALIST EXPLANATIONS OF SOCIAL
PARTICIPATION IN EVERYDAY LIFE

Tom van der Meer, Peer Scheepers & Manfred te Grotenhuis

Researchers have extensively focused on participation in formal networks, i.e. on *civic* participation that takes place within and between voluntary associations (e.g. Halpern 2005). Less attention has been paid to participation in informal networks, i.e. *social* participation. In recent years, however, attention for social participation has been on the rise. Researchers described processes of individualization as a breakdown of intimate social networks (Beck 1992), whereas others discovered increases in informal participation (Stolle and Hooghe 2005). Young cohorts were depicted emphasizing the personal and the private over the public and the collective (Putnam 2000). Other researchers described a process of informalization; young cohorts participating less in formal associations, but more in informal circles of acquaintances, friends and neighbors (e.g. Scheepers and Janssen 2003).

The extent to which individuals meet with or help friends, neighbors or colleagues informally in the intimate sphere is what we label social participation. Social participation may be characterized in terms of quantity, i.e. frequency of contact, and quality, i.e. content of contact. This distinction corresponds to a theoretical distinction proposed by Mangen, Bengtson & Landry (1988). They refer to associational solidarity (frequency of interaction between individuals) and functional solidarity (exchange of support, goods and services).

Social participation is acknowledged to have profound effects on participation in the broader public sphere. Informal social contacts may provide people with social skills (Bowlby 1988) and access to larger social networks in which they become socialized (Banfield 1958; Fukuyama 1995; Halpern 2005), and they may induce physical and mental health (Putnam 2000). Social participation also provides instrumental and expressive benefits (Lin 2001; Bian 1997; Moerbeek 2001; Mars & Altman 1992).

Some politicians and government officials aim to steer social participation by state policies; according to neo-conservative ideology, family ties and social participation in local communities should be strengthened (Van der Meer 2006). Several authors in the political and social sciences disciplines actually propose that states and their institutions should be considered as important determinants of social participation (Levi 1996; Tarrow 1996; Uslaner 2001; Onyx & Bullen 2001; Szreter 2002; Skocpol 2003). They criticize the cultural approach, which emphasizes trust relations to explain civic participation (Putnam 1993; Fukuyama 1995), thereby overlooking the important role of states in facilitating social participation. States provide the formal institutional framework within which social participation takes place (Onyx & Bullen 2001). Since states differ vastly in this facilitating role, cross-national differences may be expected. However, little empirical research has been done to actually test the impact of state institutions on various forms of participation (Parboteeah, Cullen & Lim 2004; Freitag 2006). Consequently, no more than a handful of comparative studies (e.g. Scheepers, Te Grotenhuis & Gelissen 2002; Van Oorschot & Arts 2005) have looked at the association between state institutions and social participation. Therefore, we set out to answer the following questions: (1) To what extent do the levels of social participation differ cross-nationally? (2) To what extent do state institutions determine social participation, taking individual characteristics into account? (3) To what extent is the impact of state institutions on social participation similar across social categories?

This article contributes to the literature on social participation in three ways. Firstly, it presents theoretical accounts as to how state institutions affect social participation. We derive and test hypotheses following three lines of reasoning, which provide us with contradictory and complementary views. Secondly, we take a range of state institutions into account, whereas other research has been limited to analyzing only one such institution, most notably the welfare state. By not including other state institutional measures in the analysis, one might erroneously conclude that a correlation constitutes a 'real' causal relation. Thirdly, we refine the broad concept of social participation. Contrary to previous comparative studies, we make a strict distinction between the *quantity* (frequency of contact) and the *quality* (content of the contact: providing help) of social participation. Taking advantage of recent high quality cross-national data and based on separate measures of the European Social Survey (ESS) 2002, we will test the impact of state institutions on these modes of social participation separately.

1. Theoretical Exploration of the Association between State and Social Participation

1.1 *General approach: actor-centered institutionalism*

To answer our research questions, we take up an actor-centered institutionalist approach (Scharpf 1997), which focuses on institutions as "enduring structural constraints on human behavior" (Cortell & Petersen 1999), and the choices individuals make within these constraints (Ingram & Clay 2000; Lecours 2005). We follow Hall's (1986) definition of institutions as "the formal rules, compliance procedures, and standard operating practices that structure the relationship between individuals". This definition includes both formal and informal sets of rules (North 1990). Generally, state institutions are considered to be similar, and affect the behavior of actors, rather than the other way around. Actor-centered institutionalism acknowledges that institutions can be subject to change; however, most research assumes institutional continuity (Harty 2005). State institutions are inert (Krasner 1984); they hardly change, and if they do, it is mostly through small, incremental steps (Cortell & Petersen 1999). Institutions continue to exist, even when the actors that brought about these institutions no longer sustain them. The assumption of institutional stability is considered most valid when applied to western, liberal-democratic countries (Harty 2005), not coincidentally the set of countries this article focuses on.

To explain country level differences in social participation, we specifically look at national level state institutions: general state policies and standard government practices. We consider three major theories on the relationships between state institutions and social participation. All three theories make assumptions on individuals' incentives as their starting point and transpose the individual level assumptions to the contextual level in order to formulate contextual level hypotheses. A schematic overview of the hypotheses is presented in Table 1.

Table 1: Overview of the hypotheses

Line of reasoning	Hypothesis	State level characteristic	Expected effect on social participation	Effect expected to be strongest for
Crowding out	1a/1b	Social security expenditure	−	The poor
Socio-economic security	2a/2b	Social security expenditure	+	The poor
	3a/3b	Economic development	+	The poor
Safe refuge	4a/4b	Civil rights enforcement	−	The poor
	5	Level of corruption	+	None expected
	6	Years of democracy	−	None expected

1.2 Hypotheses: Crowding out

The 'traditional' line of reasoning emphasizes the material incentives of social participation; social participation results from extensive considerations of costs and benefits. From this perspective, social participation is not a goal in itself, but a means to fulfill a higher (economic) need, to obtain an instrumental benefit. Flap (1999) signals that those who are aware of their (economic) dependency, may strive for tighter family bonds. To compensate for a lack of economic (or cultural or human) capital, they invest in their informal network ties to construct an economic safety net, implying that people with little income are more apt for social participation. Yet, this individual level hypothesis is not often corroborated by previous findings. Generally, a positive relation is found between income and social participation (Komter & Vollebergh 2002). Nevertheless, we consider this approach to social participation to be the rock bottom of the crowding out approach, which is formulated at the country level.

According to the crowding out thesis, family and friendship bonds function as a safeguard against economic hardship. In time, however, extensive states with more or less elaborate systems of social security may come to substitute the function of this economic safety net by providing social security against unemployment, disability and disease, and by offering state pensions for the old—not as charity, but as an individual right by law. Thereby, these states crowd out the role of family and friends; people no longer need to depend on their social network, but rather on the state, and therefore have less (material) incentives for social participation. Vice versa, states that lack such extensive social security systems force their citizens to rely on their families and friends and hence induce them to social participation. These hypotheses are often traced back to Tocqueville and Nisbet (van der Meer 2006) and have been tested, building on Esping-Andersen's (1990 1999) theory on welfare state regimes. They have been corroborated for a sample of elderly people in Europe (Scheepers et al. 2002). Van Oorschot and Arts (2005) formulate the crowding out hypothesis like this; "social expenditures and comprehensive social programs 'crowd out' informal caring relations and social networks, as well as familial, communal and occupational systems of self-help and reciprocity". Hence, such state programs take over the 'economic' caring tasks of social relations, but not necessarily other functions of social participation. Following this line of reasoning, we expect the crowding out effect to be most apparent in the quality of informal relations (i.e., providing help) rather than in the quantity (i.e. frequency of contact). Moreover, we expect the inverse relationship between state level social security and social participation to be stronger for people with a low income than for people with a high income, as the latter have less economic incentives for social participation to begin with. People with a low income depend more on social security than people with a high income; the crowding out effect of social security programs should be more apparent among the economically weak—i.e. the poor. We thus claim that the impact of contextual characteristics affects varying social groups differently. Hence, we propose to test the following hypotheses on the effects of state institutions:

H1a *The lower the level of social security in welfare states, the higher the level of social participation.*
H1b *There is a stronger effect of social security on social participation for the economically weak than for the economically strong—i.e. for the poor than for the rich.*

1.3 *Hypotheses: Socio-economic security*

Whereas the crowding out thesis considers social participation to be motivated by economic needs, another theory emphasizes that social participation is motivated by expressive benefits (Lin 2001), for example, belonging. Maslow (1970) proposes a pyramid of human needs in which belonging ranks rather high. He does not consider the (lower ranking) need of socio-economic security to be a goal of social participation, but rather a precondition. The general proposition in this theory is that the more these lower needs are fulfilled, the more citizens will aim to satisfy higher needs. We derive from this proposition that the more citizens feel safe and secure, be it economically or physically, the more they will look for ways to obtain a sense of belonging, possibly through social participation, e.g. with friends. Firstly, this line of reasoning provides us with an individual level hypothesis that would read, the higher citizens' income, the higher the level of social participation. There is evidence for this hypothesis (Komter & Vollebergh 2002) that contradicts the individual level hypothesis constituting the crowding out hypothesis. Secondly, we propose that states may also contribute to meet the lower needs in Maslow's pyramid by providing social security as an economic safety net for citizens. In times of hardship, citizens can rely on the welfare state to fulfill their basic needs. States that offer a high-level social security system will satisfy citizens' needs for economic security, and indirectly reinforce social participation, i.e. to meet and help others, creating a sense of belonging. Whereas, in line with the crowding out thesis, we expect a negative relationship between social security and social participation; the theory on the hierarchy of values (starting from different assumptions) proposes a positive relationship. Yet again, and for the same reasons as above, we expect the impact of social security on social participation to be stronger for the economically weak than for the economically strong. On the one hand, the well-to-do are less likely to need state arrangements to satisfy the need for socio-economic security than the poor are. On the other hand, the poor generally benefit most from social security arrangements. Hence, we propose to test contradictory hypotheses on the effects of state institutions:

H2a *The higher the level of social security in welfare states, the higher the level of social participation.*
H2b *There is a stronger effect of social security on social participation for the economically weak than for the economically strong—i.e. for the poor than for the rich.*

Building on the individual level hypothesis on income derived from the socio-economic security thesis, we like to propose that, besides the individual income, the national income may also have a positive effect on the economic and physical safety of citizens. Economic development at the national level raises the resources within a society. Wealthy countries offer more economic means and opportunities for extensive social participation. (Halman 2003). Moreover, it also has a positive impact on trust, pro-social attitudes and general feelings of reciprocity (Knack & Keefer 1997; Curtis et al. 2001; Van Oorschot & Arts 2005). Therefore, we expect countries with high levels of economic development to show high levels of social participation. Although economic development is not a state institution, we incorporate it in our study, at least as an important control, and as part of the socio-economic security thesis. Hypothesis 3 claims that:

H3a *The higher the national level of economic development, the higher the level of social participation.*
H3b *There is a stronger positive effect of economic development on social participation for the economically weak than for the economically strong—i.e. for the poor than for the rich.*

1.4   *Hypotheses: Safe refuge*

The two previous lines of reasoning consider social participation as an outcome of economic needs or expressive benefits. The safe refuge thesis does not focus on the nature of the incentives for social participation, but on the constraints. Citizens are considered to choose the best way to fulfill their needs. In some instances social participation is the best way, namely when participation in the intimate sphere is considered a safe refuge from a (distrusted) public space where public and private goals are difficult or impossible to reach (Eliasoph 1998).

Again, we start from an individual level perspective, proposing that social participation is both an end in itself (Lin's expressive benefits of social networks) as well as a means to an end (Lin's instrumental benefit of social networks). Modernization theorists (e.g. Heitmeyer 1997) propose that, over time, individuals have increasingly become free, able to choose how and to what degree they wish to participate. To the extent that individuals can more easily pursue the expressive and instrumental goals in the public sphere, they are less likely to participate in the intimate sphere (Hochschild 1997). To the extent that it is more difficult to pursue these goals in the public sphere, individuals are more likely to seek a safe refuge and socially participate in the intimate sphere.

The *safe refuge thesis* claims that the more insecure the institutional setting makes individuals feel about reaching their expressive and instrumental goals in the public sphere, the more they will use relatively secure intimate ties. Citizens feel more insecure in the public sphere to the extent that their civic autonomy comes under threat. To cope with insecurity and distrust, citizens then revert to social participation (Rose 1994). States have great powers safeguarding the autonomy of its citizens in the public sphere, as they create the institutional setting with formal and informal laws in which citizens may participate. Institutional settings that support civic autonomy actually decrease individuals' need for social participation, whereas institutional settings that do not support civic autonomy may promote the use of strong ties formed by social participation (Bian 1997). We propose some institutional settings that may be considered in determining social participation.

Firstly, social participation may be affected by the extent to which states enforce civil rights. Civil rights, like the freedom of speech and the freedom of association, are warrants for undisturbed access to the public sphere. However, to the extent that states choose not to enforce these civil rights or limit them in times of war or civic disturbances, we expect citizens to revert to social participation. We expect that states, where civil rights are hardly enforced, have a high level of social participation compared to states where civil rights are strongly enforced. The effect of limited guarantees regarding the protection of civil rights on social participation may be stronger for people with a low income than for people with a high income; financial means provide citizens with more autonomy to maneuver, thereby having less need for state guarantees. Therefore, our hypotheses read:

H4a *The weaker a state effectuates protection of civil rights, the higher the level of social participation.*

H4b *The effect of civil rights on social participation is stronger for the economically weak than for the economically strong.*

Secondly, corruption in the state bureaucracy is considered to have somewhat identical effects on social participation. Corruption hampers the freedom and impartiality of the public sphere (Transparency International 2000). Moreover, people who think of the public sphere as corrupt and politicized will have less social and institutional trust and therefore opt to participate in localized and more informal networks rather than in the broader public sphere (Eliasoph 1998). In the highly corrupt Eastern European states of Georgia and Uzbekistan, citizens mainly depend on family ties to contact officials and enter into state arrangements (Mars & Altman 1992). Therefore, we hypothesize that:

H5   *The more the state is (perceived to be) corrupt, the higher the level of social participation.*

Thirdly, in liberal democracies, civic freedoms are strongly protected by the state. In young democracies, however, social and political trust have to be gained; civil society has to emerge and political life needs to stabilize before the public sphere functions as well, and, more importantly, is *perceived* to be as safe, as in longstanding democracies, where citizens are better socialized to the system (Rose 1994). In young democracies, there is a less well-developed sense of security in the public sphere. Therefore, we expect social participation to be high in new democracies compared to longstanding democracies:[1]

H6   *The younger the democratic regime of a country, the higher the level of social participation.*

1.5   Individual level hypotheses

While testing these hypotheses, we controlled for individual level determinants that were found to be significant in previous research.

Repeatedly, it has been found that highly educated people have more pro-social attitudes and a wider social circle than lowly educated people (Bekkers & De Graaf 2006), although contrary evidence has been presented, at least amongst the elderly (Scheepers et al. 2002). However, we expect a positive association between education and social participation. Income may be considered to have a positive or a negative impact on social participation, depending on the theoretical perspective

---

[1] Likewise, we also expect differences between democratic, (former) authoritarian and (former) totalitarian regimes. Liberal democracies generally protect the public sphere, whereas authoritarian and especially totalitarian regimes tend to invade and control the public sphere. People will therefore seek refuge in the safety of the intimate sphere by social participation, in authoritarian and totalitarian regimes.

This hypothesis cannot be tested, however. A distinction to former regime type is possible, but the measure is strongly related to years of democratic rule. This makes it impossible to disentangle the effects. Fortunately, the direction of the effects is expected to go in the same direction.

that is emphasized. On the one hand, richer people may have less need for social participation than poorer people (Flap 1999); on the other hand, richer people have fulfilled their lower ranking needs (Komter & Vollebergh 2002) and hence have more means and motivation to fulfill their higher needs via social participation. Scheepers et al. (2002) found a positive relationship between income and social meetings with family members, and a negative relationship between income and social meetings with friends. Similarly, contradictory hypotheses can be applied to people who depend on social security, or to those who belong to the social class of manual workers.

For age, we expect the elderly to have less contact with friends than the younger populations would have. Younger people have both the time and the means to participate. With age, people are more constrained in terms of social participation. The length of residence in the same community is considered to positively affect social participation, most notably with reference to friendship networks; those who have resided in the same community for a longer period of time, are more likely to have built and maintained (informal) social networks (Scheepers & Janssen 2003). Urbanized communities harbor more people to participate with and hence may stimulate the level of social participation, i.e. the frequency of social contacts. Rural communities are often more closely knit, relying on each others help, inducing functional solidarity, research has shown (Scheepers et al. 2002). People who are citizens of the country they live in generally have more resources and a higher need to participate socially; they are more likely to have social contacts, being surrounded by family, and therefore have a higher need to build ongoing social contacts. They are also less likely to suffer from a language barrier.

Women may be more social than men (Komter & Vollebergh 2002). They uphold social contacts with family members, friends and neighbors. Married people have better means to manage (larger) social networks than unmarried people (Scheepers & Janssen 2003) by having more contacts and more time to help others. On the other hand, people who are not married may have a larger social circle, in the absence of a spouse (Van der Meer et al. 2006). Due to such time constraints, we expect both measures of social participation to diminish with household size and with the presence of children at home.

Repeatedly, scholars in the field of social capital have pointed to religiosity as an important determinant (Putnam 2000; Bekkers 2000). Religious people are found to have a larger and more closely-knit social network and do more volunteering, evidence that has recently been corroborated for many countries (Ruiter & De Graaf 2006). People who attend more religious services have been found to participate more in the intimate sphere (Scheepers et al. 2002). We expect Catholics and Protestants to have more informal meetings, and especially to provide more help to others, than non-religious people (Scheepers & Janssen 2003).

Moreover, we propose to test to what extent some determinants, that we like to consider intermediate (Davis 1985), actually add to the explanation of social participation. Putnam (2000) proposed that the time spent watching television is, amongst other factors, detrimental to some modes of social capital. If we generalize this proposition on time restrictions, we would propose that other activities of media consumption are likely to reduce social participation. Other individual restrictions could possibly also reduce social participation, like a lack of health, a lack of personal or financial happiness, a lack of feeling safe in one's neighborhood, and a lack of trust. We would like to take into account all these possible determinants.

2. Data & Measurements

2.1 Research design

The research questions and hypotheses in this article calls for a multilevel design. We distinguished two levels: the individual level (level 1) and the state level (level 2). The individual level data were derived from the first wave of the European Social Survey (ESS) 2002–2003, which contained questions on social participation in different modes: meeting socially with friends, relatives or colleagues; providing help, not counting (paid) work and work for voluntary organizations; and having anyone to have intimate discussions with. These questions were asked in all twenty-two countries that participated in ESS 2002: seventeen Western European countries, four former communist countries from Central Europe, and Israel. We decided to split the German sample into the former West and East Germany, in order to test the effect of democratic rule. Luxembourg was left out of the analysis, being an outlier regarding several independent variables, both at the contextual (national income—see Appendix A) and the individual level (nearly a third of the respondents in the Luxembourg sample reported that they were not a citizen of Luxembourg). This is due largely to the number

Appendix A. State level indicators

	Social security (pct GDP)	GNI per capita PPP	Years of democracy	Civil rights	Corruption
Austria	28	29888	56	7	2.2
Belgium	24	29200	82	7	2.9
Switzerland	18	34019	82	7	1.5
Czech Republic	20	16376	11	6	6.3
West Germany	29	26537	53	7	2.7
East Germany	29	26537	11	7	2.7
Denmark	31	29643	82	7	0.5
Spain	18	23046	24	7	2.9
Finland	28	27006	82	7	0.3
France	29	27684	82	7	3.7
Great Britain	22	28803	82	7	1.3
Greece	24	19599	27	6	5.8
Hungary	20	13901	11	6	5.1
Ireland	n.a.	30000	81	7	3.1
Israel	20	22166	54	5	2.7
Italy	25	26363	56	7	4.8
Luxembourg	24	55995	82	7	1.0
Netherlands	22	30088	82	7	1.0
Norway	26	36245	82	7	1.5
Poland	25	11110	11	6	6.0
Portugal	20	18684	27	7	3.7
Sweden	31	27405	82	7	0.7
Slovenia	26	18615	10	7	4.0
Mean	*24.4*	*26571*	*52.3*	*6.75*	*2.82*
Standard deviation	*3.9*	*8817*	*31.4*	*0.53*	*1.80*

of foreign employees active in the country. Eventually, we focused on 22 societies, containing a total of 38 436 respondents of 15 years and older. To a large extent, these 22 societies were comparable on general cultural and political characteristics, as they were all western or western-oriented liberal democracies. We did not weight the number of respondents within countries.

The variables have not been centered. However, we present models (2d and 3d) in which we show the standardized coefficients of our most elaborate models.

2.2 Dependent variables

We distinguished between three measures of social participation in the ESS data set.[2] We treated them as measures of the frequency and the content of social participation in the broad, informal network.

The *quantity of social participation* (or 'associational solidarity') was operationalized by asking how often respondents met socially with friends, relatives or colleagues. Answers ranged from 1 (never) to 7 (daily). The *quality of social participation* (or 'functional solidarity') was operationalized by two measures in the ESS data set. The first focused on the extent to which respondents provided help to others, outside of work and voluntary organizations. As these formal organizations were not included in the formulation of the question, the measure captured functional solidarity in an informal network. It ranged from 1 (never) to 7 (daily). The second measure of quality of social participation focused on having someone to have intimate discussions with. We considered the option of discussing personal matters with someone as a reciprocal service between the partners, and thereby an element of functional solidarity. The measure is dichotomous: either respondents claim to have anyone to have intimate discussions with, or they do not.

2.3 Independent national level determinants[3]

Although most hypotheses on welfare state effects are implicitly concerned with the level of social security, scholars tend to use the wider historical classification of welfare state regimes of Esping-Andersen (1990 1999). These ideal types encompass a multitude of elements besides social security expenditures and result in a loss in empirical data (SCP 2001; Gelissen 2001). We therefore used International Monetary Funds (IMF) statistics on *social security*. We standardized these expenditures as

---

[2] The ESS data set includes yet another measure of social participation. Respondents answer the question of how often they take part in social activities compared to others of the same age. The relative measure of frequency of social participation is positively related to the 'absolute' estimated frequency of social meetings, both at the individual level and at the contextual level. Nevertheless, we will not include the relative measure in this study. The meaning of the scores is conceptually unclear, because of the undefined 'others'. Country level differences on this measure therefore become difficult to interpret. Moreover, we stumbled on an unexpected bias: in all countries participating in the ESS, people think on average that they participate less than 'others'.

[3] For distribution of the scores over the countries, see Appendix A.

a percentage of the Gross Domestic Product (GDP). The IMF measure correlates strongly (>0.9) with both OECD and ILO data.

As a measure of *economic development*, we used GNI/Capita PPP, the national income (GNI) per head of the population (per capita) corrected for differences in price levels (Purchasing Power Parity, or PPP). We used the measure provided by IMF, which is strongly correlated (>.99) to kindred measures of the World Bank, OECD and Eurostat.

The widely used measure of *length of democratic rule*, based on Inglehart (1997), indicates how long a country has been democratic without disruption since 1920. Hence, the maximum age of a democracy in 2002 is 82. The youngest democracy in our data set is Slovenia (11 years).

Our measure of *protection of civil rights* is based on the annual index from Freedom House. Freedom House defines civil liberties "to include the freedoms to develop views, institutions, and personal autonomy apart from the state" (Freedom House Methodology 2002). Countries are ranked on a scale that ranges from 1 (no civil liberties) to 7 (high level of enforced civil liberties). Although the index has been criticized (Bollen & Paxton 2002) it is the best one at our disposal.

By absence of a cross-country measure of corruption, we used a measure of *perceived corruption*, namely the Corruption Perception Index (CPI) 2002, issued by Transparency International. The CPI is based on multiple surveys in which experts (international businesspersons, state officials and scientists) were asked to rate countries' level of corruption. The measure of corruption ranges from 0 (no corruption) to 10 (highly corrupt). The CPI correlates strongly (>.99) with the World Bank's Control Corruption Index (CCI), which is based on largely the same set of surveys.

2.4 *Independent individual level determinants*

For *education*, we used a cross-national measure on the level of education. The measure has been scaled according to strict, predefined norms for the participating countries in the ESS. It ranges from 1 (not completed primary (compulsory) education) to 7 (second stage of tertiary education (leading directly to an advanced research qualification)). *Income* was measured as the actual amount of money available to the household (net income), categorized into 12 groups (with 1 being the lowest income group and 12 being the highest). Next to the sum of the income, the *income source* was measured. We distinguished between those who get money from salaries or profit (as the reference group) and those who do not: the pensioned, the unemployed, those who depend on other social benefits, and those who depend on other sources of income.[4]

We used both *age* and age-squared in the equations, as previous studies showed curvelinear effects for age. *Length of residence* in a community is measured in years. *Level of urbanization* ranges from rural to urbanized. *Sex* has males as the reference group. Our measure of *marital status* is distinguished between those who are married (the reference group) and those who are divorced, separated, widowed or not married. *Household size* is measured as the number of people (including children) living in a household. We also know whether respondents have or have had children living in his or her household.

We introduced two individual level measures of *religiosity*: denomination and attendance to religious services. For denomination we took the non-religious as our reference group, to which we compare those from the Catholic, Protestant, Orthodox faiths as well as other religions. A quasi-metric scale ranging from never to daily measured attendance. *Citizenship* was measured by the respondents' own admission whether they were a citizen of the country they lived in.

Besides these background characteristics, we also controlled for factors that might additionally explain social participation at the individual level. First, there were measures of time constraints due to *media consumption*. We included separate measures for time people claimed to spend listening to the radio, reading a newspaper and watching television. Besides these, we also included the total amount of time people claimed to spend watching the news on television. *Lack of health* was operationalized by the subjective report of respondents regarding his or her health. We knew to which extent respondents *felt unsafe* in the neighborhoods they lived in. *Lack of social trust* was measured by the broadly used single

---

[4] Besides income source, we also constructed a broader classification based on the EGP-scheme, developed by Erickson, Goldthorpe and Portocarero (1983). In effect, we made a further distinction within the group of people who live of salaries or profit: higher professionals (as the reference group), lower professionals, routine non-manual workers, self-employed, manual supervisors/skilled manual workers, semi-unskilled manual workers. Other categories in this distinction were students, unemployed, pensioned/permanently sick or disabled, housework and others. This classification could be created for all countries, except for France.

We tested whether the EGP-classification would perform better in our models and present additional information than the variable of income source. The gain in information at the first level was, however, very small. We therefore preferred the variable income source over the EGP-classification, mainly to maximize the number of countries in the analysis.

question of whether most people can be trusted, or that you cannot be too careful in dealing with people. *Lack of happiness* was operationalized by the respondent's claim to what extent he or she was happy, taking all things into consideration. A final subjective constraint was *lack of income satisfaction*: the extent to which respondents found it comfortable or difficult to live on their current household income.

3. Analyses

We employed multi-level analysis (hierarchical modeling) (Kreft & De Leeuw 1998; Snijders & Bosker 1999) using the ML-WIN 2.0 package (Goldstein 1995). Respondents with one or more missing values on any of the variables were left out of the analyses; subsequent models were all based on the same set of respondents.

3.1 *Country level differences*

Firstly, we will briefly describe the cross-national differences in the diverse modes of social participation. Regarding two out of the three measures of social participation, there are vast differences between countries. Countries strongly differ in the level of social contacts between their citizens and on the amount of help provided to others. In all countries, however, at least 80% of the citizens claim to have someone to discuss intimate matters with. Italy (80%) and the Czech Republic (84%) are downward outliers, but are still rather high. Due to the small differences between countries, and considering the rather skewed distribution in all countries, we will refrain from testing for the impact of state institutions on having anyone to discuss intimate matters with.

On the other two measures of social participation, presented in the figures below, we do find strong cross-national differences. The frequency of meeting socially with friends, relatives and colleagues is circa 80% in Norway and Denmark, which is nearly twice as high as in Poland, Greece and Hungary. Generally, the new democracies of Central and Eastern Europe score relatively low, including former East Germany.

Help is provided regularly by over 40% of the citizens in Austria, Switzerland, the Netherlands and Germany, which is over twice as high as in Greece and the Czech Republic. The German-speaking countries are all at the high end of the spectrum of providing help, whereas the Latin Rim countries (like Italy, Spain and Portugal) are all at the low end.

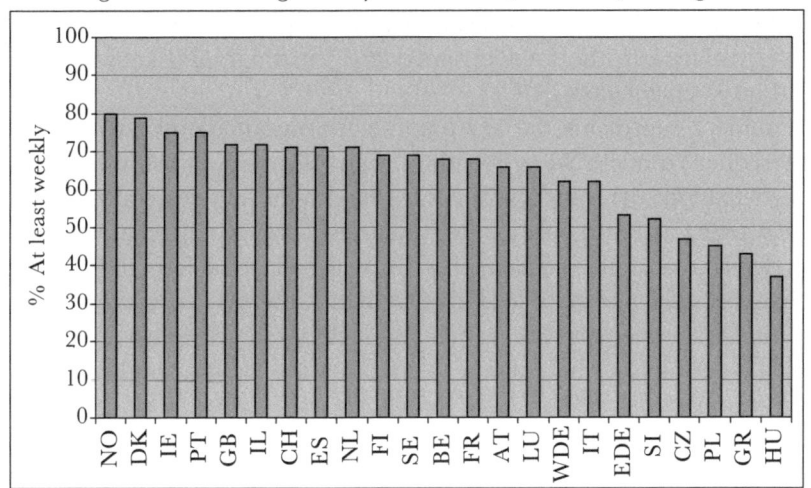

Figure 1a: Meeting socially with friends, relatives, colleagues

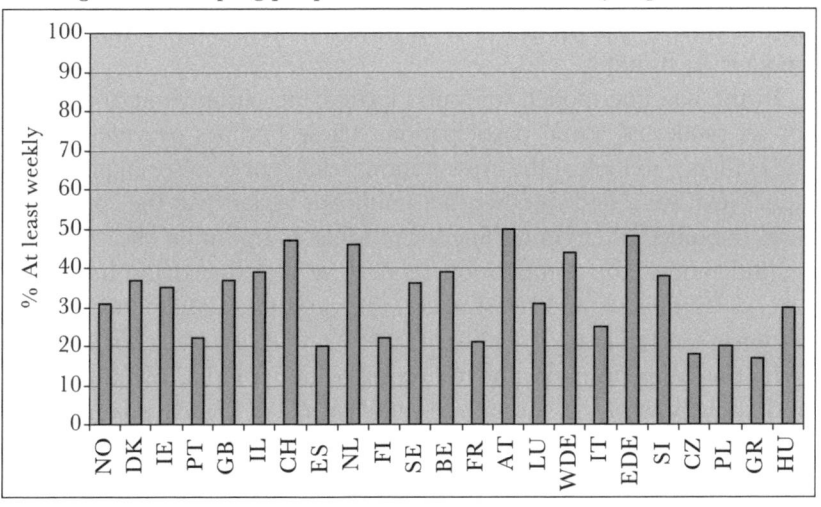

Figure 1b: Helping people outside work/voluntary organisations

3.2 *Analyses of variance*

In the next step, we tested whether the country level differences found in the descriptive analyses were significant, and to what extent the contextual variance could be explained by individual level and country level characteristics. Before we estimated the effects of these predictors in a multi-level model, we first estimated a baseline model to establish whether there is significant variance at the individual ($\sigma^2 e_{0ij}$) and at the contextual level ($\sigma^2 u_{0j}$). Moreover, we assessed the ratio of the contextual level variance to the total variance ($\sigma^2 e_{0ij} + \sigma^2 u_{0j}$), also known as the intraclass-correlation (ICC).

Table 2 represents the key parameters (variance and −2LL) of all subsequent models. Subsequently, it shows, for both measures of social participation, the (empty) *baseline model* without any determinants, the *composition model* with only the individual level background characteristics as determinants, the *full model (model A)* with individual level background characteristics and state level determinants, the *full model including individual level controls (model B)*, which also includes intermediary individual level determinants that might explain other associations, and finally the *full model including individual level controls and cross-level interactions (model C)*, which allows the slope of individual level determinants to vary and adds cross-level interactions to the equation. Firstly, we will explain to what extent these subsequent models highlight the individual and country level variances. Below, we will deal more extensively with the parameters of the models that include the state level characteristics (models A, B and C).

In the baseline model, we found significant variances at both levels for all modes of social participation. These findings provide us with the evidence to look at the cross-national differences in social participation. Next, we tested whether the significant variance at the contextual level remained after controlling for possible composition effects. In this second model, the composition model, we introduced the individual level determinants and re-estimated the variance components and the intraclass-correlation.

In both the baseline and the composition model, the individual and country level variances were significant. We found variance to be explained at both levels; hence, multilevel analysis is the appropriate tool. To ascertain whether the exercise is not merely appropriate but also sensible, we looked at the intraclass-correlation. In the baseline models, the percentage of variance at the contextual level amounted to 9.3 percent for frequency of social contacts and 7.5 percent for providing help to others. As the dependent variable was measured at the individual level, it is to be expected that most variance is at the individual level (Steenbergen & Jones 2002). The second model controlled for composition effects, but the variance at the contextual level hardly diminished. Rather, variance increased for providing help.

Table 2: Variance analyses

	Frequency of social meetings	Providing help to others
Mean	5.0	3.8
Standard deviation	1.6	1.8
N	26860	26860
Baseline model		
$\sigma^2 u_{0j}$	0.227	0.246
$\sigma^2 e_{0ij}$	2.193	3.026
Intraclasscorrelation	0.093	0.075
−2LL	97415.48	106064.30
Composition model		
$\sigma^2 u_{0j}$	0.200	0.254
$\sigma^2 e_{0ij}$	2.014	2.930
Intraclasscorrelation	0.090	0.080
−2LL	95133.93	105197.50
Deviance	2281.55	866.80
df	23	23
Significance	>0.001	>0.001
Full model (model A)		
$\sigma^2 u_{0j}$	0.075	0.128
$\sigma^2 e_{0ij}$	2.014	2.930
Intraclasscorrelation	0.035	0.042
−2LL	95113.26	105183.30
Deviance	20.67	14.20
df	5	5
Significance	0.001	0.014
Full model including controls (model B)		
$\sigma^2 u_{0j}$	0.078	0.124
$\sigma^2 e_{0ij}$	1.955	2.904
Intraclasscorrelation	0.038	0.041
−2LL	94317.09	104940.40
Deviance	796.17	242.90
df	9	9
Significance	>0.001	>0.001
Full model including controls and cross-level interactions (model C)		
$\sigma^2 u_{0j}$	0.074	0.124
$\sigma^2 e_{0ij}$	1.954	2.902
Intraclasscorrelation	0.038	0.041
−2LL	94304.74	104921.10
Deviance	12.35	19.30
df	3	3
Significance	0.006	>0.001

In other words, composition effects do not explain social participation. The intraclass-correlations, therefore, hardly diminished. In the composition models, respectively, 9 and 8 percent of the variance was at the contextual level. This percentage is sufficiently high to look for contextual level determinants in a multi-level model. Next, we specified a model including all independent determinants, both at the individual and the contextual level (model A). Following, we added to this model the determinants that we considered "intermediate" (model B): several control factors at the individual level that we theoretically expected to explain part of the association between state institutions and social participation. The decline of the loglikelihood (−2LL) divided by degrees of freedom between models was significant. In all, 'full models' variation at the contextual level was reduced (by 50 to 60 percent) because of the inclusion of direct effects of contextual determinants. Finally, we tested whether the inclusion of the cross-level interactions would additionally decrease the loglikelihood of the models, which it did. We therefore should not speak of 'the' impact of state institutions, but rather claim that their effects are stronger for some social groups than for others.

3.3 Country level effects

Now, let us turn to the results of the multiple multi-level analyses. Tables 3 and 4 provide insights in the direct as well as in the interaction effects of the individual and contextual level determinants on frequency of social contacts and on providing help to others.[5]

We are most interested in the direct effects of the state institutional determinants in Tables 3 and 4. Although model C offers most information, we will go through the models from the least to the most elabo-

---

[5] High correlations amongst the level 2 determinants (in addition to the relatively small N at level 2) in our multi-level analyses might lead to incorrect conclusions, as the effects may overlap and the coefficients might be the result of chance. To test whether this is the case or that the found coefficients on the level 2 determinants are stable, we performed perturbation analyses (Belsley 1991). Basically, we reran the statistical models one hundred times. For each of these hundred tests we introduced different, small, random errors in our measures at the country level. If the coefficients found in models B of Tables 3 and 4 are not stable but caused by multi-collinearity, we would expect that they would be affected by these small, random errors. We tested for each of the one hundred perturbations what the resulting coefficients would be in a similar hierarchical modelling procedure. We concluded that the perturbation analyses show that the effects found in models B are very stable, both in significance and in direction (for a detailed overview of the perturbation analyses and the findings, please visit http://www.ru.nl/methodenentechnieken/perturb/results/).

Table 3: Frequency of social meetings: linear hierarchical regression [a]

	A	B	C	C (Standardized)
Intercept	**5.11 (1.02)**	**4.09 (1.02)**	**3.38 (1.06)**	–
Individual level predictors				
Level of education	**0.04 (0.01)**	0.01 (0.01)	0.01 (0.01)	**0.02 (0.01)**
Income	**0.03 (0.00)**	0.01 (0.01)	**0.22 (0.06)**	**0.02 (0.01)**
Source of income (profit/salary)				
• pensioned	**0.06 (0.03)**	**0.10 (0.03)**	**0.10 (0.03)**	**0.05 (0.01)**
• unemployed	−0.02 (0.06)	0.08 (0.06)	0.08 (0.06)	0.01 (0.01)
• other social benefit	**0.14 (0.05)**	**0.25 (0.05)**	**0.26 (0.05)**	**0.04 (0.01)**
• other	**0.40 (0.08)**	**0.41 (0.08)**	**0.40 (0.08)**	**0.05 (0.01)**
Age	**−0.06 (0.00)**	**−0.05 (0.00)**	**−0.05 (0.00)**	**−0.89 (0.06)**
Age-squared (* 100)	**0.04 (0.00)**	**0.03 (0.00)**	**0.03 (0.00)**	**0.53 (0.06)**
Length of residence (* 10)	**0.04 (0.01)**	**0.03 (0.01)**	**0.03 (0.01)**	**0.06 (0.01)**
Urbanization	**0.02 (0.01)**	**0.03 (0.01)**	**0.03 (0.01)**	**0.04 (0.01)**
Sex (man)				
• woman	−0.02 (0.02)	0.02 (0.02)	0.02 (0.02)	0.01 (0.00)
Marital status (married)				
• divorced	**0.23 (0.04)**	**0.28 (0.04)**	**0.28 (0.04)**	**0.08 (0.01)**
• separated	**0.20 (0.07)**	**0.28 (0.07)**	**0.28 (0.07)**	**0.03 (0.01)**
• widowed	**0.28 (0.04)**	**0.37 (0.04)**	**0.37 (0.04)**	**0.11 (0.01)**
• unmarried	**0.19 (0.03)**	**0.24 (0.03)**	**0.24 (0.03)**	**0.10 (0.01)**
Household size	**−0.03 (0.01)**	**−0.03 (0.01)**	**−0.03 (0.01)**	**−0.05 (0.01)**
Children at home	**−0.13 (0.03)**	**−0.12 (0.03)**	**−0.12 (0.03)**	**−0.06 (0.01)**
Religion (none)				
• Catholic	0.02 (0.03)	0.03 (0.03)	0.03 (0.03)	0.01 (0.01)
• Protestant	0.02 (0.03)	−0.01 (0.03)	−0.01 (0.03)	−0.00 (0.01)
• Orthodox	−0.01 (0.10)	0.08 (0.10)	0.08 (0.10)	0.02 (0.02)
• Other	−0.03 (0.05)	0.01 (0.04)	0.01 (0.04)	0.00 (0.01)
Attendance of religious services	**0.03 (0.01)**	**0.02 (0.01)**	**0.02 (0.01)**	**0.03 (0.01)**
Citizen of country of residence	**0.10 (0.06)**	0.06 (0.05)	0.06 (0.05)	0.01 (0.01)
Lack of health		**−0.09 (0.01)**	**−0.09 (0.01)**	**−0.08 (0.01)**
Lack of social trust		**−0.02 (0.00)**	**−0.02 (0.00)**	**−0.06 (0.01)**
Time spent on watching TV		−0.00 (0.01)	0.00 (0.00)	0.00 (0.01)
Time spent on watching politics on TV		−0.00 (0.01)	−0.00 (0.01)	−0.00 (0.01)
Time spent on listening to radio		**0.01 (0.00)**	**0.01 (0.00)**	**0.03 (0.01)**
Time spent on reading newspaper		**0.05 (0.01)**	**0.05 (0.01)**	**0.06 (0.01)**
Lack of satisfaction with income		**−0.03 (0.01)**	−0.02 (0.01)	**−0.02 (0.01)**
Lack of happiness		**−0.09 (0.00)**	**−0.09 (0.00)**	**−0.18 (0.01)**
Lack of feeling safe in neighborhood		**−0.09 (0.01)**	**−0.09 (0.01)**	**−0.07 (0.01)**
State level predictors				
Social security expenditure	−2.31 (1.68)	−2.57 (1.71)	−2.41 (1.90)	−0.10 (0.06)
GPD/capita PPP (* 1000)	0.01 (0.02)	0.01 (0.01)	−0.00 (0.02)	0.06 (0.14)
Civil rights	0.12 (0.15)	0.15 (0.15)	**0.30 (0.16)**	0.07 (0.08)
Corruption	−0.10 (0.06)	−0.07 (0.06)	−0.08 (0.06)	−0.12 (0.11)
Years of democracy	0.00 (0.00)	0.00 (0.00)	0.00 (0.00)	0.10 (0.12)
Cross-level interactions				
Social security * Income			−0.04 (0.21)	−0.00 (0.01)
GNI/Capita PPP * Income			0.00 (0.00)	0.01 (0.02)
Civil Rights * Income			−0.02 (0.02)	−0.03 (0.02)

[a] Bold figures represent significant effects at the 0.05-level.

Table 4: Providing help to others: linear hierarchical regression a

	A	B	C	C (Standardized)
Intercept	1.98 (1.32)	1.71 (1.29)	1.00 (1.49)	
Individual level predictors				
Level of education	**0.05 (0.01)**	**0.02 (0.01)**	**0.02 (0.01)**	**0.03 (0.01)**
Income	0.01 (0.01)	0.00 (0.01)	0.09 (0.08)	0.01 (0.02)
Source of income (profit/salary)				
• pensioned	0.04 (0.03)	**0.07 (0.04)**	**0.08 (0.04)**	**0.03 (0.02)**
• unemployed	0.09 (0.08)	**0.14 (0.08)**	**0.14 (0.08)**	**0.02 (0.01)**
• other social benefit	**0.12 (0.06)**	**0.16 (0.06)**	**0.14 (0.06)**	**0.03 (0.01)**
• other	0.10 (0.09)	0.12 (0.09)	0.10 (0.09)	0.01 (0.01)
Age	**0.05 (0.00)**	**0.05 (0.00)**	**0.05 (0.00)**	**0.81 (0.07)**
Age-squared (* 100)	**−0.06 (0.00)**	**−0.06 (0.00)**	**−0.06 (0.00)**	**−1.01 (0.07)**
Length of residence (* 10)	**0.03 (0.01)**	**0.03 (0.01)**	**0.03 (0.01)**	**0.05 (0.01)**
Urbanization	**0.02 (0.01)**	**0.03 (0.01)**	**0.03 (0.01)**	**0.04 (0.01)**
Sex (man)				
• woman	**0.08 (0.02)**	**0.12 (0.02)**	**0.12 (0.02)**	**0.06 (0.01)**
Marital status (married)				
• divorced	**0.17 (0.04)**	**0.18 (0.04)**	**0.17 (0.04)**	**0.05 (0.01)**
• separated	0.07 (0.09)	0.06 (0.09)	0.06 (0.09)	0.01 (0.01)
• widowed	0.03 (0.04)	0.06 (0.04)	0.06 (0.04)	0.02 (0.01)
• unmarried	**0.06 (0.04)**	**0.07 (0.03)**	**0.07 (0.04)**	**0.03 (0.02)**
Household size	**0.03 (0.01)**	**0.02 (0.01)**	**0.02 (0.01)**	**0.03 (0.02)**
Children at home	**−0.06 (0.03)**	−0.04 (0.03)	−0.04 (0.03)	−0.02 (0.02)
Religion (none)				
• Catholic	**−0.16 (0.03)**	**−0.15 (0.03)**	**−0.15 (0.03)**	**−0.07 (0.02)**
• Protestant	**−0.06 (0.03)**	**−0.08 (0.03)**	**−0.08 (0.03)**	**−0.03 (0.01)**
• Orthodox	0.08 (0.12)	0.13 (0.12)	0.12 (0.12)	0.03 (0.03)
• Other	**−0.11 (0.06)**	−0.09 (0.05)	−0.09 (0.06)	−0.02 (0.01)
Attendance of religious services	**0.16 (0.01)**	**0.15 (0.01)**	**0.15 (0.01)**	**0.23 (0.01)**
Citizen of country of residence	**0.16 (0.07)**	**0.14 (0.07)**	**0.13 (0.07)**	**0.02 (0.01)**
Lack of health		**−0.03 (0.01)**	**−0.04 (0.02)**	**−0.04 (0.01)**
Lack of social trust		−0.00 (0.00)	−0.00 (0.00)	**−0.01 (0.01)**
Time spent on watching TV		**−0.05 (0.01)**	**−0.06 (0.01)**	**−0.10 (0.01)**
Time spent on watching politics on TV		**0.04 (0.01)**	**0.04 (0.01)**	**0.04 (0.01)**
Time spent on listening to radio		**0.02 (0.00)**	**0.02 (0.00)**	**0.06 (0.01)**
Time spent on reading newspaper		**0.07 (0.01)**	**0.07 (0.01)**	**0.09 (0.01)**
Lack of satisfaction with income		0.02 (0.02)	**0.03 (0.02)**	0.02 (0.01)
Lack of happiness		**−0.03 (0.01)**	**−0.03 (0.01)**	**−0.05 (0.01)**
Lack of feeling safe in neighborhood		**−0.06 (0.01)**	**−0.06 (0.02)**	**−0.05 (0.01)**
State level predictors				
Social security expenditure	0.98 (2.20)	0.74 (2.16)	1.76 (2.74)	−0.02 (0.08)
GNI/Capita PPP (* 1000)	**0.06 (0.03)**	**0.06 (0.03)**	**0.09 (0.03)**	**0.34 (0.18)**
Years of democracy	**−0.01 (0.00)**	**−0.01 (0.00)**	**−0.02 (0.00)**	**−0.40 (0.15)**
Civil rights	−0.13 (0.20)	−0.10 (0.19)	−0.17 (0.24)	−0.06 (0.11)
Corruption	**−0.19 (0.08)**	**−0.17 (0.08)**	**−0.13 (0.07)**	**−0.30 (0.14)**
Cross-level interactions				
Social security * Income			−0.17 (0.17)	−0.00 (0.01)
GNI/Capita PPP * Income			−0.00 (0.00)	**−0.04 (0.02)**
Civil Rights * Income			0.01 (0.02)	0.01 (0.02)

[a] Bold figures represent significant effects at the 0.05-level.

rate. Firstly, we focus on the overall effects in model A that we nuance and specify below in our description of model C. In model 3A and 4A (Tables 3 and 4), we find (some) state institutions to be significant determinants for both modes of social participation, after taking into account the individual level effects.

Let us first have a look at the effects of social security expenditure on which we formulated contradictory hypotheses (1a versus 2a). We find that the effects of social security expenditures are not significant for both the quantity (meeting) and the quality (helping) of social participation, consequently refuting both hypotheses, the crowding out thesis (H1a) as well as the hypothesis on the economic safety (H2a). Yet, the effect of social security on meeting reaches significance at the .10 level, indicating some rather weak evidence in favor of the crowding out hypothesis (H1a).

Economic development is not significantly related to frequency of meetings, but is significantly related to providing help to others. The higher the state level of economic development, the more people are inclined to provide help to each other in the intimate sphere. This finding supports, at least partially, hypothesis H3a.

Hypothesis H4a focused on the state level enforcement of civil rights. We find that the respective parameters do not reach significance; state level enforcement of civil rights does not significantly determine frequency of social meetings nor the extent of providing help to others. These findings clearly refute this hypothesis.

Next, we find that the state level of corruption is a significant determinant of help provision; in countries characterized by a high level of corruption, people tend to provide help to others less often. Although not significant at the .05–level, the state level of corruption is a significant determinant of social meetings at the .10–level. The effect is in the same direction; in countries characterized by a high level of corruption, people tend to have fewer meetings with others. Both findings clearly refute hypothesis H5. Apparently, people in such countries perceived to be corrupt are not only likely to distrust their state, but moreover, are also less likely to seek refuge in the intimate sphere, as captured by this measure.

Finally, we take a look at the effects of the age of a democracy, referred to in hypothesis 6. It appears to be unrelated to having social meetings, but is inversely related to providing help to others. This supports this hypothesis; people in longstanding democracies provide less informal help to others than newly developed democracies. Yet, although significant at the .01-level, effectively the impact of democracy on help provision takes a lot of time to prove. On estimate, having eighty years of democracy accounts for an average decrease of approximately one point on our informal help provision scale.

In short, hypotheses H1a, H2a and H4a are refuted, as there are no significant effects. Hypothesis H5 is refuted as well, because the (perceived) state level corruption has a negative, instead of a positive effect on providing help in the larger social network. Hypothesis 3a, is partially corroborated, as we find evidence for the relationship between economic development and providing help to others. Hypothesis 6 on the length of democratic rule is also partially supported, as far as it concerns providing help to others. Model 3D, which displays standardized coefficients, demonstrates that years of democratic rule is the strongest determinant of help provision, followed by economic development and level of corruption.

3.4 *Individual level effects*

Table 3 shows that the level of education and income are positively related to meeting others socially; the higher people's income or education, the higher the frequency of social contacts. Table 4 shows that for providing help to others, only education has a positive effect. Next, we find that people who depend on social benefits generally have more social contacts than working people. Yet, when it comes to providing help, only those with 'other social benefits', significantly and positively differ from people with wages or profit. As the accompanying parameters show, age generally has a downward slope for meeting others; young people participate most strongly, and the older one gets the less one participates. After a certain age (around retirement, due to less constraints), people are likely to meet others more frequently. We find the opposite pattern on providing help to others; the older people get, the more help they provide, which decreases after the age of approximately 42 years (probably due to more constraints related to age). Models 2D and 3D show that age is relatively the strongest determinant of both modes of social participation. Besides age, people have more social meetings and provide more help, the longer they have lived in their community of residence and in urbanized surroundings.

Table 3 shows that there are no significant differences between men and women for frequency of meetings. Yet, according to our results in Table 4, women do provide significantly more help to others than men.

We find that non-married people have *more* meetings with others and provide more help than married people do (although differences between married versus separated and widowed people are not significant for providing help). Moreover, having children has an additional negative effect on social participation. Surprisingly, household size has a negative effect on meetings, but a positive effect on providing help to others. Apparently, people in large households have less time or needs to meet with others, but more means to provide help to others informally.

Those who attend religious services more often have more social meetings and provide more help to others. This rather strong effect of church attendance reduces differences between non-religious people and those who consider themselves belonging to a religious denomination, when it comes to social meetings, to non-significance; and moreover, this rather strong effect creates the image that Catholics, Protestants or people belonging to other religions provide less help. Finally, citizenship is positively related to having social meetings and to providing help.

3.5 *Controlling for intermediate determinants*

In models B of both Tables 3 and 4, we add some extra complexity to our models. We include so-called intermediate determinants referring to individual constraints regarding both measures of social participation. In line with expectations, lack of health, happiness, and feelings of safety, all have negative effects on social participation. Lack of social trust and income satisfaction has a negative effect on the frequency of meeting with others, but do not reach significance regarding providing help. As for media use, listening to the radio or reading the newspaper have a positive, rather than a negative effect on either measure of social participation. Most likely, instead of the expected (negative) time constraint effect, there are (positive) pro-social selection effects at play. Watching television negatively impacts help provision, but does not affect having meetings in this context. Watching politics on the television positively impacts help provision, but does not affect having meetings either. For a more detailed study of the effects of media use, see Chapter 6 by Schmitt-Beck.

We are also curious whether these effects presented in model B actually explain some of the effects found in model A of Tables 3 and 4. At the individual level, these intermediate determinants reduce or explain effects of education, income and citizenship on social meetings, and of having children on providing help. At the contextual level, the negative effect of corruption on social meetings (significant at the .10 level) becomes insignificant when we include these determinants. Apparently, in corrupt societies, citizens have more social or psychological constraints (lack of feelings of safety, social trust, happiness) than in non-corrupt societies. The state level effects on providing help, on the other hand, are hardly diminished by the introduction of these determinants.

3.6 *Cross-level interactions*

Finally, building on our previous findings we set out to answer our third research question in model C of Tables 3 and 4: to what extent is the impact of state institutions similar across social categories? We introduce the cross-level interaction effects to the models to test hypotheses H1b, H2b, H3b and H4b. We insert all cross-level interaction terms simultaneously into the models.[6] Model C of Tables 3 and 4 tell us that the effects of state institutions on either mode of social participation are not similar across social categories.

We do not find any evidence that the effect of social security expenditure is either more strongly negative or more strongly positive for people with a low income than for people with a high income; the interaction term is insignificant. This refutes both hypothesis H1b and hypothesis H2b. The interaction effect of state level enforcement of civil rights and individual level income is not significant either, when we also include the other interaction effects. This supports hypothesis 4b, after the main effect had already refuted hypothesis 4a. However, if we leave out the other non-significant cross-level interaction effects in table 3, the interaction effect of civil rights enforcement and income is significant and negative. The direction of the effect suggests that the impact of civil rights is stronger for people with a low income (i.e. 0.29 for the lowest income group) than for people with a high income (i.e. −0.04 for the highest income group). However, we should be very careful to interpret this effect as it becomes non-significant once we control for other cross-level interaction effects.

---

[6] If we do not include all other interaction terms simultaneously, but rather in a step-wise fashion, we would find that the interaction effect of civil rights and individual income is significant for providing help to others. Likewise, the interaction effect of economic development and individual income is significant for having social meetings. However, when rigorously controlling for the other interaction terms, these effects loose significance.

We do find, in model C of Table 4, that the interaction effect of state level economic development and individual income is significant and negative for providing help to others, supporting hypothesis 3b. In other words, the positive impact of economic development at the national level on providing help to others is stronger for poor people (0.080–0.004 * 1 = 0.076 for the lowest income group) than for rich people (0.080–0.004 * 12 = 0.032 for the highest income group). At the same time, the interaction effect might be interpreted in another way; differences between income categories in terms of help provision vary across societies with different state levels of economic development. The higher a state's level of economic development, the smaller the differences between income categories in terms of providing help. Vice versa, the lower a state's level of economic development, the bigger the differences between income categories.

In general, we find that state institutions matter a lot. A brief example resulting from our tables would make this claim clearer. Let us compare the estimated level of help provision by two socially identical women. Both women are 40 years old, married, employed with a medium income (6) and are devout Protestants who go to church at least once a week. Yet, they live in different countries, namely Denmark and the Czech Republic. Based on model C in Table 4, we can estimate their level of help provision. For the woman from Denmark, we estimate a score of 5.06 (which is in the range of once a week). For the woman from the Czech Republic, the score is substantially lower, namely 3.73 (which is somewhat less than several times a month). These differences between socially identical women underpin the importance of state institutions in explaining help provision.

4. Summary and Discussion

This contribution studies the impact of a range of state institutions on social participation in a broad and informal social network. More specifically, we focus on the associational and functional aspects of social participation. We take up an actor-centered institutionalist approach to answer three research questions on state effects. The first is to what extent social participation differs cross-nationally. Descriptive analyses show large differences between countries in the associational aspect of social participation, i.e. the frequency of informal social meetings. The functional aspect of social participation, i.e. the extent to which individuals provide help to others, outside of organized voluntary work, differs cross-nationally as well. A third measure of social participation does not show such large country level differences; almost all people in all countries (varying from 80% in Italy to over 90% in most countries) claim to have someone to discuss intimate matters with. We therefore focus on the first two modes of social participation.

The second question we set out to answer is to what extent state level institutions determine these modes of social participation. This study demonstrates that some state institutions do have a significant impact on social participation, also when we control for other individual level determinants.[7]

We proposed to test three lines of reasoning as to how state institutions might determine social participation: the crowding out thesis, the economic safety thesis and the safe refuge thesis.

Speaking in strict statistical terms, the empirical evidence contained in this contribution does not corroborate the crowding out thesis. Yet, we found that social security expenditure has a weak ($p<.10$) negative relationship with the frequency of social meetings and in some of the additional analyses, testing for robustness of our results, we actually found a somewhat stronger ($p<.05$) negative relationship, implying that the state level of social security reduces the frequency of social meetings among citizens. These, admittedly non-convincing, findings together with previous cross-national evidence, sometimes supporting and sometimes rejecting this crowding out thesis (Scheepers et al. 2002; Van Oorschot & Arts 2005), may probably induce researchers to set out

---

[7] Next to answers to our research questions, we additionally looked for other determinants (or constraints) of social participation. We found at the individual level that some characteristics actually increase both modes of social participation, like the level of education, not being married, the length of residence in a community, the level of urbanization and the frequency of church attendance. We also found rather consistently that some individual level constraints reduce social participation, like a lack of happiness and a lack of income satisfaction. A rather odd pattern came up regarding age effects: the young appeared to have more frequent social meetings than the elderly up to a certain age, but the young provided less help than the elderly, again up to a certain age. Rather inconsistent were the effects we found on other constraints: one is that a lack of social trust reduced providing help to others but had no effect on social meetings; the other is that the time spent watching TV had a positive effect on providing help to others but no effect on the frequency of social meetings. The latter finding may be considered at odds with the partial explanation proposed by Putnam (2000) that, at least in the United States, the time spent watching TV is detrimental to social capital. Apparently, the hours that Europeans spend on TV watching do not refrain them from helping others.

for more rigorous tests on even more extensive databases to disprove or prove this theory.

Consequently, the results of this contribution offer mixed support for the second line of reasoning, the socio-economic security thesis. If we focus on other indicators of socio-economic security, then the main finding is that the state level of economic development is significantly and positively related to the functional aspect of social participation, i.e. providing help. Although the direct effect of state level social security expenditure on providing help to others never comes near significance, we would like to mention that this relationship is positive rather than negative, contributing to the controversial character of this hypothesis.

We also find somewhat mixed support for the safe refuge thesis. A lack of state level enforcement of civil rights does not increase social participation. The length of democratic rule is significantly related to providing help (negatively, as expected), but not to having social meetings. Finally, the level of corruption is a strong determinant of social participation. Yet, the effects we found are contrary to the expectations we formulated in line with the safe refuge thesis. We find that state level corruption has a negative impact on having social meetings in the social circle as well as on providing help to others. Apparently, in corrupt societies, citizens do not seek their refuge in the informal ties of the broader social network. It is unclear whether we should consider these findings to be a refutation of this line of theorizing, or rather that we should refine the theory. Possibly, citizens in corrupt societies seek their safe refuge only in the most secure ties, that is, within the nuclear family and among the very best friends whom they can trust blindly, rather than in broader circles (Van der Meer et al. 2006). The measure of social participation that we used for this study does not limit the informal social circle to the primary and most intimate contacts. Respondents may simply consider these 'others' to constitute a too broad group of informal intimate contacts to test the safe refuge thesis. Then, the crucial test for this line of theorizing should focus on real intimate, primordial social contacts with family members or with best friends.

Our third research question looks at the impact of state institutions across social groups. We tested whether this impact is the same for the economically weak as for the economically strong. We found that it would be wrong to refer to the impact of state institutions on either mode of social participation as a single term. Rather, the impact of state institutions on the social participation of the poor is stronger than on that of the rich. Economic development at the national level has a stronger positive effect on the help provision by the poor than by the rich. Tentatively we can also claim that civil rights enforcement has a stronger positive effect on social meeting for the poor than for the rich.

Parallel to this interpretation of the cross-level interaction effects, we can also look at them from a different, but equally valid, point of view. The cross-level interaction effects simultaneously show that the effect of individual level income on social participation is conditioned by state level characteristics. From this perspective, this association is significantly less strong in societies with more economic prosperity at the national level, and in societies where civil rights are more strongly protected.

These findings imply that even those who are not interested in the impact of state level characteristics, as such, should take the following into account; the strength and possibly even the direction of the individual level association between income and social participation is partly determined by the institutional environment. Especially in non-comparative analyses, it would therefore be improper to look at this association without taking the conditioning role of state institutions into account.

References

Banfield, E. (1958): *The moral basis of a backward society*. Glencoe: The Free Press.
Beck, U. (1986/1992): *Risk society, towards a new modernity*. London: Sage Publications.
Bekkers, R. (2000): Kerklidmaatschap en participatie in vrijwilligerswerk; een kwestie van psychologische dispositie of sociale organisatie? *Sociologische Gids* 47: 268–292.
Bekkers, R. / de Graaf, N.D. (2006): Education and prosocial behavior (submitted).
Belsley, D.A. (1991): *Conditioning diagnostics, collinearity and weak data in regression*. New York: John Wiley & Sons.
Bian, Y. (1997): Bringing strong ties back in: indirect ties, network bridges and job searches in China. *American Sociological Review* 62: 366–385.
Bollen, K. / Paxton, P. (2000): Subjective measures of liberal democracy. *Comparative Political Studies* 33: 58–86.
Bowlby, J. (1988): *A secure base: Clinical applications of reflexive sociology*. Chicago: University of Chicago Press.
Cortell, A.P. / Petersen, S. (1999): Altered states: explaining domestic institutional change. *British Journal of Political Science* 9: 177–203.
Curtis, J. / Baer, D. / E. Grabb, E. (2001): Nations of joiners: Explaining voluntary association membership in democratic societies. *American Sociological Review* 66: 783–805.
Davis, J. (1985): *The logic of causal order*. Beverly Hills/London/New Delhi: Sage Publications.
Eliasoph, N. (1998): *Avoiding Politics: How Americans Produce Apathy in Everyday Life*. Cambridge: Cambridge University Press.

Erikson, R., / Goldthorpe, J. / Portacarero, L. (1983): Intergenerational class mobility and the convergence thesis in England, France and Sweden. *British Journal of Sociology* 34: 303–343.
Esping-Andersen, G. (1990): *Three worlds of welfare capitalism*. Cambridge: Polity.
——— (1999): *Social foundations of post-industrial economies*. Oxford: Oxford University Press.
Flap, H. (1999): Creation and returns of social capital, a new approach. *La Revue Tocqueville* 20: 5–26.
Freedom House Methodology (2002): http://freedomhouse.org/template.cfm?page=35&year=2002, downloaded 04.10.2006.
Freitag, M. (2006): Bowling the state back in: Political institutions and the creation of social capital. *European Journal of Political Research* 45: 123–152.
Fukuyama, F. (1995): *Trust: The social virtues and the creation of prosperity*. New York: The Free Press.
Gelissen, J.P.T.M. (2001): *Worlds of welfare, worlds of consent? Public opinion on the welfare state*. Amsterdam: Thela Thesis.
Goldstein, H. (1995): *Multilevel statistical models*. London: Edward Arnold.
Hall, P. (1986): *Governing the economy: the politics of state intervention in Britain and France*. Cambridge: Polity Press.
Halman, L. (2003): Volunteering, democracy, and democratic attitudes. In: P. Dekker / L. Halman (eds.) *The values of volunteering*. New York: Kluwer Publishers, 179–198.
Halpern, D. (2005): *Social Capital*. Malden: Polity Press.
Harty, S. (2005): Theorizing institutional change. In: André Lecours (ed.) *New institutionalism: Theory and analysis*. Toronto: University of Toronto Press.
Heitmeyer, W. (eds.) (1997): *Was treibt die Gesellschaft auseinander?* Frankfurt am Main: Suhrkamp.
Hochschild, A.R. (1997): *The time bind: When work becomes home and home becomes work*. New York: Metropolitan Books.
Inglehart, R. (1997): *Modernization and postmodernization: cultural, economic and political change in 43 societies*. Princeton: Princeton University Press.
Ingram, P. / Clay, K. (2000): The choice-within-constraints new institutionalism and implications for sociology. *Annual Review of Sociology* 26: 525–546.
Knack, S. / Keefer, P. (1997): Does social capital have an economic pay-off? A cross-country investigation. *The Quarterly Journal of Economics* November: 1251–1288.
Komter, A. / Vollebergh, W. (2002): Solidarity in Dutch families. Family ties under strain? *Journal of Family Issues* 23: 171–188.
Krasner, S.D. (1984): Approaches to the state: alternative conceptions and historical dynamics. *Comparative Politics* 16: 233–246.
Kreft, I. / de Leeuw, J. (1998): *Introducing multilevel modeling*. London: Sage.
Lecours, A. (2005): New Institutionalism: Issues and Questions. In: André Lecours (ed.) *New institutionalism: Theory and analysis*. Toronto: University of Toronto Press.
Levi, M. (1996): Social and unsocial capital: a review essay of Robert Putnam's *Making democracy work*. *Politics and Society* 24: 45–55.
Lin, N. (1992): Social Resources Theory. In: E.F. Borgatta / M.L. Borgatta (eds.) *Encyclopedia of Sociology*, Volume 4. New York: Macmillan.
——— (2001): *Social Capital: A theory of structure and action*. London/New York: Cambridge University Press.
Mangen, D.J. / Bengtson, V.L. / Landry, P.H. (eds.) (1988): *Measurement of intergenerational relations*. Newbury Park: Sage.
Mars, G. / Altman, Y. (1992): A Case of a Factory in Uzbekistan; Its Second Economy Activity and Comparison with a Similar Case in Soviet Georgia. *Central Asian Survey* 11: 101–112.
Maslow, A.H. (1970): *Motivation and personality*. New York: Harper & Row.
Moerbeek, H. (2001): *Friends and foes in the occupational career*. Utrecht: ICS.

North, D.C. (1990): *Institutions, Institutional Change and Economic Performance*. New York: Cambridge University Press.
Onyx, J. / Bullen, P. (2001): The different faces of social capital in NSW Australia. In: P. Dekker / E. Uslaner (eds.), *Social capital and participation in everyday life*. London/New York: Routledge, 45–58.
Parboteeah, K.P. / Cullen, J.B. / Lim, L. (2004): Formal volunteering: a cross-national test. *Journal of world business* 39: 431–442.
Putnam, R. (1993): *Making democracy work: civic traditions in modern Italy*. Princeton: Princeton University Press.
——— (2000): *Bowling alone: The collapse and revival of American community*. New York: Simon & Schuster.
Rose, R. (1994): Post-communist democracies and the problem of trust. *Journal of Democracy* 5: 18–30.
Ruiter, S. / de Graaf, N.D. (2006): National context, religiosity and volunteering: results from 53 countries. *American Sociological Review* 71: 191–210.
Scharpf, F.W. (1997): *Games real actors play. Actor-centered institutionalism in policy research*. Boulder, CO: Westview.
Scheepers, P. / Janssen, J. (2003): Informal aspects of social capital: developments in the Netherlands 1970–1998. *The Netherlands' Journal of Social Sciences* 39: 87–106.
Scheepers, P. / te Grotenhuis, M. / Gelissen, J. (2002): Welfare States and Dimensions of Social Capital. Cross-National Comparisons in European Countries. *European Societies* 4: 185–207.
SCP (2001): *On worlds of welfare: institutions and their effects in eleven welfare states*. Den Haag: SCP.
Skocpol, Th. (2003): *Diminished democracy: from membership to management in American civic life*. Norman: University of Oklahoma Press.
Snijders, T. / Bosker, S. (1999): *Multilevel Analysis: An introduction to basic and advanced multilevel modelling*. London: Sage.
Steenbergen, M.R. / Jones, B.S. (2002): Modeling multilevel data structures. *American Journal of Political Science* 46: 694–713.
Stolle, D. / Hooghe, M. (2005): Inaccurate, exceptional, one-sided or irrelevant: the debate about the alleged decline of social capital and civic engagement in Western societies. *British Journal of Political Science* 35: 149–168.
Szreter, S. (2002): The state of social capital: Bringing back in power, politics, and history. *Theory and society* 31: 573–620.
Tarrow S. (1996): Making social science work across space and time: a critical reflection on Robert Putnam's *Making democracy work*. *American Political Science Review* 90: 389–397.
Tocqueville, A. (2000 [1835–1840]): *Democracy in America*. Chicago: University of Chicago Press.
Transparency International (2000): *TI Source Book—chapter 15*.
Uslaner, E. (2001): Volunteering and social capital: how trust and religion shape civic participation in the United States. In: P. Dekker / E. Uslaner (eds.), *Social capital and participation in everyday life*. London/New York: Routledge, 104–117.
Van der Meer, T.W.G. (2006): Staat en gemeenschap in conservatief perspectief. In: H. Pellikaan / S. van der Lubben (eds.) *Ruimte op rechts? Conservatieve onderstroom in de Lage Landen*. Utrecht: Spectrum.
Van der Meer, T.W.G. / Scheepers, P. / te Grotenhuis, M. (2006): Family ties: a new institutionalist approach to social participation (submitted).
Van Oorschot, W. / Arts, W. (2005): The social capital of European welfare states: the crowding out hypothesis revisited. *Journal of European Social Policy* 15: 5–26.

CHAPTER THREE

IS ALTRUISM MORE EFFECTIVE WHERE IT IS REQUIRED MORE? COLLECTIVITY-ORIENTATION AND INVOLVEMENT IN INTEREST, ISSUE, AND RELIGIOUS ASSOCIATIONS[1]

Heiner Meulemann

Modern societies are differentiated societies. Therefore, men must move continuously between spheres of society. We commute daily from home to work or school, and we less often emigrate from home to foreign provinces such as friends or clubs, churches or theatres, holiday resorts or election cabins. Life extends from the private to the public sphere. On the one hand, everyone is anchored in the harbor of the family. On the other hand, a community of private persons will survive only when there is a degree of public life. At a minimum, the subsistence means for every person must be available and the vicissitudes of living together with other communities must be managed. Thus, two domains of public life, the economy and the polity, develop where formal organizations, administrations of the state, of firms, of parties, and of churches, are established to be entered by every private person eventually.

Yet, between the harbor of private life and the public stages of economic and political organizations, there is another, less formally organized sphere of public life: the civil society. Looking at the society, it stretches from kinship and neighborhood covering all sorts of groups, clubs, and associations, to economic and political associations, that is, trade unions, pressure groups, and parties. Looking from the viewpoint of the person, it fits in between leisure and work, freedom and necessity. In brief, private life, civil society, and organized society constitute three layers of social and personal life. Yet, only the lowest and highest layers are strongly crystallized—as a household of a family or as an organization in the economy or the polity. In between, there are many and manifold associations of persons. They serve diverse

---

[1] I am grateful to Tilo Beckers, Peter Graeff, Jan Marbach and Andreas Schmitz for their helpful comments.

needs, they organize themselves less or more strongly, and they are more or less connected with large-scale organizations. Just as in the solar system, the planetoids between Mars and Jupiter, the civil society is fitted nicely between the family and organized public life. Variety is the earmark of civil society.

Located in between private and organized public life, the civil society serves as a bridge from one to the other (Warren 2001: 56–59). It contributes to the social integration of the society in two ways. Firstly, it provides avenues from private life to organized social life. One learns how to articulate interests in the student association or in the tennis club in order to be able to act politically in a trade union or a political party (Paxton 2002; Stolle 2003: 22–28). Secondly, it exonerates organized social life from the provision of social services not readily produced in the family. The larger the intermediate sphere of associations of a society, the better the prospects of its social integration. For these reasons, associations have been extensively studied in comparative perspective by social scientists (Anheier / Salamon 2001; Curtis / Baer / Grabb 2001; Schofer / Fourcade-Gourinchas 2001; Gabriel et al. 2002; van Deth 2006).

In most of these studies, however, involvement in associations has been treated summarily, without regard to the specific kinds of associations. The planetoids have been treated—so to speak—as a single planet.[2] There is no objection against this as long as the first function of associations is only considered. To provide a learning arena for political action, a human rights movement is just as suitable as the youth group of a political party. Yet, a summary treatment becomes problematic as soon as the second function is considered. Some associations intend, more strongly than other associations, to serve needs beyond the immediate interests of their members. Therefore, associations can be classified according to whether they more strongly serve the immediate aims of their members or general goals of a community, that is, according to their self- or collectivity-orientation (Parsons / Shils 1951). Self-orientation seeks to gratify the self more than others.

---

[2] Warren (2001: 127, 136–137) charts associations according to three theoretically derived dimensions: ease of exit, life domain, and goods provided, but overshoots the mark ending up simultaneously with too many kinds of associations and too many empty cells in their classification. Moreover, his classification refers to the level of institutions and ignores the level of persons' motives, which, in my opinion, has to be regarded first.

Collectivity-orientation seeks to gratify others more than the self. As everybody must look out for oneself first, self-orientation can be more or less complemented by collectivity-orientation. Therefore, the polarity can be labeled by the pole not being taken for granted: collectivity-orientation.[3]

Yet, collectivity-orientation is a factor not only used to classify associations, but people and societies as well. In the following, therefore, the classification of associations according to their collectivity-orientation will be developed analytically in order to empirically examine whether involvement in these kinds of associations depends differently on the collectivity-orientation of persons and of societies. In section one, the classification of associations is justified and hypotheses on the impact of persons and of countries on the involvement in associations are proposed. In section two, the impact of persons will be tested, and in section three, the impact of persons and countries.

1. Design of the Research

1.1 *Three kinds of associations and two forms of involvement*

The first kind of association serves the needs of its members. They produce a good to be consumed by its members, and by nobody else. Thus, a tennis club provides facilities for its members. Accordingly, I become an active member if I want to play tennis and a passive member if I want to meet people. Involvement is motivated by the expectation of personal gratification. The second kind of association serves the needs of people who are not members. These associations produce a good, not to be consumed by the members, but to the benefit of the society, even of humankind or of nature. For example, people not in the labor force are involved with sick people in hospitals through visits and other activities, or retired teachers offer their services in supplementary afternoon teachings for weak students, or an association fights for the rights of unjustly imprisoned people around the world, for the rights of animals or fights for environmental causes. Involvement is motivated by the will to benefit others. As the first kind of association serves the interests of its members, and the second kind serves the interests

---

[3] In any case, it is assumed that associations intend to fulfil a positive function for this range of interests.

of others, that is, an issue its members identify with, I will call them *interest* and *issue* associations.⁴ As involvement in interest associations is motivated by the expectation to share the products, and involvement in issue associations is motivated by the identification with the interests of others, involvement in issue associations is more collectivity-oriented than involvement in interest associations.

A third kind of association squares the distinction between self- and collectivity-orientation: *religious associations*. Religion, at the same time demands the service of the interests of others and serves the interests of its believers. It responds to the limits of self-orientation by demanding collectivity-orientation, and it engenders its own form of self-orientation.

Self-orientation is self-determination, that is, the tendency to guide action more strongly by the preferences of the persons, than by the rules of the institutions. Yet, self-determination is limited by conditions of the human kind, illness and death, unexplainable mischief and unavoidable injustice, which every individual comes across eventually. These conditions highlight the religious question of where a person comes from and will go to. It is answered by religious dogma, which cannot be proven, but must be believed. Yet, someone who believes the dogma must also accept the limits of self-determination. Religion justifies the metaphysical self-restraint of man's self-image before it demands the moral self-restraint of man's selfishness. Religion, as such, independently of, yet possibly enforced by, the morale of brotherly love, justifies collectivity-orientation. Just as obvious as the limits of the self,

---

⁴ In three empirical studies, a similar distinction has been made: "associational volunteering for" the volunteers' association vs. "program volunteering on behalf of" an association and in favour of some issue (Wilson 2000: 216); "old" associations vs. "new" ones "specializing on claims and identities" (Wessels 1997: 200; Schofer / Fourcade-Gourinchas 2001: 813); "traditional political associations" vs. "new social movements" (van Deth / Kreuter 1998: 140–147). Also four theoretical treatises make a similar distinction: Janoski (1998: 14) distinguishes between "interest groups" and "welfare associations"; to these, he adds three other forms: political parties, social movements, and religious bodies. Erlinghagen (2000: 261–263) distinguishes between "self-help volunteering" mainly for members and "altruistic volunteering" mainly for non-members of the association. Putnam / Goss (2002: 11) distinguish between "inward" and "outward looking social capital" and "groups", which "promote interests of their members" or "concern themselves with public goods". Finally, on the aggregate level "service functions" to "deliver direct services" and "expressive functions" of "values, interests and beliefs" have been distinguished for associations (Salamon / Sokolowski / List 2003: 22).

are the obligations of the self. For this reason, religious associations are similar to issue associations.

However, religions also provide goods to be consumed by members only, namely the certainty of salvation, or, in secular language, of meaning in life. In order to pursue this goal, religions invest in the public of non-members and take stakes in secular, that is, political, cultural, and value conflicts. In this respect, religious associations are similar to interest associations. Thus, religious associations are a hybrid kind, which serves as an issue association as well as an interest association. Involvement in them is more collectivity-oriented than involvement in interest associations, but less collectivity-oriented than involvement in issue associations.

Just as these three kinds of associations, two forms of involvement can be analyzed with reference to self- or collectivity-orientation: *belonging* and *engagement*. *Belonging* means membership and participation. Considering it is what the association was formed to provide, it is self-oriented only in interest associations. Yet, because it always has some side effects, as the enjoyment of social contacts and of inner satisfaction, it is self-oriented in interest *and in issue* associations. *Engagement* requires spending time or money. As it costs more than belonging, it is collectivity-oriented in issue *and in interest* associations. Yet, as it is geared to more distant people in issue than in interest associations, it is collectivity-oriented only in issue associations. Across the board, then, engagement is *more* collectivity-oriented than belonging.

If the civil society is divided according to the collectivity-orientation of its associations, then, interests and issues, and secular and religious interests and issues, are the demarcation lines. They structure the civil society, just as status structures private life or power structures public life. Collectivity-orientation is an aim of associations, and a motive of persons. However, it is also a norm of the social order of societies. In particular, collectivity-orientation will be required more or less strongly by different political regimes and by different religious traditions. Collectivity-orientation, therefore, affects involvement on the level of *persons*, as well as on the level of *countries*.

1.2 *Data and dependent variables*

Data from the European Social Survey 2002 (www.europeansocialsurvey.org) will be used, which is comprised of 22 countries. Of these countries, Switzerland and the Czech Republic did not survey involvement in associations, furthermore, Germany was spilt up into the former East and West divisions, thereby resulting in 21 societies. Austria, Belgium, Denmark, Spain, France, Finland, Greece, Israel, Ireland, Italy, Luxembourg, the Netherlands, Portugal, Sweden, the United Kingdom, and West Germany as the Western countries—and East Germany, Hungary, Poland and Slovenia as the Eastern countries. The total sample size is n = 38959. Analyses within societies are based on samples weighted demographically, analyses in Europe are weighted additionally to give each society the same sample size of n = 2000.

Regarding the question of involvement in associations, it was asked: "For each of the voluntary associations I will now mention, please use this card to tell me whether any of these apply to you now or in the last 12 months, and, if so, which. (Card)—A member of such an organisation.—Participated in an activity arranged by such an organisation.—Donated money to such an organisation.—Done voluntary (unpaid) work for such an organisation." These four forms of involvement were asked for eleven kinds of associations resulting in 44 dummy variables, which had to be reduced.

As for forms of involvement, membership and participation have been combined for *belonging* (BELO), and donation of money and voluntary work have been combined for *engagement* (ENGA), for each kind of association. There were two justifications for this. Conceptually, members or participants *take* the opportunities supplied by the association and donators and voluntary workers *give* to the association. Empirically, membership and participation as well as donation and volunteering correlate more strongly amongst each other than with the variables of the other pair, for each kind of association.

As for the kinds of associations, parties have been excluded because they are more a part of the organized social life than of the civil society. Of the remaining ten associations, seven were classified as *interest*, and two as *issue* associations, namely humanitarian and environmental/peace/animal associations. The seven interest associations, furthermore, were subdivided according to the interest they served, into two *professional* ones—trade unions and business/professional/farmers associations—and five *private* ones—sports clubs, consumer associations, scientific/educational/teachers' associations, social clubs, and cultural associations. Finally, *religious* associations were a single item.

The two forms have been considered for the four kinds so that eight variables remained. In order to retain as much comparability between the four kinds as possible, the forms have, as in similar studies (Gabriel et al. 2002: 46), not been counted and summed up. If someone belongs, for example, to five of the five private associations, they get a score of 1, just as one who belongs to only one of the five. Although, one may be tempted to regard more associations as an indicator of more collectivity-orientation, the budget restriction on a person's time and energy contradicts such an interpretation. The percentages of both forms of involvement in each kind of association are given in Table 1.

Table 1: Forms of involvement according to the kind of association in 21 European countries 2002, in %

Form	Kind		Issue	Religion
	Interest			
	Professional	*Private*		
Belonging	28.4	50.8	12.3	15.1
Engagement	4.4	18.3	15.7	7.8

In professional associations, belonging is more than six times as frequent as engagement, and in private associations almost three times as frequent. In issue associations, however, belonging is lower than engagement while in religious associations belonging is again higher than engagement, but to a much lower degree than in professional and private associations. For professional, and to a lesser degree private associations, belonging is instrumental for personal aims and remains socially "virtual". For issue, and to a lesser degree religious associations, engagement serves as a gate to belonging. This fits together with the principle of our classification; belonging and interest associations indicate the dominance of self-orientation, engagement and issue as well as religious associations indicates the dominance of collectivity-orientation.

As professional associations show only a minimal level of engagement, they will no longer be considered in the following analyses, so that engagement and belonging in private, issue and religious associations remain as the dependent variables.

1.3 *Hypotheses and measurements: Persons*

Attitudes: Collectivity-orientation
Collectivity-orientation is a value, a cognitive standard to evaluate a broad range of actions. It demands gratification of others as well as the self. This leads to the *first* hypothesis: involvement in associations should increase with collectivity-orientation, and this should be stronger

for issue and religious associations, which mainly provides goods for others, than for interest associations, which mainly provides goods for its members. If post-materialism is an indicator of collectivity-orientation insofar as it transcends the needs of the person in favor of the goals of the society, there is some empirical evidence for its positive impact on membership in associations (Halman / Pettersson 2003: 181) and also on its stronger impact on issue rather than on interest associations (Schofer / Fourcade-Gourinchas 2001: 820). Collectivity-orientation will be considered here in three ways; directly as a value, as behavior indicating the value, and as an attitude closely connected with the value.

As a value, collectivity-orientation was measured *directly* with reference to both poles, the self and the collectivity. Self-orientation seeks to gratify the self more than others and can be split up into two types according to the gratification sought after; the fulfillment of subjective needs and the attainment of an objective standard. If gratifications of subjective needs are sought after, one may speak of hedonism; if gratifications through attainments are sought after, one may speak of achievement orientation. Hedonism has only one and immediate goal, the self; achievement is a goal beyond the self whose attainment can be gratifying for the self. Collectivity-orientation seeks to gratify others more than the self and is labeled altruism in everyday language.

Hedonism, achievement and altruism have been measured in the items of the Schwartz inventory. Schwartz (2002: 253) groups hedonism, stimulation and achievement under "self-enhancement" and juxtaposes them to "self-transcendence", which includes benevolence, so that this axis corresponds to the opposition of self- and collectivity-orientation. In order to eliminate personal response tendencies, responses have been transformed into deviations from the personal mean. Of the 18 bivariate correlations between hedonism, achievement and altruism (that is, benevolence) with participation or engagement in private, issue or religious associations, eight were smaller than absolutely .03, and none was greater than absolutely .07. Therefore, value variables have not been included in the following analyses.

As behavior indicating the value, time used for television watching indicates self-orientation, which implies a negative impact on involvement. It restricts activity and reduces life to the passive reception of other people's experiences. Rather than to strive for one's own or other people's goals, the self is absorbed with, and confined in the pleasures of vicarious experiences. Although, this holds independently of content, it holds more strongly if the content is entertainment rather than information. Television use has been measured by the following question: "how much time do you spend, all in all, on an average working day watching television?", with responses ranging from "no time at all" (score 0) to "more than three hours a day" (score 7). This was followed by the question: "and again on an average weekday, how much of your time watching television is spent watching news or programs about politics and current affairs?", with the same response options. After subtracting the score of political use from the score of total use, a rough score of *TV entertainment use* resulted, which was, as all further variables, used in the following analyses.

As an attitude closely connected with the value, religiosity is considered. As religion implies the acceptance of personal self-restriction, religiosity—the identification of a person with religion—should further collectivity-orientation. There is indeed some evidence for the impact of different aspects of religiosity—belonging to a church (Curtis / Baer / Grabb 2001: 795; Smidt 1999: 189; Reitsma et al. 2006), service attendance (Bühlmann / Freitag 2004: 340; Gabriel et al. 2002: 108–118, 138; Norris 2002: 185; Norris / Inglehart 2004: 187–189; Meulemann / Beckers 2004a: 66; Smidt 1999: 189; Wilson / Musick 1997: 704, 708) or diffuse religiosity (Schofer / Fourcade-Gourinchas 2001: 819, 820; Halman / Pettersson 2003: 181)—on involvement in associations.

Religiosity has been measured by church membership. As membership is not formally institutionalized in all European countries, the question referred to the identification: "do you consider yourself as belonging to any particular religion or denomination?" If yes, the denomination was asked whom in all countries (except Greece, where 93% were Orthodox and Israel, where 53% were Jewish) was predominantly Catholic or Protestant (including other Christian denominations). Accordingly, two dummy variables were formed for the identification with the *Catholic* or *Protestant* churches, with all other churches and non-identification as the base category for all countries (including Greece and Israel).

Furthermore, religiosity has been measured by two behaviors and two attitudes: "apart from special occasions such as weddings and funerals, about how often do you attend religious services nowadays?" "Apart from when you are at religious services, how often, if at all, do you pray?" "Looking at this card (of life domains as family, friends, leisure, politics, work, voluntary associations, and religion), how important is each of these factors in *your* life?" "Regardless of whether you belong to a particular religion, how religious would you say you are?" Responses ranged from 1 to 7 or from 0 to 10. As these four measures form a single dimension (Billiet / Welkenhuysen-Gybels 2004), they have been combined with equal weight into an additive *index of religiosity*.

Other Attitudes

An attitude is the tendency to act with reference to an object—for example, to join or to work for an association. This tendency, in turn, may result from a norm to perform the action (Ajzen / Fishbein 1980: 84). As this norm refers to associations in general, it should further involvement in associations independently of their character. From this, the *second* hypothesis follows: involvement in associations of each kind should increase equally with the strength of the norm to be involved in an association. The *subjective norm* to do volunteer work was ascertained by the following question: "to be a good citizen, how important would you say it is for a person to be active in voluntary associations (among other requirements)?", to which responses were given on a scale from 0 to 10.

Someone who has had positive experiences with other people is more prone to sacrifice something for them. Over time, moreover, positive experiences with others are built into trust in others. Trust, in turn, increases the propensity to do something for others. For, the presence of the other is no longer required for altruistic action. Someone who trusts, gives with the expectation that rewards will return on a longer chain of relations. Trust is no longer geared to "the other", but to the "generalized other" (Mead 1977: 217): my fellow persons will respond to my advances eventually. From this, the *third* hypothesis follows: involvement in associations of each kind should increase equally with trust in other people. Indeed, trust increases associational membership in many nations (Uslaner 2002: 38–43; Bühlmann / Freitag 2004: 340; Schofer / Fourcade-Gourinchas 2001: 820) and voluntary work in Germany (Meulemann / Beckers 2004a: 66).

Trust extends from the fellow person one encounters almost daily, to the institutions of the society one is subject to. *Trust in fellow persons* has been asked with three questions. (1) "Generally speaking, would you say that most people can be trusted, or that you can't be too careful in dealing with people?" (2) "Do you think that most people would try to take advantage of you if they got the chance, or would they try to be fair?" (3) "Would you say that most of the time people try to be helpful or that they are mostly looking out for themselves?" Answers were given on a scale from 0 to 10. As the three questions tap the same dimension (Kunz 2004: 207), an additive index was constructed. *Trust in the society at large* is indicated by political interest, that is, by the inclination to care for its most important domain: "how interested would you say you are in politics?", with four response options.

Resources
Resources are life chances, that is, production means for action. They are measured on a socially agreed upon scale and are in this sense "institutionalized". A resource that one needs to sustain actions is money. Yet, as for involvement in associations, money is needed only to become a member, whereby sustaining a membership requires devotion. Much more than being directly instrumental for, money indirectly motivates toward involvement; it does not reduce the costs of involvement, but the opportunity costs. It becomes easier to join or to do unpaid work in the ninth hour of the workday, if one has earned money in the first eight hours.[5] Alternatively, one may consider money as a symbol of success and of integration in the community, both of which facilitate involvement. From either of these arguments, the *fourth* hypothesis follows. Involvement in associations should depend positively on the income of a person.

The *income* was ascertained by the following question: "using this card (which contained 12 levels headed by a letter), if you add up the income from all sources, which letter describes your household's total net income?" As nearly 20% of the sample did not respond to this question, the country specific mean has been assigned to the missing values. Furthermore, the *subjective income* was ascertained by the following question: "which of the descriptions on this card comes closest to how you feel about your household's income nowadays? Living comfortably on present income (score 4), coping on present income (3), finding it difficult on present income (2), and finding it very difficult on present income (1)."

While money is a resource used and used up in action, other resources are used and are *not* consumed, such as knowledge or relations, human

---

[5] Theoretically, the opposite argument may be launched as well. The more one earns, the higher the costs not to work for money. The more one has earned in the first five hours of the day, the more difficult it becomes to do unpaid work from the sixth hour onwards. Yet according to this reasoning one would never join and never do voluntary work; at least, it implies a negative impact of income on involvement. This, however, contradicts all prior research. Income had a *positive* impact on involvement in Germany, the US, Spain and Sweden (Meulemann / Beckers 2004a: 64; Wilson / Musick 1997: 704; Halman / Pettersson 2003: 181).

capital or social capital. Human capital is as useful for unpaid involvement in associations as it is for paid work in employment. Social capital serves as an information channel as well as an incentive for involvement. A person, who knows many people, can ask where to go and what to do; and what others do may be a model for his or her actions. From this, the *fifth* hypothesis follows: involvement in associations should increase with the human and social capital of a person. There is indeed much evidence for the impact of education in the USA (Wilson / Musick 1997: 704; Lam 2002: 413, 416, 418), Switzerland (Bühlmann / Freitag 2004: 340) and in many other nations (Curtis / Baer / Grabb 2001: 795; Schofer / Fourcade-Gourinchas 2001: 820; Halman / Pettersson 2003: 181; Reitsma et al. 2006), and also some evidence for the impact of social relations (Wilson / Musick 1997: 704) on volunteering.

The *human capital* was ascertained by the following question: "what is the highest level of education you have achieved?" The country-specific schemes of certifications have been put together according to the ISCED classification of 7 levels. The *social capital* has been asked with and without reference to groups: "how often do you meet *socially* with friends, relatives or work colleagues?", and: "compared to other people your age, how often would you say you take part in social activities?" Responses were scaled 1 to 7 or 1 to 5 and have been combined with equal weight in an additive index.

Furthermore, social demographic variables have been extensively examined in bivariate analyses. Neither the occupational life cycle nor the family life cycle nor the housing environment had even minor correlations with belonging or engagement. Therefore, only *gender* and *age groups* have been controlled in the following analyses.

Pattern
As issue and religious associations are assumed to be more collectivity-orientated than interest associations, the first and second hypothesis predict that involvement in issue and religious associations is *more strongly* determined by collectivity-orientation than involvement in interest associations. However, as respective norms prescribes involvement in no matter what kind of organizations, moreover as trust facilitates pro-social action in general, and finally as the same amount of resources are needed to become a member and to volunteer in each kind of association, the third to six hypotheses should affect involvement *similarly* in each kind of association. This will be called the *pattern hypothesis*.

1.4 *Hypotheses and measurements: Countries*

Belonging to a country may affect individual action on two levels. Firstly, the *social order* consists of *norms*, which require that something must be done. Norms are incorporated in institutions, for example love and faithfulness in the family; together, all the institutions of a country form its social order. Norms of the social order are largely shared by the people. In order to show how the social order affects a specific target action, the relevant norms have to be named. Then, the social order, just as any other norm held by a person, can be understood as a *direct* guideline to individual action, and different social orders as incorporating collectivity-orientation to varying degrees.

Secondly, the *opportunity structure* comprises *supplies*, which allows that something can be accomplished. Just as the social order is largely shared by everybody, so is the opportunity structure equally available to everybody. Yet, as norms directly mould action, supplies form an environment, which restricts or facilitates action. In order to show how this holds for a specific target action, the social mechanisms have to be found through which the appropriate supply has been accumulated during the societal development. Just as the opportunity level or the resources of a person, the opportunity structure does not mould individual action directly, but *indirectly* opens a range of options.

The social order as well as the opportunity structure refers to three societal domains: politics, economics and culture. For each, accordingly, three hypotheses on the effects of country membership on individual action can be formulated.

Social order

The social order is represented, firstly, by four types of *political regimes*, which underscores collectivity-orientation with different strengths. A *social democratic* and a *liberal* regime both encourage collectivity-orientation—the former "top-down" through political regulations, the latter "bottom-up" through stimulating societal initiative. Social democratic regimes morally and politically propagate involvement and provide direct support for it; liberal regimes foster an ethic of volunteering from within the civil society, by giving leeway to civil society. However, *traditional corporatist* regimes appropriate the tasks potentially served by the civil society and, therefore, discourage collectivity-orientation. These three types refer to Western Europe. In the former *Eastern Bloc*, the state dominated the society by morally, and often legally, enforcing membership in associations, and controlled what remained of public life by supervisory agencies. In these countries, people might still today show a lower level of involvement in associations than in Western European countries (Curtis / Baer / Grabb 2001: 792, 794, 798; Schofer / Fourcade-Gourinchas 2001: 809).

The social order is represented, secondly, by the *economic individualization*, as measured by the Economic Freedom Rating (EFR, Gwartney / Lawson 2003: 11). The more a social order socializes economic action by regulations of the state or large-scale socio-political organizations, the more people are relieved from the responsibility of their own fate; as everybody is taken care of, nobody needs to take care of the other. Therefore, collectivity-orientation will have a weaker and less prominent position in the social order; EFR should affect involvement positively.

The social order is represented, thirdly, by the *Catholic* or *Protestant* tradition. Catholicism is organized "top-down" in a hierarchical, centralized, and authoritarian bureaucracy; Protestantism organizes itself "bottom-up" in egalitarian communities. Yet, an authoritarian culture, just like a social order de-emphasizing economic individualization, exonerates the believer from responsibilities, while an egalitarian culture, just like a social order emphasizing economic individualization, instigates everybody to work for the community. Therefore, Protestantism should more strongly encourage collectivity-orientation and, consequently, involvement, than Catholicism (Curtis / Baer / Grabb 2001: 785, 796).

In each of the three domains, the measures are indicators for a broad consensus within a society, which underscores collectivity-orientation and implies an obligation for involvement. They affect action in just the same manner as the collectivity-orientation of a single citizen, namely as a norm.

Opportunity structure
The opportunity structure is represented, firstly, by the *democratic stability*, as measured by the years a democracy has been established in a country. Democracy separates the sphere of politics from the spheres of economics, civic life, and culture. Yet, the longer democratic rules are established in politics, the more they are implanted also in other spheres, and the more associations therein will flourish. Thus, democratic stability enhances opportunities for involvement.

The opportunity structure is represented, secondly, by the level of *economic progress* of a country, as measured by the gross domestic product per capita. As development means professional and social differentiation, it increases the number of associations within a country, that is, the opportunities for involvement (Halman / Pettersson 2001: 88, Curtis / Baer / Grabb 2001: 796; Schofer / Fourcade-Gourinchas 2001: 809). Democratic stability and economic progress are developmental variables; their increment should increase the number and the forms of associations required for involvement.

The opportunity structure is represented, thirdly, by the cultural pluralization of a country, as measured by the Herfindahl index of *denominational heterogeneity*; for this, the percentages from responses to the question to which church one feels they belong to in the ESS 2002, including no church at all, has been used.[6] As each social sphere seeks to follow its specific imperative more efficiently, differentiation between spheres leads to differentiation within spheres; this, in turn, fosters the growth of the number and kinds of associations. Thus, denominational heterogeneity enhances the supply of associations and the opportunities for involvement.

In each of these three domains, the measures are indicators for the *supply* of associations, which for lack of reliable data (Paxton 2002: 261–262; Salamon / Sokolowski / List 2003: 10), cannot be measured directly. In each of these three domains, moreover, the opportunity structure of associations is produced by the same societal development, namely social differentiation, which is the core of modernization. Modernization implies differentiation, which increases the supply of associations so that involvement is facilitated.

---

[6] The Herfindahl index is an index of *homogeneity*; it measures the probability that a member of a denomination will meet a member of the same denomination (Iannaccone 1991). As cultural pluralization is the concept to be measured here, the unaffiliated are included also. Moreover, the complement value (to 1) is computed, so that the index measures *heterogeneity*. In this form, it has also been computed using the data of Barrett et al. (2001). The ESS-based index produces higher heterogeneity than the index based on Barrett et al., probably because it refers to the *feeling* of belonging rather than to its bureaucratic registration. Taking this into account, both indices produced similar figures, apart from the Netherlands and Luxembourg where the ESS-based index is high (.63 and .55) while the index according to Barrett et al. is low (.18 and .19). As such a low religious cultural heterogeneity seems inadequate for both countries, we choose the ESS-based index. Furthermore, the ESS allowed us to distinguish between Western and Eastern Germany. As East Germans are either Protestant or not affiliated, the heterogeneity is lower (.45) than in West Germany (.71). Over the 22 countries, both measures correlate r = .60.

Pattern
If involvement in issue and religious associations is more strongly determined by collectivity-orientation than involvement in interest associations, a social order, which requests collectivity-orientation, should have a stronger impact on involvement in issue and religious associations than in interest associations. However, the opportunity structure of a society provides the supply for each kind of association equally, and should, therefore, have the same effect on each. This will be again called the *pattern hypothesis*.

2. RESULTS: PERSON LEVEL

The logistic regressions of involvement in interest, issue and religious associations on attitudes, resources, and social-demographic variables are presented in Table 2. After weighting each of the 21 countries to n = 2000, the sample contained 38 943 cases; accordingly, 7.3% of the cases had missing values on any of the independent variables. Due to the enormous sample size, almost every coefficient is significant; therefore, coefficients not significant at least at the 0.1%-level are set in small type italics. Furthermore, standardized coefficients are represented by stars indicating their size, so that coefficients can also be compared column wise.

As for the *collectivity-orientation*, time spent on TV entertainment programs has, in accord with the *first* hypothesis, a negative impact on involvement in secular associations, which is, as the standardized coefficients show, fairly small. Yet, the *pattern hypothesis* of a stronger impact on involvement in issue than in private associations is not confirmed.

Identification with the Catholic Church lowers involvement in secular associations; and identification with the Protestant Church heightens it. Although the negative effect of Catholicism is often not significant, the opposition of effects holds throughout. Yet, identification with either church heightens involvement in religious associations, and more strongly so for the Protestant Church. Compared to Catholicism, then, Protestantism increases involvement in every kind of association. The index of religiosity lowers involvement in private associations, leaves involvement in issue associations unaffected, and increases involvement in religious associations. As the standardized coefficients show, the effects of religiosity and of Protestantism on the involvement in religious associations are the strongest of all. Here, the *first hypothesis* is confirmed only for

Table 2: Logistic regression of involvement in associations on attitudes, resources, and social demographic variables: multiplicative coefficients

	H	C	Private: BELO	Private: ENGA	Issue: BELO	Issue: ENGA	Religion: BELO	Religion: ENGA
Constant			.009	.004	.003	.004	.001	.0002
Attitudes: Collectivity-orientation								
TVEnt	–	8	.972	.954	.934	.953	*.970*	.979
Catholic	+	2	*.970*	.951	*.882*	.860	2.048*	2.160*
Protestant	+	2	1.524	1.395	*1.062*	1.243	5.290**	3.609**
Religious	+	11	.904**	.950	*.980*	*1.001*	1.393***	1.423***
Other attitudes								
SubjNorm	+	11	1.160**	1.141*	1.144*	1.065*	*1.016*	1.030
Trust	+	11	1.101*	1.073	1.078	1.106*	1.107*	1.075
PolInterest	+	4	1.241*	1.191	1.370*	1.371*	1.165	1.195
Resources								
Income	+	12	1.219**	1.112*	1.111*	1.124*	1.100*	1.103*
SubjInc	+	4	1.144	1.166	1.128	1.199	*1.068*	*1.055*
Education	+	7	1.223**	1.110	1.230*	1.206*	1.082	1.092
SocCapit	+	8	1.348*	1.312*	1.175*	1.131	1.198*	1.187*
Social demography								
Male	?	2	1.255	1.281	.679*	.661*	*1.083*	*1.038*
Age-25	?	2	*.900*	.743	*.962*	.720	*1.193*	*.789*
Age-45	?	2	*.846*	*1.001*	*.972*	*.931*	*1.026*	*.895*
Age-65	?	2	*.917*	1.043	1.120	.885	1.007	.960
R^2–Collectivity			.147	.086	.092	.083	.225	.177
R^2–Other Attitudes			.077	.037	.029	.036	.050	.042
R^2–Attitudes, both			.204	.111	.102	.096	.250	.199
R^2–Resources			.243	.107	.099	.109	.027	.018
R^2–Resour+Attitudes			.305	.154	.144	.142	.270	.214
R^2–Total			.308	.160	.151	.152	.271	.216

H = Hypothesis. C = N of categories.—Reference groups: Denominations: none and all others; age: 66+.
*** Standardized coefficients absolutely > 2, ** > 1.5, * > 1.2. Coefficients in small italics: not significant at $p<.001$.

Protestantism, and the *pattern hypothesis* of a stronger effect of religiosity on involvement in issue than in private associations is not confirmed. Nevertheless, a pattern of differential effects of religiosity emerges. Its strong positive effect on involvement, taken for granted in prior research, holds only for religious associations; on secular associations, it has a much weaker and often negative effect. In particular, religiosity constitutes no motive for involvement in secular value issues (Halman / Pettersson 2001: 84; Lam 2002: 412, 416; Reitsma et al. 2006).

As the R^2-values for the four variables indicating collectivity-orientation show, the *pattern hypothesis* of a *greater* impact on issue than interest associations is confirmed neither for belonging nor for engagement. Rather, belonging to interest associations is more strongly determined than engagement in interest associations and both forms of involvement in issue associations. As these R^2 values furthermore show, collectivity-orientation has much less impact on secular than on religious associations.

As for the *other attitudes*, the *subjective norm* has, in accord with the *second hypothesis*, a positive impact on all forms and kinds of involvement. Yet, as the standardized coefficients show, it is strong only for private and issue associations. The two *trust* variables have, in accord with the *third hypothesis*, a positive impact on all forms and kinds of involvement. Political interest has a stronger impact on both forms of involvement in issue than in private associations. Obviously, the political affinity of issue associations reinforces the impact of political interest on involvement. As the standardized coefficients show, there is only one consistently strong impact, namely, of political interest on involvement in issue associations.

As the R^2-values for the three other attitudes show, the *pattern hypothesis* of an *equal* impact is confirmed for engagement, but not for belonging. As these R^2 values furthermore show, subjective norms and social experiences have much more impact on secular than on religious associations.

As for *resources*, they all have a positive impact on all the forms and kinds of involvement, in accord with the *forth and fifth hypothesis*. As the standardized coefficients show, income, education and social capital are strong predictors of both forms of involvement in all kinds of associations, while subjective income is only a weak predictor.

As the R^2-values for the four resources show, the *pattern hypothesis* of an *equal* impact is confirmed for engagement but not for belonging, which is better to predict for private than for religious associations. Looking back to the regression coefficients, one finds two particularly strong differences. Firstly, one unit of social capital increases belonging in private associations by 35%, yet, in issue associations only by 18%; private associations rely on neighbors and friends, issue associations rely on value identifications. Secondly, one unit of income class increases belonging in private associations by 22%, yet, in issue associations only by 12%; income is an entrance gate for a golf club, but hardly for Amnesty International. As these R^2 values furthermore show, resources have much more impact on secular than on religious associations; economic, human and social capital is needed to get involved in secular associations, but religions have the community of believers to draw volunteers for their associations from.

As for *socio-demographic predictors*, men are more often involved in private, women in issue associations, and both equally often in religious associations; and age does not matter.[7] As the R^2-values show, they only minimally increase the predictability of involvement.

In sum, each of the five hypotheses is confirmed at least for some indicators. However, the pattern hypothesis is clearly disconfirmed. Instead, an unexpected pattern of effects emerges. Involvement in secular associations results from subjective norms, trust, and resources, but not from religiosity. However, involvement in religious associations does not need norms, trust, and resources. It rests on the pre-commitment of religious membership and devotion. Religiosity is not transformed into secular involvement, and religious associations do not need secular means and incentives.

3. Results: Person and Country Level

The effects of the countries on the level of involvement, the regression intercepts, is estimated together with the effects of person variables in an *intercept model* of a *hierarchical regression*, which combines a regression on person variables with a regression of the intercepts on country variables. As the dependent person variables are dichotomous, logistic regressions *without an error term* are computed on the person level. As the dependent country variable, the intercept, is continuous, linear regressions *with an error term* are computed on the country level.[8]

---

[7] Norris / Davis (2007: 255–256, 260) find a slight curvilinear effect for age on mere membership in all kinds of associations such that it is highest in the middle age group. This is no longer visible in our results, which combine membership and participation on the one hand and differentiates between kinds of associations on the other hand.

[8] Computations have been made with HLM6 and restricted "penalized quasi-likelihood" estimations (Raudenbush / Bryk / Congdon 2004: 103–106).

3.1 Country level

Due to the small number of countries, separate regressions had to be computed for the social order and the opportunity structure. Furthermore, as the two social order dimensions overlap considerably—many of the social democratic countries are also Protestant and many of the traditional corporatist countries are also Catholic[9]—separate regressions for political regime and religious tradition are computed controlling for the same person level variables as in Table 2, except for TV entertainment, subjective income and age. Of these three regressions, the country variable coefficients are presented in Table 3. The table will be regarded in three ways. *Firstly*, the hypotheses will be tested by looking at the raw coefficients row wise, *secondly*, the relative strength of the predictors will be assessed by looking at the standardized coefficients column wise, and *thirdly*, the pattern hypothesis will tested by looking at the explained variances.

Testing the hypotheses: Raw Coefficients
Looking at *political regime*, the three West European types facilitate each of the six variables of involvement more than the former Eastern bloc. As predicted, the advantage of the liberal and the social democratic regime is mostly bigger than the advantage of the traditional corporatist regimes. Yet, the former advantages are seldom significant, and the latter advantage is substantially negligible. Pooling the three West European regimes produces a positive effect for each dependent variable, although never significant below the 5% level. However, if one takes into account the small sample of countries, the consistency of the effects seems more important than the lack of significance.

---

[9] *Liberal*: Ireland, United Kingdom; *social democratic*: Denmark, Finland, Israel, Norway, Netherlands, Sweden; *traditional corparatist*: Austria, Belgium, Spain, France, Greece, Italy, Luxembourg, Portugal, West Germany: *Eastern bloc*: East Germany, Hungary, Poland, Slovenia. This follows Curtis / Baer / Grabb (2001: 790) and Janoski (1998: 23). Greece was classified as traditional corporatist according to information on legal regulation from the European website MISSOC; Luxembourg was classified traditional corporatist because of its long economic union with Belgium; Israel was classified as social democratic according to its founders' traditions.—*Catholic*: Austria, Belgium, Spain, France, Ireland, Italy, Luxembourg, Portugal, Hungary, Poland, Slovenia; *Protestant*: Denmark, Finland, Sweden, United Kingdom, East Germany; *Mixed*: Netherlands, West Germany; *religiously homogeneous otherwise*: Greece, Israel. This follows Curtis / Baer / Grabb (2001: 790).—As can be seen for the above: of the 11 Catholic countries and the 9 traditional corporatist countries, 7 are both; off the 6 Protestant countries and 6 social democratic countries, 4 are both. Simultaneous typologies in both dimensions did not fare better than each alone.

Table 3: Hierarchical logistic regression of involvement in associations on the social order and the opportunity structure of countries: multiplicative coefficients

	H	C/SD	Private: BELO	Private: ENGA	Issue: BELO	Issue: ENGA	Religion: BELO	Religion: ENGA
Raw-Coefficients								
Tau without			.958	.795	.644	.795	.628	.590
Social Order: Political Regime								
Constant			.0003	.007	.001	.003	.001	.066
Liberal	++	2	1.214	1.402	1.138	1.322	1.742	4.447**
SocDem	++	2	3.162'	1.924	2.709*	2.730	2.366**	1.796
TradCor	+	2	1.270	.874	1.990	1.221	1.029	.946
EcoFreeR	+	.49	2.842*	1.443	1.806	1.661	1.741	.825
Tau			.781	.780	.480	.676	.437	.514
% red			18.5	1.9	25.5	15.0	30.4	12.9
Social Order: Religious Tradition								
Constant			.003	.185	.006	.134	.002	.036
Catholic	−	2	.423*	.358**	.796	.384**	.568	.621
NL-WG	?	2	1.313	1.158	1.645'	1.445'	1.592*	2.260*
GR-ISR	?	2	.390	.173***	.344	.145*	.384	.376
EcoFreeR	+	.49	2.272'	.931	1.578	1.113	1.607	.961
Tau			.798	.580	.544	.464	.440	.520
% red			16.7	27.4	15.5	41.6	19.9	11.9
Opportunity structure								
Constant			.049	.018	.021	.026	.017	.009
YearDem	+	29	1.012*	1.005	1.010***	1.008'	1.011'	1.005
GDPpc	+	9.83	1.057**	1.031	1.047***	1.043	1.003	.987
Hetero	+	.15	9.275**	8.813'	2.289	2.944	2.950	5.619
Tau			.227	.488	.137	.397	.546	.617
% red			76.3	38.6	78.7	50.1	13.1	0.0
Standardized Coefficients								
Social Order: Political Regime								
Liberal			1.06	1.11	1.04	1.09	1.18	1.56**
SocDem			1.70'	1.35	1.58'	1.59	1.49**	1.31
TradCor			1.13	0.93	1.42	1.11	1.01	0.97
EcoFreedR			1.67*	1.20	1.34	1.28	1.31	0.91
Social Order: Religious Tradition								
Catholic			1.56^{-1}*	1.69^{-1}**	1.12^{-1}	1.64^{-1}**	1.33^{-1}	1.28^{-1}
NL-WG			1.09	1.04	1.16'	1.12'	1.15*	1.28*
GR-ISR			1.33^{-1}	1.69^{-1}***	1.37^{-1}	1.79^{-1}*	1.33^{-1}	1.33^{-1}
EcoFreedR			1.49'	0.97	1.25	1.05	1.26	0.98
Opportunity structure								
YearDem			1.41*	1.16	1.33***	1.26'	1.37'	1.16
GDPpc			1.72**	1.35	1.57***	1.51	1.03	0.88
Hetero			1.40**	1.39'	1.13	1.18	1.18	1.30

H = Hypothesis. C/SD = N of categories for qualitative variables, Standard deviation for quantitative variables
Reference groups: for liberal, social democratic and traditional corporatist regimes: Eastern bloc; for Catholic countries, NL-WG, GR-ISL: Protestant countries.
Standardized coefficients with exponent −1: negative effect
*** $p < .001$, ** $p < .01$, * $p < .05$, ' $p < .10$

Even 13 years after the demise of state socialism, the civil society is still stronger in West than in East European societies. Furthermore, this is clearly a system effect of the old social order because the person variables through which the old social order may affect involvement have been controlled for. Although state socialism has suppressed religion and destroyed trust in public affairs, the lack of these personal conditions of involvement cannot be made accountable for the differences between Western and Eastern countries.[10]

Looking at *religious tradition*, Catholic countries always and often significantly lag behind Protestant ones, as predicted. Yet, the two denominationally mixed countries, Netherlands and West Germany, facilitate involvement even more than the Protestant ones, while the two homogeneous countries, Greece and Israel, lag even more behind—although both tendencies are not often significant. Involvement is rank ordered according to heterogeneity and, additionally in the middle, according to denomination; it is highest in the heterogeneous countries, medium in the predominantly Protestant countries, followed by the predominantly Catholic countries, and lowest in the homogeneous countries.

The third variable of the social order, the Economic Freedom Rating, was an additional predictor in the regression on regimes and in the regression on religious traditions. In both regressions, it has a positive impact as expected, yet a strong and significant one only on belonging to private associations.

Looking at the *opportunity structure*, each of its three variables show the expected positive effects on involvement in secular associations, which is often substantial and significant, but none has an effect on involvement in religious associations. Looking more closely at secular organizations, years of democracy and gross domestic product have a stronger effect on belonging than on engagement. Obviously, social differentiation widens the supply of private as well as issue associations so that people will simply seize the opportunities to belong. Yet, engagement requires more than opportunities, namely personal motivation. Often, opportunities are sufficient for belonging, yet, not even necessary for engagement.

In sum, the effects of the social order and the opportunity structure are mostly as expected. Liberal and social democratic West European

---

[10] This is in contrast to Curtis / Baer / Grabb (2001: 798) where the significantly lower level of membership and of voluntary work in Eastern bloc countries vanished when economic development and years of democracy had been controlled for.

regimes and Protestant traditions form a normative frame, which all citizens of a given country bear in mind and often follow. In addition, social differentiation provides the opportunity structure for secular, yet, not for religious organizations.

Relative strength of predictors: Standardized Coefficients
For each of the six dependent variables, none of the ten independent variables sticks out as a particularly strong and consistent predictor. However, the advantage of the social democratic countries in comparison to the Eastern bloc and the disadvantage of Catholic countries in comparison to the Protestant ones, are almost always the strongest effects. As the Social Democratic and the Protestant countries are largely the same, these effects are the same. Furthermore, the gross domestic product is always among the four strongest effects on involvement in private and issue associations.

As for the social order, then, social democratic regimes and Protestant countries, together with mixed traditions, are prominent in favoring involvement in *all* kinds of associations. As for the opportunity structure, the gross domestic product is prominent in favoring involvement in *secular* associations. Protestant tradition, backed by social democratic policy, furthers every involvement; and social differentiation, which provides the supply of secular associations, furthers involvement in secular associations.

Testing the pattern hypothesis: Explained Variances
The Tau values represent the estimated error of the intercept over the countries. In the first line of Table 3, the Tau value for the random intercept model without country predictors is presented, which serves as a yardstick for the Tau values of the three models with predictors. To make the Tau values comparable between different dependent variables, the percentage of the error reduction relative to the random intercept models are presented immediately below the respective Tau values.

If one compares the *Tau values between the three models within each dependent variable*, the opportunity structure affects involvement in private and in issue associations much more than the two sets of predictors of the social order. Yet, the social order affects involvement in religious associations more than the opportunity structure. That is, the border between kinds of associations runs not between interest associations and issue as well as religious associations, but between secular and religious associations. If one compares the *percentage reduction of Tau values between dependent variables within each model*, both models of the social order do not consistently affect involvement in issue and religious associations more strongly than in private associations. However, the opportunity structure affects involvement in private and issue associations more strongly than in religious associations. Again, the border between kinds of associations runs not between interest associations and issue as well religious associations, but between secular and religious associations. Whichever way one looks at it, the pattern hypothesis is not confirmed; social orders, which more strongly emphasize collectivity-orientation, do not heighten collectivity-oriented involvement in a country. Yet, the opportunity structure strongly heightens involvement in secular, and not at all in religious associations. Why is this so?

Seemingly, social differentiation has a stronger impact on the growth of civic associations than on the development of religion. On the one hand, it increases the supply of associations not in general, but predominantly, of interest and issue associations. It broadens the alternatives of occupational careers and of leisure time and the possible conflicts according to political, economic, educational and cultural differences, so that the number of interest associations rises. For the same reason, domestic and global problems increase in number and become increasingly aware to the public, so that the number of issue association rises. As societies grow and differentiate internally, then, the supply of associations, which serve interests and express issue identifications, will increase. On the other hand, religions develop according to their own logic, namely the conceivable answers to the religious question, which follows societal differentiation dimly at best. Specifically, European countries in recent decades did not develop along this line; although people have retreated from the churches, which are the bearers of religious associations and resorted to seeking personal answers to the religious question (Jagodzinski / Dobbelaere 1995). Rather than increase with societal differentiation, the country level of involvement in religious associations should decrease with the secularization of countries.

As for the effects of the opportunity structure, then, secular and religious associations are set apart from each other in a similar way as on the level of persons. On the person level, involvement in secular associations depends on resources and attitudes, and involvement in religious associations depends on religiosity. On the country level, involvement in secular associations increases with the societal supply,

Table 4: Comparison between the multiplicative coefficients Catholic and Protestant between logistic regressions on person level (P) and on person and country level (P + C)

	Private				Issue				Religion			
	BELO		ENGA		BELO		ENGA		BELO		ENGA	
	P	P+C	P	P+C	P	P+C	P	P+C	P	P+C	P	P+C
Cath	1.01	1.14	.99	1.13	.88	.68	.89	.90	2.04	2.03	2.18	2.14
Prot	1.58	1.30	1.47	1.26	1.08	.91	1.30	1.04	5.28	3.12	3.72	2.87

and involvement in religious associations is stronger where it is favored normatively by the social order, either directly as in Protestant teaching and in social democratic policies or indirectly as in liberal policies, which stress individual self-realization. Altogether, involvement in secular associations seems more strongly a matter of opportunities, while involvement in religious associations is more strongly a matter of norms on both levels.

3.2 *Person level*

In each of the regressions in Table 3, the same predictors as in Table 2, except TV entertainment, subjective income and age, are controlled. They had nearly the same coefficients, except the identification with the Catholic and the Protestant church. Table 4, therefore, compares these coefficients between the hierarchical regression on religious traditions, that is the second model of Table 3, and a regression with exactly the same person level predictors only.

As the comparison shows, the positive effect of being Protestant is reduced once the religious tradition of countries is controlled for, so that the difference between the denominations disappears for private and issue associations and is reduced for religious associations. This is due to the fact that countries with a Protestant tradition, at the same time have a high percentage of Protestants and a high level of involvement. Once countries are pooled, therefore, the effect of the Protestant tradition is attributed to being Protestant. The differences of the person level regressions are, completely for private and issue associations, partly for religious associations, spurious. In truth, Protestants are not more inclined to get involved in private and issue associations than Catholics; and both only very weakly. In truth, furthermore, Protestants are still more, but not overwhelmingly, inclined to get involved in religious associations than Catholics; and both still very strongly.

On the person level, then, denominations do not affect involvement in secular associations, but in religious associations.[11] However, on the country level, the Protestant tradition affects involvement in all kinds of associations. The different teachings of the churches are not reflected in different secular involvements of their believers, yet they build up a national tradition, which guides the involvement of each citizen alike, including the one who has a different creed. Furthermore, each church is successful across countries in mobilizing its members to get involved in religious associations.

While religious denominations have different effects on involvement on the person and the country level, two other variables encompassing both levels have the same impact on both, as a comparison between Table 2 and 3 shows. *Firstly*, income as well as gross domestic product further involvement in secular associations. Wealthy people are more often involved than poorer people—no matter whether "people" means persons or countries. Those that have more money are more inclined to be involved and there are more opportunities for involvement in wealthier than in poorer countries. Economic resources of the person and the economic development of a society similarly increase the involvement in associations. *Secondly*, trust, as well as the longevity of democracy, further involvement in secular associations. Those that trust their fellow humans will be more involved in civic associations, and a democratic tradition broadens the opportunities of civic associations. Positive experiences of a person with their fellow citizens and the accumulation of stable and reliable social interaction patterns in a society both increases involvement in associations.

---

[11] This contradicts the results of Norris / Inglehart (2004: 187, 189) based on the World Value Surveys (WVS) of 76 countries, which show that attendance of religious services has a positive impact on membership in religious and non-religious associations. There are three reasons, which can account for the difference. Firstly, the WVS includes many more countries with non-Christian traditions than the ESS in which the relations could be stronger while it does not hold in European countries. Secondly, Norris and Inglehart indicate religiosity by church attendances only and do not control for the "other attitudes" on the person level so that the effect of church attendance may have taken over the effects of these other variables. Thirdly, Norris and Inglehart do not control for religious tradition on the country level such that again the effect of church attendance may have taken over the these effects.

4. Conclusion

To test the empirical fruitfulness of the analytical distinction of associations according to their collectivity-orientation, it was examined whether involvement in issue, interest, and religious associations is differently determined by the collectivity-orientation of *people*, as well as by the collectivity-orientation implied by the social order of *countries*.

As for *people*, interest, issue and religious associations could not be distinguished according to the effects of collectivity-orientation. Rather than interest from issue and religious associations, the border within civil society separates secular from religious associations. There is no religious, but also no secular collectivity-oriented motive for involvement in secular, and specifically in issue associations, but there is a religious motive for involvement in religious associations. Secular civil society does neither profit from secular values nor from religion; religion furthers involvement only in its own domain, where involvement reflects self-orientation as much as collectivity-orientation. Contrary to what has been shown in studies of involvement, which did not distinguish between kinds of associations, religiosity does not transfer into public virtues.

Moreover, while involvement in interest and issue associations was equally strongly determined by norms, social experiences and resources, involvement in religious associations was not affected at all by these factors. Obviously, involvement in secular associations is a matter of feasibility, yet involvement in religious associations is a matter of conviction.

As for *countries*, interest associations could not be distinguished from issue and religious associations according to the effects of the social order. However, interest and issue associations must be distinguished from religious associations according to the effects of the opportunity structure. The opportunity structure more strongly increased involvement in interest and issue associations than in religious associations. As for the effect of the opportunity structure, there is a borderline between secular and religious associations. Just as on the person level, involvement in secular associations is a matter of feasibility and involvement in religious associations, a matter of conviction, on the country level, involvement in secular associations is more a matter of the opportunity structure and involvement in religious associations more a matter of the social order.

If one looks at the determinants of involvement on the person as well as on the country level, then, the border runs not between interest and issue, but between secular and religious associations. The pattern hypothesis was not verified, neither on the person nor on the country level. The variety of the civil society can be captured by the concept of collectivity-orientation analytically, yet not empirically. If one restricts the civil society to secular associations, their recruitment is very homogeneous; if one includes religious associations, one lumps together fairly differently recruited kinds of associations and this holds within as well as between countries.

References

Ajzen, Icek / Fishbein, Martin (1980): Understanding Attitudes and Predicting Social Behavior. Englewood Cliffs, New Jersey: Prentice Hall.

Anheier, Helmut K. / Salamon, Lester M. (2001): Volunteering in cross-national perspective: Initial comparisons. *Civil society Working Paper 10. Available from the Centre for Civil Society Studies at the Institute for Policy Studies at the Johns Hopkins Universit.*

Barrett, David B. / Kurian, George T. / Johnson, Todd M. (2001): World Christian Encyclopedia. A comparative survey of churches and religions in the modern world. Oxford: Oxford University Press.

Billiet, Jaak / Welkenhuysen-Gybels, Jerry (2004): Assessing Cross-National Equivalence in the ESS: The case of religious Involvement, Paper prepared at the European Conference on Quality and Methodology in Official Statistics. Mainz.

Bühlmann, Marc / Freitag, Markus (2004): Individuelle und kontextuelle Determinanten der Teilhabe an Sozialkapital. Eine Mehrebenenanalyse zu den Bedingungen des Engagements in Freiwilligenorganisationen. *Kölner Zeitschrift für Soziologie und Sozialpsychologie* 56: 326–349.

Curtis, James E. / Baer, Douglas E. / Grabb, Edard G. (2001): Nations of Joiners: Explaining Voluntary Association Membership in Democratic Societies. *American Sociological Review* 66: 783–805.

Erlinghagen, Marcel (2000): Informelle Arbeit. Ein Überblick über einen schillernden Begriff. *Schmollers Jahrbuch* 120: 239–274.

Gabriel, Oscar W. / Kunz, Volker / Roßteutscher, Sigrid / Deth, Jan W. van (2002): Sozialkapital und Demokratie. Zivilgesellschaftliche Ressourcen im Vergleich. Wien: WUV-Universitätsverlag.

Gwartney, James / Lawson, Robert (2003): Economic Freedom of the World. 2003 Annual Report. Vancouver: Fraser Institute. www.freetheworld.com.

Halman, Loek / Pettersif, Thorleif (2001): Religion and social capital in contemporary Europe: Results from the 1999/2000 European Values Study. 66-93 in: *D. O. Moberg / R.L. Piedmont* (eds.). Research in the Social Scientific Study of Religion, Volume 12. Leiden: Brill.

Halman, Loek / Pettersson, Thorleif (2003): Religion and social capital revisited. 162–184 in: *Halman, Loek / Riis, Ole (eds.)*. Religion in Secularizing Society. The Europeans' Religion at the End of the 20th Century. Leiden / Boston: Brill.

Iannaccone, Laurence R. (1991): The Consequences of Religious Market Structure. *Rationality and Society* 3: 156–177.

Jagodzinski, Wolfgang / Dobbelaere, Karl (1995): Secularization and Church Religiosity. 76-119 in: *van Deth, Jan / Scarbrough, Eleanor (eds.).* The impact of Values. Beliefs in Government Volume Four. Oxford: Oxford University Press.
Janoski, Thomas (1998): Citizenship and civil society. A framework of rights and obligations in liberal, traditional, and social democratic regimes. Cambridge: Cambridge University Press.
Kunz, Volker (2004): Soziales Vertrauen. 201–228 in: *van Deth, Jan (ed.).* Deutschland in Europa. Wiesbaden: Verlag für Sozialwissenschaften.
Lam, Pui-Yan (2002): As the Flocks Gather: How Religion Affects Voluntary Association Participation. *Journal for the Scientific Study of Religion* 41: 405–422.
Mead, George Herbert (1977): On Social Psychology. Chicago.
Meulemann, Heiner / Beckers, Tilo (2004a): Das sichtbare und das verborgene Element—Häufigkeiten und Hintergründe von Ehrenamt und privater Hilfe in Deutschland im Jahre 2002. *Soziale Welt* 2004: 51–74.
Meulemann, Heiner / Beckers, Tilo (2004b): Ehre in unterschiedlichen Ämtern. Der Einfluss von Ressourcen und Einstellungen auf die Übernahme eines Ehrenamtes in Dienstleistungs- und Wohlfahrtsvereinen in Deutschland im Jahre 2002. 109–136 in: *Michael Bayer / Sören Petermann (Hrsg.),* Soziale Struktur und wissenschaftliche Praxis im Wandel. Festschrift für Heinz Sahner. Wiesbaden: VS Verlag für Sozialwissenschaften.
Norris, Pippa (2002): Democratic Phoenix. Cambridge: Cambridge University Press.
Norris, Pippa / Inglehart, Ronald (2004): Sacred and Secular. Cambridge: Cambridge University Press.
Norris, Pippa / Davis, James (2007): A continental divide? Social Capital in the US and Europe. 239–264 in: *Jowell, Roger et al. (eds.).* Measuring Attitudes Cross-National. Lessons from the European Social Survey. London: Sage.
Parsons, Talcott / Shils, Edward A. (eds.) (1951): Toward A general Theory of Action. Theoretical Foundations for the Social Sciences. New York: Harper.
Paxton, Pamela (2002): Social Capital and Democracy: An Interdependent Relationship. *American Sociological Review* 67: 254–277.
Putnam, Robert D. / Goss, Kristin A. (2002): Introduction. 3–20 in: *Putnam, Robert D. (ed.)* Democracies in Flux. Oxford: Oxford University Press.
Raudenbush, Stephen W. / Bryk, Anthony S. / Congdon Richard T. (2004): HLM6: Hierarchical Linear and Nonlinear Modeling. Chicago; Scientific Software International.
Reitsma, Jan / Scheepers, Peer / te Groetenhuis, Manfred (2006): Dimensions of individual religiosity and volunteering in Europe. Paper available from j.reitsma@maw.ru.nl.
Salamon, Lester M. / Sokolowski, S. Wojciech / List, Regina (2003): Global Civil Society: An Overview. Baltimore: John Hopkins Center for Civil Society Studies. Also: www.jhu.edu/~ccss.
Schofer, Evan / Fourcade-Gourinchas, Marion (2001): The structural Contexts of Civic Engagement: Voluntary Association Membership in Comparative Perspective. *American Sociological Review* 66: 806–828.
Schwartz, Shalom (2002): A proposal for measuring value orientations across nations. Chapter 7 of: European Social Survey. Development of the Core Questionnaire.
Smidt, Corwin (1999): Religion and Civic Engagement: A Comparative Analysis. *Annals of the American Academy of Political and Social Science* 565: 176–192.
Stolle, Dietlind (2003): The sources of Social Capital. 19–42 in: *Hooghe, Marc / Stolle, Dietlind (eds.)* Generating Social Capital. Civil society and Institutions in comparative Perspective. New York: Palgrave Macmillan.

Uslaner, Eric M. (2002): The moral foundations of Trust. Cambridge: Cambridge University Press.
van Deth, Jan (2006): Democracy and Involvement. The benevolent aspects of social participation. 101–129 in: *Torcal, Mariano / Monter, Jose Ramon* (eds.). Political Disaffection in Contemporary Democracies. London: Routledge.
van Deth, Jan / Kreuter, Frauke (1998): Membership of voluntary associations. 135–155 in: *van Deth, Jan (ed.).* Comparative Politics. London / New York: Routledge.
Warren, Mark E. (2001): Democracy and Association. Princeton University Press: Princeton—Oxford.
Wessels, Bernhard (1997): Organizing capacity of societies and modernity. 198–219 in: *van Deth, Jan* (ed.). Private groups and public life, London / New York: Routledge.
Wilson, John (2000): Volunteering. *Annual Review of Sociology* 26: 215–240.
Wilson, John / Muzick, M. (1997): Who cares? Towards an integrated theory of volunteer work. *American Sociological Review.*

CHAPTER FOUR

EXPLAINING SOCIAL TRUST: WHAT MAKES PEOPLE TRUST THEIR FELLOW CITIZENS?

Katja Neller

Putnam (1993: 167) defines the core components of social capital as social trust, involvement in social networks or associations, and norms of reciprocity (or civic norms). While associational involvement represents the *structural* aspects of the concept of social capital, social trust and civic norms form its *attitudinal* or *cultural* components (e.g. van Deth 2003: 80).

On the *individual-level*, trust refers to expectations of future behaviors and is mainly based on beliefs about the trustee's competence and sense of responsibility (Coleman 1988; Gambetta 1988; Misztal 1996). To trust means to rely on others to meet their obligations and not to be taken advantage of (Misztal 1996: 16ff., 24). Researchers like Braithwaite (1998) differentiate exchange-orientated and community-orientated forms of trust. Exchange-orientated forms of trust deal with expectations of reliability, accountability and competence of the object of trust. Community-orientated forms of trust focus on sharing the same social identity, norms and values, the feeling of being respected and the belief that other people take into account the interests of others when acting (see also Hardin 1998; Tyler 1998). Putnam (2000: 134) characterizes the individual-level consequences of social trust as follows: "I'll do this for you now, without expecting anything immediately in return and perhaps without even knowing you, confident that down the road you or someone else will return the favor".

On the *aggregate-level*, social trust is considered an important resource of societies to promote cooperation. "Trust lubricates cooperation. The greater the level of trust within a society, the greater the likelihood of cooperation. And cooperation itself breeds trust" (Putnam 1993: 171, see also Almond/Verba 1963: 227ff.). Cooperation, in turn, is considered a basic factor for integration, building and maintaining democracy, economic prosperity and other societal and individual benefits.

In the following, the focus will be on *generalized* social trust in other people as a special kind of trust. This type of "thin" trust is more general than "thick" trust, defined as trust in single persons like friends or relatives. Another important characteristic of generalized trust is that it is horizontal—contrary to vertical trust in political elites or institutions (e.g. Delhey/Newton 2004: 152).

Research on social trust was promoted as a side effect of the extensive debate on social capital during the last years (e.g. Badescu/Uslaner 2003; Cook 2001; Cook et al. 2005; Hardin 2002; Ostrom/Walker 2003; Sztompka 1999; Uslaner 2002; Warren 1999). The ongoing interest in this phenomenon may also result from a "widely shared, though largely implicit, diagnosis of basic problems of public policy and the steering of social coordination, and ultimately the maintenance of social order itself" (Offe 1999: 42).

If social trust is such an important personal and country-level resource, it is important to know about the factors generating it. Most of the empirical analysis conducted so far concentrates on individual-level determinants. However, it is clear that the number of studies analyzing micro-level factors explaining generalized social trust in a *systematic* way, is still surprisingly low (Kunz 2004: 210). One basic result of these studies is that micro-level factors account only for a small part of the variance of social trust. In sum, the explanatory power of these micro models is more or less disappointing (see, for example, results presented in Delhey/Newton 2002; Freitag 2003; Gabriel et al. 2002; Kunz 2004; Zmerli/Newton/Montero 2007). One reason for this could be the fact that none of the individual-level models tested so far integrates variables representing *all* relevant approaches discussed in the literature on determinants of social trust. Therefore, this chapter aims first at testing an integrated micro model of possible factors explaining why people trust others or not, analyzing the effects of as many variables representing different hypotheses as possible.[1]

The number of empirical studies testing country or macro-level variables as determinants of social trust is even lower than the numbers of studies using a micro-level perspective. The basic results of these studies are that the levels of socio-economic development and wealth, the degree of social

---

[1] Naturally, there will be some limitations due to the ESS data used here. The questionnaire for the first wave of the ESS contains variables to operationalize a significant part of, but not all of the possible determinants of social trust (see part 3.1 of this chapter).

(in)equality, the kind of political and institutional settings (e.g. age of democracy, consensus democratic structures, type of welfare state), the existence of a civic society network and the inclusion of people in this network, and Protestant (non-Catholic) religious traditions, seems to be the most important contextual factors (Bornschier 2001; Freitag/Bühlmann 2005; Gabriel et al. 2002; Inglehart 1997; Kunz 2004).

Multilevel explanations of social trust in a comparative perspective, combining individual and country-level factors, have only been performed in exceptional cases so far.[2] Freitag/Bühlmann (2005) show in their multilevel analysis of the 1995–1997 World Value Survey Data, that social equality (measured by distribution of incomes), an independent judiciary, and a consensual political setting (measured by the existence of a system of proportional representation), generate social trust and boost the positive effects of education, satisfaction with life and low television consumption, on social trust.

Against this background, the second aim of this chapter is to develop a concept to explain social trust that integrates individual-level and macro-level approaches, assessing the additional benefit of using a multilevel model compared to a micro-level model.

The analysis proceeds in several steps. As a starting point for further analysis, the first question is: do all Europeans trust their fellow citizens in a similar way or are there significant differences in the display of social trust between European countries? Then, a comprehensive individual-level model explaining social trust is developed by testing different hypotheses. If this individual-level model does not lead to satisfactory results in explaining why people trust others or not, country differences (macro-level indicators) will be considered as additional determinants. To keep the multilevel model as small as possible, different contextual factors will be tested in an explorative analysis; firstly to find those that represent the relevant dimensions best. In the last step, the final micro model, the significant variables found by testing several individual-level approaches simultaneously, is combined with country-level factors (that

---

[2] As a part of a study on contextual effects on electoral turnout at a German municipal election, Schmitt-Beck (2005) performed a multilevel analysis of social trust, including individual-level data from a survey conducted in Duisburg in 2004 and district level macro data. He found that males are more trusting than females and that higher levels of formal education, knowledge about local politics, satisfaction with democracy, trust in the city council, external efficacy in respect to local elites, political self-confidence, membership in voluntary organizations and living in a more affluent neighborhood (= contextual factor) contribute to higher levels of social trust.

result from the explorative analysis of the macro determinants) in a multilevel analysis. After having exhausted the potential of the micro-level determinants, this design will illustrate the *additional* power of country-level differences to explain social trust.

1. Levels of Social Trust in Europe

In the literature on social trust, there is a broad discussion about the adequate ways to operationalize generalized social trust (Gabriel et al. 2002: 56f.; Glaeser et al. 2000; Keele 2004; Kunz 2004: 202f., 223; Paldam 2000; van Deth 2003). One of the main concerns however, is that, due to data restrictions, most studies have to rely on a single indicator with quite a narrow scale of response options to measure the feeling of trust people have for their fellow citizens. This way of operationalization and its consequences for the reliability and validity of the measurement of social trust has been strongly criticized, especially in respect to comparative survey data sets.

Fortunately, in the European Social Survey (ESS), there is more than one indicator used to measure trust in other people. In sum, there are three variables covering various aspects of the concept of generalized interpersonal trust. The first indicator is the standard variable used in empirical research: "generally speaking, would you say that most people can be trusted, or that you cannot be too careful in dealing with people?" The second indicator taps into the dimension of fairness: "do you think that most people would try to take advantage of you if they got the chance, or would they try to be fair?" The third indicator deals with the dimension of solidarity and helpfulness: "would you say that most of the time people try to be helpful or that they are mostly looking out for themselves?" For every item, the respondents could give their answers using an 11–point scale ranging from 0 to 10, where 0 was the negative pole and 10 the positive one. Factor analyses for ESS (Kunz 2004: 206) and other data (e.g. Brehm/Rahn 1997) show that these items form one dimension. Taking into account these results for the following analysis, generalized social trust was measured by an additive index, combining the three indicators. The range of the index was recoded, covering now values from −5 to +5. According to findings of methodological studies on the measurement of social trust (see above), this index allows minimizing the effects of possible measurement errors.

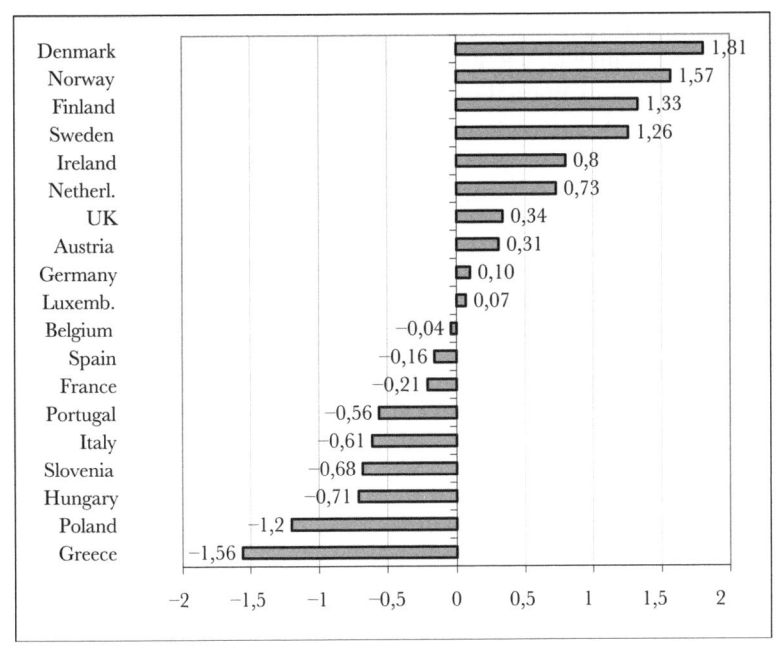

Denmark	1,81
Norway	1,57
Finland	1,33
Sweden	1,26
Ireland	0,8
Netherl.	0,73
UK	0,34
Austria	0,31
Germany	0,10
Luxemb.	0,07
Belgium	−0,04
Spain	−0,16
France	−0,21
Portugal	−0,56
Italy	−0,61
Slovenia	−0,68
Hungary	−0,71
Poland	−1,2
Greece	−1,56

Source: European Social Survey, Round 1. Additive index (trust other people; fairness; solidarity, see above). Mean values of a scale ranging from −5 (most people cannot be trusted) to +5 (most people can be trusted). Data weighted for sample design effects. Standard deviation: between 1.55 (Norway) and 2.00 (Greece, Austria, Slovenia).

Figure 1: Social trust in Europe, 2002–2003

Figure 1 shows results for the index of social trust in those 19 countries later included in the multilevel analysis: Austria, Belgium, Denmark, Finland, France, Germany, Hungary, Greece, Ireland, Italy, Luxembourg, the Netherlands, Norway, Poland, Portugal, Slovenia, Spain, Sweden and the United Kingdom. Some of the countries participating in the first round of the ESS in 2002/2003 were not considered for this analysis and, therefore, were not included in Figure 1: Israel, Switzerland and the Czech Republic. Israel was excluded to restrict the analysis to European countries only. For Switzerland and Czech Republic, no data on associational membership was available in the international data set. Since membership was a crucial variable for explaining the level of social trust, these countries had to be excluded.

The analysis of the social trust index reveals an impressive variety of high, middle and low trust societies. Results known from several other studies comparing levels of trust throughout Europe (e.g. Gabriel et al. 2002) are confirmed once again. The *most trusting societies* can be found in Scandinavia. Denmark, Norway, Finland and Sweden show the highest mean values. This group is followed by Ireland, the Netherlands, the United Kingdom and Austria. Germany, Luxembourg and Belgium show levels of social trust quite close to 0, the middle of the index scale. The *low trust societies* are all located in the South and East of Europe. In general, there seems to be a considerable gap between West and East Europe and North and South Europe as well (further details see e.g. Kunz 2004: 208f.).

To explain these differences between countries and regions within Europe, individual and country-level factors should be accounted for. In the following chapters, various approaches discussed in the literature are considered.

2. Explaining Social Trust: Individual-Level Factors

Up until now, there has been no established theory or generally accepted model explaining the generation of social trust (e.g. Freitag 2003). Therefore, the following part of this chapter summarizes the different schools of thought, approaches and hypotheses discussed in the literature to create an integrated individual-level model of potential determinants of generalized trust. Additionally, for every hypothesis, its operationalization in the ESS is described.

2.1 *Hypotheses. What explains social trust on the level of individual persons?*

So far, the studies by Gabriel et al. (2002), Delhey/Newton (2002, 2004), Freitag (2003), Freitag/Bühlmann (2005) and Kunz (2004) prove to be the most detailed research discussing and testing a great variety of competing hypotheses about individual-level origins of social trust. The following summary is heavily based on these contributions. Additionally, there are significant studies discussing and analyzing some *selected* variables as possible determinants. For reasons of length constraints, only some of these can be mentioned here.

According to Delhey/Newton (2002), Kunz (2004), Rothstein/Stolle (2002) and others, potential factors determining why people trust others or not can be grouped into two basic categories: firstly, person-centered or personality-centered approaches and secondly, structural or society-orientated approaches.

2.1.1 *Person-centered approaches*

General characteristics of persons

Gender and age are included in nearly all studies on determinants of social trust. Some researchers concluded that men are more likely to have a higher level of social trust than women (e.g. Newton 1999), while others found no consistent effects of gender (e.g. Gabriel et al. 2002). In the following analysis, gender will be included as a general control variable. The same will be done with age. The relevance of this variable is related to Putnam's (e.g. 2000) argument about civic generations in the United States. In general, older people are expected to trust *more* (e.g. Stolle 1998). Nevertheless, taking into account findings like those presented by Gabriel et al. (2002), the effect of age is very different when comparing countries. Since older people are more likely to show feelings of insecurity and a fear of crime, which possibly affects their level of social trust, it also seems plausible to expect a negative effect of increasing age. Consequently, different hypotheses and operationalizations using several dummy variables representing various age categories (< 30; young, 30–60; middle-aged, 60+; old) will be tested.

Socioeconomic factors—resources

According to findings presented in research literature, the most important individual level determinant of social trust is "success" (e.g. Newton 1999; Gabriel et al. 2002). Success is a consequence of and reflected in individual resources like education, income and professional status. The general hypothesis is that the higher the socioeconomic status and the stock of resources, the higher the level of social trust (e.g. Verba et al. 1995). As pointed out by Putnam (e.g. 1995) and others, higher levels of education are related with a bigger capacity to accept different people and to establish contacts, which increases social trust. Income and social status are considered as basic variables to explain why people are more or less trusting because "the richer the individual and the higher the professional status, the less costly it is if he or she might be wrong" (Stolle 1998: 512). Education is included in the analysis by asking how long the individual has spent in full-time education. Income is operationalized using an item with different categories of household net income, ranging from 1 (less than 1800 Euro a year) to 12 (120000 Euro or more). Social and professional status is measured by the ISEI-index (International Socio-Economic Index of Occupational

Status), calculated from the ISCO-codes provided in the ESS data set.[3]

Personal well-being
Besides success, Delhey and Newton (2002: 5) consider satisfaction with life and happiness as central components of their "success and well-being theory", to explain social trust. This theory stresses the importance of adult life experiences (see also Freitag 2003; Inglehart 1990). High levels of subjective well-being are considered as reflections of special individual emotional characteristics, having positive effects on the perception of the world outside and of other people (e.g. Kunz 2004: 211; Brehm/Rahn 1997). This also influences the level of social trust. The arguments and findings of Uslaner (2003b, using World Value Survey data for 1990–1995), point in a similar direction. He shows that optimism, which is closely related to the subjective level of well-being, is the most powerful determinant of trust in both the East and the West. Satisfaction with life and the degree of happiness are comprised in an additive index measuring subjective personal well-being. Well-being and, therefore, social trust, can be affected by negative events in personal life (e.g. Brehm/Rahn 1997). These negative events are measured by three different variables: if the respondent or a member of his/her household has been the victim of a crime in the last five years, the respondent has been divorced, or he or she was unemployed for more than 12 months. These items are included in an index, ranging from 0 (experienced none of these events) to 3 (all 3 negative experiences made).

Civic norms and morality
Besides networks of civic engagement, Putnam names norms of reciprocity as the basic source of social trust in complex modern settings (Putnam 1993: 170f.). Morality in general, is also considered as a factor having effects on the level of social trust. Freitag (2003: 947) summarizes the considerations of Fukuyama (2000), Uslaner (2002) and others as follows: "a society in which people strongly believe in moral principles is expected to have a large stock of social trust". Shared social and moral values are basic prerequisites to enable people to cooperate,

---

[3] Because of the high degree of missing cases for the income variable, its effect has to be tested in a separate model additionally. Due to missing data, no ISCO-codes are available for France. So, for testing the respective effects, France is not included in the analysis.

which in turn generates trust (e.g. Fukuyama 1999). These aspects can be tested using some ESS variables on dimensions of "good citizenship": the importance of helping other people who are worse of than oneself, the frequency of actively providing help for other people, and the importance of always obeying laws and regulations. These items were summarized in an additive index.

Liberalism—Cosmopolitanism
Liberal, ideological or cosmopolitan orientations can also help generate a higher level of social trust. Individuals who are more open-minded, tolerant and less fearful of difference are more likely to develop social trust by interacting and cooperating with others (e.g. Brehm/Rahn 1997; Freitag 2003, with further references). This dimension will be measured by support for the statement that it is better for a country to share a variety of religions, and disagreement with the statement that it is better for a country if almost everyone shares the same customs and traditions, comprised into an additive index.

Religious orientations
Religion is another kind of network one can be integrated into. Additionally, special forms of religious orientations are said to be closely connected to the support for social norms and morality (e.g. Kunz 2004). The hypothesis following the argumentation of Putnam (e.g. 2000) is that Protestants show higher levels of social trust than Catholics. The egalitarian, horizontal and liberal culture of Protestantism and its community orientation increases the probability of people developing trust in their fellow citizens, along Protestant beliefs. Empirically, religious involvement, *in general*, shows consistent, but weak effects (e.g. Gabriel et al. 2002). In contrast, comparing countries in respect to the effects of religious *denominations* on the level of social trust leads to very inconsistent results (Gabriel et al. 2002). In the ESS, the dimension of religious involvement can be measured using two variables: church attendance (scale ranging from never to at least once a week) and religiosity (not at all religious to very religious). For the effect of different religious denominations, a dummy variable for being Protestant (or not) will be tested.

Media use
Putnam (1995, 2000) attributes the decline of social capital to the diffusion of television. He argues that watching television makes people

lethargic and prevents them from taking part in associations (generating social trust, see above). From his point of view, television also leads to a loss of trust in others by spreading mostly negative news, thus promoting a pessimistic view of the world. Most of the existing empirical studies on the relationship between television watching and social trust found significant, but rather weak negative relationships (see the contribution of Schmitt-Beck in this volume). Besides television, Putnam (1995) also discusses the effect of reading newspapers on social trust. In contrast to his assumptions and findings on the consequences of television watching, reading newspapers is associated positively with trusting people. According to these results, a negative effect of television use (measured by the time spent watching television on an average weekday) and a positive effect of newspaper use (measured by the time spent reading newspapers on an average weekday) is expected for the following analysis.

2.1.2 *Structural approaches*

Social integration and networks
Referring to Toqueville, one of Putnam's (1993, 2000) basic expectations is that associational involvement is a central source of social trust. Experiences with others while interacting within these social networks, practicing civic norms, are generalized to other social relationships (e.g. Gabriel et al. 2002; Freitag 2003; Badescu/Neller 2007). Numerous empirical studies have shown that the relationship between social trust and associational membership is, in countries where it exists at all, weak (Delhey/Newton 2002; Gabriel et al. 2002; Newton 1999, 2001; Uslaner 2000).

Some scholars have discussed the assumption that all types of associations should have the same ability to generate social trust, in contrast to the expectation that some types of organizations could have a higher impact than others (Eastis 1998, Stolle/Rochon 1998). Putnam (e.g. 2000: 22) differentiates between *bonding* and *bridging* social capital. The former is exclusive, generated by social networks of quite homogenous groups. The latter is inclusive and assigned to social networks of socially heterogeneous people. These bridging associations, cutting across social divisions, being rather egalitarian or horizontal than hierarchical, are said to be more powerful in generating social capital. Since they are more inclusive, outward looking and encompass people across different social divides (Putnam 2000: 22), their potential to generate social trust seems to be higher than the capacity of bonding organizations (see also e.g. Rothstein/Stolle 2002). Taking this into account, associational membership is included in the analysis in different forms; firstly, as being a member of a bridging organization (or not) and, secondly, as being a member of a bonding organization.[4] Additionally, according to Putnam's (1993, 2000) assumptions and the findings of Stolle (1998) and others about the effect of the activity level in associations on their capacity to create trust, the degree of involvement is taken into account.

Since time spent within associations is, in sum, rather marginal, other networks such as family, friends, work colleagues, local, community, and neighbors, should also be considered in this context (Gabriel et al. 2002; Kunz 2004; Roßteutscher 2000). In view of this, the micro-level analysis will also comprise variables referring to marital and employment status (married/not married; unemployed/employed) and the question of having friends. People that are married, employed and have friends, meeting with them regularly, are expected to have a higher level of social trust.

Size of community and duration of residence
Urbanization leads to an increase in the isolation of individuals. According to the assumptions of Putnam (e.g. 2000), the lowest level of trust in others is likely to be found in the inner areas of big cities, higher levels are typical for smaller communities. As exceptions to this linear relationship, Putnam (2000) names rural communities and towns with less than 10,000 inhabitants. The ESS includes a variable describing whether the respondent lives in a house or a farm on the countryside, in a small village or a town, in the suburbs or in a big city. These categories are transformed into several dummy variables to operationalize Putnam's hypothesis on the effect of community size. Since it takes time to develop social trust, the duration of residence should also be taken into account. For the analysis, a dummy variable including two categories (having lived in the area for up to 10 years and having lived in the area for more than 10 years) will be used.

---

[4] *Bridging organizations*: Sport clubs; clubs for outdoor, cultural or hobby activities; consumer organizations; automobile clubs; organizations for humanitarian aid, human rights, minorities or immigrants; organizations for environmental protection, peace, animal rights; religious or church organizations; organizations for science, education or teachers and parents; other social clubs. *Bonding*: trade unions; business, professional or farmers organizations; political parties.

Discrimination and belonging to a minority group
Being a member of a minority group increases the risk of discrimination. The feeling of discrimination and the notion of being unequal to other members of the society increases the belief that other people are unfair, not helpful and dishonest (e.g. Brehm/Rahn 1997; Kunz 2004). In the ESS, people were asked if they would describe themselves as being a member of a group that is discriminated against in their country, and whether they belong to a minority ethnic group in their country. These two items will also be included in the later analysis.

Public security
According to Delhey/Newton (2002), socially homogeneous societies are characterized by low levels of conflict and a high sense of public safety. In this view, based on empirical findings for 1999–2001, they emphasize the importance of the feeling of security for generating social trust. The dimension of public security is measured by using an ESS question that asks respondents about their feelings of safety when walking alone in their area after dark.

Satisfaction with democracy and the economic situation
Utilizing a top-down-perspective, political culture research argues that a stable and functioning democracy contributes to the establishment of a valid base for generating trust between people. This base is provided by democratic structures that keep check on opportunistic behavior and enhance the level of personal security (e.g. Kunz 2004: 214; Delhey/Newton 2002). An economic situation perceived as bad fosters the consequences of existing inequalities, enhances the pressure of competition and promotes pessimistic views of an insecure future. This makes trusting others more difficult (e.g. Brehm/Rahn 1997; Kunz 2004). These two aspects are included using items measuring the degree of satisfaction with the way democracy works in the country of the respondent and his or her satisfaction with the present state of the national economy.

Political Trust
Political trust is included as another individual-level predictor to determine social trust, even if the causal direction of influence between social and political trust has not been finally defined from a theoretical and empirical perspective (e.g. Newton 1999). Researchers like Rothstein and Stolle (2003), Freitag (2003, 2006) or Freitag/Bühlmann (2005) argue

that trust in political institutions plays an important role in explaining individual levels of social trust. Freitag/Bühlmann (2005: 591), for example, point out that political institutions perceived as being fair, just and incorruptible help minimize personal uncertainty in dealing with unknown persons. In this way, trust in institutions can help generate trust in others.

Due to strong correlations, satisfaction with democracy (see above) and trust in political institutions have to be tested in alternative models. To identify separate effects on social trust in one model, including both of these variables, is quite problematic (Kunz 2004: 214). For the final optimized model, only one of these two alternative determinants, showing higher explanatory power for social trust, will be used. Two additive indices will be used. One includes trust in justice and police, the other consists of trust in parliament and politicians. These indices reflect different dimensions of political trust (e.g. Gabriel 1999), defined as trust in the *institutions of the constitutional state* and as trust in *institutions involved in everyday political life and party politics*.

Particular hypotheses discussed in the literature on social trust will *not* be tested in the following analysis. The first one of these concerns *family socialization sources*. Even though the influence of the family, during the process of socialization, seems to be a crucial one in the development of trusting attitudes (e.g. Stolle 1998), it is not possible to test the respective hypotheses. There is no data included in the ESS questionnaire to operationalize this dimension. The same problem appears for the concept of *postmaterialism*. Inglehart (1997) argues that people with postmaterialistic values should be more trusting. According to the results of Uslaner (2003b, based on World Value Survey data 1990–1995) and others, postmaterialism is in fact one of the most important variables to predict social trust. Unfortunately, Ingleharts standard items were not included in the ESS, so the effect of sharing postmaterialist values on the level of generalized social trust cannot be tested in this analysis.

2.2 *Results of the individual-level analysis*

Using data for the nations included in Figure 1, various regression analyses were performed to find an optimized "best" individual-level model to explain social trust. The best model is defined as one that explains an amount of variance as high as possible, utilizing the least number of variables necessary. The regression analyses to find this model were done in several steps. Initial analyses were calculated for

Table 1: Micro-level determinants of generalized social trust
(final model, regression coefficients, pooled analysis)

	unstandardized	Standardized
Intercept	−3.88	
Personality-centered approaches:		
Resources: education	.04	.10
Well-being	.23	.21
Religion: Protestant	56	.12
Society-centered approaches:		
Membership	.48	.12
Trust in legal system and police (index)	.10	.12
Trust in parliament + politicians (index)	.20	.21
R^2/corr. R^2		.27/.27
N		32202

All coefficients significant, $p < 0.001$, data weighted (design weight and standardized sample size for all countries for pooled regression analysis N = 2000).

each country separately, including all possible determinants described in chapter 2.1. Only variables being statistically significant ($p < .001$) and reaching standardized beta coefficients of at least .10 or higher in at least 13 of the 19 countries were kept in the model. In the next step, the number of variables was reduced by checking for correlations between the determinants. The final individual-level model was, once more, checked for pooled and country data as well.

Table 1 shows the results for the pooled analysis and the final model. Only a few of the determinants tested remain in the final, optimal model. The most basic variables to determine the level of social trust represent personality-centered approaches as well as society-centered approaches. Taking a closer look at the variables representing the personality-centered approaches, it proves that a higher educational level, a higher degree of personal well-being and the fact that someone feels a sense of belonging to the Protestant religion, makes him or her significantly more trusting in others. Looking at the determinants representing society-centered approaches, the most important factors fostering social trust are trust in the legal system and in the police force, trust in a country's parliament and politicians, and membership in an organization.

Comparing the values of the standardized regression coefficients leads to the result that the degree of satisfaction with personal factors (life as a whole, happiness) and trust in political institutions (parliament and politicians) are overall the most important factors to explain individual levels of social trust.

These findings confirm some of the results presented earlier, for example, by Inglehart (1990), Uslaner (2000), Freitag/Bühlmann (2005) and Kunz (2004, with ESS data). Kunz (2004) follows a quite similar strategy to find an integrated model to explain social trust, using a somewhat smaller base of different approaches and variables included in the model.[5] One of the main differences to the strategy used here is that Kunz analyzes the consequences of membership, activity and relationships within organizations calculating *separated* effects of four types or voluntary organizations: sports and leisure time, socio-cultural, political, and economic.

Additionally, he uses indices counting the *number* of memberships and friendships within organizations. He ends up with a model quite similar to the one identified here, but with a basic difference. Kunz (2004: 220f.) concludes that membership, activity and friendships in voluntary associations do not matter for explaining social trust. In the model presented here, "pure" membership (dummy variable, counting whether someone is a member in any organization or not) has a considerable effect on social trust. Contrary to the assumptions of Putnam (2000) and others, the separate analysis of bridging and bonding organizations and of the impact of various degrees of activity in associations leads to the finding that these distinctions do not make a real difference. This confirms the results presented by Freitag/Bühlmann (2005). The effect of being a member in bridging organizations on the level of social trust is somewhat higher than the effect of being a member in a bonding association. However, best results are obtained for the index *not* differentiating between these types of organizations. The same holds true for degree of activity. Testing the effect of various levels of involvement and of having friends in organizations (for all organizations and separately for bridging and bonding ones) did not improve the model.

An interesting result supplementing the findings presented by Freitag/Bühlmann (2005) is the importance of trust in political institutions such

---

[5] Besides some differences in the operationalization of variables, he did not include indicators measuring the professional status, liberalism and urbanization. Concerning the factors of perception of political settings, Kunz concentrated on testing satisfaction with democracy and state of economy as determinants of social trust, but did not check for the effect of political trust.

as parliament and politicians. While the analysis of Freitag/Bühlmann is limited to the positive effects of trust in institutions of the juridical system (police and legal system), the findings presented here show that trust in institutions involved in everyday political life seems to be even more important in explaining social trust.

In sum, the optimal model presented in Table 1 explains a total amount of variance of 27 percent. This is not bad, but not very impressive either. Consequently, after having exhausted the potential of individual-level approaches to explain generalized social trust, it seems to be necessary and promising to try alternative strategies of analysis, taking into account context or country-level factors.

3. Explaining Social Trust: Country-Level Factors

3.1 *Hypotheses: Fixed effects—random intercepts*

What explains social trust on the level of countries? In the following part of this chapter, different hypotheses will be discussed and operationalized (for further information on the main country-level variables also see appendix). The focus will be on the *institutional approaches* developed and/or tested by Stolle (1998, 2003), Rothstein/Stolle (2002), Kumlin/Rothstein (2005), Freitag/Bühlmann (2005). and others.

Political/institutional settings
Stolle (2003: 30ff.) summarizes the findings of various studies on the effect of political and institutional settings on social capital as follows: the most important factors for generating high levels of social capital and generalized social trust are democracy, a high level of political rights and civil liberties, a low repression level, social equality as a consequence of a strong welfare state and a trustworthy state.

In respect to democracy, research literature is divided regarding the causal direction of influence. Scholars like Almond/Verba (1963) and Muller/Seligson (1994) conclude that generalized trust is rather a *product* of democracy than a cause of it. This is empirically confirmed, for example, by Gabriel et al. (2002). According to their findings, the duration of democratic experience plays a central role as a macro-level factor explaining social trust: the higher the age of a democracy, the higher the level of social trust. However, results presented by Letki and Evans (2005) show that in the case of post-communist countries, the process of democratization resulted in a *decrease* of social trust. For the following analysis, the age of democracy will be measured by a variable counting the years of the existence of a democratic regime in each country since 1919.

To create social trust (or social capital, in general), political institutions should be inclusive, that is they should have effective mechanisms to include and protect societal minorities (Gabriel et al. 2002; Freitag/Bühlmann 2005; Freitag 2006). Inclusiveness is a characteristic feature of consensual democratic settings. In these institutional settings, minorities have better chances to be integrated (e.g. Lijphart 1999). According to the findings of Gabriel et al. (2002), consensual democratic structures lead to higher levels of social trust. Findings of Freitag/Bühlmann (2005) regarding effects of the existence of a system of proportional representation point in the same direction. For the following analysis, an index differentiating between majoritarian democracies and consensus democracies will be used (classification according to information provided by Lijphart 1999; Ismayr 2002; Bandelow 2005).

In the view of Stolle, Rothstein (Stolle 1998, Rothstein/Stolle 2002) or Offe (1996), social trust is not only influenced by the aspects discussed above, but also by differences in national institutional settings. "These differences result from the distinct values about inclusion and exclusion that are filtered through the educational system as well as the set of welfare institutions" (Stolle 1998: 513). More inclusive welfare institutions lead to a lower level of social inequality. This hypothesis is also discussed regarding political institutions in general. If these institutions are impartial, un-biased, just, incorruptible and inclusive, they can help generate social trust (Kumlin/Rothstein 2005; Freitag/Bühlmann 2005; Rothstein/Stolle 2002, 2003). The impartiality and efficiency of these institutions influences how people experience feelings of safety, how they make inferences from the system and public officials to other citizens, how they observe the behavior of others and how they experience discrimination (Rothstein/Stolle 2002: 27; Kumlin/Rothstein 2005). In an analysis done with data from Sweden, Kumlin and Rothstein (2005: 360f.) conclude that one explanation for why Sweden and other Scandinavian countries have such high levels of social trust could be the fact that relatively few Scandinavians experience selectively distributed public welfare and service, whereas many encounter universal agencies. "The creation of universal-type institutions can thus be seen as a way for governments to make investments in social capital" (Kumlin/Rothstein 2005: 361). Freitag/Bühlmann (2005) argue in a similar way. According to their considerations, justness, fairness, incorruptibility and impartiality are important characteristics for institutions to uphold to have the potential to foster social trust. Institutions with these properties create a social context characterized by security and credibility whereby unfair or un-cooperative behavior will be sanctioned.

Universalistic institutions can be associated with low levels of *social inequality* and special *welfare state settings* (Freitag/Bühlmann 2005; Kumlin/Rothstein 2005). The equal distribution of resources is considered a key factor in making people believe that they share a common destiny. Against this background, low levels of social inequality are crucial for high levels of social trust. "In highly unequal societies, people will stick with their own kind. Perceptions of injustice will reinforce negative stereotypes of other groups, making trust (...) more difficult" (Uslaner 2003b: 85; Boix/Posner 1998; Brehm/Rahn 1997, etc.). Performing macro analyses, e.g. Uslaner (2003a, 2003b) and Gabriel et al. (2002), the strong relationship between social trust and social inequality is emphasized. According to findings of a multilevel analysis presented by Freitag/Bühlmann (2005), social inequality is one of the most important contextual factors explaining trust in other people. Following Uslaner (2003b), Freitag/Bühlmann (2005) and others, social inequality will be measured using the GINI index of income inequality (World Bank data for 2002). Special welfare state settings can help minimize (the effects of) social inequality. This could also contribute to higher levels of social trust in countries with special forms of welfare systems. To test the influence of welfare state settings, the typology developed by Esping-Andersen (1990) is used. Esping-Andersen distinguishes between liberal welfare states, which support market forces and offer only a minimum of social security, conservative welfare states which offer social security but support status differences and traditional family forms, and universal welfare states which offer social security and aim at greater equality in the public and private sphere. For the analysis, a dummy variable coded 1 for universal welfare states and 0 for all others is used.

A large part of the aspects described above can be summarized using the term *good governance*. Governance comprises the process of decision-making and the implementation of decisions. *Good* governance comprises a set of different characteristics like participation, rule of law, transparency, responsiveness, consensus orientation, equity, inclusiveness, effectiveness, efficiency and accountability. The World Bank data set provides six governance indicators, developed by Kaufmann et al. (e.g. 2005). These indicators include six dimensions of governance: *voice and accountability*, measuring political, civil and human rights, *political instability and violence*, measuring the likelihood of violent threats to or changes in government, including terrorism, *government effectiveness*, measuring the competence of the bureaucracy and the quality of public service, *regulatory burden*, measuring the incidence of market-unfriendly policies, *rule of law*, measuring the quality of contract enforcement, the police, and the courts, as well as the likelihood of crime and violence, and *control of corruption*, measuring the exercise of public power for private gain, including both petty and grand corruption and state capture. Index values for 2002 (www.worldbank.org/wbi/governance/govdata) will be used as additional aggregate measures for the multilevel analysis.

In addition to the various institutional approaches presented so far, some other country-level factors will be tested as control variables.

Socioeconomic development—wealth
While Putnam (e.g. 1993) argues that social capital leads to economic growth and prosperity, other researches state that wealth is a factor to explain why some nations are more trusting than others (e.g. Gabriel et al. 2002, Stolle 2003). This problem of causal relationships can not be discussed in detail or analyzed in this contribution. Socio-economic development or wealth will be treated as an independent variable to explain social trust. According to the findings of macro-level analysis performed by Gabriel et al. (2002) and others, the level of socioeconomic development or wealth of a nation belongs to the most important factors explaining the aggregated level of social trust of different societies. The Gross Domestic Product (GDP) per capita in the year of the survey (2002) will measure this dimension.

Cultural fragmentations—cleavages
According to Knack/Keefer (1997), societies with high levels of social polarization and ethnically diverse societies are more likely to develop deep cleavages that have the power to exert a negative influence on social trust. Delhey/Newton (2002) also emphasize the effect of cleavages on social trust. In the following analysis, the effect of social and cultural fragmentation will be tested using different measures. Ethnic diversity is operationalized by an ethnic homogeneity index calculated using the population share of the seven largest ethnic groups in the respective country (data for most recent year, von Barrata 2002). The number of cleavages in a society is also reflected in the degree of fractionalization of the party system. This can be measured by the Rae-Index (Rae 1968).

Post-communist societies
According to some researchers, post-communist societies are characterized by a "syndrome of distrust" (Sztompka 1996: 46), affecting personal relationships amongst citizens and relationships between citizens and political elites as well. Generalized social trust seems to be too risky in such systems. Trust is limited to close family members and intimate friends (Uslaner 2003b). Additionally, since the communist regimes suppressed and destroyed voluntary associations, the conditions for effects of membership and activity in organizations are quite different in the East European countries (Kunz 2004). A broad variety of empirical studies and results presented for the ESS data in section one of this chapter prove that citizens of former communist countries of Central and Eastern Europe show less trust in their fellow citizens than those living in Western Europe. For the macro data set, a variable indicating that a country is a post-communist society will be used.

Opportunity structure—density of associational networks
The density of the network of voluntary organizations in a country can be seen as an opportunity structure. A higher number of associations increase the possibility and chance to take part in one of these networks. Involvement in associations itself is considered a crucial factor for generating social trust. Since an international measure of membership data based on associational registers information is missing, the national share of citizens being members in an organization, calculated from ESS data, is used as a proxy variable.

Protestant/Catholic societies
As scholars like Knack/Keefer (1997), Inglehart (1999) and Fukuyama (1995) argue, Protestantism is an important factor for higher levels of social trust and the creation of social capital. What is the reason for this? Putnam (1993) and Seligman (1997) state that trust will not develop in highly stratified, hierarchical cultures. Since the Protestant church has historically been more egalitarian (e.g. Putnam 1993; Uslaner 2003a), Protestant societies are dominated by horizontal networks fostering trust. The Catholic Church is dominated by hierarchical structures. Therefore, traditionally Catholic societies are characterized by vertical networks. These networks are rather obstructive for generating social trust. Empirical findings (e.g. Uslaner 2003a) show that Protestant societies are more trusting. For the multilevel analysis, a variable indicating the percentage of Protestants in each country will be used (values calculated from Barrett 1982).

3.2 Hypotheses: Cross-level interaction—slope effects

Following the argumentation presented by Maas/Hox (2004) concerning the assumptions of performing multilevel analyses, a minimum of 10 level-2 units is sufficient, but for calculating fixed effects or random intercepts only. For calculating random slopes models with effects of cross-level interactions, at least 30 level-2 units are necessary. However, according to the findings of Freitag/Bühlmann (2005), a test of at least some slope effects seems important and justified from a theoretical and empirical perspective—even if the results for the ESS data should not be "over-interpreted", due to the limited number of countries and the problems resulting from this.

Two hypotheses were tested for interaction effects. The first one is, in countries with high degrees of social inequality (measured by the GINI-index), the effect of well-being on generalized trust in others is weaker. Freitag/Bühlmann (2005: 594), argue that only in countries with an almost equal distribution of income, generalized social trust can develop from satisfaction with life, or generally speaking, well-being. Success and satisfaction with life leads to a better ability when dealing with risks, including the risk of trusting others (e.g. Kunz 2004: 211; Inglehart 1999; Putnam 2000: 332ff.). Using World Value Survey data, Freitag/Bühlmann (2005: 594), can also show that in countries with high levels of income inequality, the positive effect of subjective well-being on social trust is smaller. A second hypothesis, also derived from findings presented by Freitag and Bühlmann (2005: 594; in respect to trust in and fairness of the judicial system), is that the effect of trust in political and juridical institutions on social trust is stronger in those countries with higher values regarding the index of good governance. The reason behind this is that living in a reliable, functioning environment of good governance fosters an atmosphere of trust in institutions with possible spill over effects on social trust.

4. COMBINING INDIVIDUAL AND COUNTRY-LEVEL FACTORS: RESULTS OF A MULTILEVEL MODEL EXPLAINING SOCIAL TRUST

In preliminary analyses, all country-level variables were tested in an explorative way. Only the variables with a significant impact on social trust were kept for further model calculations. Due to high correlations between the indicators, the different aspects measuring the quality of governance were comprised in one index of "good governance". Additionally, because of high correlations with the years-of-democracy-factor and based on the results of the multilevel model statistics, the variable indicating whether a country was a post-communist society was excluded. In the next step, further analyses were performed using the remaining indicators separately and simultaneously.

Several models were calculated with the final set of variables, starting out with the so-called baseline or empty model, followed by the level 1 individual model, a multilevel model with fixed effects only, and a final multilevel model including cross-level interaction or slope effects.

The first column of Table 2 shows the empty or baseline model. It does not introduce any explanatory variables, but decomposes the total variance of the outcome variable into two levels (e.g. Hox 2002): the individual level and the country-level variance of social trust. Calculating this model, the existence of a significant amount of variance in the baseline level of social trust across countries can be tested. The Intra-Class Correlation Coefficient (ICC) of .21 shows that there is a considerable part of variation that can be explained using country-level variables.

The individual-level model in the second column of Table 2 includes all variables of the final or optimal micro model presented in Table 1. The pattern of individual-level effects corresponds to the results of the regression analysis presented in Table 1. The significant decrease in the deviance value shows that the optimal micro-level model specified works quite well, but there is still a highly significant part of individual and country-level variance left, to be explained. The drop in the ICC value indicates that a considerable part of the cross-country variation of social trust is due to compositional effects. This means a considerable part of country-levels differences of social trust results from differing distributions of individual-level independent variables across countries. However, the amount of country-level variance remaining is highly significant. Since the potential of micro-level predictors was exhausted previously, now, country-level indicators will be introduced in the model.

The third column of Table 2 presents the results of the multilevel model with fixed effects only. It includes all variables of the optimal micro-level model and only those country-level predictors that proved to be significant in a multiple test for all macro variables remaining after the initial exploratory analysis described above. The only country-level determinants left to be included in this multilevel model are the indexes of good governance, the degree of income inequality (GINI-index) and the existence of a Protestant tradition, measured by the share of Protestants in each country. The effect coefficients and the increase in

Table 2: Explaining generalized social trust: a multilevel model

	Base-line model	Level 1– individual-level model	Level 1 + Level 2– multilevel model Fixed effects	Level 1 + Level 2– multilevel model Cross-level interaction
Fixed effects				
General intercept	.16	.16	.15*	.14*
Resources/success: education		.03***	.03***	.03*** (0.06)
Well-being		.17***	.17***	.18*** (0.17)
Religion: Protestant		.10***	.10***	.10*** (0.05)
Membership		.11***	.11***	.11*** (0.05)
Trust in legal system and police		.10***	.10***	.11*** (0.12)
Trust in parliament and politicians		.18***	.18***	.18*** (0.20)
Contextual factors				
Good governance			1.04***	1.00*** (0.21)
Income Inequality			−1.52*	−2.04* (−0.05)
% Protestants			.36*	.31* (0.04)
Interaction effects tested				
Good governance and trust indices				n.s.
Income inequality * wellbeing				−.06** (− 0.02)
Variance components				
Individual-level	3.15	2.65	2.65	2.65
Context level	.82***	.37***	.07***	.07***
Wellbeing Slope				.001***
Variance explained				
Individual-level		.16	.15	.16
Context level/Context+interact. eff.		.56	.91	.91
ICC	.21	.12	.03	.03
Deviance	128185.30	122681.29	122650.98	122615.23
Number of estimated parameters	3	6	12	15
N individual-level/context level			32139/19	

*** p < .0001, ** p < .01, * p < .05. n.s.: not significant. All independent variables entered grand mean centered. Unstandardized coefficients, in brackets (for final model with interaction effects): standardized coefficients. Data weighted (equal number of cases for each country). RML estimation.

the variance explained at the macro-level clearly show the substantial impact of these contextual factors. Social trust is significantly higher in countries scoring high on the good-governance-index, in countries showing lower levels of income inequality, and in societies sharing a Protestant culture. For example, a country ten scale points above the grand mean of good governance, ten scale points above the grand mean of income inequality and 10 percentage points above the grand mean of percentage of Protestants has a predicted intercept of .15 + 1.04*1−1.52*0.10 + 0.36*0.10 = 1.07. Therefore, the mean value of this country is heightened nearly one point on the eleven point scale of social trust.

The findings for income distribution support presented, for example, by Freitag and Bühlmann (2005), while the results for Protestant culture, confirms assumptions and findings of Putnam (1993), Inglehart (1999), Uslaner (2003a) and others. However, the improvement in the model statistics is mainly due to the good governance factor. Hence, in respect to the influence of country-level determinants, the main result of the multilevel analysis is that, considering a variety of possible contextual variables, the most important remaining macro determinants explaining social trust are factors reflecting basic *institutional country settings*. Using somewhat different indicators, this finding is compatible with results presented by Freitag and Bühlmann (2005) and the assumptions of Rothstein/Stolle (2002) and others; political-institutional settings are relevant for the generation of social trust. Therefore, even if the research literature is divided regarding the direction of causal influence, the statement of Letki and Evans (2005: 523) seems to hold true: "social trust is linked with institutional performance".

The fourth column of Table 2 presents the results of the *final* multilevel model, including the findings for testing the two hypotheses for possible slope effects elaborated above. Before calculating this final model, another analysis was completed to check if the slopes for subjective well-being and the two trust indices vary significantly. The results are not presented in the table, but this random slopes model showed that there is enough variance in the slopes to be explained. Thus, it is worthwhile to test the two hypotheses on cross-level interaction effects elaborated in Part 3.2 of this chapter.

Calculating these cross-level interactions leads to a further small improvement for the deviance value, even if the amount of variance explained does not change. While no significant slope effect for good governance and the trust indices can be found, the first hypothesis is supported by the analysis. In a country one point above the mean value of the social inequality index (mean value of GINI index, see appendix), the effect of well-being is weakened by the amount of the interaction effect (−.06). Therefore, in sum, the effect of well-being on social trust is only .12. As a result, in countries with higher levels of social inequality, an increase in subjective well-being has a weaker positive effect on social trust than in countries with lower levels of social inequality. This result supports findings presented by Freitag/Bühlmann (2005: 595).

In sum, comparing the relative explanatory power of individual-level and contextual level variables shows that even if in the final multilevel model, the contextual level variance can be explained very well using the macro indicators specified, the remaining amount of individual-level variance not explained is still very high. This supports the necessity of looking for other individual-level approaches not included in the model yet.

5. Conclusion

Even if its curative powers as the "chicken soup of social life" (Uslaner 2002: 1) have been sometimes oversold, generalized social trust is considered a basic individual and societal resource. If this kind of trust is this important, it is crucial to know how to generate it. According to the expanding research literature of the last decade, sources of social trust can be found on the individual and the country-level as well.

In this chapter, different levels of social trust *within* countries and differences in social trust *between* countries were explained by combining micro and macro-level factors. Since not only personality traits or other individual characteristics determine the orientations and behavior of individuals, but also their social and political context (e.g. Snijders/Bosker 1999), the method of multilevel analysis seems to be an adequate strategy to integrate these perspectives. In this view, the basic aim of this chapter was to find the most adequate explanation for the degree of trust people have in their fellow citizens.

On the micro-level, the optimized model found is one including personality-centered approaches as society-centered approaches. People with higher levels of education, a stronger feeling of personal well-being, a sense of belonging to the Protestant community, being a member of an association and showing higher levels of trust in political and juridical institutions, are more trusting in their fellow citizens. In sum, even if some basic micro-level factors determining social trust were identified, the amount of variance explained by the final individual-level model is still quite unsatisfactory. Therefore, in a next step, context variables were combined with individual-level factors within a multilevel model.

Empirical findings presented in social research literature so far, support the statement of Inglehart (1999: 88) that social trust is a "relatively enduring characteristic of given societies". As Inglehart (1999), Gabriel et al. (1999), Kunz (2004), Freitag/Bühlmann (2005) and others argue, this leads to the assumption that individual-level factors can only *partly* explain the differences in national levels of social trust. Additionally, cultural, historical and political factors reflecting country-specific aspects have to be taken into account. The result of the multilevel analysis performed confirms this view. Testing a great variety of contextual determinants, the most important macro factors remaining are the index of good governance, comprising the aspects of participation, rule of law, transparency, responsiveness, consensus orientation, equity, inclusiveness, effectiveness, efficiency and accountability, and an index of social inequality. Good governance on the country-level is reflected in positive orientations (trust) towards political institutions, actors and the judicial system on the individual-level. The same holds true for social inequality and subjective well-being. Taking the perspective of the micro-level analysis, political trust and well-being are the most important individual-level determinants of social trust. This illustrates how the link between the micro and the macro-level effects found in the multilevel analysis works. In respect to the two slope effects tested, only one proved to be significant: in countries with higher degrees of income inequality, an increase in subjective well-being has a weaker positive effect on social trust than in countries with a more equal distribution of income.

Good governance and low degrees of social inequality both contribute to a societal climate that helps create social trust by reducing personal risks and establishing sanctions. In societies with high levels of good governance and a low degree of inequality, the probability of making negative experiences—in general as well as with institutions and other people—is lower. These findings are especially important for those countries in which the resource of social trust is rather scarce. To raise the level of social trust, it seems most important to improve the quality of governance and to find concepts to establish higher degrees of social equality. This is a crucial task for political elites and future concepts of political engineering.

However, the multilevel analysis performed also proved that even testing a great variety of different approaches, the remaining amount of individual-level variance not explained is high. This leads to the conclusion that there are some important predictors not included in the optimal model yet. One of these predictors could be variables tapping the dimension of socialization. Following the argumentation of social psychologists like Erikson (1950) or Allport (1961), social trust is a core personality trait learned in early childhood, changing only slightly in later life as a result of different experiences (for empirical results see Uslaner 2000). Nevertheless, as Stolle (2003: 28) states, the family "has been largely left out of the discussion about social capital". In sum, the focus of empirical research on explaining social trust has clearly been on those approaches emphasizing the importance of later life experience on social trust. This is partly because most data sets, including the ESS, do not include questions about the process of socialization or about parenting concepts. To include these aspects in future micro and multilevel research on social trust could be a promising strategy to find out more about the sources of social trust.

References

Allport, Gordon W. (1961): Pattern and Growth in Personality. New York: Holt, Rinehart and Winston.
Almond, Gabriel A. / Verba, Sidney (1963): The Civic Culture. Political Attitudes and Democracy in Five Nations. Newbury Park: Sage.
Badescu, Gabriel / Uslaner, Eric M. (2003): Social Capital and the Transition to Democracy. London/New York: Routledge.
Badescu, Gabriel / Neller, Katja (2007): Explaining Associational Involvement. 158–187 in: van Deth, Jan W. / Montero, Jose Ramon / Westholm, Anders (eds.): Citizenship and Involvement in European Democracies: A Comparative Analysis (Routledge Research in Comparative Politics), London/New York: Routledge.
Bandelow, Nils (2005): Konsensdemokratische Elemente im Baltikum, http://www.nilsbandelow.de/kd05fo12.pdf.
Barrett, David B. (1982): World Christian Encyclopedia. A Comparative Study of Churches and Religions in the Modern World Ad 1900–2000. Oxford/New York. Oxford University Press.
Boix, Charles / Posner, Daniel N. (1998): Social Capital: Explaining its Origins and Effects on Government Performance. British Journal of Political Science 28: 686–693.
Bornschier, Volker (2001): Gesellschaftlicher Zusammenhalt und Befähigung zur Gesellschaftsbildung—Determinanten des generalisierten Vertrauens im explorativen Vergleich demokratischer Marktgesellschaften. Swiss Journal of Sociology 27: 441–473.
Braithwaite, Valerie (1998): Communal and Exchange Trust Norms: Their Value Base and Relevance to Institutional Trust. 46-74 in: Braithwaite, Valerie / Levi, Margaret (eds.): Trust and Governance. New York: Sage.
Brehm, John / Rahn, Wendy (1997): Individual-Level Evidence for the Causes and Consequences of Social Capital. American Journal of Political Science 41: 999–1023.
Campbell, William Ross (2004): The Sources of Institutional Trust in East and West Germany: Civil Culture or Economic Performance? German Politics 13: 401–418.
Cook, Karen S. (ed.) (2001): Trust in Society. New York: Russell Sage Foundation.
Cook, Karen S. / Hardin, Russell / Levi, Margaret (2005): Cooperation without Trust? New York: Russell Sage Foundation.

Coleman, James S. (1988): Social Capital in the Creation of Human Capital. American Journal of Sociology 94: 95–120.
Delhey, Jan / Newton, Kenneth (2002): Who Trusts? The Origins of Social Trust in Seven Nations. Discussion Paper FS III 02–402 Berlin: WZB.
——— (2004): Determinanten sozialen Vertrauens. Ein international vergleichender Theorientest. 151–168 in: Klein, Ansgar / Kern, Kristine / Geißel, Brigitte / Berger, Maria: Zivilgesellschaft und Sozialkapital: Herausforderungen politischer und sozialer Integration, Wiesbaden: VS Verlag.
Eastis, Carla M. (1998): Organizational Diversity and the Production of Social Capital. One of These Groups Is Not Like the Other. American Behavioral Scientist 42: 66-77.
Erikson, Erik H. (1950): Childhood and Society. New York: Norton.
Esping-Andersen, Gösta (1990): The Three Worlds of Welfare Capitalism. Cambridge: Polity Press.
Freitag, Markus (2003): Social Capital in (Dis)Similar Democracies. The Development of Generalized Trust in Japan and Switzerland. Comparative Political Studies 36: 936-966.
——— (2006): Bowling the State back in: Political Institutions and the Creation of Social Capital. European Journal of Political Research 45: 123–152.
Freitag, Markus / Bühlmann, Marc (2005): Politische Institutionen und die Entwicklung generalisierten Vertrauens. Ein internationaler Vergleich. Politische Vierteljahresschrift 46: 575–601.
Fukuyama, Francis (1995): Trust. The Social Virtues and the Creation of Prosperity. London: Hamish Hamilton.
——— (1999): The Great Disruption. New York: Free Press.
——— (2000): The Great Disruption. Human Nature and the Reconstitution of Social Order. New York: Free Press.
Gabriel, Oscar W. (1999): Integration durch Institutionenvertrauen. Struktur und Entwicklung des Verhältnisses der Bevölkerung zum Parteienstaat und zum Rechtsstaat im vereinigten Deutschland. 199–235 in: Friedrichs, Jürgen / Jagodzinski, Wolfgang (eds.): Soziale Integration. Special issue 39 of Kölner Zeitschrift für Soziologie und Sozialpsychologie. Wiesbaden / Op-laden: Westdeutscher Verlag.
Gabriel, Oscar W. / Kunz, Volker / Roßteutscher, Sigrid / van Deth, Jan W. (2002): Sozialkapital und Demokratie. Zivilgesellschaftliche Ressourcen im Vergleich. Wien: WUV-Universitätsverlag.
Gambetta, Diego (1988): Trust. Making and Breaking Cooperative Relations. Oxford: Blackwell.
Glaeser, Edward. L. / Laibson, David / Scheinkman, Jose A. / Soutter, Christine L. (2000): Measuring Trust. Quarterly Journal of Economics 115: 811–846.
Hardin, Russell (1998): Trust in Government. 9–27 in: Braithwaite, Valerie / Levi, Margaret (eds.): Trust and Governance. New York: Russell Sage Foundation.
——— (2002): Trust and Trustworthiness. New York: Russell Sage Foundation.
Hox, Joop J. (2002): Multilevel Analysis. Techniques and Applications. Mahwah, NJ: Erlbaum.
Inglehart, Ronald (1990): Culture Shift in Advanced Industrial Societies. Princeton: Princeton University Press.
——— (1997): Modernization and Postmodernization. Cultural, Economic, and Political Change in 43 Societies, Princeton/New Jersey: Princeton University Press.
——— (1999): Trust, Well-Being and Democracy. 88–120 in: Warren, Mark E. (ed.): Democracy and Trust. Cambridge: Cambridge University Press.
Ismayr, Wolfgang (ed.) (2002): Die politischen Systeme Osteuropas. Wiesbaden: Leske + Budrich.
Kaufmann, Daniel / Kraay, Aart / Mastruzzi, Massimo (2005): Governance Matters IV. Governance Indicators for 1996-2004. World Bank Policy Research Working Paper 3630.

Keele, Luke (2004): Macro Measures And Mechanics of Social Capital. In: http://users.ox.ac.uk/~polf0034/socap.pdf, download date: 22.11.05.
Knack, Stephen / Keefer, Philip (1997): Does Social Capital have an Economic Payoff? Quarterly Journal of Economics 112: 1251–1288.
Kumlin, Staffan / Rothstein, Bo (2005): Making and Breaking Social Capital. The Impact of Welfare State Institutions. Comparative Political Studies 38: 339–365.
Kunz, Volker (2004): Soziales Vertrauen. 201–227 in: van Deth, Jan W. (ed.): Deutschland in Europa. Ergebnisse des European Social Survey 2002–2003. Wiesbaden: VS Verlag.
Letki, Natalia / Evans, Geoffrey (2005): Endogenizing Social Trust: Democratization in East-Central Europe. British Journal of Political Science 35: 515–529.
Lijphart, Arend (1999): Patterns of Democracy: Government Forms and Performance in Thirty-Six Countries. New Haven: Yale University Press.
Maas, Cora J. M. / Hox, Joop J. (2004): Robustness Issues in Multilevel Regression Analysis. Statistica Neerlandica 58: 127–137.
Misztal, Barbara A. (1996): Trust in Modern Societies. The Search for the Bases of Social Order. Cambridge: Polity Press.
Muller, Edward N. / Seligson, Mitchell A. (1994): Civic Culture and Democracy: The Question of Causal Relationships. American Political Science Review 88: 635–652.
Newton, Kenneth (1999): Social and Political Trust in Established Democracies. 169–187 in: Norris, Pippa (ed.): Critical Citizens. Oxford: Oxford University Press.
——— (2001): Trust, Social Capital, Civil Society, and Democracy. International Political Science Review 22: 201–214.
Offe, Claus (1999): How Can We Trust Our Fellow Citizens? 42–87 in: Warren, Mark E. (ed.): Democracy and Trust. Cambridge: Cambridge University Press.
Ostrom, Elinor / Walker, James (eds.) (2003): Trust and Reciprocity. Interdisciplinary Lessons from Experimental Research. New York: Russell Sage Foundation.
Paldam, Martin (2000): Social Capital: One or Many? Definition and Measurement. Journal of Economic Surveys 14: 628–653.
Putnam, Robert D. (1993): Making Democracy Work. Civic Traditions in Modern Italy. Princeton, NJ.: Princeton University Press.
——— (1995): Tuning in, Tuning out: The Strange Disappearance of Social Capital in America. PS—Political Science and Politics 28: 664–683.
——— (2000): Bowling Alone. New York: Simon and Schuster.
Rae, Douglas W. (1968): A Note on the Fractionalization of Some European Party Systems. Comparative Political Studies 1: 413–418.
Roßteutscher, Sigrid (2000): Associative Democracy. Fashionabel Slogan or Constructive Innovation? 172–183 in: Saward, Michael (ed.): Democratic Innovation. Deliberation, Representation and Association. London/New York: Routledge.
Rothstein, Bo / Stolle, Dietlind (2002): How Political Institutions Create and Destroy Social Capital: An Institutional Theory of Generalized Trust. Paper presented a Collegium Budapest, Project on Honesty and Trust: Theory and Experience in the Light of Post-Socialist Experience, November 22–23, 2002.
——— (2003): Social Capital, Impartiality and the Welfare State: An Institutional Approach. 191–209 in: Hooghe, Marc / Stolle, Dietlind (eds): Generating Social Capital. Civil Society and Institutions in Comparative Perspective. New York: Palgrave Macmillan.
Schmitt-Beck, Rüdiger (2005): Contextual Effects on Electoral Turnout at a German Municipal Election. Paper prepared for the Workshop "Local Participation in Different Contexts" at the ECPR Joint Sessions of Workshops, University of Granada/Spain, 14–19 April 2005.
Seligman, Adam B. (1997): The Problem of Trust. Princeton, NJ: Princeton University.

Snijders, Tom A.B. / Bosker, J. Roel (1999): Multilevel Analysis. An Introduction to Basic and Advanced Multilevel Modeling. London et al.: Sage.
Stolle, Dietlind (1998): Bowling Together, Bowling Alone: The Development of Generalized Trust in Voluntary Associations. Political Psychology 19: 497–526.
――― (2003): The Sources of Social Capital. 19–42 in: Hooghe, Marc / Stolle, Dietlind (eds.): Generating Social Capital. Civil Society and Institutions in Comparative Perspective. New York: Palgrave Macmillan.
Stolle, Dietlind / Rochon, Thomas R. (1998): Are All Associations Alike? American Behavioral Scientist 42: 47–65.
Sztompka, Piotr (1996): Trust and Emerging Democracy. Lessons from Poland. International Sociology 11: 37–62.
――― (1999): Trust. A Sociological Theory. Cambridge: Cambridge University Press.
Tyler, Tom R. (1998): Trust and Democratic Governance. 269–294 in: Braithwaite, Valerie / Levi, Margaret (eds.): Trust and Governance. New York:Russell Sage.
Uslaner, Eric M. (1999): Morality plays: Social capital and Moral Behavior in Anglo-American Democracies. 213–239 in: van Deth, Jan W. / Maraffi, Marco / Newton, Kenneth / Whiteley, Paul (eds.): Social Capital and European Democracy. London: Routledge.
――― (2000): Producing and Consuming Trust. Political Science Quarterly 115: 569–90.
――― (2002): The Moral Foundations of Trust. Cambridge: Cambridge University Press.
――― (2003a): Trust, Democracy and Governance: Can Government Policies Influence Generalized Trust? 171–190 in: Hooghe, Marc / Stolle, Dietlind (eds): Generating Social Capital. Civil Society and Institutions in Comparative Perspective. New York: Palgrave Macmillan.
――― (2003b): Trust and civic Engagement in East and West. 81–94 in: Badescu, Gabriel / Uslaner, Eric M. (eds.): Social Capital and the Transition to Democracy. London/New York: Routledge.
van Deth, Jan W. (2003): Measuring Social Capital: Orthodoxies and Continuing Controversies. International Journal of Social Research Methodology 6: 79–92.
von Barrata, Mario (ed.) (2002): Der Fischer Almanach. Frankfurt: Fischer.
Verba, Sidney / Schlozman, Kay Lehman / Brady, Henry E. (1995): Voice and Equality: Civic Voluntarism in American Politics. Cambridge, Mass.: Harvard University Press.
Warren, Mark E. (ed.) (1999): Democracy and Trust. Cambridge: Cambridge University Press.
Zmerli, Sonja / Newton, Kenneth / Montero, José, Ramón (2007): Trust in People, Confidence in Political Institutions, and Satisfaction with Democracy. 35–65 in: van Deth, Jan W. / Montero, José Ramón / Westholm, Anders (eds.): Citizenship and Involvement in European Democracies, London/New York: Routledge.

6. Appendix

Global country variables (variables not constructed by an aggregation of individual-level variables in the ESS data set): Descriptives

	Mean / %	Standard Deviation	Range
Age of democracy (years of democracy since 1919)	66,68	23,87	72
Majoritarian / consensus democracy; 0: majoritarian democracy; 1: one dimension consensus; 2: two dimension consensus	0: 16% 1: 58% 2: 26%	—	2
Social inequality: GINI index	0,29	0,04	0,14
Welfare state typology (Esping-Andersen)	0,21	—	1
Good Governance index	1,11	0,65	1,29
Wealth: gross domestic product (GDP) per cap.	22,09	7,30	34,32
Ethnic homogeneity index	0,82	0,17	0,60
Rae-Index	0,75	0,87	0,35
Post-communist society	0,16	—	1
Protestant/Catholic society: % of protestants (data from Barrett 1982)	0,28	0,37	0,99

CHAPTER FIVE

WHAT DETERMINES CITIZENS' NORMATIVE CONCEPTION OF THEIR CIVIC DUTIES

Bas Denters and Henk van der Kolk

In an era in which social scientists ponder the implications of globalization (Sassen 1999) and shifts in governance (Pierre 2000; Pierre and Peters 2000; Rhodes 1997) there is a renewed interest in issues of social and political citizenship. In 1978, van Gunsteren claimed that 'the concept of citizenship has gone out of fashion among political thinkers' (van Gunsteren 1978). In the beginning of the 1990s, however, citizenship had become fashionable once again (Kymlicka 2002: 284; Kymlicka and Norman 1994: 352).

The return of an interest in issues of citizenship is not a matter of coincidence. Oftentimes the notion of citizenship has been defined in direct relation to the nation state (Sassen 2002) and therefore it should not come as a surprise that Castells observes that "[t]he blurring of boundaries of the nation state" is likely to confuse the definition of citizenship (Castells 1997, p. 309). This confusion is reinforced by the fragmentation or even hollowing out (Peters 1993) of the state and the increasing importance of complex networks in public decision-making. This not only creates problems of governability and accountability (Van Kersbergen and Van Waarden 2004), but it also compounds the definition of civic rights and obligations vis-à-vis an ever more amorphous, diffuse state.[1] Against this background, it is natural that academics of various disciplinary fields have adopted the intellectual challenges of rethinking notions of contemporary citizenship (Isin and Turner 2002). This literature is almost, by necessity, normative in its approach and sets out to develop new conceptions of citizenship or to amend traditional visions in such a way as to gear these toward the modern age.

With the re-emergence of citizenship as a central notion, the meaning of the concept seems to have changed. In the influential conception

---

[1] Kymlicka and Norman mention some additional reasons why citizenship became the 'buzz word' of the 1990s.

by T.H. Marshall, citizenship was defined in terms of a set of civil, political and social rights.[2] For many people, citizenship is merely 'the right to have rights' (Kymlicka 2002: 288). More recently, however, this conception was complemented by conceptions in which 'duties and responsibilities', as well as 'identities' played a more prominent role (Kymlicka 2002: 288; Kymlicka and Norman 1994).[3] These new conceptions, stemming from various political backgrounds such as the New Right political philosophy and Communitarianism, stressed, according to Galston, general virtues like law abidingness and loyalty, economic virtues like a strong work ethic and the importance of self-reliance, social virtues like independence, and political virtues like the willingness to engage in public discourse (Galston 1991: 221–224).

Different normative theories of citizenship have stressed the importance of distinct duties. One reason for these differences is related to two different views on citizenship. The 'classical', sometimes called the 'Aristotelian' view, stresses the importance of the 'intrinsic value' of an active involvement in both state and society (Kymlicka 2002: 287). This view stresses the importance of duties related to an active involvement in both politics and society. A more 'liberal' viewpoint puts a smaller emphasis on 'participation as duty'. Participation should be merely 'instrumental', while assigning it an intrinsic value will easily lead to 'a coercive form of state perfectionism', forcing people to be active (Kymlicka 2002: 299). Both the 'classical' and the 'liberal' conceptions of citizenship, however, stress the importance of at least *some* involvement, since the state cannot function with at least public reasonableness, a critical attitude to authority, and the obligation not to break the law (Kymlicka 2002: 300).

Although this chapter deals with issues of contemporary citizenship, it is more prosaic in its aims. We will look into ways in which contemporary citizens define their position vis-à-vis their state and their society. As Conover et al. stated in 1991, '[r]ecent political and

---

[2] A recent discussion of citizenship as rights and governmental policies defining these rights can be found in Howard 2006. This author also stresses the idea that 'duties' are not something recently introduced in the discussion of citizenship. 'Liberal citizenship' not only implies 'rights' but also several 'duties' like 'the obligation to pay taxes' and the 'willingness to serve in the military' (Howard 2006: 444).

[3] Conover, Crewe and Searing also use the distinction between 'rights', 'duties' and 'identities' to present their empirical analysis of people's citizenship conceptualizations. It may be useful to distinguish between 'duties' and 'virtues' as well (Conover, Crewe, and Searing 1991).

philosophical debates [about citizenship; BD/HvdK] have an air of unreality about them, because they are being conducted in what is virtually an empirical void' (Conover, Crewe, and Searing 1991: 801). Moreover, despite some attempts to analyze 'citizenship' empirically, the number of empirical studies devoted to citizenship is rather limited.[4] Our ambitions are therefore not devoid of importance, since it will be interesting to see whether the changes in state and governance and the ensuing intellectual reorientation on the nature of citizenship are reflected in a state of confusion or even civic anomie amongst contemporary mass publics.

In this chapter, two empirical questions are asked. The first descriptive question asks how citizens in contemporary European democracies define their social and political obligations. In dealing with this question, we will begin by comparing the mass publics in various European democracies in terms of the strength of their allegiance to the aforementioned social and political obligations. We will also look into the 'structure' of citizenship; do citizens who consider their social duties important, also have a stronger sense of duty with regard to political obligations, and are these structures robust across various countries.

The second question is explanatory. The issue addressed is which factors impact upon the strength of citizens' allegiances to various civic obligations. In this analysis, we look into explanatory factors at two levels: individual factors and national factors. We develop some hypotheses that will, on the one hand, help us identify potentially important factors from both levels of analysis and, on the other hand, will provide theoretically plausible expectations regarding the possible impact of these factors.

This chapter begins with a discussion of citizenship, describing various aspects of citizenship in Europe (section 1). We then proceed with a discussion of factors potentially influencing different aspects of citizenship, which is elaborated in section 2. In section 3, the data is analyzed and the findings are summarized with conclusive remarks.

---

[4] For example, Almond and Verba have empirically studied aspects of both liberal (passive) and classical (active) aspects of citizenship (Almond and Verba 1989: 117) Jennings and Niemi have asked respondents to describe the 'idealized good citizen' (Jennings and Niemi 1981) and Conover et al. have used 'focus group studies' to study different conceptions of citizenship (Conover, Crewe, and Searing 1991). More recently several authors have used survey data to study notions of citizenship (Denters, Gabriel, and Torcal 2004; Rose 1995; Rose and Stahlberg 2000; Roßteutscher 2004).

1. CITIZENSHIP IN EUROPE

1.1 What do we mean by 'citizenship'?

In our view, citizenship is a status that situates individuals in a social and political context.[5] In this contribution, we will concentrate on civic *obligations*; to be more precise we will deal with citizen's normative conceptions about the obligations inherent in their role as citizen. The obligations of citizens pertain to oneself, to other members of a particular society and to the political authorities governing the society (Prior, Stewart, and Walsh 1995). A generally accepted list of 'virtues' however, is lacking (Roßteutscher 2004: 180).

Political citizenship has several aspects. The first aspect is the status of a person obliged to respect the laws and orders issued by the political authorities. This obligation is characteristic for all ordered political societies, either democratic or non-democratic. We shall call this the 'law abiding' aspect of citizenship (Denters, Gabriel, and Torcal 2004: 3). In operational terms, it is the *importance of always obeying laws and regulations*. Secondly, it is the status of a political *actor*, who should "take an active interest and participate in the conduct of public affairs" (Parekh as cited in (Weale 1999: 191). In operational terms, this means, first, *forming an independent opinion on public issues*. This active aspect of political citizenship also stresses *the importance of voting in an election*, and *the importance of being active in politics*.

From a narrow perspective, citizenship can be defined in political terms only, i.e. the obligations of citizens toward the state. Especially under the current conditions, however, where there is a shift of governance, whereby the balance between responsibilities of individual citizens, civic society, market organizations in the care for the common weal and governments are redefined; a narrow definition of citizenship as 'political' norms is unsatisfactory. We will therefore not only take political aspects of citizenship into account, but also some social aspects. The social aspects of citizenship are defined in terms of people's normative conceptions about their role towards other members of society;

---

[5] According to Kymlicka and Norman, this is only part of citizenship. 'Citizenship is not just a certain status, defined by a set of rights and responsibilities. It is also an identity, an expression of one's membership in a political community' (Kymlicka and Norman 1994: 369). In this contribution we shall ignore the 'identity part' of citizenship.

in operational terms: *the importance of solidarity with people worse off*, and the *importance of participation in voluntary organizations*.

1.2   *Describing citizenship in Europe*

The data used in this chapter are derived from the European Social Survey 2002 (www.europeansocialsurvey.org), which is comprised of 22 countries. Israel is excluded in order to restrict the analysis to European countries, while the German case has been split into Eastern and Western groups, resulting in a sample of 22 countries; Austria, Belgium, Denmark, Spain, France, Finland, Greece, Ireland, Italy, Luxembourg, the Netherlands, Norway, Portugal, Sweden, Switzerland, United Kingdom, and West Germany as West-European countries—and Czech Republic, East Germany, Hungary, Poland and Slovenia as East-European countries. After doing some preliminary tests of the data, we were forced to exclude Switzerland and the Czech Republic due to some missing data with respect to important independent variables (see below). Hence, we ended up analyzing data from 20 countries. The aforementioned elements of citizenship were measured asking; 'to be a good citizen, how important would you say it is for a person to support those who are worse off than themselves, vote in elections, always obey laws and regulations, form their own opinion, independently of others, be active in voluntary organizations and be active in politics?' Citizens were able to answer on an 11-point scale ranging from 0 (extremely unimportant) to 10 (extremely important).

The mean support for the various statements related to elements of citizenship in all European countries is presented in Figure 1. This figure, in which the means represented start at 2 instead of 0 to increase contrasts, clearly shows that the general statement of a good citizen being one who is active in politics is, on average, least supported in all European countries. Being active in a voluntary organization is valued more, but still less than other aspects of citizenship in all European countries. This means that the two most demanding norms are supported less than less demanding norms like 'voting in elections' and 'obeying laws'.

The averages presented here should not hide the fact that individuals have different opinions about these norms; the standard deviation for all statements in all countries shows a substantial disagreement within countries. Systematic country differences, based on these averages, are less easy to observe. Variation between countries, especially looking at

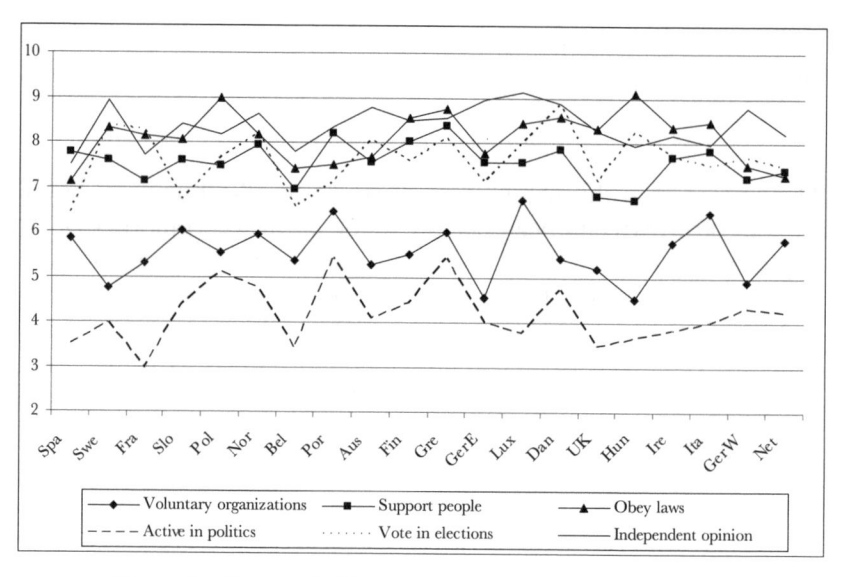

Figure 1: Norms of citizenship in twenty European countries

the four norms valued most—to support people who are worse off than themselves, to vote in elections, to obey laws and regulations, and to form an opinion independently of others—is limited.

1.3 *Patterned differences*

Before looking at individual and country differences, it is useful to see whether the aforementioned aspects of citizenship can be meaningfully reduced to a limited number of empirical factors. In order to see whether there are indeed some more general '*dimensions* of citizenship', we conducted a factor analysis based on the full sample. The outcome of this analysis corresponds nicely with some theoretical ideas from citizenship studies.

In a factor analysis, which explains about 58% of the total variance in the six aspects of citizenship, we can extract two factors. The first factor consists of voting in elections, obeying laws and regulations, and forming an opinion independent from others. The second factor consists of being active in voluntary organizations and being active in politics. One item loads on both factors; to support people who are worse off than they are.

Table 1: Rotated solution of six aspects of citizenship

To be a good citizen:	Component 1	Component 2	$H(i)^2$
How important to support people worse off	,443	,412	0,365
How important to vote in elections	,685	,273	0,543
How important to always obey laws/regulations	,776	–,013	0,602
How important to form independent opinion	,685	,109	0,481
How important to be active in voluntary organizations	,139	,843	0,730
How important to be active in politics	,105	,844	0,724
Eigen values (component)	2,383	1,062	
Total variance explained			57,4%

Principal Component Analysis. Rotation Method: Varimax with Kaiser Normalization.

The factor solution nicely fits the 'classical'-'liberal' divide mentioned in the introduction.[6] It also fits nicely in at least some of the empirical results from citizenship studies. To cite Conover et al., who did some focus group studies to better understand the meaning citizens give to the word citizenship; 'the most liberal of our discussants are mainly concerned with rights, though they accept that citizens have a set of core duties (obeying the law, paying taxes, voting, and defending the country). They part company with their more communitarian [classical; BD/HvdK] neighbors over the nature of responsibilities toward public involvement and community service' (Conover, Crewe, and Searing 1991: 825). The factors we found seem to correspond with this idea. Since the issue of 'supporting people less well off' did not fit theoretically or empirically, we decided to drop this aspect of citizenship in the subsequent analyses.[7]

---

[6] Based on the same data, Roßteutscher finds the same factors which she labels 'Representative' and 'Participatory'. She includes the statement 'to support people who are worse off than themselves' in the first dimension (Roßteutscher 2004: 188). Almond and Verba used a rather similar distinction between 'active participation in local community' and 'more passive community activities' (Almond and Verba 1989: 129).

[7] In the ESF project 'Citizenship, Involvement and Democracy', Denters et al. used a more differentiated approach based on a forced three factor solution in which 'supporting people less well off' (a statement we ignored in the final solution) together with

Using the full sample, the two factors form weak yet acceptable scales. The 'classical' scale (alpha 0.64) and the 'liberal' scale (alpha 0.68) will therefore be used in the subsequent analyses. We should, however, not hide the fact that this factor solution does not perform equally well in all country samples. The classical scale drops (slightly) below 0.5 (alpha) in six countries. The 'liberal' scale is generally stronger and drops below 0.5 (alpha) in one country only (Italy).

Since this contribution is devoted to the effect of contextual factors on citizenship, we also tested whether the two resulting scales show some variation between countries. The analysis of variance shows that these country differences are indeed significant, although the between country variance is rather limited. About 7 percent of the total variance in the liberal scale and about 5 percent in the variance of the classical scale can, at this moment, be attributed to country differences. Whether these differences are to be attributed to country characteristics or to composition effects, remains to be seen. The least we can say is that there is indeed some variation at the macro level.

Closer inspection of the data finally reveals that the relationship between the liberalism scale and the classical scale is as expected. Support for liberal duties is 'necessary' for supporting classical duties, but not sufficient. Virtually no one who does *not* support liberal values supports the classical values. In the rest of this paper, we shall focus on these two dimensions of citizenship.

2. Explaining Citizenship

In the literature on the development of citizenship and comparable orientations like interpersonal trust, we can distinguish different schools of thought, each stressing different factors. (Denters, Gabriel, and Torcal 2004; Mishler and Rose, 2001). One group of scholars stresses the importance of socializing agents and groups Other scholars focus on the political and institutional context in which people live. Although the two approaches are sometimes presented as rival explanations (Mishler and Rose 2001: 31), we will see them as complementary and

---

one other item forms a separate factor which they named 'solidarity'. They also found that 'law abidingness' and 'forming an independent opinion', two items we see as part of the 'liberal' aspect of citizenship are two different factors.

we will empirically assess their relative contribution to the explanation of citizenship.

2.1 *Individual level explanations*

Scholars focusing on the social characteristics of individuals trace the values underlying citizenship partly to early socialization in families, by friends, in voluntary groups and in schools. Citizenship is an imprint of early socialization and can best be understood by looking at the circumstances under which people are raised. We can expect that children are raised differently and that the societal integration of their parents has an impact on their values. We will therefore see whether some characteristics of parents affect citizenship. In this context, we shall look at the (highest) level of *education of the parents*.

Many philosophers and social scientists have stressed the impact of *schooling*. The economist Friedman, for example, argues that 'a stable and democratic society is impossible without a minimum degree of literacy and knowledge on the part of most citizens and without widespread acceptance of some common set of values. Education can contribute to both' (Friedman and Friedman 1962). Researchers have focused on the question of whether schooling and especially (but not exclusively), civic education, fosters acceptance of some common set of norms and duties (Almond and Verba 1989: 117–135). Although many scholars admit that 'schools historically have often been used to promote deference, chauvinism, xenophobia and other illiberal and undemocratic vices' (Kymlicka 2002: 307), we hypothesize that in most European societies, education fosters self-reflection and thus the acceptance of at least some liberal values like obeying laws and regulations and to form an opinion independent of others.

Scholars have also focused on *generational differences*, observing a general decline in turnout due to cohort effects (Denters, Gabriel, and Torcal 2004; Kymlicka 2002: 293; Roßteutscher 2004: 190). The idea is that each generation is affected by circumstances during its 'constitutive years'. Testing this idea in a comparative study is difficult since the 'circumstances under which people grow up' are not the same for the same generations in different countries. An analysis in which we make country specific distinctions between cohorts in 21 countries is virtually impossible. We therefore follow Roßteutscher, who suggests focusing on three important years in the history of Europe: 1945 (the end of WWII), 1968 (the 'cultural' revolution) and 1989 (the fall of the

Berlin Wall). We will compare four different generations, each having their formative years in a specific period. We will make a distinction between those experiencing their formative period, being 10 years or older before 1945, (born before 1935 being raised during the years of crisis and war); people having their formative years before 1968 (born between 1935 and 1958, having their formative years after the war, during a period of reconstruction); people having their formative years before 1989 (born between 1958 and 1979, living in relative affluence in the West and under communist rule in the East) and finally, those born after 1979 and formed in the post-cold war era. As we shall argue below, we expect that generational differences will be different in the countries we have studied.

Others have focused on socialization later in life. In line with Alexis de Tocqueville, and more recently, Almond and Verba (1989), it is argued that *civic associations* provide a permanent training ground for the values, norms, and civic skills necessary for a healthy democracy. 'It is in the voluntary organizations (...) that we learn the virtues of mutual obligations' (Kymlicka 2002: 305). A point also stressed by authors like Robert Putnam. According to Putnam, such associational memberships are a form of social capital and as such, membership in civic associations is likely to be closely linked to peoples' support for civic values and norms (Putnam 2000; Putnam, Leonardi, and Nanetti 1993). This is not to say that the empirical claim that 'civil society is the seedbed of civic virtue' is uncontested. 'It may be that in the neighborhood that we learn to be good neighbors, but neighborhood associations also teach people to operate on the 'Not In My Backyard' principle when it comes to the location of group homes or public works' (Kymlicka 2002: 305). Nevertheless, there is, at least, some empirical support regarding membership and involvement producing support for citizenship norms. 'We find, that (...) forms of associational involvement make a modest contribution to the shaping of civic norms in many of the countries under analysis' (Denters, Gabriel, and Torcal 2004).

An important issue in the argument on voluntary organizations is related to *church membership*. On the one hand, it is argued that church membership, like membership in all kinds of voluntary organizations, stimulates citizenship. On the other hand, however, it is argued that at least some churches teach deference to authority and intolerance of other faiths (Kymlicka 2002: 305). We therefore take active church membership as an additional potential antecedent to civic norms.

In addition to childhood socialization and to socialization through current involvement in voluntary organizations, some people feel more 'attached' to the nation state than others do. *People belonging to groups that are rejected by others* may lose their willingness to comply to the societal norms and values (Conover, Searing, and Crewe 2004). In the literature, several authors have stressed the importance of *legal* citizenship (Howard 2006). The number of people in the dataset having no or a limited legal status, however, is extremely small, we therefore do not develop this idea further.

A final factor is *employment*. This factor has been stressed by various authors. Theorists of the 'New Right' have often praised the market as a school of civic virtue (Kymlicka 2002: 304). Others, however, claim that the 'market' may teach initiative, but not a sense of social responsibility and duty. Having a paid job, however, may have the same effect as being active in a voluntary organization. A job, at least in many cases, can be conceived as a permanent training ground for the norms and civic skills necessary for a healthy democracy. Furthermore, a final argument to include having a job and an income as explanatory factors is the fact that these aspects of human life gives people a stake in society. If you are well integrated and self reliant, you will more easily develop the concept of duty to uphold the fundamental order of society.

2.2 *Country level explanations of citizenship*

A second approach traces citizenship to contextual origins. This approach concentrates on characteristics of the 'objective' macro-contexts in which people function and on the individual perception and evaluation of these contexts (Denters, Gabriel, and Torcal 2004; Freitag 2006; Maloney, Smith, and Stoker 2000; Mishler and Rose 2001). As we have stressed in the introduction, the fragmentation of the nation state and the growing complexity of national decision-making may have had a profound impact on the values of individuals. Not all states state are alike in this respect, and we therefore expect systematic national differences in citizenship orientations. Empirical analysis has shown that there is at least some variance left to be explained at the macro level, however, it is difficult to find precise ways to capture and observe this. We will therefore identify some factors that may affect citizenship without hypothesizing about the precise relationship between the explanatory variables and the dependent variable.

Firstly, a factor potentially explaining country differences directly, is the disparity in affluence levels, measured by GDP per capita (or *purchasing power parities*), of each country. In political science, there is a long-agreed upon idea that feelings of legitimacy and attachment to the state are related to affluence. If there is a certain level of living standards to be protected, people will adopt a 'stake' in the current system, thereby creating an environment where people are willing to obey and express support for the present government.

Secondly, we observe, as an explanatory factor, the *age of democracy*, in which we distinguish between 'old' democracies (continuously democratic since at least 1945), countries that became democratic (again) in the 1970s and 1980s (Greece, Portugal and Spain) and finally countries that became democratic after the fall of the Berlin Wall in 1989 (East European countries). We expect that citizenship is stronger in older democracies. In these countries, the long existing 'civil society' will have created civic norms. In the new democracies, this process has been interrupted or at least been strongly affected by years of dictatorship. We also think the age of democracy will have an impact on the relationship between age and allegiance to civic norms, thus creating an interaction effect between age, age of democracy and citizenship.[8]

A larger (and more interesting, while changeable) set of factors potentially contributing to citizenship can be found in the institutional formation of a state. In a recent contribution, Markus Freitag (2006) has argued that the character of democratic institutions may have an important effect on the creation of social capital in political communities. Although Freitag focuses on associational involvement, we think that his arguments may also be relevant for the normative component of social capital in the form of people's endorsement of civic norms. In the footsteps of Lijphart (Lijphart 1998; Lijphart 1975/1968), Freitag has argued that a consensus democracy, with its high degree of decentralization (Freitag 2006: 132) and its system of power-sharing (Denters, Gabriel, and Torcal 2004; Freitag 2006: 132–133), is conducive for the accumulation of social capital. Decentralization 'ensures differentiated rights and sustains the recognition of identities and the accommodation of given cultural differences, thus harboring multifaceted interests'.

---

[8] A well-known fact is that old democracies in Europe are also relatively 'rich' democracies. Especially because the number of countries is relatively small, this means there is a potential multi-collinearity problem. We will therefore test these hypotheses separately and discuss potential multi-collinearity problems.

Moreover, a consensus democracy is also characterized by "inclusiveness and its rules and institutions [that] aim at broad participation in policies". This creates a setting in which various groups and minorities have opportunities to voice their opinions and to advocate their interests. "Majoritarian systems on the other hand "are exclusive and formulate policies in a less deliberative way" (Freitag 2006: 132–133). On this basis, Freitag hypothesizes that decentralization and power-sharing will make people more politically active, more active in civic associations and 'generally more civic minded'. In line with these considerations, we will test the hypothesis that the two dimensions of consensus democracy developed by Lijphart (*decentralization* and *power-sharing*) are also relevant when applying it to people's allegiance to key civic duties.[9]

3. ANALYSIS

3.1 *Multi-level modeling; individual level results*

As we already noted, based on a one-way analysis of variance, the between country variance is small compared to the within country variance. The 'empty model' of our multi-level model, presented in the first columns of Table 2 summarizes some of its characteristics. This will be used as a base line model.

The multi-level model using all individual characteristics explains only a small part of the individual level variance. This is of course partly due to the lack of 'attitudes and opinions' in our model. Of course, a model including all kinds of attitudes such as 'political alienation' or 'political interest' would have improved the level of explained variance. We think, however, that these more specific attitudes are probably consequences rather than explanations of citizenship duties and we therefore did not include this kind of individual level characteristics in our model.

The individual level characteristics we did include in our first multi-level model explain citizenship and more specifically the *liberal component of citizenship*, in the expected directions. Only 'having work' does not contribute to our explanation of support for liberal duties. The effect of education of the parents is not very large. Since education is measured on a seven point scale, an additional school level raises the level of adherence to liberal duties (on a scale from 0 to 10) only 0.03

---

[9] Data are from (Armingeon and Careja 2004; Lijphart 1998; Roberts 2006).

Table 2: Multi-level model with individual characteristics only, explaining *liberal citizenship* (significant relationships bold)

	Empty model			Individual characteristics model		
	b	s.e.	beta	B	s.e.	Beta
Constant	**8,31**	**0,10**		**8,34**	**0,10**	–
Education of parents	–			**0,03**	**0,01**	0,03
Generation 2: born 1935–1958	–			**–0,21**	**0,03**	–0,06
Generation 3: born 1959–1979	–			**–0,56**	**0,03**	–0,17
Generation 4: born after 1979	–			**–0,72**	**0,03**	–0,15
Education	–			**0,08**	**0,01**	0,07
Civic associations	–			**0,19**	**0,02**	0,06
Church involvement	–			**0,19**	**0,02**	0,06
Belonging to group rejected by others	–			**–0,10**	**0,04**	–0,02
Having work	–			–0,03	0,02	–0,01
Intra-country correlation		0,07			0,08	
R-square level-1 (individual)	–				4,77%	
R-square level-2 (country)	–				–1,58%[10]	
N (weighted)		32.444			32.444	

Dependent variables: Liberal citizenship is a scale (0–10) based on adding answers to three statements regarding voting, obeying laws and forming an independent opinion.
Explanatory variables: Education of parents (–3 to 3), the highest level of education of either father or mother, based on country specific coding and recoded by ESS into a seven point scale; generational differences (4 categories, oldest generation is the reference category, based on year of birth of respondent; Education (–3 to 3); civic associations (dichotomy; 0 or 1) originally based on the number of associations the respondents are actively involved in. Since this variable was extremely skewed towards 0, the variables did not allow a comparison between full time involvement in one organization and superficial involvement in two or three organizations, and because several analyses showed the estimation results were not different for the full scale, we decided to recode the answers into a simple dichotomy; church involvement (a dichotomy, 0 or 1) was based on the attendance of services (regular of not), since this aspect of religiosity came closest to our theoretical expectation; belonging to group rejected by others (dichotomy, 0 or 1), based on a direct question, other operationalizations based on legal citizenship and the country where the parents were born appeared to be skewed and bivariate analyses showed this operationalization could not be used in a meaningful analysis; having work (dichotomy, 0 or 1), based on activities in the last week.
Countries: Austria, Belgium, Denmark, Spain, France, Finland, Greece, Ireland, Italy, Luxembourg, the Netherlands, Norway, Portugal, Sweden, United Kingdom, and West Germany as West-European countries—and East Germany, Hungary, Poland and Slovenia as East-European countries.
Estimation: Since MLWin does not simply provide standardized coefficients, the Z-scores were computed and a normal regression was done in MLWin using the Z-scores. Since Z-scores were computed without taking missing data into account, small differences between actual beta's and estimated beta's can occur. R-squares are based on Snijders and Bosker 1999: 101–104.

[10] The explained variance is negative, indicating that between country variance increases when the individual variables are added. This is an extra indication that the individual level model does not fit the data well (Snijders and Bosker 1999: 104 and 123–124).

Table 3: Multi-level model with individual characteristics only, explaining *classical citizenship* (significant relationships bold)

	Empty model			Individual characteristics model		
	b	s.e.	beta	B	s.e.	Beta
Constant	4,85	0,11	–	4,57	0,119	–
Education of parents	–			–0,02	0,01	–0,01
Generation 2: born 1935–1958	–			0,10	0,04	0,02
Generation 3: born 1959–1979	–			**–0,22**	**0,05**	**–0,05**
Generation 4: born after 1979	–			–0,03	0,05	–0,00
Education	–			**0,08**	**0,01**	**0,05**
Civic associations	–			**0,66**	**0,03**	**0,13**
Church involvement	–			**0,53**	**0,03**	**0,10**
Belonging to group rejected by others	–			0,06	0,05	0,01
Having work	–			–0,05	0,03	–0,01
Intra-country correlation	0,05			0,05		
R-square level-1 (individual)	–			4,02%		
R-square level-2 (country)	–			1,84%		
N (weighted)	35.366			32.382		

Dependent variables: Classical citizenship is a scale (0–10) based on two statements regarding political and social involvement.
Other entries of this table: see Table 2.

points (slightly less than 0.3 percent points). Individual education adds slightly more. People, who feel that the societal majority rejects their group, express somewhat weaker support for liberal duties. This is also as expected, although the effect is rather small. The most important individual level explanatory factors are associated with 'social capital' characteristics and 'generation'.

Being an active member of at least one organization contributes 1.5 percent points to liberal duties and being an active church member does the same. According to our interpretation of the data, this means that people actively involved in either a social organization or a church (and especially those actively involved in both), more strongly support duties like 'voting', 'obeying laws' and 'forming an independent opinion'.

The biggest differences can be found between the three generations that we have distinguished. Since we have used the oldest generation as a reference category, the data shows that every younger generation is indeed, less supportive of liberal duties. The (negative) 'effect' of being born after 1979 on support for liberal duties on a scale ranging from 0 to 10, is –0.72.

Table 4: country level differences (descriptives) (N = 20)

	Mean	Range		Standard deviation
		Min	Max	
GDP in PPP	27.063	10.719	60.150	10.198
Executive party dimension	0,07	−1,50	2,42	0,99
Federal unitary dimension	0,08	−2,20	1,41	0,98

Explanatory variables at the macro level: Gross Domestic Product (GDP) in Purchasing Power Parities (PPP) is based on IMF data (2002). In order to simplify interpretation of the coefficients, before doing the actual estimations, we divided this number by 10.000, followed by centering the data around the mean; The two 'power-sharing' dimensions are completely based on the original operationalization of Lijphart, as explained in the main text (Lijphart 1998). Since Lijphart does not give data for East European countries, we first of all used the data from (Armingeon and Careja 2004), averaging the post 1989 data. Since this dataset does not contain a comparable measure for all variables used in the operationalization of Lijpharts two dimensions of power-sharing, we also used the coding of (Roberts 2006), cross checking similar coding. Low levels is the 'consensus' end of the scale. Since we standardized the scores based on all ESS countries, the mean is slightly lower than 1 and the variance is not exactly equal to 1.

The explanation of the *'classical' part of citizenship* is less convincing. Several factors contributing to stronger liberal duties, do not lead to stronger classical duties. Support for 'classical' values, for example, is not substantially stronger within the generation that dominated the universities in the 1960s than it is within the youngest generation. The contribution of social involvement to the support of citizenship duties is stronger, but we should be aware of the potential (at least partly) endogeneity problem when explaining this aspect of citizenship. Social involvement will not just lead to stronger support for civic duties; people having the conviction that they should be involved will also be more active. Unfortunately, however, we cannot solve this problem with the available synchronic data. Since the effect of social participation on liberal duties is probably less vulnerable for this endogenous effect, we think there is an effect on classical duties as well, albeit less than estimated in our study.

3.2 *Describing country level differences*

The first two characteristics of the countries we will use in the multi-level analysis are straightforward. The Gross Domestic Product per capita (corrected using Purchasing Power Parities) is a well-known variable and the classification of democratic heritage in a three-fold classification is straightforward. Nevertheless, Luxembourg is an extreme case with respect to GDP in PPP per capita. We have to consider this when estimating the effect of this variable on citizenship.

The classification of countries, based on their institutional setup, is more complicated. In his work, Lijphart argues that ten characteristics of countries can be summarized in a two dimensional map. The first five characteristics are the proportionality of the electoral system, the effective number of political parties, the number of parties represented in cabinets, the dominance of parliament over the executive, and the level of corporatism. These institutional features, according to Lijphart, form one dimension ranging from 'majoritarian' to 'concensus' democracies. The second group consists of the level of decentralization, bicameralism, constitutional rigidity, judicial review and finally, central bank independence. These country features also form a dimension ranging from 'unitary' to 'federal'. Lijphart subsequently standardizes the scales found. We do the same and plot the two dimensional conceptual map of democracy in the same way as Lijphart (Lijphart 1998: 248).

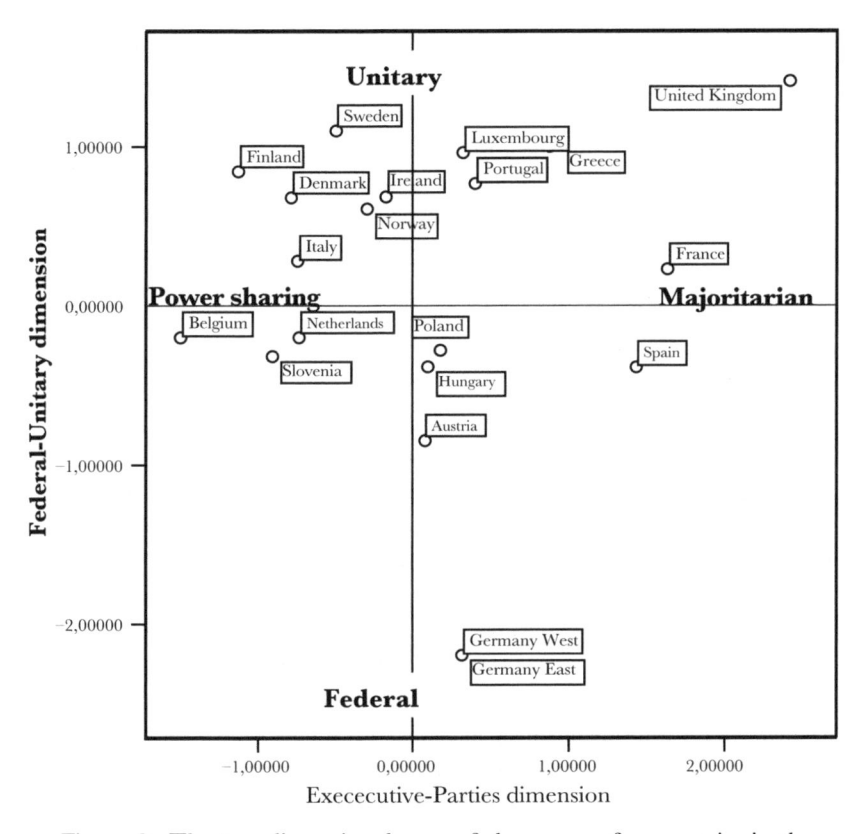

Figure 2: The two dimensional map of democracy for countries in the present study (N = 20)

Given the two dimensional map, the potential impact of Germany (East and West) is large. We will consider this when estimating the coefficients.

3.3 Multi-level modeling: fixed effects

Estimating the model with the threefold classification of democracies (older democracies as the reference category), does not yield significant effects; support for liberal or classical duties is not substantially lower in newer than it is in older democracies. In the subsequent analyses, we have therefore dropped the variable 'age of democracy'. Another macro factor potentially affecting support for liberal duties is the affluence of society. Our estimations, however, also show that GDP (per capita) does not have a significant effect on either liberal or classical aspects of citizenship. Dropping Luxembourg (an outlier on this variable), does not change this. We therefore conclude that GDP per capita, like age of democracy, does not have an effect on support for liberal values.

After dropping both age of democracy and GDP per capita, we included the two dimensions of democratic institutions developed by Lijphart. The results of this model are presented in Table 5. As the results show, there is no significant effect of power-sharing (the executive-parties dimension) or of centralization on liberal citizenship. This means our preliminary expectations do not account for the differences in aspects of liberal citizenship in European countries.

The same holds for the analysis of classical aspects of citizenship. Neither the age of democracy, nor GDP, nor elements of power-sharing and centralization are significantly related to this aspect of citizenship in Europe.

3.4 Multi-level modeling: random effects

After fitting the fixed effects model, we proceeded by allowing the effects of the various explanatory values to vary across countries.[11] We expected, for example, that the effect of belonging to a specific generation would be different in different countries (see above). We also expected that these differences would be largest for the older generations. Since the number of countries in our study is small, this

---

[11] Since the number of countries is small, while the number of respondents within countries is large, a multi-level analyses with a random slope analysis is of limited value. We therefore analysed the individual level model for all countries separately to see whether some relevant and interpretable differences in the various effect parameters were available.

Table 5: Micro—macro level explanations of *liberal and classical citizenship* (significant relationships bold). Only the model with Lijpharts variables reported.

	Liberal citizenship			Classical citizenship		
	B	s.e.	beta	B	s.e.	Beta
Constant	8,33	0,09	–	8,348	0,098	–
Micro variables						
Education of parents	**0,03**	**0,01**	**0,03**	-0,02	0,01	-0,01
Generation 2: born 1935–1958	**-0,21**	**0,03**	**-0,06**	**0,10**	**0,04**	**0,02**
Generation 3: born 1959–1979	**-0,56**	**0,03**	**-0,17**	**-0,22**	**0,05**	**-0,05**
Generation 4: born after 1979	**-0,72**	**0,03**	**-0,15**	-0,03	0,05	-0,00
Education	**0,08**	**0,01**	**0,07**	**0,08**	**0,01**	**0,05**
Civic associations	**0,19**	**0,02**	**0,06**	**0,66**	**0,03**	**0,13**
Church involvement	**0,19**	**0,02**	**0,06**	**0,53**	**0,03**	**0,10**
Belonging to group rejected by others	**-0,10**	**0,04**	**-0,02**	0,06	0,05	0,01
Having work	-0,03	0,02	-0,01	-0,05	0,03	-0,01
Macro variables						
Executive party dimension	-0,04	0,10	-0,02	-0,11	0,11	-0,05
Federal unitary dimension	0,15	0,09	0,09	0,18	0,11	0,07
Intra-country correlation		0,07			0,04	
R-square level-1 (individual)		5,70%			4,73%	
R-square level-2 (country)		11,04%			4,32%	
N		32.444			32.382	

additional analysis can only be tentative and exploratory. We therefore focused on direct effects only.

Our analysis shows that generational differences in support for *liberal citizenship* are stable across all countries we have analyzed; in virtually all countries, every younger generation is less supportive of the values of liberal citizenship. The decline in support, however, is clearly different across countries. These differences cannot be related to democratic heritage; the decline in support for liberal citizenship does not systematically decrease in new, middle and old democracies. We therefore have to reject this expectation.

Our analysis also shows that in the individual level explanation of liberal citizenship, the effect of the education of parents (a rather weak effect in the overall model), substantially varies across countries, seems to be absent in several countries, but is never negative. The direct effect of education also varies and is in one country even negatively related to liberal values. The differences found, however, are difficult to interpret. Neither GDP nor democratic heritage or institutional differences are related to the differences in effects. Comparable observations can be made when looking at the varied effects of social participation and church involvement. These effects are always positive (albeit not always significant) in all countries that we have observed. The (relative) effects, however, are diverse.

The effect of feeling discriminated against on support for liberal citizenship is also different in the various countries we have studied. The *effect* is especially (but not exclusively) strong in both regions of Germany. However, since the number of people claiming they are discriminated against in both regions is extremely small, we should not try to over-interpret these results.

Our analysis of support for *classical values* does not yield clear interpretable indications of inter-country differences in effects. The overall fixed effects analysis showed a positive impact of social participation and church membership on support for classical values. In addition, the generation born between 1959 and 1979 seems to be less supportive of these values. These relationships are, largely, the same for all countries, although the age effect varies across countries. This variance, again, is not clearly related to one of the country level variables we studied.

4. Conclusion and Discussion

In this paper, we analyzed two aspects of citizenship. Liberal citizenship was defined as the obligation to obey laws, to form an independent opinion and to vote in elections. Classical citizenship was defined as the importance to be active in voluntary organizations and the importance to be active in politics. This aspect was called 'classical' because it refers to the idea that a person can only become a citizen by being socially and politically active, an idea strongly defended by theorists like Aristotle. Our empirical analysis clearly confirms these two aspects theoretically, although the dimensionality is not necessarily robust across nations. After constructing one single scale for both types of citizenship, we found that liberal citizenship is clearly more supported than classical citizenship. Moreover, Europeans clearly differ to the extent that they support both aspects of citizenship.

In an empirical analysis of the individual level factors related to both liberal and classical citizenship, we focused on aspects of socialization (education of parents, generation to which a person belongs), education, social and economic involvement (social activities, church involvement and having work or not), and social integration (the extent to which a person belongs to a group rejected by others). Differences in citizenship were not strongly related to these individual level characteristics. Only a small percentage of the variance could be attributed to these factors. A study of the differences between countries on the mean level of support for citizenship values (fixed effects) and on the effect of individual characteristics on citizenship (slope differences) did not contribute significantly to the explanation of the individual level differences.

The poor quality of the individual level model seems to add to the confusion about citizenship. In the introduction, we observed that after at least two thousand years of thinking about 'citizenship', a general acceptance of citizenship duties is still lacking. After this study (and previous empirical studies focusing on citizenship), we have to conclude that a clear picture on the sources of citizenship is lacking as well. The effect of individual education, for example, exists, but seems to be quite small. We therefore not only have to better define what we mean by citizenship, but we also have to keep looking for sources of citizenship. The decline of the nation state is not only confusing citizenship definitions, but will eventually also have an effect on the level of citizenship in the various European countries. Only when we know what factors contribute to citizenship, this trend can be reversed. In looking for factors stimulating citizenship, we should not primarily look at the institutional level of countries. We have observed that the biggest differences are found not between countries, but within countries. This is not to say that the context does not matter. It may well be that citizenship is created in neighborhoods or municipalities. Future research should be conducted observing the impact of these contexts on citizenship.

REFERENCES

Almond, Gabriel A. / Verba, Sidney (1989): *The civic culture: political attitudes and democracy in five nations*. Newbury Park, Calif.: Sage Publications.

Armingeon, K. / Careja, R. (2004): Comparative Data Set for 28 Post-Communist Countries, 1989–2004. In: http://www.ipw.unibe.ch/content/forschungsgruppen/prof_armingeon/societal_conflicts/index_ger.html. Berne: Institute of Political Science, University of Berne, 2004.

Conover, Pamela Johnston / Crewe, Ivor M. / Searing, Donald D. (1991): The Nature of Citizenship in the United States and Great Britain: Empirical Comments on Theoretical Themes. *The Journal of Politics* 53 (3):800–832.

Conover, Pamela Johnston / Searing, Donald D. / Crewe, Ivor (2004): The Elusive Ideal of Equal Citizenship: Political Theory and Political Psychology in the United States and Great Britain. *The Journal of Politics* 66 (4):1036–1068.

Denters, S.A.H., / Gabriel, O. / Torcal, M. (2004): Norms of Good Citizenship (final draft).
Freitag, Markus (2006): Bowling the state back in: Political institutions and the creation of social capital. *European Journal of Political Research* 45 (1):123–152.
Friedman, M. / Friedman, R.D. (1962): *Capitalism and Freedom* Chicago: University of Chicago Press.
Galston, W. William A. 1991. *Liberal purposes: goods, virtues, and diversity in the liberal state.* Cambridge / New York etc.: Cambridge University Press.
Howard, M.M. (2006): Comparative citizenship; an agenda for cross-national research. *Perspectives on Politics* 4 (3):443–456.
Isin, Engin F. / Turner, Bryan S. (eds.) (2002): *Handbook of Citizenship studies*. London etc.: Sage.
Jennings, M. Kent. / Niemi, Richard G. (1981): *Generations and Politics; a panel study of young adults and their parents*. Princeton, New Jersey: Princeton University Press.
Kymlicka, W. (2002): *Contemporary political philosophy: an introduction*. second ed. Oxford: Oxford University Press.
Kymlicka, W. / Norman, W. (1994): Return of the Citizen—a Survey of Recent Work on Citizenship Theory. *Ethics* 104 (2):352–381.
Lijphart, A. 1998. *Patterns of Democracy; Government forms and performance in Thirty-Six Countries*. New Haven and London: Yale University Press.
Lijphart, A. (1975/1968): *The politics of accommodation; pluralism and democracy in the Netherlands*. Berkeley: University of California press.
Maloney, W. / Smith, G. / Stoker, G. (2000): Social capital and urban governance: adding a more contextualized 'top-down' perspective. *Political Studies* 48:802–820.
Mishler, William / Rose, Richard (2001): What Are the Origins of Political Trust?: Testing Institutional and Cultural Theories in Post-communist Societies. *Comparative Political Studies* 34 (1):30–62.
Peters, B.G. (1993): Managing the hollow state. In: *Managing public organizations: lessons from contemporary European experience*, edited by K.A. Eliassen / J. Kooiman. London etc.: Sage.
Pierre, J. (ed.) (2000): *Debating Governance: Authority, Steering, and Democracy*. Oxford: Oxford University Press.
Pierre, J. / Peters, B. Guy (2000): *Governance, politics, and the state*. New York: St. Martin's Press.
Prior, D. / J. Stewart / K. Walsh. 1995. *Citizenship: Rights, Community & Participation*. London: Pitman Publishing.
Putnam, R.D. (2000): *Bowling alone: the collapse and revival of American community*. New York: Simon & Schuster.
Putnam, R.D. / Leonardi, R. / Nanettim, R.Y. (1993): *Making democracy work: civic traditions in modern Italy*. Princeton: Princeton University Press.
Rhodes, R.A.W. (1997): *Understanding Governance: Policy Networks, Governance, Reflexivity and Accountability* Buckingham: Open University Press.
Roberts, A. (2006): What Kind of Democracy Is Emerging in Eastern Europe? *Post Soviet Affairs* 22 (1):37–64.
Rose, L.E. (1995): *The notion of local citizenship: Is it meaningful? How does it relate to local governance?*: Paper prepared for the workshop on the 'Changing local governance of Europe', ECPR Joint Sessions of Workshops, Bordeaux.
Rose, L.E., and K. Stahlberg (2000): Municipal identification and democratic citizenship: A Finnish-Norwegian Comparison. In *Festschrift for Dag Anckar on his 60th Birthday on February 12, 2000*: Abo Akademi University Press, Abo.
Roßteutscher, S. (2004): Die Rueckkehr der Tugend? In: *Deutschland in Europa*, edited by J.W. v. Deth. Wiesbaden: Verlag für Sozialwissenschaften.
Sassen, S. (1999): *Globalisering. Over mobiliteit van geld, mensen en informatie*. Amsterdam: Van Gennep.

Sassen, S. 2002. The repositioning of citizenship: emergent subjects and spaces for politics. *Berkeley Journal of Sociology* 46 (?): 4–25.
Snijders, T. / Bosker, R. (1999): *Mutilevel Analysis. An introduction to basic and advanced multilevel modelling.* 2000 reprinted ed. London etc.: Sage Publications.
van Gunsteren, H.R. (1978): Notes towards a Theory of Citizenship. In: *Democracy, consensus and social contact*, edited by P. Birnbaum / J. Lively / G. Parry. London: Sage.
Van Kersbergen, K. / Van Waarden, F. (2004): 'Governance' as a bridge between disciplines: Cross-disciplinary inspiration regarding shifts in governance and problems of governability, accountability and legitimacy *European Journal of Political Research* Volume 43 (2):143–171.
Weale, A. (1999): *Democracy*. Houndmills etc.: MacMillan Press.

CHAPTER SIX

MASS MEDIA AND SOCIAL CAPITAL IN EUROPE:
EVIDENCE FROM MULTILEVEL ANALYSES[1]

Rüdiger Schmitt-Beck

The notion of democracy can be conceived differently. However, all notions of democracy concur that assigning independent mass media a key role is one of the vital traits of a system of government where leaders are ultimately accountable to the people (Scammell 2000). Without a free press, it would be impossible for citizens to gain the 'enlightened understanding' that Dahl considers one of the key requirements of genuinely democratic decision-making, and the foundation of elected leaders' legitimacy (Dahl 1998). It is no small paradox then, that, as Kepplinger (1998: 225–6) notes, the freedom of the press might also become dysfunctional for democracy, bearing—while nonetheless remaining one of its key components—a potential to undermine its support in society.

For three decades now, the mass media in Western democracies have continuously been criticized for being potentially harmful to democracy. This chapter explores the most recent contribution to this debate; the hypothesis, put forward by Putnam (1995, 2000), that television erodes modern democracies' social capital. Putnam argues that television-watching is detrimental to social capital because it absorbs time that citizens no longer have available for civic engagement, and because it has psychological consequences that are harmful for people's motivation to participate in collaborative activities. Although less prominently, Putnam also considers the role of the printed press for social capital. His view concerning newspapers is far more sanguine. While television, especially televised entertainment, is clearly assigned the role of the 'bad guy' in Putnam's narrative of civics and its blessings for modern societies, newspapers are unequivocally seen as the 'good guy'.

---

[1] The author is indebted to Martin Elff for methodological advice at an early stage of this research.

The purpose of this paper is to test these claims' validity for 19 European countries. In contrast to previous research on this topic, my analysis applies a wider scope. It not only focuses on micro level effects of individual media usage on media users' stocks of social capital. Rather, the present explorations expand this rather limited perspective by inquiring the individual-level consequences of country-specific macro patterns of media consumption, which may be seen as indicative for the operation of processes of indirect, socially mediated effects of mass media on social capital.

Starting from a pure individual-level model like those typical of existing research in this field, it will be tested whether social capital is also responsive to styles of media usage that characterize societies as a whole. It is hypothesized that, regardless of any possible individual-level effects of media usage, individuals' social capital is, to some degree, also dependent on the media consumption habits of the respective societies in which they are embedded. Hence, members of societies where television consumption is high, and where televised entertainment has a strong attendance, are expected to display lower levels of social capital than members of societies that pay less attention to the audiovisual medium and its entertainment programs. In contrast, people belonging to societies where many citizens read the papers are expected to display higher levels of social capital than others, again independently of their own reading habits. Whether such phenomena play a role with regard to the relationship between media usage and social capital cannot be decided by means of pure individual-level analysis. Only by comparing individuals *as members of specific societies that differ in their aggregate television and newspaper consumption*, can such macro-micro relationships be decided. This requires the application of techniques of multilevel analysis (Hox 2002; Rosar 2003; Luke 2004).

Locating Putnam's propositions in the context of the more general theme of 'media malaise' in subsection 1.1, the chapter starts with a detailed discussion of Putnam's propositions about media effects on social capital in subsection 1.2. The related evidence that has been accumulated so far is then reviewed in subsection 1.3. Subsequently, the main hypothesis of the present paper, depicting media effects on social capital in terms of contextual effects, is developed in subsection 1.4. The remainder of the paper is devoted to a test of this hypothesis with regard to both television and the printed press, using data from the 2002 ESS, supplemented with data from television broadcasters' audience research and from press statistics. Subsection 2.1 describes the data used for that purpose. The dependent variable is discussed in subsection 2.2, the independent and control variables are described in sections 2.3 and 2.4. Replicating previous studies' dominant approach, subsection 3.1 presents pure individual-level analyses, assessing the role of direct exposure to television as well as newspapers for social capital. Findings suggest a significant, though clearly minor role of media consumption as a production factor of social capital, with signs of relationships corresponding to Putnam's expectations. Subsection 3.2 then turns to multilevel analyses aimed at exploring whether, how and to what extent aggregate features of media consumption within different European societies contribute to these societies' members' social capital, over and above these persons' individual media usage.

1. The Media and Modern Democracy

1.1 *A new voice in the 'media malaise' choir*

Since Robinson published his seminal paper in the mid-1970s, the notion of a media-induced political 'malaise' has gained wide and constant currency among political scientists (Robinson 1976). While most of this literature narrowly revolves around effects of the news media's political coverage on their audience's political attitudes (Delli Carpini 2004), in recent years a new version of this general theme has emerged that applies a broader perspective by tying in with a lively debate on the private prerequisites of public life. Echoing Tocqueville's classic statements about American democracy in the 19th century (De Tocqueville 1990), authors like Almond and Verba (1963), Inglehart (1997), and in recent years, Putnam (1993), argue that for a democracy to function well, it is necessary for its citizens to be tied together by a dense web of interactions, mutual trust, and reciprocity. Following this approach, the private is political, and "[t]he prospects for a democracy in which men do not get along well with one another, do not trust one another, and do not associate with one another is uncompromising" (Lane 1959: 163). At the core of this debate is the concept of '*social capital*', introduced by Coleman (1990: 300–21), and widely popularized by Putnam (1993, 2000).

The notion of social capital "refers to features of social organization, such as trust, norms, and networks, that can improve the efficiency of society by facilitating coordinated action" (Putnam 1993: 167). Social capital appears in three forms. All of them refer to ways of how the members of societies are tied to one another, indicating that social capital is a relational concept. Two of these dimensions are attitudinal, one of them concerns structures that emerge out of and at the same time channel persons' behavior. The structural component refers to people's embeddedness in *networks* of social interaction, and specifically to their active social participation and civic engagement with and for others (Putnam 1993: 171–6). Voluntary associations are seen as an especially important manifestation of the structural component of social capital (Gabriel et al. 2002: 38–42). *Social trust* and *norms of reciprocity* are the two attitudinal components of social capital (Putnam 1993: 171–6). In Putnam's words, "citizens in a civic community, though not selfless saints, regard the public domain as more than a battleground for pursuing personal interests" (Putnam 1993: 71). Accordingly, they are prepared to give one another the benefit of the doubt, hold community obligations, cooperation, and empathy in high esteem, and generally display pro-social rather than selfish orientations. In many respects, social capital is believed to be a valuable asset of modern democratic societies (Putnam 1993, 2000). To analyze the 'production factors' of social capital (Gabriel et al. 2002: 97–144) in order to understand what stimulates the generation of social capital, and what reduces it, must therefore be considered a major task for political science research. This is where the role of media enters the picture.

1.2 The media and social capital: hypotheses

According to Putnam (1995, 2000), with regard to the creation and sustenance of social capital in contemporary democracies, one of the most dangerous developments has been the expansion of television over the past decades; an allegation that turned the social capital debate into one of the most recent voices in the 'malaise' choir of political communication research (Delli Carpini 2004: 402–4). How does television erode a society's social capital? Putnam proposes three hypotheses to support his claim (Putnam 1995: 678–80, 2000: 237–46). The *time-displacement hypothesis* argues that television watching consumes citizens' precious spare time. People who watch a lot of television are 'homebodies'. Time that otherwise might be used for socializing and maintaining social networks is now spent in front of the television set, isolated in the private space of one's living room. Television consumption thus displaces time that otherwise could be used for the production of social capital in its structural forms. According to the *lethargy hypothesis*, "[t]elevision has psychological effects that inhibit social participation" (Putnam 2000: 237). Watching the tube is often a habitually used means for momentary escape, bringing a few flickers of light into the bleak lives of people who feel unhappy and bored. It is, according to Putnam, the cheapest way of averting boredom, and overall a rather unsatisfying experience. Pleasing only as long as it lasts, television produces lethargy, inertia, and, ultimately, passivity in social matters, undermining any impulse for civic engagement that there otherwise might have been. It offers a pseudo-personal environment that may even replace its viewers' real social relationships.

While these two hypotheses focus on the specific usage that people make of the medium, and on the damaging consequences this may entail for their civic engagement, the *'mean world' hypothesis* refers to the content experienced by the television audience. Much of what is broadcast is, according to Putnam, capable of undermining civic motivations. The representation of the world that heavy television users are confronted with regularly, is likely to increase pessimism and create a cynical worldview. Putnam derives this hypothesis from Gerbner's studies about television's 'cultivation' effects (Gerbner et al. 1994). This research starts from the assumption that television, with its entire programming, has become one of the key socialization agencies in modern society. In particular, for people who watch a lot of television, its content becomes a surrogate social environment from which they adopt beliefs about the functioning of society. "Glued to the tube" for much of their available time, they derive their views of the social world not from real social experiences with other people, but from what they see on the screen. Heavy consumers thus subjectively live in a different world than those who watch less television and live real social lives. This becomes important for social capital because television content is, according to 'cultivation' research, a 'mean world', full of materialism, selfishness, cynicism, and crime. Subjectively, being a member of such a society cannot be conducive for the creation of trust and norms of reciprocity. Rather, it may nurture distrust and the notion that only selfishness gets one ahead.

Remarkably, *newspapers* occupy a very different role in Putnam's view of the civic world. Reading the papers, for Putnam, counts as an important civic activity. His understanding is clearly inspired by Tocqueville who saw newspapers as a crucial precondition for the creation of civic associations. Through their information and publicity function, they can create broad awareness of certain ideas and occurrences in society, around which associations then can be formed. "[N]othing but a newspaper can drop the same thought into a thousand minds at the same time. [...] [I]f there were no newspapers there would be no common activity. [...] [T]here is a necessary connection between public associations and newspapers: newspapers make associations, and associations make newspapers." (De Tocqueville 1990/II: 111–2) Newspapers may create a sense among their readers that their concerns are not personal and individual but shared by many others, to the point that they can even exert pressure on their individual readers to conform to the group that they feel to be a member of. "A newspaper represents an association; it may be said to address each of its readers in the name of all the others." (De Tocqueville 1990/II: 114) This understanding of the newspapers' civic function is clearly echoed in Putnam's statement "that newspaper reading and good citizenship go together" (Putnam 2000: 218; see also Putnam 1993: 92–3, 1995: 678).

In his early contributions, Putnam painted an almost Manichean picture of good and bad media. "The basic contrast is straightforward: newspaper reading is associated with high social capital, TV viewing with low social capital." (Putnam 1995: 678) Quickly, criticism was leveled at this undifferentiated conception of the media, pointing out that Putnam's view of television, as one monolithic block was inadequate, overlooking the fact that the medium offers a variety of programs, which may play different roles for social capital (Norris 1996). Responding to this, Putnam (2000) sharpened his hypothesis stating that it is not necessarily television per se that is harmful to social capital, and in any case, television news must be exculpated. Rather, the damaging consequences of television consumption mostly concern entertainment programs. "Nothing [...] is more broadly associated with civic disengagement and social disconnection than is dependence on television for entertainment." (Putnam 2000: 231)

1.3 *The media and social capital: existing evidence*

Putnam's bold claims spurred a small boom of more or less thorough inquiries into the relationships between media use and social capital. Several of these analyses confirm that in the United States the amount of television viewing is indeed negatively, though weakly linked to various aspects of social capital. Some studies found such effects for social trust (Brehm and Rahn 1997; Shah 1998; Gabriel et al. 2002: 120), though others were unable to detect significant relationships (Uslaner 1998; Shah et al. 2001a; Lee et al. 2003). Civic engagement in voluntary associations and socializing activities were also occasionally found to be negatively related to the amount of time spent watching television (Moy et al. 1999; Shah et al. 2001a), though again other analyses were unable to reproduce this effect (Brehm and Rahn 1997; Uslaner 1998; Shah 1998; Shah et al. 2001b; Gabriel et al. 2002: 107–19). Several European (de Hart and Dekker 1999; Hooghe 2002; Arnold and Schneider 2004; Freitag 2003a, 2003b), and Japanese (Freitag 2003b), as well as broad comparative studies (Norris 2000b; Gabriel et al. 2002: 97–144; Freitag and Bühlmann 2005), likewise found a negative effect of viewing television on interpersonal trust. However, no similarly clear-cut relationship emerged between television viewing and civic engagement as well as norms of reciprocity.

On the whole, while varying with regard to the data used, operationalizations of dependent and independent variables, and control variables included in the models, most existing studies found negative and significant, though usually slight relationships between the time spent watching television and social capital. Findings that were more consistent were reported for newspapers. Both American and European studies agree that reading newspapers is indeed an important correlate of social capital in its various manifestations (Brehm and Rahn 1997; Moy et al. 1999; Shah 1998; Shah et al. 2001a, 2001b; de Hart and Dekker 1999; Norris 2000b; Lee et al. 2003). Several studies took into consideration that watching television is not a uniform experience because different people may seek different genres from the variety offered by television. They found partly complex patterns of relationships. Watching 'hard' news on television appeared sometimes (Norris 2000b; Shah et al. 2001a; Hooghe 2002), though not always (Shah 1998; Shah et al. 2001b; Lee et al. 2003), to be positively linked to social capital.

Distinguishing different types of programs within the broad spectrum of televised entertainment, Shah (1998; see also Shah et al. 2001b; Lee et al. 2003) and Hooghe (2002) observed that consumption of some, though not all types of programs was indeed correlated negatively with social trust or civic engagement. In a German study, a general preference for television entertainment was found to be negatively related to social capital (Arnold and Schneider 2004). Remarkably, the type of broadcaster also seemed to play a role. In a Belgian study, Hooghe (2002) distinguished respondents who favored programs from public broadcasters from those who considered private television more attractive, and found that the latter were weaker on social capital. Although in stark contrast to the European dual broadcasting systems, public television plays only a marginal role in the United States. Watching public television and more specifically watching the news on public television was found to be positively, and significantly related to several indicators of social capital (Uslaner 1998; Lee et al. 2003).

In sum, several, though not all, existing studies from various countries suggest that at the individual level, and in cross-sectional perspective, the amount of time spent watching television is negatively, though rather weakly, linked to various manifestations of social capital. Some scattered evidence indicates that the (slightly) damaging effect of television on social capital might be less a consequence of television usage as such, but rather of using this medium primarily for the purpose of entertainment. The observation of a positive relationship between following public affairs programming and social capital indicates that the type of content used is indeed of some relevance, although these relationships are also not consistent and strong. Some sporadic findings also suggests that public television—which compared to private broadcasters, usually places more value on information and less value on entertainment programming (Pfetsch 1996; European Audiovisual Observatory 2005/V)—might have beneficial effects on social capital. Newspapers, on the other hand, appear quite unequivocally as the civic "hero", portrayed by Tocqueville in the 19th century, and agreed upon by his contemporary intellectual successor, Robert Putnam.

1.4 *The media and social capital: a case for contextual effects?*

While largely, though by no means unequivocally in line with Putnam's hypotheses, these findings do not seem to justify any dramatization of the impact of media consumption on modern democracies' social capital. The effects that could have been observed are simply too small. Many other factors have, meanwhile, been identified by numerous studies looking at the background of social capital and its components with regard to social trust, norms of reciprocity, and social networks, together being far more substantial than that of citizens' usage of the media. In particular, the concerns expressed about the potentially damaging role of television seem not to be significantly affirmed, while the positive role of the press has been uniformly confirmed.

In the conclusion of a recent Belgian study on Putnam's television hypothesis, which arrived at a similar prognosis, Hooghe raised an interesting point. He argued that the difficulties to find evidence for the validity of Putnam's hypothesis at the individual level do not necessarily mean that it is entirely meaningless. Zero or almost-zero findings in individual-level analyses of survey data must not preclude the possibility that such effects could exist at the macro level (Hooghe 2002: 89). It is conceivable that the impact of television on a society may have changed it to such a degree that individual-level differences cease to be important. To illustrate this point he uses the example of associations that no longer offer opportunities for joint activities because organizers find it too frustrating, given their experience of declining attendance. In such a situation, even television avoiders will no longer be able to take part in organizational activities, not because they lack the necessary time and motivation, but because of the lack of opportunities for such activities. None of the existing studies, including Hooghe's own, approaches empirically this type of macro-micro argument, because they all rely exclusively on individual-level data. Yet, following this strand of thought further is certainly a worthwhile endeavor.

The notion of social capital always refers to citizens' connections to their fellow citizens (Coleman 1990: 300–21). Due to this inherently relational characteristic, social capital may be especially susceptible to contextual effects that come about through directly experienced or observed social interaction (Books and Prysby 1991). If one's social environment changes in ways that no longer are conducive to the production of social capital, even citizens whose personal characteristics would otherwise predispose them to display the highest levels of social capital may find themselves incapable to sustain and actively live their civic orientations. Social networks cannot be created and nurtured by one person alone, it needs others to connect and interact with. However, if others are kept from socializing by *their* television usage, no networks can be built and sustained.

Similarly, if a person were as altruistic and trusting as anyone could possibly be, but would rarely or never experience the trustworthy and altruistic nature of others due to the fact that television may have undermined trust and a sense of reciprocity, he or she would probably at some point also become less trusting as well as unconditionally altruistic. If Putnam is right about the detrimental role of television, societies that, overall, spend much of their disposable time on watching television, particularly televised entertainment, will tend to have low stocks of social capital. However, if it is also true that social capital is not only dependent on citizens' media habits but also on endogenous processes of auto-feedback (Putnam 1993: 177–81), then, under such circumstances, a vicious circle will arise, further eroding the remaining pockets of social capital, even among those who are less fond of television, simply because their social capital is constantly undermined by other people, and eventually leading to a leveling at the bottom. An analogous, though reverse argument can be constructed with regard to the advantageous role of the printed press. If the press contributes to the growth of social capital, and if social capital is indeed contagious and self-nurturing, then a high newspaper penetration of a society, by means of similar processes of endogenous contagion, will trigger a virtuous circle of spreading social capital, even among those who do not, themselves, bother to read the papers.

2. Data and Variables

2.1 *Data*

Using data from the first wave of the European Social Survey (ESS), fielded in 2002, the present paper seeks to shed some new light on the puzzling relationship between media consumption and social capital. Data from almost all the European countries where the ESS was conducted, will be used. Israel as a non-European country is excluded, since the assumption of at least a basic contextual similarity between the countries included in the study cannot be upheld in this case. Unfortunately, Switzerland and the Czech Republic must also be excluded because one of the variables used for the construction of the dependent variable is missing in these countries' ESS data (membership in voluntary associations). Respondents, who are residents of ESS countries but nationals of other countries, are excluded from the analyses. Hence, the findings presented below are representative for the population of citizens residing in their home countries, aged 16 and above, of 16 West European countries (Austria, Belgium, Denmark, Finland, France, Germany, Greece, Ireland, Italy, Luxembourg, the Netherlands, Norway, Portugal, Spain, Sweden and the United Kingdom) and three East Central European countries (Hungary, Poland and Slovenia). The design weight will be used throughout. In addition, weights are applied to equalize the sample sizes of all countries to the average number of cases of 1,600, to adjust for the fact that samples are considerably larger in some countries than in others.² This is to ascertain that the results of the analyses give an accurate picture of the average situation across all included countries that is not arbitrarily biased by differing sample sizes, giving countries with larger samples more weight in the results than those with smaller samples. For the multilevel analyses, the ESS data will be supplemented by aggregate data taken from national statistics of media use, described below in more detail.

2.2 *Dependent variable*

Operationalizing social capital is not a straightforward task. There is no such thing as a canonical, tried and tested standard operationalization of social capital, or even, for that matter, of its various components (van Deth 2002). To grasp the multidimensionality of the concept while at the same time keeping models parsimonious, the present study uses an index that includes all three dimensions of social capital—social trust, reciprocity norms, and social networks—as dependent variable. Although some dimensional analyses were performed, it is not the goal of this chapter to scrutinize the internal consistency of the concept of social capital. Like other, more thorough analyses of its empirical integrity (e.g., Gabriel et al. 2002: 37–96), these analyses suggest that interrelationships are actually rather weak.³ However, as these dimensions are all integral components of the multidimensional construct of social capital, their combination into one summary measure appears a theoretically appropriate way to proceed (Norris 2002: 146–9; Gabriel et al. 2002: 131–5). This *Index of Social Capital (ISC)* is built in an additive way and indicates the number of different facets of the construct with which individual respondents are equipped.

The first component of the ISC is based on a measure of *social trust*. It is derived from an additive index composed of respondents' assessments on 11-point scales of three questions. The first question being, "generally speaking, would you say that most people can be trusted, or that you cannot be too careful when dealing with people?" The second question; "do you think that most people would try to take advantage of you if they got the chance, or would they try to be fair?" Finally,

---

² Unweighted sizes of active samples range from 1,079 in Luxembourg to 2,799 in Germany.
³ Intercorrelations (Pearson's r) between the four variables discussed below do not exceed .27 (pooled analysis for all included countries).

the third question; "would you say that most of the time people try to be helpful or that they are mostly looking out for themselves?" The unidimensionality of these items has been ascertained by means of a principal components analysis, the scale's α-reliability is .77. The index' range is 0 to 30. About a third of all respondents have high values on this trust measure, between 19 and 30. For constructing the ISC, a dummy variable is created, assigning these respondents a value of 1. The reciprocity norm is represented by a measure of *altruism*: "not counting anything you do for your family, in your work, or within voluntary organizations, how often, if at all, do you actively provide help for other people?" Answers are registered on a 7-point scale. About a third of all respondents achieve values of 5 to 7, indicating that they help other people at least once a week. They are assigned a value of 1 on a corresponding dummy variable.

Socializing in the form of meeting with other people is an important way of generating and maintaining social networks. It can be measured by the question: "how often do you meet socially with friends, relatives or work colleagues?", again using a 7-point scale. Respondents with values of 6 or 7, i.e. those who met other people several times a week or daily, are assigned a value of 1 on a corresponding dummy variable. This is the case for about 45% of all respondents. The fourth variable concerns another dimension of social networks—*membership in voluntary associations*. It registers, again as a dummy variable, whether respondents are members of at least one of a whole series of leisure organizations (sports clubs or clubs for out-door activities; organizations for cultural or hobby activities; social clubs, clubs for the young, the retired/elderly, women, or friendly societies), interest organizations (trade unions; business, professional, or farmers' organizations; consumer or automobile organizations), and cultural or religious organizations (organizations for humanitarian aid, human rights, minorities, or immigrants; religious or church organizations; organizations for science, education, or teachers and parents). About two thirds of all respondents report being a member of at least one such association.

The ISC is a count over these four dummy variables, and its range is, accordingly, 0 to 4.[4] A value of 4 indicates that the respective respondent is a well equipped 'social capitalist' (Gabriel et al. 2002:

---

[4] Intercorrelations (Pearson's r) between the four dummy variables range from .03 (trust and altruism) to .21 (trust and association membership).

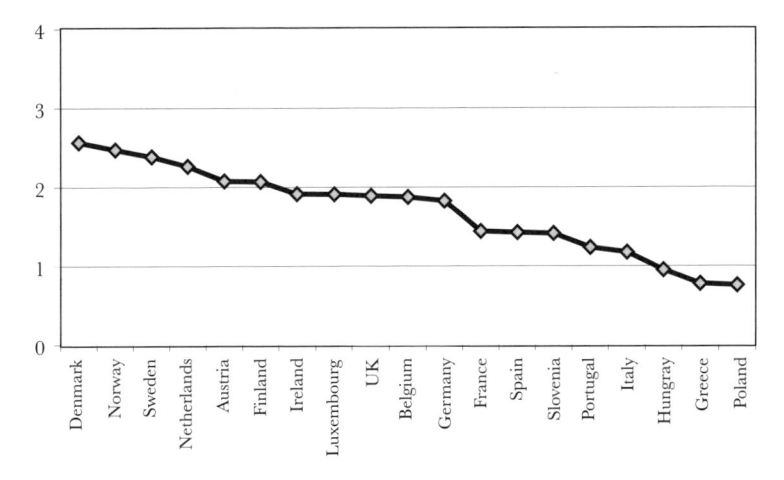

Figure 1: Social capital in Europe (country means)

131–5): He or she is a member of at least one voluntary association, often meets other people, is very trusting, and frequently helps other people. In contrast, a value of 0, indicates the absence of all of these various facets of social capital. Values in between indicate moderate degrees of 'social capital'. Figure 1 displays the mean levels of 'social capital' in the countries analyzed in this study.[5] The results vary widely. Scandinavians are, on average, about three times better equipped with social capital in its different forms than the Polish or the Greeks are.

2.3 Independent variables: micro level

The ESS includes a small question battery to register respondents' media usage. To measure the *amount of their total television consumption*, ESS respondents were asked: "on an average weekday, how much time, in total, do you spend watching television?" Answers were registered on an 8-point scale ranging, in half-hour intervals, from 0 = no time at all, to 7 = more than 3 hours. One of the most important points of view that has repeatedly been put forward in the debate on television's role for social capital, is the necessity to distinguish various forms of television consumption, especially the usage of information and entertainment programs. The latter is believed to be particularly detrimental to social capital. The ESS includes a variable that refers to

---

[5] Overall mean with countries weighted equally: 1.71 (SD = 1.12).

televised political information, but no question concerning entertainment content. However, the information question can be used to obtain at least an indirect measure of consumption of televised entertainment. Respondents were asked how much time they usually spent "watching news or programs about politics and current affairs". This again, was measured in half-hour intervals. Relating this variable to respondents' total television usage by expressing consumption of political programs as a share of total consumption, one can obtain a measure of the degree to which television usage is dominated by viewing political information (cf. Klingemann and Voltmer 1989). The variable resulting from this transformation ranges from 0, for respondents who never watch politics on television (regardless of whether they never watch television at all or just watch exclusively non-political content), to 1.0, for respondents who devote their entire television time exclusively to political content. By inverting this variable and taking into account respondents' total television usage, a new variable can be generated that registers *non-political television usage*, and thus an estimation of the amount of time spent watching television that is devoted to entertainment. The resulting variable correspondingly ranges from 0, for respondents who never watch entertainment programs (either because they never watch television or because they exclusively attend to political content), to 1.0, for respondents who devote their entire television time exclusively to non-political content. Usage of *newspapers*, is measured similarly. One variable registers the self-reported *total time* that is devoted to reading the papers on an average day; the other measures the proportion of this usage that is devoted to *non-political content*. Unsurprisingly, non-political usage overall plays a much smaller role in newspaper reading than in watching TV.

In seeking to arrive at an adequate understanding of the role of media usage as an individual-level production factor for social capital, it is essential that competing explanations for observed relationships be ruled out as much as possible. Hence, a broad range of control variables must be included in the multivariate models that will be designed to assess the impact of the media variables on the ISC. At the individual level, this concerns both factors that are known to influence people's media usage and factors that are connected to individuals' social capital. The problem of selectivity bias, notorious in media effects research using cross-sectional data, requires that factors be included in the models, which are well-known correlates of patterns of television and newspaper usage. In particular, this concerns sociodemographic attributes like *age, gender, levels of formal education, household income* and *household structures*.

The same factors must also be included in order to control for competing explanations of the amount of social capital held by the respondents. Age and gender are standard control variables in virtually all models of social capital. Individuals' social integration and social status have emerged as important predictors of their levels of social capital (Gabriel et al. 2002: 104–7). The former concerns variables such as *church attendance*, and *community size*. Higher levels of social capital are expected for respondents who attend service often, and live in smaller communities. *How long* they have been living in the same area may also play a role, the expectation being that extended periods of residence are beneficial to the development of social capital (Uslaner 1998; Hooghe 2002). Education and household income are important correlates of social status. It is assumed that higher-status individuals who are better equipped with socio-economic and intellectual resources will display higher levels of social capital (Newton 1999; Freitag 2003b). In contrast, people who are *unemployed* and thus command relatively few resources may be rather poorly equipped with social capital.

Since people's *time budgets* can be assumed to play an important role as preconditions for civic activity (Putnam 1995: 668–9, 2000: 189–203; Shah 1998; Hooghe 2002), several temporal variables like the time consumed by *employed respondents'* as well as *spouses' jobs*, by *housework*, and by *caring for children* will be included as controls.[6] If respondents' household time budgets are highly constrained by working long hours, by housework or by childcare, they can be expected to be less able to engage in civic activities like helping others or in social participation more generally. Occasionally fear of crime has been assumed detrimental to the attitudinal components of social capital (Brehm and Rahn 1997; Shah 1998). An important reason for developing fear of crime is certainly the previous personal or indirect *experience of crime*. The negative impact of such an event might, to perhaps a lesser degree, even extend to the behavioral components of social capital. Finally, it can be expected that people who are dissatisfied with their lives tend

---

[6] At the same time, these variables implicitly also measure whether respondents' are gainfully employed and married—two important aspects of social integration that cannot be included separately into the models because this would create multicollinearity.

to withdraw from civic activities, and may develop a less sanguine outlook on their social environment (Brehm and Rahn 1997; Uslaner 1998; Shah 1998; Shah et al. 2001b). Hence, self-reported *life satisfaction* will also be included among the control variables of the multivariate models discussed in the following section.

2.4 Independent variables: macro level

To supplement the four indicators of respondents' individual media usage described above, we need aggregate measures of their entire societies' media habits. Concerning television, data of high quality are fortunately provided by television broadcasters' media research. Broadcasters' audience data are highly valid, since they are based on direct behavioral measurement of actual individual television usage, using electronic devices—so called people-meter systems—that are hooked to television sets in selected panel households, and continuously register the actual consumption of each household member in extremely small time-intervals (1 second in most countries). Luxembourg is, due to its small size, the only ESS country where this costly technique is not used. Instead, audience data are obtained by means of CATI surveys using the diary technique (Schulz 2000; IP International Marketing Committee 2003: 27–30). A useful macro indicator for the time devoted to watching television by members of a society is audiences' *average total daily television viewing time (in 2002).*[7] This data reveals that television usage differs strikingly across Europe. Hungary and Poland lead the field with an average daily viewing time per person of more than four hours (268 resp. 246 minutes). At the other end of the scale is Luxembourg with just about two hours and 20 minutes (141 minutes) average daily viewing time (mean = 195.3, SD = 35.6). It is to be expected that citizens

---

[7] Source: IP International Marketing Committee (2003: 26). The populations of the audience data are not all similar, due to national traditions of audience research. They mostly refer to television viewers aged 15 and above, but in a few countries, they also include younger viewers. In addition, it is not clear from the available documentation whether and where this data includes the non-national resident population. However, on the whole, this does not present a serious drawback with regard to the data's usability for the present purpose. For culturally segmented Belgium, the television macro data are differentiated by language region, since both television programming and usage habits differ substantially between these regions. As there are also substantial differences in television consumption between East and West Germany (Berg and Ridder 2002), these regions are also distinguished in the analyses (Source of East and West German data: http://www.ard.de/intern/basisdaten/fernsehnutzung/fernsehnutzung_20im__ _23220_3Bberblick/-/id=55024/bxj2vh/).

of countries where more time is spent in front of television screens, social capital will be less wide spread.

Apart from television time, it is also desirable to have a measure of content-specific consumption. Audience research does not provide cross-nationally comparable data regarding usage of specific types of programming. What does exist, however, is data on usage of specific channels. Of particular interest, are the respective *audience or market shares of public (and, by way of implication, private) broadcasters* in each country.[8] Public channels exist in all European countries except Luxembourg, where public channels from neighboring countries are available. The market share of a channel is the percentage of the population tuned into this particular channel from those watching television at a particular time (Schulz 2000: 117). Such shares can easily be calculated using the data that is continuously collected by organizations undertaking audience research, and they can be aggregated in any desirable way, be it over time or across channels, or both. The data used in this paper is the audience shares of all public channels within each country or region, cumulated for the year 2002.[9]

Several studies of programming structures as well as content analyses of specific programs have shown that public broadcasters' programming differs considerably from private broadcasters (Pfetsch 1996; European Audiovisual Observatory 2005/V). The latter are guided by a commercial logic, and their programming policies follow the principle of audience maximization. They seek to offer programming that attracts the largest possible audiences, in order to be able to demand higher prices from the advertising industry being their prime source of revenue. Consequently, their programming is usually dominated by light entertainment, while information, especially 'hard' political information, is relegated to a rather marginal role. In contrast, public television stations are usually, at least to some degree, kept free from market pressures by means of public subsidies or audience fees. They are, to varying degrees, dependent on governments or political parties, and required to adhere to norms and standards in their programming that are fixed in codices,

---

[8] In dual broadcasting systems, private broadcasters' audience shares are the inverse of public broadcasters' audience shares.
[9] Source: IP International Marketing Committee (2003: 18). Data for East and West Germany are taken from Darschin and Gerhard (2003) and include children aged 3 and above.

charters and broadcasting laws, and monitored by special supervisory bodies (Humphreys 1996: 111–58).

The BBC's well-known slogan nicely captures the mission of public broadcasters: to inform, entertain, and educate (http://www.bbc.co.uk/info/purpose/). Entertainment does play a role for public broadcasters that is, by no means, marginal. However, it is not the only or even dominant purpose, and the other two tasks are of a kind that is certainly at odds with the imperatives guiding private broadcasters' programming. In addition, even regarding their entertainment programming, public broadcasters are typically required to meet certain standards of quality (Humphreys 1996: 121). Following this line of argument, it can be assumed that a society that spends a small amount of its overall television time watching the programs of public broadcasters is exposed to, on the whole, more of the kind of content that Putnam considers damaging to social capital. Accordingly, I expect individual social capital to be higher in societies where public televisions' audience shares are larger, and, inversely, shares are smaller with respect to private broadcasters. Some individual-level findings from the studies reviewed above (cf. section 2.3) support this expectation. Within Europe, there are large differences regarding the degree to which audiences attend to public broadcasters' programs. Denmark tops all other countries with an audience share of public channels of 71.1%. In Greece, on the other hand, public television accounts for just 12.5% of total television consumption (Mean = 37.3, SD = 13.3). Remarkably, the average amount of time spent watching television and the audience shares of public broadcasters are virtually unrelated ($r = -.11$).

Lastly, we need a measure for the varying importance of the printed press in European countries. Standardized circulation figures of daily newspapers are best suited for that purpose. Accordingly, in my analysis, I include the *average daily circulation of newspapers per 1000 inhabitants (in 2002)* as a measure of the degree to which newspapers penetrate European societies.[10] Again, numbers are varying extremely, from 71 in Greece, to 705 in Norway. Norway leads the field within European countries, alongside other Scandinavian countries, and, together with Japan, is one of the most newspaper-saturated countries of the world. In general, there is a clear North-South divide in newspaper reading. Circulation rates also tend to be rather small in the new democracies

---

[10] Source: Hasebrink and Herzog (2004: 145).

of East Central Europe, but still more significant than the Mediterranean countries (mean = 294, SD = 159). Individual stocks of social capital are expected to be higher in countries where more people read newspapers. The (aggregate) correlation of this variable with television time is negative and rather strong (−.61), indicating that more time is spent on watching television in countries where fewer people read newspapers (cf. Norris 2000a: 85–7 for similar findings). The correlation with public television market shares is positive, but much smaller (.27). While these three macro indicators nicely correspond to three of the individual-level measures of media use, it would be ideal to also have a measure of non-political (or political) newspaper consumption. However, no such indicator is available. Hence, the ensuing multilevel analyses will focus on two measures of aggregate television consumption and one of newspaper usage.

Since only 21 macro-level cases are available for the multilevel analyses, there is not much room for contextual control variables. At least one obvious factor will be included in the ensuing analyses—a dummy variable registering whether a country (or region) is an *old or a new democracy*. The latter encompass Hungary, Poland, Slovenia, and East Germany. Due to their specific historic trajectory, new democracies can be expected to display generally lower levels of social capital (Rose 1994).

3. Analyses and findings

3.1 *Individual-level analyses*

Table 1 displays estimates from a series of OLS models that include all four individual-level media variables: total television time; the proportion devoted to non-political, presumably mostly entertainment programs; time spent reading newspapers; and the share of this time that is, correspondingly, devoted to reading non-political articles. The first model predicts respondents' ISC values, i.e. their endowment with various components of social capital, exclusively from their media consumption. The second model additionally includes the whole array of control variables. Looking first at the pure media model, it becomes obvious that media use is indeed related to social capital, and that all relationships are in the expected directions. Social capital shrinks as more time is spent watching television, and as non-political content becomes more dominant with regard to the share of the television usage

Table 1: Media usage and social capital in Europe: individual-level models

	B		Beta	
	Media only	Media plus controls	Media only	Media plus controls
Constant	1.87***	.85***		
Television viewing time (0–7)	−.05***	−.02***	−.09	−.03
Share of non-pol. usage in TV viewing (0–1)	−.17***	−.18***	−.04	−.05
Newspaper reading (0–7)	.15***	.09***	.17	.11
Share of non-pol. usage newspaper reading (0–1)	−.13***	−.07**	−.04	−.02
Male (1/0)		−.03*		−.01
Age (in years)		−.005***		−.08
Secondary education (1/0)		.20***		.09
Household net income (1–12)		.10***		.23
Community size (1–3)		−.03***		−.02
Lived in area more than 10 years (1/0)		−.06***		−.03
Church attendance (0–5)		−.02**		−.02
Time consumed by job (0–3)		−.01		−.01
Time consumed by spouse's/partner's job (0–3)		−.06***		−.07
Unemployed (1/0)		−.03		−.01
Housework (1/0)		.02		.01
Children in household (1/0)		−.14***		−.06
Victim of crime (1/0)		.06**		.02
Life satisfaction (0–10)		.10***		.19
Adj. R^2	.04	.19		
(N)	(24,662)			

*** $p < .001$; ** $p < .01$; * $p < .05$; + $p < .10$.
Note: The design weight is used, and all national samples are standardized to an average sample size of 1,600. The reported N is unweighted.

that respondents attend to. Remarkably, with regard to non-political content, the same applies to newspapers. In contrast, individuals' stock of social capital tends to increase as they invest more time in studying the papers. With an R^2 of 4%, this model's explanatory power is not overwhelming, but neither is it altogether negligible. Nevertheless, there is no denying that the beta coefficients are anything but impressive, with the exception of time spent on reading newspapers.

Adding control variables leads to further declining effect sizes for most media variables. None become insignificant, but this is largely due to the enormous number of cases available in the pooled ESS dataset. The remaining effects are minuscule, with the exception of time spent reading newspapers. In other words, the results are similar to what has already been concluded by numerous previous studies from many countries. Table 1, thus, simply confirms the conclusion drawn from the review of existing research in section 2.3. On the whole, this analysis does not lend much support to the notion that media usage is an important production factor of social capital in Europe, and above all, to the conclusion that a large amount of television consumption can undermine individuals' social capital. Other explanatory variables seem more influential than even newspaper reading, with household income and life satisfaction clearly standing out. The explanatory power of this more complete model is about five times larger than the pure media model. Starting from this pure individual-level model, we now turn to a multilevel analysis.

3.2 *Multilevel analyses*

The multilevel models displayed in Table 2 are so-called random intercept models (Hox 2002).[11] The chosen modeling strategy proceeds in three steps (cf. Rosar 2003 for this logic of analysis and related terminology). The first column displays a baseline or 'empty' model (*E model*), to check for the existence of significant variance in the baseline levels of social capital across countries. Comparable to an analysis of variance, this model tests whether the intercepts of country-specific models of social capital, without any explanatory variables, differs significantly. If that were not the case, there would be no variation that could be explained by country-level media variables, or any other country-level variables, for that matter.

However, this is clearly not the case. European societies differ markedly with regard to their members' average levels of social capital.[12] According to Table 2, there is substantial, highly significant cross-country variance. Its share of the total variance, expressed in the Intra-Class Correlation Coefficient, ICC, is about 24%. The next step is to see

---

[11] HLM 6.0 was used for these analyses (cf. Raudenbush et al. 2004).
[12] The increase of the intercept in Table 2 as compared to Table 1, is a result of the Grand Mean centering applied to all independent variables in Table 2.

whether these country differences are the consequence of cross-national differences in the distributions of individual-level independent variables. The estimates in the second column of Table 2 show to what degree this is the case. These are the findings from a so-called *I model*, i.e. a model that includes exclusively individual-level predictors. It includes all significant independent variables from the individual-level model displayed in Table 1. The drop in the ICC value as compared to the *E model* indicates to what degree the cross-country variation of social capital is due to compositional effects, that is, differing distributions of important independent variables across countries. Although the ICC decreases moderately to .20, the remaining country-level variance in the dependent variable is still highly significant. Hence, it makes sense to carry on and test for the effects of independent country-level aggregate variables. The individual-level predictors' explanatory power amounts to about 7% of the individual-level variance, and 27% of the cross-country variance.

The model displayed in the third column of Table 2 is an extension of this model (except for a few control variables that were dropped because they appeared no longer significant in the *I model*). This is the first of two *C models* (*i.e.*, complete models) that include not only the four individual-level media variables as well as all significant micro level control variables, but also country-level predictors. In the first *C model*, these are the two aggregate television variables, as well as the dummy variable distinguishing old from new democracies. Strikingly, both media variables are highly significant, and signs are in the expected directions. Clearly, not only respondents' personal usage of the audiovisual medium counts for their social capital, but also how much and in what ways it is generally used in the societies they are members of. Their stocks of social capital tend to shrink as their fellow citizens attend more frequently to television, but they get broader if this consumption tends to concentrate on public television.

According to the second *C model* that additionally includes aggregate data on European societies' newspaper penetration stocks of social capital, it also tends to be more extensive among citizens of countries where many people read the papers. While including newspaper distribution in the model does not affect the impact of public television's market share, the effect of average television time decreases somewhat. This comes as no surprise, as we have seen above, that newspaper readership and television time are quite strongly negatively correlated. However, even after introducing this additional media variable, aggregate television time remains an important predictor of social capital. In addition, in the last model there is also a marginally significant positive effect of being a citizen of an old democracy that was suppressed when aggregate newspaper usage was not included in the model. On average, citizens of old democracies have somewhat more social capital at their disposal than citizens of the post-Communist new democracies of East Central Europe and East Germany.[13]

According to the standardized coefficients shown in the last column of Table 2, Europeans' stocks of social capital are somewhat broader if they read newspapers, and marginally smaller if they watch a lot of television, especially entertainment programs, and also if they read more non-political than political reports in the papers. However, these relationships are no match to the effects of the patterns of media use of the social environments they find themselves in. Their social capital tends to be considerably smaller if they happen to live in a society whose members are on average heavy consumers of television, and it tends to be considerably larger if their society is deeply penetrated by newspapers. These two effects are the largest in the entire model, surpassing even the effects of age and life satisfaction that in this analysis appear strongest at the level of individuals.[14] The kind of programming European societies watch on television also plays a role, although a smaller one. Persons living in countries where citizens overall watch more public television tend to be endowed with more social capital than those living in regions where private broadcasters dominate the screen. Compared to the *I model*, the four aggregate variables decrease the unexplained cross-country variance of social capital by another

---

[13] A corresponding intercept as outcome model, predicting changes in country means of the ISC only from country characteristics, produced (with all predictors Grand Mean centered, except the old vs new democracy dummy) the following equation: Mean country-level ISC = 1.49–.006*Average TV Viewing Time + .001 * Public TV Audience Share + .001 * Newspapers Average Daily Distribution + .26 * Old Democracy. All predictors were significant with $p<.05$ or better. The model's context level R^2 amounted to .84. This model predicts differences in country means on the 4-point scale of the ISC between countries with the lowest and the highest values amounting to .42 for TV time, .59 for Public TV's audience shares, and 64 for newspaper distribution. The difference between old and new democracies is .26.

[14] That household income no longer displays a strong beta coefficient in this analysis suggests that the estimates displayed in Table 1 were due to compositional effects, caused by substantial income differences between countries that also differed with regard to social capital. Including an aggregate measure of average income in the multilevel models should prove this.

Table 2: Media usage and social capital in Europe: multilevel models

	E model	I model	C model (TV only)	C model (TV and newspapers)	C model (TV and newspapers) - Beta -
Fixed effects					
Constant	1.70***	1.70***	1.51***	1.51***	
Average total television viewing time (min. per day)			−.008***	−.005**	−.15
Public channels' audience share (%)			.001**	.001*	.09
Newspapers average distribution per day (per 1,000 inhab.)				.001**	.18
Old democracy (1/0)			.21	.23+	.09
Television viewing time (0–7)		−.02**	−.02**	−.02**	−.03
Share of non-political usage in TV viewing (0–1)		−.11*	−.11*	−.11*	−.03
Newspaper reading (0–7)		.06***	.06***	.06***	.07
Share of non-political usage in newspaper reading (0–1)		−.09***	−.09***	−.09***	−.03
Male (1/0)		.01			
Age (in years)		−.007***	−.007***	−.007***	−.12
Secondary education (1/0)		.17***	.17***	.17***	.08
Household net income (1–12)		.02***	.02***	.02***	.05
Community size (1–3)		.00			
Lived in area more than 10 years (1/0)		.09***	.09***	.09***	.04
Church attendance (0–5)		.06***	.06***	.06***	.07
Time consumed by spouse's/partner's job (0–3)		−.04***	−.04***	−.04***	−.04
Children in household (1/0)		−.06**	−.06**	−.06**	−.02
Victim of crime (1/0)		.07***	.07***	.07***	.03
Life satisfaction (0–10)		.06***	.06***	.06***	.12
Variance components					
σ_e^2	0.899	0.837	0.837	0.837	
τ_0^2	0.288***	0.209***	0.073***	0.045***	
ICC	.24	.20	.08	.05	
R^2 individual level		.07	.07	.07	
R^2 context level		.27	.75	.84	
Deviance	69095.93	67393.69	67379.84	67386.61	

*** $p < .001$; ** $p < .01$; * $p < .05$; + $p < .10$.

Notes: Table entries are unstandardized regression coefficients, except for the last column. Restric Maximum Likelihood estimation was used for the analyses. All independent variables are c tered at Grand Mean. The design weight is used, and all national samples are standardize average sample size of 1,600. N of respondents (unweighted) = 25,254, N of countries/regi = 21. Degrees of freedom in all models = 2.

57%. Consequently, the share of remaining cross-country variance in the total unexplained variance of the ISC drops to just about 5%.

In sum, these findings prove that expanding the scope of analysis beyond the level of individuals was worthwhile. With regard to individual social capital, it is not entirely irrelevant to what degree and how Europeans personally use television and especially the press. However, media consumption patterns of the countries they happen to live in appear much more powerful as predictors of their individual stocks of social capital—irrespective of their own usage.

4. Conclusion

Introducing the notion of social capital to political science, Robert Putnam has, in recent years, stimulated lively debates about civics and its benefits for modern democracies' social, economic, and political functioning. One of these debates concerns an interesting new angle to the 'malaise' argument that, for the last three decades, has been a constant theme of political communication research. According to Putnam, television, especially its entertainment programs, is to be accused of destroying modern societies' precious social capital, by wasting people's time, by making them apathetic, and by creating a cynical outlook at the social world. While television emerges mostly—with the single exception of its public affairs programs—as a force of evil from this reasoning, newspapers are highly appreciated as the embodiment of civics. Yet, existing research, so far, proves unable to underpin these claims with impressive empirical substance.

Against this state of affairs, this paper attempted to break new ground by expanding the scope of analysis to include macro-micro relationships. The relational core of the construct of social capital, and its self-nurturing character, that is a consequence of this attribute (Putnam 1993: 177–81), gave rise to the assumption that media effects on social capital may be an area with a particularly high likelihood of contextual effects, supplementing, and perhaps even surpassing individual-level effects of direct exposure. According to this reasoning, media can also have indirect effects on social capital, reaching even those who do not care about watching much television or reading the papers by way of their experiences with those fellow citizens who do, and who have—if Putnam is right—been transformed by their media exposure. In a society saturated with entertainment television, in all likelihood people—even television abstainers—will tend to meet more heavy users, and their experiences with them will, in turn, tend to be rather unpleasant, being, on average, anti-social. Even if they avoid meeting them, they will inevitably witness how they behave socially. Since social capital is fed by experience, contagion through disagreeable social interaction will thus contribute to its further erosion. A similar process will take place in a society composed of heavy readers of newspapers. Just the effect will be the opposite: a virtuous instead of a vicious circle.

To deal empirically with social processes such as these, pure micro level analyses of the type commonly used are inadequate. Rather, multilevel modeling, taking appropriate indicators of aggregate media usage of entire societies into account, is the preferable way to proceed. The findings presented in the previous section suggest this to be a worthwhile endeavor. Clearly, social capital is broadest not so much among respondents who themselves watch little television, but amongst those who live in countries where people generally do not spend much time attending to the screen. At the same time, irrespective of personal styles of media use and of all other individual attributes that were explored in this paper, levels of individual social capital are on average higher in countries where many people read a newspaper. Hence, switching from a pure micro level to multilevel analysis, thereby accepting the notion that media effects may also be indirect and to some degree independent of citizens' individual media habits, provides the basic Putnam theme that television is the 'bad guy', and the printed press is the 'good guy', with empirical support that is less ambiguous and more substantial than most findings from previous studies of the same topic.

Although weaker, there is some evidence that the type of content watched is also relevant. While television generally seems to be indeed damaging to social capital, the particular content on television that is watched by a society appears to be relevant, too. Individuals' stocks of social capital are positively related to the audience shares of public television. The greater the amount of society's television time spent watching programs on public channels, the more developed the social capital of its members, irrespective of their own viewing habits. Often, public broadcasting is explicitly assigned the task of contributing to different societal groups' mutual understanding, and ultimately, nothing less than the integration of a society (Jarren et al. 2001: 35–45). The findings reported above suggest that it is not without success in fulfilling such functions. Accordingly, a polity interested in high levels of social capital among its citizens should try to create incentives to abstain from television, and to refer to the printed press instead. To the degree that this cannot be achieved, it should deem public rather than commercial television preferable.

References

Almond, Gabriel A./Verba, Sidney (1963): The Civic Culture. Political Attitudes and Democracy in Five Nations. Princeton/NJ: Princeton University Press.

Arnold, Anne-Katrin/Schneider, Beate (2004): TV Kills Social Capital? Eine kritische Auseinandersetzung mit der Sozialkapitalforschung von Robert Putnam. Publizistik 49: 423–438.

Berg, Klaus/Ridder, Christa-Maria (eds.) (2002): Massenkommunikation VI. Baden-Baden: Nomos.

Books, John W./Prysby, Charles L. (1994): Political Behavior and the Local Context, New York: Praeger.

Brehm, John/Rahn, Wendy (1997): Individual-Level Evidence for the Causes and Consequences of Social Capital. American Journal of Political Science 41: 999–1023.

Bühlmann, Marc/Freitag, Markus (2004): Individuelle und kontextuelle Determinanten der Teilhabe an Sozialkapital. Eine Mehrebenenanalyse zu den Bedingungen des Engagements in Freiwilligenorganisationen. Kölner Zeitschrift für Soziologie und Sozialpsychologie 56: 326–349.

Coleman, James S. (1990): Foundations of Social Theory. Cambridge/Mass.: Harvard UP.

Dahl, Robert A. (1998): On Democracy. New Haven/London: Yale University Press.

Darschin, Wolfgang/Gerhard, Heinz (2003): Tendenzen im Zuschauerverhalten. Fernsehgewohnheiten und Fernsehreichweiten im Jahr 2002. Media Perspektiven 4: 158–166.

De Hart, Joop/Dekker, Paul (1999): Civic engagement and volunteering in the Netherlands. In: van Deth, Jan W., Maraffi, Marco, Newton, Kenneth/Whiteley, Paul F. (eds.): Social Capital and European Democracy. London/New York: Routledge.

De Tocqueville, Alexis (1990) [1840]: Democracy in America, Vol. I and II. New York: Vintage.

Delli Carpini, Michael X. (2004): Mediating Democratic Engagement: The Impact of Communications on Citizens' Involvement in Political and Civic Life. In: Kaid, Lynda Lee (ed.), Handbook of Political Communciation Research, Mahwah/NJ: Lawrence Erlbaum, 395–434.

European Audiovisual Observatory (ed.) (2005): Yearbook, Vol.V, Strasbourg: EAO.

Freitag, Markus (2003a): Beyond Tocqueville: The Origins of Social Capital in Switzerland. European Sociological Review 19: 217–232.

―――― (2003b): Social Capital in (Dis)Similar Democracies. The Development of Generalized Trust in Japan and Switzerland. Comparative Political Studies 36: 936–966.

Freitag, Markus/Bühlmann, Marc (2005): Politische Institutionen und die Entwicklung generalisierten Vertrauens. Ein internationaler Vergleich. Politische Vierteljahresschrift 46: 575–601.

Gabriel, Oscar W./Kunz, Volker/Roßteutscher, Sigridvan/Deth, Jan W. (2002): Sozialkapital und Demokratie. Zivilgesellschaftliche Ressourcen im Vergleich. Wien: WUV.

Gerbner, George/Gross, Larry/Morgan, Michael/Signorielli, Nancy (1994): Growing Up with Television: The Cultivation Perspective. In: Bryant, Jennings/Zillmann,

Dolf (eds.): Media Effects. Advances in Theory and Research. Hillsdale/NJ: Lawrence Erlbaum.
Hasebrink, Uwe/Herzog, Anja (2004): Mediennutzung im internationalen Vergleich. In: Hans-Bredow-Institut (ed.), Internationales Handbuch Medien 2004/2005, Baden-Baden: Nomos, 136–158.
Hooghe, Marc (2002): Watching Television and Civic Engagement.Disentangling the Effects of Time, Programs and Stations. Harvard International Journal of Press/Politics 7: 84–104.
Hox, Joop (2002): Multilevel Analysis. Techniques and Applications. Mahwah/NJ: Lawrence Erlbaum.
Humphreys, Peter (1996): Mass Media and Media Policy in Western Europe. Manchester: University of Manchester Press.
Inglehart, Ronald (1997): Modernization and Postmodernization. Cultural, Economic, and Political Change in 43 Societies. Princeton/NJ: Princeton University Press.
IP International Marketing Committee (ed.) (2003): Television 2003. International Key Facts. Paris: CMI.
Jarren, Otfried/Donges, Patrick/Künzler, Matthias/Schulz, Wolfgang/Held, Thorsten/Jürgens, Uwe (2001): Der öffentliche Rundfunk im Netzwerk von Politik, Wirtschaft und Gesellschaft, Baden-Baden: Nomos.
Kepplinger, Hans Mathias (1998): Die Demontage der Politik in der Informationsgesellschaft. Freiburg/München: Alber.
Klingemann, Hans-Dieter/Voltmer, Katrin (1989): Massenmedien als Brücke zur Welt der Politik. Nachrichtennutzung und politische Beteiligungsbereitschaft. In: Max Kaase/Winfried Schulz (Hg.): Massenkommunikation. Theorien, Methoden, Befunde. Opladen: Westdeutscher Verlag, 221–238.
Lane, Robert E. (1959): Political Life. Why and How People Get Involved in Politics. New York: Free Press.
Lange, Bernd-Peter (1980): Kommerzrundfunk versus Integrationsrundfunk. Zur ordnungspolitischen Legitimation alternativer Organisationsmodelle von Rundfunkveranstaltern. Media Perspektiven 3: 133–144.
Lee, GangHeong/Cappella, Joseph N./Southwell, Brian (2003): The Effects of News and Entertainment on Interpersonal Trust: Political Talk Radio, Newspapers and Television. Mass Communication and Society 6: 413–434.
Luke, Douglas A. (2004): Multilevel Modeling, Thousand Oaks: Sage.
Moy, Patricia/Scheufele, Dietram A./Holbert, R. Lance (1999): Television Use and Social Capital: Testing Putnam's Time Displacement Hypothesis. Mass Communication and Society 2: 27–45.
Newton, Kenneth (1999): Social and Political Trust in Established Democracies. In: Norris, Pippa (eds.): Critical Citizens. Global Support for Democratic Governance. Oxford: Oxford University Press.
Norris, Pippa (1996): Does Television Erode Social Capital? A Reply to Putnam. PS—Political Science and Politics 29: 474–480.
——— (2000a): A Virtuous Circle. Political Communications in Postindustrial Societies. Cambridge: Cambridge University Press.
——— (2000b): The Impact of Television on Civic Malaise. In: Pharr, Susan J./Putnam, Robert D. (eds.): Disaffected Democracies. What's Troubling the Trilateral Countries? Princeton/NJ: Princeton University Press.
——— (2002): Democratic Phoenix. Reinventing Political Activism. Cambridge: Cambridge University Press.
Pfetsch, Barbara (1996): Convergence through Privatization? Changing Media Environments and Televised Politics in Germany. European Journal of Communication 11: 427–451.
Putnam, Robert D. (1993): Making Democracy Work. Civic Traditions in Modern Italy. Princeton/NJ: Princeton University Press.

—— (1995): Tuning In, Tuning Out: The Strange Disappearance of Social Capital in America. PS—Political Science and Politics 28: 664–683.

—— (2000): Bowling Alone. The Collapse and Revival of American Community. New York: Simon & Schuster.

Raudenbush, Stephen/Bryk, Anthony/Cheong, Yuk Fai/Congdon, Richard (2004): HLM 6: Hierarchical and Nonlinear Modeling. Lincolnwood/IL: Scientific Software International.

Robinson, Michael J. (1976): Public Affairs Television and the Growth of Political Malaise: The Case of "The Selling of the Pentagon". American Political Science Review 70: 409–432.

Rosar, Ulrich (2003): Die Einstellung der Europäer zum Euro. Ein Anwendungsbeispiel der Mehrebenenanalyse als Instrument komparativer Umfrageforschung. In: Pickel, Susanne/Pickel, Gerd/Lauth, Hans-Joachim/Jahn, Detlef (eds.): Vergleichende politikwissenschaftliche Methoden. Wiesbaden: Westdeutscher Verlag, 221–246.

Rose, Richard (1994): Postcommunism and the Problem of Trust. In: Journal of Democracy 5: 18–30.

Scammell, Margaret (2000): Democracy and the Media. In: Scammell, Margaret/Semetko, Holli (eds.): The Media, Journalism and Democracy. Aldershot: Ashgate.

Schulz, Winfried (2000): Television Audiences. In: Wieten, Jan/Murdock, Graham/Dahlgren, Peter (eds.): Television Across Europe. London: Sage, 113–134.

Shah, Dhavan V. (1998): Civic Engagement, Interpersonal Trust, and Television Use: An Individual-Level Assessment of Social Capital. Political Psychology 19: 469–496.

Shah, Dhavan V./Kwak, Nojin/Holbert, R. Lance (2001a): "Connecting" and "Disconnecting" with Civil Life: Patterns of Internet Use and the Production of Social Capital. Political Communication 18: 141–162.

Shah, Dhavan V./McLeod, Jack M./Yoon, So-Hyang (2001b): Communication, Context, and Community. An Exploration of Print, Broadcast and Internet Influences. Communication Research 28: 464–606.

Shah, Dhavan V./Schmierbach, Michael/Hawkins, Joshua/Espino, Rodolfo/Donavan, Janet (2002): Nonrecursive Models of Internet Use and Community Engagement: Questioning Whether Time Spent Online Erodes Social Capital. Journalism & Mass Communication Quarterly 79: 964–987.

Uslaner, Eric M. (1998): Social Capital, Television, and the "Mean World": Trust, Optimism, and Civic Participation. Political Psychology 19: 441–467.

van Deth, Jan W. (2003): Measuring social capital: orthodoxies and continuing controversies. International Journal of Social Research Methodology 6: 7.

PART TWO

CONSEQUENCES OF SOCIAL CAPITAL

CHAPTER SEVEN

POLITICAL INVOLVEMENT AND SOCIAL CAPITAL

Jan W. van Deth[1]

Democracy relies on the willingness and competence of citizens to be involved in political decision-making processes. From Pericles onwards, virtually every political theorist considered a lack of interest in politics among citizens as a burden on democracy. Without a minimum level of curiosity about issues of a political nature, citizens would not have the awareness regarding the opportunities available to them to articulate their interests and to contribute to collective decision-making. Politically involved citizens will be more informed than their less-involved counterparts, their attitudes and expectations will be more consistent, and they will be more willing to actually engage in political decision-making procedures. The debate is about the *degree* of involvement in democratic systems—not about the requirement of citizens' involvement (cf. Berelson et al. 1954: 307; Almond and Verba 1963: 474–9; Barber 1984: 117).

Usually political involvement among citizens is explained using socio-structural factors (such as education, age, and gender) and socio-cultural factors (such as value orientations and efficacy) at the individual-level. Yet well-documented cross-national differences regarding the levels of political involvement in several countries cannot be explained in this way. Two strategies have been developed to deal with this puzzle. Firstly, social capital—broadly defined as networks and opportunities to mobilize resources—is presumed to solve many problems, including a lack of political involvement among citizens, combining socio-structural and socio-cultural factors. Mainly relying on Tocquevillian arguments, many authors argue that social capital implies greater concern about collective problems and opportunities among citizens. Cross-national

---

[1] I am very grateful to Tamara Schupp for her assistance during all phases of preparing and analyzing the data used in this chapter. Furthermore, I would like to thank Heiner Meulemann and the other contributors to this volume for their stimulating comments on earlier versions of this contribution.

differences in political involvement, therefore, can be connected to, at least partly, distinct levels of social capital. A second strategy takes a completely different approach. Here, cross-national differences in political involvement are related to different degrees of politicization in distinct societies. In general terms, the politicization thesis states that the level of political involvement among citizens is a positive and monotonous function of the relevance of societal and political arrangements in a society. The persistent cross-national differences in political involvement and the seemingly inconsistent trends observed in several countries, then, can be contributed to the result of different levels of politicization in these societies.

At first sight, the social-capital approach can be tested using conventional statistical models for individual-level data, whereas the politicization approach requires the use of aggregate-level or multi-level models combining individual and contextual factors to explain cross-national differences in political involvement. This depiction, however, overlooks the ambiguous conceptualization of social capital as both an individual resource and a collective phenomenon. In this chapter, social capital will be understood in both ways, that is, aspects of social capital will be introduced at the micro-level as individual resources and at the macro-level as collective phenomena.[2] Moreover, if social capital is understood as a collective phenomenon, it is expected to contribute significantly to our understanding of political involvement in several countries.

Following the twofold goals of the explorations presented here—tracing the relevance of social capital and of politicization to explain cross-national differences in political involvement at various levels—the analyses proceed in several steps. In the first section, several aspects and measures of political involvement in European countries are presented and the degree of *cross-national variation* is determined. Whether *micro-level models* including a number of individual antecedents can explain political involvement, is considered in the second section. In section three, indicators of social capital are included in these models separately in order to trace their impact. Furthermore, to test the politicization the-

---

[2] In order to distinguish these two variants clearly, Esser (2000) proposes two different terms to replace social capital: "Beziehungskapital" ("relational capital") and "Systemkapital" ("system capital"). For the 'public-good aspect of social capital' see also the early remarks by Coleman (1990: 315–7). Notice that the distinction refers to the location of the social capital concept applied and not to the distinction between micro and macro approaches (cf. van Deth 2003: 83–4).

sis, indicators for socio-economic development and the degree of state intervention in each country are examined as contextual factors, and social capital factors (as aggregated indicators) are combined separately for similar reasons mentioned in section two. In the final step of the analyses in section four, *a multi-level model* is designed with the relevant micro-level determinants at the individual-level as well as indicators for both the politicization of society and the degree of social capital at the macro-level.[3]

The analyses presented here are based on the first wave of the *European Social Survey* (ESS; 2002–2003). This wave includes information collected in 22 countries. Since one of our main indicators for social capital—membership in voluntary associations—is not available for Switzerland and the Czech Republic, these two countries are not considered. Furthermore, Israel is excluded in order to restrict the analyses to European countries only. The final set of countries include 19 states: Austria, Belgium, Denmark, Finland, France, Germany, Hungary, Greece, Ireland, Italy, Luxembourg, the Netherlands, Norway, Poland, Portugal, Slovenia, Spain, Sweden, and the United Kingdom.

1. MEASURING POLITICAL INVOLVEMENT

1.1 *Aspects and Instruments*

Political interest is defined in several ways and concepts like *interest in politics, political involvement, psychological involvement*, and *political apathy* are used to cover the same phenomenon.[4] Political interest is defined as the "...degree to which politics arouses a citizen's curiosity" (van Deth 1990: 278). Understood in this way, political interest is 'paying attention' to political phenomena, which is "a prerequisite for learning anything" that might give citizens the opportunity to participate

---

[3] The multi-level models presented here are similar to the longitudinal multi-level analyses of cross-national differences in political interest and political apathy seen in *Eurobarometer* data used in other studies (see van Deth and Elff (2001 and 2004)). In contrast to these earlier analyses, a much broader concept of political involvement is used here. Furthermore, the statistical analyses include much more efficient estimation procedures for the micro- and macro-level effects and the impact of social capital at various levels. For the general strategy behind the main for steps in the analyses presented here see Langer (2004: Ch. 5).

[4] For distinct definitions and demarcations of the concept political interest and related concepts see Sigel and Hoskin (1981: Ch. 3–6), Bennett (1984: 31–9), Gabriel (1986: 179–82), van Deth (1990: 276–82), or Zaller (1992: 43 and 333–6).

in politics (Lupia and McCubbins 1998: 22), and which is required for "building an informed citizenry" (Delli Carpini and Keeter 1996: 175). Political interest is understood here as a specific variant of the more general concept of political involvement, which refers to the willingness of individuals to take notice of politics, irrespective of possible advantages or disadvantages. Political involvement as a broader concept covers four distinct aspects and measures. Political interest is usually measured with a simple straightforward question regarding the degree of political interest on the one hand, and a question about the frequency of engaging in political discussions with friends and family, on the other. Given that curiosity about politics might be closely related to the importance of political phenomena, two other instruments for measuring the relevance of politics in absolute and relative terms are used here. More specifically, the indicators selected as the four aspects of political involvement are subjective political interest, frequency of political discussions, personal importance of politics, and saliency of politics.

Subjective political interest
The most commonly used way to avoid complications concerning the distinction between interest in politics and behavioral utterances or consequences of interest, is to register *subjective political interest*. Variants of a straightforward instrument to register this form of political involvement have been used in many studies, in a number of countries, since the early voting studies in the 1940s (Lazarsfeld et al. 1948: 24–5). This instrument is based on the self-description of the respondent regarding his or her degree of interest in politics. The question used in the ESS for *subjective political interest* is: "how interested would you say you are in politics—are you very interested, quite interested, hardly interested, or, not at all interested?" Similar, but not identical questions have been used in many countries and in many studies. The exact wording of the question and/or the number of responses offered varies.

Frequency of political discussions
A second indicator of political involvement is based on the *frequency of political discussions* with friends and family, at the workplace or in clubs and organizations. For this indicator, the ESS uses the following question: "how often would you say you discuss politics and current affairs: every day, several times a week, once a week, several times a month, once a month, less often, or never?" This instrument, too, has been

used in many countries. Concerning analyses of the development of cross-national differences in political involvement, this indicator is very popular (cf. van Deth and Elff 2001 and 2004).

Personal importance of politics
Even when people consider political phenomena interesting or speak frequently about political or public matters, it is not clear how important politics is for them personally. Many citizens will be more concerned with more important, relevant, fascinating, or less threatening or occupying matters than politics. In the ESS, the personal relevance of various areas of life is measured with the following question and items: "how important is each of these things in your life: family, friends, leisure time, politics, work, religion, and voluntary organizations? (for each item: extremely unimportant = 0 and extremely important = 10)." This measure offers a straightforward indicator of the importance and relevance of politics for the respondent personally. By utilizing the score, we obtain a measure for a third aspect of political involvement: the *personal importance of politics*.

Saliency of politics
The indicator for the personal importance of politics reflects the relevance of politics without considering other areas of life. Similar (rating) scores from this measure for respondents, however, can have clearly different meanings if we neglect the importance of other areas. What is required is a measure of the *relative relevance of politics* (or *saliency*), that is, we need an indicator based on the position of politics among other areas of life (rankings). In order to measure this relative position, a procedure is used that reflects the position of politics among the other items scored by the respondent (see van Deth 2000 and 2001). Each respondent has rated each of the seven areas of life mentioned above on an 11-point scale. If politics obtains the highest score of these seven ratings, then, politics is relatively important for this respondent—irrespective of the absolute level of his or her score. If politics obtains the lowest score of the seven ratings, then politics is clearly unimportant. In this way, we can compute the relative position of politics amongst the other areas of life—or *political saliency*—for each respondent.[5]

---

[5] Since ties are almost unavoidable, the resulting score for political saliency is partly based on the average score for all items obtaining the same absolute score as politics.

The four aspects of political involvement—subjective interest, political discussions, political importance, political saliency—measured independently, enable distinct analyses of cross-national variations regarding political involvement in Europe. Instead of combining these four measures into a single measure, they are treated here as analytically and conceptually distinct aspects of political involvement. Obviously, empirical relationships are hard to avoid (Klingemann 1979: 264; van Deth 2000).

1.2 *Political Involvement in Europe*

Early voting studies depicted the average citizen as not strongly involved in politics (cf. Berelson et al. 1954: 24; Campbell et al. 1960: 91, 102–3). Recent studies also highlight that the absolute levels of political involvement in most countries are still rather low. Empirical analyses concerning trends of political involvement in Europe, arrive at the conclusions that, on average, only one out of every six European citizens frequently discusses politics with his or her friends, whilst every third citizen is completely unconcerned with this topic (cf. Inglehart 1990: 353–4; Topf 1995: 61; van Deth 1991: 204 and 1996: 386–7; van Deth and Elff 2004: 481). Yet, Dalton concludes that for the period since 1945, "…the trend of increasing political interest in advanced industrial democracies is unmistakable" (2006: 25; see also Kaase and Marsh 1979: 36). Other authors challenge this conclusion and emphasize that for many Western European countries in the last decades, it can be seen that political interest increases in some countries, decreases in others, and shows trendless fluctuations in remaining countries (van den Broek and Heunks 1993; Gabriel and van Deth 1995; Topf 1995; van Deth 1996; van Deth and Elff 2000). Moreover, a trend of decreasing political interest can be observed in the United States (Bennett 1984: 552; van Deth 1990: 282; Miller and Shanks 1996: 107–11).

Even though the debate about long-term trends in political involvement has not arrived at any conclusionary end, all studies show that the level of political involvement differs clearly between various coun-

---

For instance, a respondent rating family and work with the scores 9 and 7 respectively, and politics with score 4, whereas all other items are scored 2, obtains a score of 3 on the scale for political saliency, since only two areas of life are more important than politics. If, however, he or she had rated leisure time with a score of 4 as well, the score for political saliency would become 3.5 (the average of rank 3 and 4 that politics and leisure time posit together).

tries. On the one hand, we have the well-established democracies in countries such as Switzerland, Belgium, the Netherlands, Germany, and Denmark that usually display very high levels of involvement. On the other hand, much less involvement is found among citizens in the newer democracies in Southern Europe (Spain, Portugal) and Eastern Europe (Poland, the Czech Republic). Even if extensive statistical controls are implemented to neutralize compositional effects of cross-national differences regarding socio-economic background factors, considerable differences can be observed in the levels of political involvement among citizens in various countries (van Deth and Elff 2004).

Applying the four measures to cover four aspects of political involvement, the existence of substantial cross-national differences are unambiguously confirmed in the *European Social Survey*. Figure 1 shows the percentages from respondents in the 19 European democracies selected. For each country, the share of citizens who express a relatively high level of political interest, who are frequently involved in political discussions, who attach great importance to politics, and who consider politics salient, are shown. The four indicators clearly show that the level of political involvement is high in the Netherlands, Germany, and Denmark, whereas it is extremely low in Italy, Greece, and Spain. For all other countries, the four aspects show varying degrees of political involvement, depending on the indicator selected. For instance, respondents in Luxembourg appear to discuss politics rather frequently and attach significant importance to politics; however, both their level of subjective interest and the saliency of politics are modestly illustrated. Another exceptional case is Greece, combining a very high level of political importance with low scores on each of the other three indicators. Apparently, the four aspects of political involvement do not just detect similar features of the same phenomenon, but suggest considerable differences between the countries depending on the specific aspect of involvement taken into account. The most evident cross-national differences can be observed for the level of subjective political interest. In the Netherlands, Germany, and Denmark, more than sixty percent of the respondents clearly pay attention to politics—the corresponding figure in Italy, Greece, and Spain is about half that!

At face value, the cross-national differences in subjective political interest presented in Figure 1 are particularly evident. Much less obvious is the variation between the countries regarding the indicators for the frequency of political discussions or for the importance and the saliency of politics. In addition to the distinct levels of political involvement as

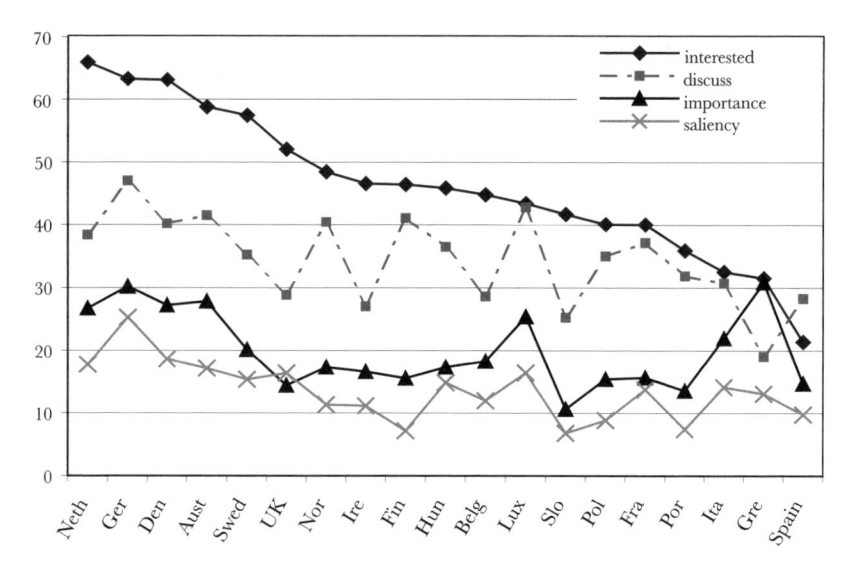

[Figure: line graph showing percentages across countries Neth, Ger, Den, Aust, Swed, UK, Nor, Ire, Fin, Hun, Belg, Lux, Slo, Pol, Fra, Por, Ita, Gre, Spain for four variables: interested, discuss, importance, saliency]

The graph shows the percentages of the variables: Subjective interest (categories 3–4 of 4), Discuss politics (categories 6–7 of 7), Importance of politics (categories 8–11 of 11), and Political saliency (categories 1–4 of 7).

Figure 1: Political involvement in Europe (in percentages)

indicated by the percentages shown in Figure 1, so-called empty models (or intercept-only models) are computed to estimate the intercepts and the variance components between and within the countries (Hox 2002: 16). As can be seen from the variance components in Table 1, the differences between the countries are mainly due to the variance within each country. For the four aspects of political involvement, about 4–6 percent of the population variances can be attributed to differences between the countries, whereas a much more considerable part of the differences are related to factors within the countries.

Although the distribution of political involvement in Europe appears to be highly country-specific, these differences seem to be related to factors within each country. The rough clustering of countries in the well-established democracies of North-Western Europe on the one hand, and the younger democracies in Southern Europe on the other, suggests that systemic factors are accountable for at least part of the cross-national differences, and that contextual factors should be considered to explain the orientations of individual citizens in distinct countries. Yet, the figures presented in Table 1, strongly emphasize the relevance of within-country explanations. The results presented in Figure 1 and

Table 1: Cross-national differences in political involvement
(Multi-level analyses; Empty-models)

	Empty-Models	
	Variance between	Variance within
Subjective interest	.061	.934
Discussion frequency	.037	.957
Importance of politics	.039	.965
Saliency of politics	.045	.981

N = 24,544.

Table 1 seems to point in different directions. Figure 1 suggests clear cross-national differences in political involvement, which, roughly speaking, reflects systemic distinctions between older and younger democracies in North-Western and Southern Europe respectively. Yet, it is clear from Table 1 that an explanation for these cross-national differences is mainly located at the individual-level. Paying attention to contextual factors to explain cross-national differences in political involvement, then, does not seem to be important until individual-level approaches have been considered extensively.

2. Individual-Level Explanations of Political Involvement

Political involvement can be attributed to a number of factors at the individual-level. Since we want to account for as much variation as possible at that level before contextual factors are considered, the first step is to search for all individual features that might contribute to this goal. In a second step, measures for various aspects of social capital (understood as an individual resource in this section), are introduced. In this way, individual-level explanations for each of the four aspects of political involvement, as well as the specific contributions of social capital can be estimated. The explanatory factors for political involvement can be recapitulated in five broad categories: socio-demographic factors, political orientations, satisfaction, media consumption, and social capital.

Explanations of political involvement usually begin with factors related to the *socio-demographic characteristics* of people. From the early roots of empirical political research, individual resources related to these characteristics appear to be important. Typically, higher educated men in their middle ages, are much more involved in politics than women, the less educated, the young, and the old. Therefore, we include in our analyses, as the most relevant factors at the individual-level, gender, education, and age.[6] Since the young and the old are more concerned with matters other than politics, the square of age is included in order to take possible curvy-linear effects of age into account. Furthermore, income defines an important part of the socio-economic status of an individual (together with education), and is especially relevant for explanations of political involvement in terms of resources. Finally, church attendance is included. People who are engaged in religious organizations are usually more socially integrated and are more willing to be politically involved, than other people (see Milbrath und Goel 1977; Verba, Schlozman, and Brady 1995; van Deth 1990; van Deth and Elff 2000; Pattie, Seyd, and Whiteley 2004: 92–6; Hadjar, Becker 2006).

Several *political orientations* can be considered as a second set of explanatory factors of political involvement at the individual-level. People who place themselves more to the left on a political left-right scale are more interested in social change than other people are. This interest generally implies a higher degree of attentiveness to political phenomena. Besides, if people consider themselves able to have some impact on political processes (internal efficacy), or if they consider the political process, in principal, open for interventions by people like themselves (external efficacy), then they will be much more involved in politics than other people are (Milbrath and Goel 1977; Verba, Schlozman and Brady 1995).

A third set of explanatory factors, the *level of satisfaction*, is introduced. Only when people are more or less satisfied with the way democracy functions in their society (that is, that they are not clearly alienated from the system), can it be expected that they are willing to pay attention to politics. For other areas of life, satisfaction is more difficult to relate to political involvement. Discontent with the economic situation might stimulate attentiveness for social and political development, but it is not clear what impact satisfaction with life in general can have on political involvement. The distinctions between the four aspects of political involvement are relevant here. Whereas, subjective political interest and political discussion frequency are unlikely to be strongly affected,

---

[6] Brief descriptions of questions, categories, and codes are presented in footnotes to the tables below.

political importance and saliency seem to be much more dependent on satisfaction (van Deth 2000: 130).

Nowadays, virtually nobody has direct experience with political actors or institutions. Instead, all information is selected and passed on by the mass media. Political involvement, then, is likely to depend on the consumption of this media by citizens; people showing higher levels of *media consumption*, are more likely to be politically involved than other people. Reading newspapers and watching television can be seen as indicators for the consumption of political information, and so measures for general media consumption are included as a fourth block of factors relevant for political involvement at the individual-level (see Chapter 6 by Rüdiger Schmitt-Beck in this volume).[7]

The final block of relevant factors for political involvement incorporates several aspects of *social capital*. Social capital consists of structural as well as cultural aspects (van Deth 2003). Structural aspects concern the degree of (informal) social contacts the respondent has, as well as his or her membership in voluntary associations. Regarding associations, the distinction between three broad types appeared to be highly relevant for political involvement: sports/leisure time associations, interest groups, and cultural organizations (Gabriel et al. 2002: 159–65). Cultural aspects of social capital are measured by the support for civic norms and values. Finally, the degree of social trust is included in the analyses as an indicator of the cultural aspects of social capital (see Uslaner 2002 for an extensive overview and discussion).

The first attempt to explain the level of political involvement of citizens is through the use of 14 factors, included in the first four blocks of indicators, as a base model for further elaborations, leaving the social capital factors aside. The results of the multiple regression analyses for each of the four aspects of political involvement are presented in the left-hand columns of the four parts in Table 2. Relatively strong effects can be observed for the conventional socio-demographic factors of gender and education, and these effects are all in the expected direction (males and higher educated people are more involved). For age, the picture is somewhat less clear, with increasing levels of subjective interest, importance and saliency of politics among older

---

[7] The data also includes information about the consumption of political information (and not only media consumption in general). Since the consumption of political information can be considered as another indicator of political involvement, these variables are not used as determinants of political involvement here.

people, whereas discussion frequency shows the expected curvy-linear relationship with age. Surprisingly, income does not seem to be very relevant for political involvement (after education, age, and gender are included in the models). People engaged in church activities appear to consider politics as not very salient (negative coefficients) or, to phrase this observation differently, it seems, for some, religion plays a much more important role than politics does (cf. van Deth 2006: 111). Among the factors included in the remaining three blocks, consistent substantial effects can be noted for efficacy (especially external efficacy) and for newspaper reading. As expected, people with higher levels of efficacy and people reading newspapers are more involved in politics than less efficacious people or people not reading newspapers. Television watching does not seem to be related to political involvement. The total amount of variance explained by these base models range from 14 to 23 percent, which is not very impressive, however usual for these types of analyses.

In order to assess the contribution of social capital to the explanations of the various aspects of political involvement, the base models presented in Table 2 are extended with a block of social capital indicators. The results are modest. Although several coefficients are significant, the impact of the six factors is limited (as indicated by the standardized regression coefficients for each variable). Only support for civic norms and values seem to have some impact on subjective interest, discussion frequency, and the importance of politics. For these three aspects of political involvement, the addition of social capital variables leads to an improvement of the models. The maximum gain is obtained for the importance of politics (an improvement of 4 percentage points). Apparently, social capital offers a modest contribution to the explanation of political involvement at the individual-level after the conventional socio-demographic factors, efficacy, and mass media consumption are taken into account. Especially for the explanation of political saliency, social capital does not seem to be relevant.

Since a rather extensive number of variables have been included in the models at the individual-level summarized in Table 2, not much can be expected from further attempts to improve our explanations by searching for additional individual features. Instead, alternative approaches focusing on contextual and systemic factors, seems to be more promising. In particular, social capital understood as a collective good might prove to be relevant for political involvement in several countries.

Table 2: Micro-level antecedents of political involvement
(Complete models; standardized linear regression coefficients; pooled, weighted analyses)

	Subjective interest		Discussion		Importance		Saliency	
	Base Model	SoCap. Model	Base Model	SoCap. Model	Base Model	SoCap. Model	Base Model	SoCap. Model
Socio-demogr. factors:								
-Gender: Male	.12***	.13***	.08***	.08***	.06***	.07***	.10***	.10***
-Education	.24***	.23***	.21***	.19***	.09***	.09***	.09***	.09***
-Age	.19***	.15***	.03***	.02***	.07***	.04***	.13***	.13***
-Age-squared	−.04***	−.04***	−.11***	−.11***	−.01	−.01	.09***	.09***
-Income	.05***	.04***	.05***	.04***	.03***	.03***	.02***	.03***
-Church attend.	.01*	−.01*	.00	−.02***	.06***	.04***	−.24***	−.25***
Political orientations:								
-Left-right	−.04***	−.04***	−.03***	−.03***	−.03***	−.03***	−.06***	−.06***
-Internal efficacy	.09***	.08***	.06***	.05***	.12***	.10***	.05***	.05***
-External efficacy	.19***	.17***	.10***	.08***	.17***	.16***	.10***	.11***
Satisfaction with:								
democracy	.03***	.02***	.04***	.02**	.10***	.08***	.02**	.02**
economy	−.06***	−.06***	−.08***	−.07***	−.05***	−.02**	−.04***	−.03***
life in general	.01	−.01	.01	−.01	.02*	.00	−.05***	−.05***
Media consumption:								
TV viewing	.00	.00	−.04***	−.03***	.04***	.04***	.03***	.03***
Newspaper	.14***	.13***	.11***	.10***	.09***	.08***	.08***	.08***
Social capital:								
Social trust		.00		−.02**		−.03***		−.04***
Social contacts		−.01*		.05***		.00		−.02***
Norms/values		.14***		.14***		.20***		.04***
Leisure/sport		.03***		.02***		.01*		.02***
Interest groups		.00		.02***		−.01*		−.01
Cultural organis.		.06***		.05***		.01		.00
Variance								
explained (corr.)	.210	.232	.135	.160	.111	.149	.142	.145
N (weighted)	27,500		27,468		27,484		27,484	

Significance: ***<.001, **<.01, *<.05; standard weight for each country N = 2000, including the whole of Germany.

Dependent variables: subjective interest: 4-point-scale (1–4), discussion frequency: 7-point-scale (1–7), importance: 11-point-scale (0–10), and saliency: 6-point-scale (1–6). Independent variables: Gender: 0 = female, 1 = male; Education: years; Age and Age-squared: years; Income: 12 categories with means for missing values; Church attendance: 7-point-scale (0–6); Left-right placement: 11-point-scale (0–10; left = 0); Internal efficacy: Additive index of two items about the subjective assessment of the complexity of politics; External efficacy: Additive index of two items about the assessment of the responsiveness of the political system; Satisfaction with democracy, economy, or life in general: 11-point-scales (0–10); TV viewing: total time of watching TV; Newspaper reading: total time of reading newspapers; Social trust: Additive index of three trust items, index range: 0–30; Social contacts: 7-point-scale (1–7); Norms and values: Additive Index of four good citizen items, index range: 0–40; Leisure/sport organization, Interest groups, or Cultural organizations: Count of membership in three types of voluntary organizations.

3. Macro-Level Explanations of Political Involvement

Basically, cross-national differences in political involvement reflect differences in aggregate figures (means and proportions obtained for the various national citizenries as presented in Figure 1) for specific aspects of involvement. After considering micro-level explanations for these differences, we now turn to relationships at the macro-level. In a preliminary step, the most relevant factors detected at the micro-level, are selected and included in so-called optimal models (that is, models that explain the maximum amount of variance with a minimum number of variables).[8] For the estimates at the macro-level, the aggregated figures for the variables selected for the optimal models are used in order to explain the aggregated figures for the four aspects of political involvement. Furthermore, aggregate figures for three context factors (economic development, government consumption, and state intervention) are included too. Concerning the models at the individual-level, the social capital factors will be added separately, in order to trace the specific contribution of these factors to the explanation of cross-national differences at the macro-level.

3.1 *Selecting Individual-Level Factors*

The base models at the individual-level included 14 variables; for the social capital models this number increased to 20 variables (see Table 2). Even without adding contextual factors, it is clear that we cannot estimate models including 14–20 variables with a maximum number of 19 cases (countries). In a first attempt to reduce the number of factors, the four base models are estimated for each country separately instead of using the results of the pooled analyses. For each of the four aspects of political involvement, those factors are selected for further analyses that reach statistical significance ($p < .001$) in at least 13 of the 19 countries in these analyses. Initially, the combined list of these significant factors comprises no less than 12 of the 14 variables of the base model. Since many of these variables are correlated, further cuts appear to be possible without reducing the amount of variance explained in each country.

---

[8] To identify the optimal models, multiple regressions similar to those presented in Table 2 are estimated for each country. All variables, which were significant in at least 13 countries are kept. In this way, the number of variables is reduced from 20 to eight.

Finally, for each of the four aspects of political involvement, similar optimal models are estimated again for the pooled data set (see Table 3). As in the previous section, the social capital factors are combined in a second step separately.

The optimal models in Table 3 include the most relevant individual-level factors for political involvement. These factors are not only relevant for the pooled analyses of all countries, but also for each country separately. Obviously, both the conclusions about the impact of various factors discussed at the end of Section 2, and the results about the contributions of social capital factors are underlined by the results obtained with the models presented in Table 3. The eight variables included in the base models explain a satisfying part of the variance—especially for the level of subjective interest. For this type of interest and for discussion frequency, the most important determinant is the level of education, whereas the strongest predictors of importance and saliency of politics are, respectively, internal efficacy and church attendance. Yet, the social capital variables are not able to improve the base models considerably; the maximum increase obtained by adding these six variables is 4.5 percentage points for the importance of politics. With the exception of the support for civic norms and values, the standardized regression coefficients for the social capital variables in Table 2 and 3 are very low and virtually identical.

The base models presented in Table 3 include all eight factors that are theoretically and statistically relevant for the explanation of political involvement at the micro-level. The fact that the addition of social capital factors appears to be rather unimportant at this level, could be due to a misspecification of social capital as an individual feature. This brings us to the selection of contextual factors for the explanation of political involvement in Europe.

3.2 *Selecting Contextual Factors*

Contextual factors for cross-national differences in political involvement include social capital factors as well as factors relevant for the politicization thesis. Regarding social capital, we already identified six aspects. The operationalization of politicization is more complicated and involves several steps. In earlier analyses of contextual factors using the *Eurobarometer* data concerning the frequency of political discussions as a dependent variable at the individual-level, politicization was operationalized with cleavage structure, state intervention, openness of the political

Table 3: Micro-level antecedents of political involvement
(Optimal models; standardized linear regression coefficients; pooled, weighted analyses)

	Subjective interest		Discussion		Importance		Saliency	
	Base Model	SoCap. Model	Base Model	SoCap. Model	Base Model	SoCap. Model	Base Model	SoCap. Model
–Gender	.12***	.13***	.08***	.09***	.07***	.08***	.10***	.10***
–Education	.26***	.23***	.23***	.21***	.11***	.10***	.09***	.09***
–Age	.18***	.15***	.04***	.03***	.08***	.04***	.14***	.13***
–Age squared	–.06***	–.05***	–.13***	–.12***	–.01*	–.01*	.09***	.09***
–Church attend.	.00	–.02***	–.01	–.03***	.05***	.03***	–.25***	–.26***
–Internal efficacy	.09***	.08***	.07***	.05***	.12***	.10***	.05***	.05***
–External efficacy	.20***	.17***	.11***	.08***	.22***	.19***	.10***	.11***
–Newspaper	.15***	.14***	.12***	.10***	.10***	.09***	.08***	.08***
Social capital:								
–Social trust		.00		–.03***		–.01		–.05***
–Social contacts		–.01		.06***		.00		–.02***
–Norms & values		.14***		.14***		.21***		.04***
–Leisure/sport		.04***		.03***		.02***		.03***
–Interest groups		.01*		.03***		.00		–.01
–Cultural organis.		.05***		.05***		.01		.00
Variance explained (corr.)	.226	.251	.147	.177	.118	.161	.137	.142
N (weighted)	35,099		35,014		35,040		35,040	

Significance: ***<.001, **<.01, *<.05. See Table 2 for weight variables.

system, and control capacity of the state. Moreover, economic development was operationalized as a fifth cluster of macro-level factors.[9] These previous analyses clearly identified two main groups of macro-level factors regarding the explanation of cross-national differences in political involvement: economic development and state intervention. For these reasons, the analyses here are restricted to these two main macro-level factors in addition to the social capital factors.

---

[9] An extensive overview of the specification of the various data sources, concepts, dimensions, sub-dimensions, and indicators used, is presented by van Deth and Elff (2001: 42–68). An electronic version of this document (MZES Working Paper 36) is accessible from: http://www.mzes.uni-mannheim.de/publications/wp/wp_start.html.

Social capital
For the six social capital factors used in the analyses at the individual-level discussed above, the argument for using aggregate indicators for the same factors is straightforward. In a society where the aggregate-level of social trust is high, for each individual, the impact of having a high level of trust will be stronger, since he or she will gain a lot, with little risk, by trusting other people. Since this conditional relationship between trust and involvement seems the most plausible from an individual perspective, we will not introduce the level of trust as a contextual factor. Furthermore, this simplification has the advantage of restricting the number of variables to the, theoretically, most important relationships. The aggregate-level of trust in a society, then, can be seen as a conditional factor for the impact of trust on political involvement at the micro-level. In a similar way, the impact of civic norms and values at the micro-level most likely depends on the aggregate-level of the support for these norms and values; that is, relatively strong support for these norms and values will be especially relevant in countries where the general level of support is already relatively high. On the other hand, it does not yield success for an individual when norms and values supported by some, are not met with the same support by others.

For the structural aspects of social capital, the argument is identical; the impact of social contacts and of engagement in various types of voluntary associations at the individual-level depends, respectively, on the aggregate-level of social contacts and engagement available. For each of these social capital factors, the aggregate-level in a country functions as a conditional factor on the relationships between social capital and political involvement—that is, I restrict this part of the analyses to slope models and do not deal with intercept models.

Economic development
Although the exact causal factors and mechanisms are still disputed, economic development has been identified as a strong determinant of political involvement in many studies since the 1950s. Usually, the dual and interlinked processes of 'modernization' and 'democratization' are used as the main explanations in this area. Since economic development affects a large number of other factors (education, position of women, secularization, mass media consumption), it is modeled here as a conditional factor on the constant in the regression models.

Economic development can be measured in various ways. A straightforward indicator is GDP per capita in the year of our surveys (2003).

However, economic development is a long-term phenomenon with time-lagged consequences, and therefore GDP per capita, at constant prices, and purchase power parities to the US Dollar in the period 1970–2003, are implemented here. Furthermore, the sectoral composition of the workforce can be seen as an indicator of economic development (proportion of workforce in several sectors). A principal components analysis used to test whether these indicators form a common dimension shows that all variables have high loadings on the component, which explains more than eighty percent of the variance. However, there is no reliable data on sectoral composition of the workforce for several countries. In order to obtain a straightforward indicator for economic development, the principal components analysis is repeated based on the two GDP measures only. A summary indicator of economic development is constructed from the scores on the first principal component of this analysis, which recovers more than 97 percent of the total variance (communalities .973). These results are clearly in line with the results obtained earlier for a much longer period of time (van Deth and Elff 2001: 65–6).

State intervention

State intervention is a core aspect of the politicization thesis; the higher the degree of state intervention, the higher the chances are that citizens will be confronted with state activities, and the more likely it is that their interests are affected by these activities. As with economic development, state intervention is related to a large number of other factors (such as education, position of women, mass media consumption), and, similarly, it is modeled here as a conditional factor on the constant in the regression models.

State intervention refers to the degree to which the state is involved in economic and social processes in a country. Three ways of state-involvement can be distinguished: the degree to which governmental institutions extract resources from general society, the degree to which they provide benefits and services, and the proportion of the workforce employed by governmental institutions and state-owned firms ('public sector'). Government receipts, as a proportion of the gross national product, can be seen as an indicator of the degree to which the state extracts resources from society, whereas government final consumption expenditure, as a proportion of the gross national product, is an indicator of the degree to which the state provides benefits and services. The proportion of the workforce employed by government institutions and state-owned firms indicates the degree the state is directly involved in societal and economic processes.

Principal components analyses do not confirm the earlier results obtained for the much longer time-period, where a clear one-dimensional structure of the three indicators was detected (van Deth and Elff 2001: 66). In the present analyses, however, the first principal component recovers only 54 percent of the variance. A closer look reveals that the indicator for government receipts does not fit into the simple structure (communality of .020). Dropping this indicator would severely restrict the validity of the resulting measure, and therefore this strategy proves not an acceptable alternative. A plausible explanation for the apparent inconsistencies between the previous findings and the results obtained with the more recent data is based on the countries selected. While the previous analyses relied on West European countries only, the present exercises deal with a mixture of West and Central European countries. The figures for government final consumption appear to be very different for these two groups of countries. In fact, our previous result of a one-dimensional structure can be easily replicated for the West European countries with recent data, but not for the other countries. After considering various options to deal with this problem, the best strategy seems to be the use of two distinct indicators: one for government final consumption and another for direct state intervention, based on the combination of the two other indicators. For this last measure of direct state intervention, the factor scores of the single factor consisting of government receipts and proportion of the working force in public services are computed.

3.3 *Macro-Level Models for Political Involvement*

Having selected the relevant micro-level and macro-level factors for the explanation of political involvement, we are now able to consider the relationships between the aggregate variables (see Langer 2004). Plainly, we cannot estimate multivariate models with 17 variables (eight of the base model, six for social capital, and three for politicization) with about the same number of cases available (countries). A reduction in the number of variables can be based on an inspection of the bivariate coefficients for each of the 17 variables and each of the four aspects of political involvement. The three distinct measures for engagement in three distinct types of voluntary associations appears to be highly correlated at the aggregate-level and can be replaced by a single measure. Yet, the problems seem to be concentrated on the two measures of efficacy, and reducing the number of measures for associational activities does not solve these complications. In a second step, then, the measures for efficacy had to be excluded.[10]

4. A MULTI-LEVEL APPROACH

The analyses so far resulted in more or less satisfactory estimates for the determinants of political involvement at the individual-level. However, the macro-level factors identified in Section 3.2 are simply not presumed to be related at the aggregate-level. Especially, the various aspects of social capital can be depicted as contextual factors that have a conditional impact on specific relationships at the micro-level. A multi-level model that takes these findings into account consists of various parts. Firstly, we reduce the number of micro-level factors further by deleting the impact of age from our models. This variable does not seem to be very relevant and has caused complications by the estimates of several models. In this way, eight independent variables at the micro-level regarding the explanation of cross-national differences in political involvement (four base model variables and four social capital variables), are selected. Secondly, we have three macro-level indicators for the degree of politicization of a society (economic development, government consumption, and direct state intervention). Finally, we have four social capital variables conceptualized at the macro-level, which function as conditional factors for the respective aspects of social capital (trust, norms and values, contacts, and engagement in voluntary associations). A simple multi-level base model includes the eight micro-level variables only (with individual-level effects and compositional effects). In addition, the effects predicted by the politicization thesis are included in a model that consists of the base model and the three contextual factors selected. In the last step, the four social capital factors are included as conditional factors at the macro-level. Notice that in this way, the social capital factors do not have an impact on the dependent variables directly. Since social capital is conceptionalized here as both an indi-

---

[10] In a final attempt to reduce the number of variables, the total block of socio-demographic variables was replaced with indicators for internal and external efficacy only. The results obtained with these models show similar problems as obtained with the 13 variables mentioned.

vidual resource and as collective good (see Esser 2000), these two effects are modeled explicitly in order to trace the consequences of both types of social capital as clearly as possible.[11] Adding compositional effects of social capital would make it very difficult to disentangle the effects of these theoretically defined concepts as micro and as contextual factors. In this way, we might not reach the maximum levels of variance explained, but gain a clear insight into the explanatory power of our theoretically defined concepts.

The first round of model estimates includes separate analyses for the three models for each of the four aspects of political involvement.[12] The (standardized) results of these computations are presented in Table 4a/b. The first point to note is that large parts of the cross-national differences in political involvement are directly linked to the distributions of the individual factors. About three-quarters of the variance in subjective political interest and 86 percent of the variance in political saliency can be explained at this level. Gender, education, and media consumption are strong determinants of political involvement, while political saliency is highly dependent on church attendance. The impact of social capital factors at the individual-level is clearly visible regarding the support for norms and values and for membership in voluntary associations.

The four contextual models in Table 4a/b provide the empirical information for an appraisal of the politicization thesis. For these models, the simple base models are extended with the three contextual factors selected. As can be seen from both the effect parameters and the increases in the variances explained at the macro-level, the impact of the three contextual factors is limited and virtually none of the coefficients is statistically significant. Remarkable are the negative signs for the impact of state intervention. Apparently, political involvement is *lower* in countries with high levels of state intervention. Since this result is especially vital for the importance of politics, state intervention seems to allow citizens to attach less importance to politics than in countries where the state is less active. Politicization at the societal level—conceptualized as state intervention—apparently implies a depoliticization of engagement at the individual-level. This might be bad

---

[11] This means that for the four social capital factors considered as contextual effects, so-called 'slope models' are estimated whereas 'intercept models' are not take into account.

[12] All estimations are carried out with MLwiN.

Table 4a: Multi-level antecedents of political involvement (standardized regression coefficients)

	Subjective interest			Discussion		
	Base Model	Context Model	SoCap. Model	Base Model	Context Model	SoCap. Model
Optimal Model:						
–Gender	.21***	.21***	.21***	.31***	.31***	.31***
–Education	.05***	.05***	.05***	.12***	.12***	.12***
–Church attendance	.00	.00	.00	-.05***	-.05***	-.05***
–Newspaper reading	.11***	.11***	.11***	.13***	.13***	.14***
–Social trust—micro	.01***	.01***	.01***	.00	.00	.00
–Social trust—context			.00			.00
–Social contacts—micro	-.01***	-.01***	-.02**	.07***	.07***	.07***
–Social contacts—context			.00			.00
–Norms/values—micro	.03***	.03***	.03***	.05***	.05***	.05***
–Norms/values—context			.00			.00
–Organizations—micro	.07***	.07***	.07***	.16***	.16***	.16***
–Organizations—context			.00			.00
Societal context:						
–Economic development		.00	.00		-.07	-.17*
–Gov. consumption		.00	.00		.01	.00
–State intervention		-.02	.01		-.06	.01
Variance parameters:						
–Micro-level factors	.594***	.594***	.591***	3.194***	3.194***	3.166**
–Random intercept	.022**	.022**	.071**	.110**	.095**	.066**
Variance explained (micro)	.142	.142	.220	.136	.132	.299
Variance explained (macro)	.522	.522	-0.543	.236	.340	-3.604

Significance: ***<.001, **<.01, *<.05. Economic development: factor scores (GDP); Government consumption: means; State intervention: factor scores (government receipts and proportion of workfa employed in public sector); see Table 2 for definitions of dependent and independent variables use here at the micro-level.

news for those in favor of fashionable assertions about a lack of political involvement among citizens, but these findings seem to support the idea that state activities enable citizens to focus on other themes and areas of interest rather than politics. That causes and effects are difficult to disentangle is underlined here by the fact that economic development contributes to higher levels of the importance and the saliency of politics. One might expect that these two aspects of political involvement are also negatively related to economic development (that is, in highly

Table 4b: Multi-level antecedents of political involvement (standardized regression coefficients)

	Importance			Saliency		
	Base Model	Context Model	SoCap. Model	Base Model	Context Model	SoCap. Model
Optimal Model:						
−Gender	.39***	.39***	.39***	.18***	.18***	.21***
−Education	.06***	.06***	.07***	.01***	.01***	.01***
−Church attendance	.03*	.03*	.03*	−.14***	−.14***	−.13***
−Newspaper reading	.22***	.22***	.22***	.08***	.08***	.08***
−Social trust—micro	.03***	.03***	.03***	.00*	.00*	.00*
−Social trust—context			.00			.00
−Social contacts—micro	.02	.02	.01	−.02***	−.02***	.02***
−Social contacts—context			.00			.00
−Norms/values—micro	.11***	.11***	.11***	.01***	.01***	.01***
−Norms/values—context			.00			.00
−Organizations—micro	.11***	.11***	.13***	.01***	.01**	.03***
−Organizations—context			.00*			.00
Societal context:						
−Economic development		.06	−.02		.09*	.02
−Gov. consumption		.00	−.01		.00	.00
−State intervention		−.33*	−.36**		.07*	−.04
Variance parameters:						
−Micro-level factors	5.359***	5.359***	5.342***	.743***	.743***	.740***
−Random intercept	.278**	.211**	.408*	.018**	.014**	.600***
Variance explained (micro)	.125	0.113	.150	.060	0.054	.818
Variance explained (macro)	−.139	.135	−0.672	.514	.622	−15.216

Significance: ***<.001, **<.01, *<.05. See Table 4a for details.

developed countries, politics is less relevant), but that interpretation is not confirmed by the results presented in Table 4a/b. Apparently, the importance and saliency of politics seem to depend on relatively high levels of economic development, and on low levels of state intervention. The results for the inclusion of social capital factors as conditional factors are very disappointing. Whereas, the individual-level factors (that is, social capital understood as an individual resource) contribute to the explanations, the conceptualization of social capital as a collective good does not add anything to our models. Even more disappointing, is the result that inclusion of norms and values as a conditional factor has a disruptive effect on the models estimated with negative levels of explained variance for the final solutions. Since all these results indicate the highly problematic role social capital as conditional factors play, no further model specification is considered here.

The results obtained strongly corroborate the relevance of individual factors to explain political involvement and the cross-national differences in involvement. The addition of indicators for the politicization of society has minor effects only, whereas the final addition of the four social capital factors in a multi-level model, leads to a rejection of the idea that social capital should be understood as a conditional factor for political involvement. As with the addition of the contextual variables in the second step, most coefficients for the conditional effects of social capital are not significant. Furthermore, in order to present the impact of these factors, we had to extend the information presented using three instead of two decimals (which means that they refer to very small slopes). For the explanation of cross-national differences in political involvement, then, social capital is mainly relevant if it is understood as an individual resource. The conceptualization of social capital at the macro-level (specified as conditional effects) does not seem to contribute to the explanation of these differences.

5. Conclusions

Levels of political involvement appear to be surprisingly different in European countries. Apparently, neither the firm establishment of democratic institutions nor the rapid rise in competencies (education) among mass publics, has led to a convergence of the levels of political involvement. Only at a very general level, systemic differences can be noted between the settled democracies of North-Western Europe and the newer democracies of Southern Europe. This north-south distinction in political involvement is much more evident than an east-west line of demarcation.

Political involvement compromises subjective interest, frequency of political discussion, the importance of politics, and the saliency of politics. Starting with the presumption, that individual features (i.e. standard socio-demographic variables) are not sufficient to explain cross-national differences in political involvement, the major aims of the analyses presented in this chapter were twofold. First, we wanted to see whether social capital contributes to political involvement of citizens, understanding social capital both as an individual resource and as a contextual factor. Secondly, the idea that cross-national differences in political involvement are related to differences in the level of politicization in these countries is tested. In order to analyze these expectations in appropriate ways, models at the micro- and macro-level are estimated. Furthermore, a multi-level model is designed including individual factors, aspects of social capital conceptualized as individual resources and as contextual factors, and contextual factors signifying the degree of politicization in each country.

The relevance of distinguishing between the four aspects of political involvement is underlined by the different findings for each of these four aspects. Cross-national differences in each of these aspects can be mainly attributed to individual-level factors (gender, education, church attendance, efficacy, and media consumption), and to the cross-national differences in the distribution of these factors. In particular, church attendance appears to be highly relevant for political saliency, whereas people with higher levels of efficacy and people following politics in the news, are more involved in politics than less efficacious people or people not following politics in the mass media. However, the general pattern suggested by the findings of our more sophisticated approaches, is rather disappointing. Of the social capital factors, only the support for norms and values seem to contribute to the explanation of political involvement, after the conventional antecedents at the individual-level are taken into account. Neither social capital understood as an individual resource, nor social capital understood as a conditional effect at the macro-level, appears to be very relevant for the explanation of any of the four aspects of political involvement. Particularly, the use of social capital at the macro-level is disappointing. Similar conclusions can be seen for the impact of contextual factors based on the politicization thesis. Here, too, the additional variance explained is modest only and the interesting effects are mainly restricted to the negative impact of state intervention on the importance attached to politics.

Conclusions based on the more sophisticated multi-level models estimated here, are all jeopardized by the apparent instability of the solutions obtained. Estimation procedures appear to be highly vulnerable for the inclusion of specific factors (especially, but not only, related to efficacy, social trust, and social norms), and even the amounts of variances explained do not always increase when the number of variables is extended. Despite these evident warnings, it is probably not too perilous to state that individual factors contribute most to the explanation of political involvement in Europe. The attempts to count for cross-national differences in involvement with macro-level factors do not seem to be very promising. The multi-level models tested here underline the relevance of conventional individual-level factors. Cross-national differences in political involvement are mainly due to differences in the distributions of these factors in the various countries.

The evident statistical complications encountered in these analyses do not allow for definite conclusions about cross-national differences in political involvement in Europe. The most promising analyses for further improvements, however, seem to be located at the individual-level. In other words, political involvement probably depends more on the characteristics of individual citizens than on features of the social, economic, and political situations encountered. Apparently, social capital and politicization do not have much to offer, in addition to the conventional explanations available, to increase our understanding of political involvement.

REFERENCES

Almond, Gabriel A./Verba, Sidney (1963): The Civic Culture: Political Attitudes and Democracy in Five Nations. Princeton: Princeton University Press.

Barber, Benjamin R. (1984): Strong Democracy. Participatory Politics for a New Age. Berkeley: University of California Press.

Bennett, Stephen E. (1984): Apathy in America, 1964–1982: A new measure applied to old questions. Micropolitics 3 (4): 499–545.

Berelson, Bernard R./Lazarsfeld, Paul F./McPhee, William N. (1954): Voting: A Study of Opinion Formation in a Presidential Campaign. Chicago: University of Chicago Press.

Campbell, Angus/Converse, Philip E./Miller, Warren E./Stokes, Donald E. (1960): The American Voter. New York: John W. Wiley & Sons.

Coleman, James S. (1990): Foundations of Social Theory. Cambridge. Mass.: The Belknap Press of Harvard University Press.

Dalton, Russel J. (2006): Citizen Politics. Public Opinion and Political Parties in Advanced Industrial Democracies. Washington DC: CQ-Press.

Delli Carpini, Michael X./Keeter, Scott (1996): What Americans Know About Politics and Why It Matters. New Haven, CT: Yale University Press.

Esser, Hartmut (2000): Soziologie: Spezielle Grundlagen. Band 4: Opportunitäten und Restriktionen. Frankfurt and New York: Campus.

Gabriel, Oscar W. (1986): Politische Kultur, Postmaterialismus und Materialismus in der Bundesrepublik Deutschland. Opladen: Westdeutscher Verlag.

Gabriel, Oscar W./Kunz, Volker/Roßteutscher, Siegrid/van Deth, Jan W. (2002): Sozialkapital und Demokratie: Zivilgesellschaftliche Ressourcen im Vergleich. Wien: WUV Universitätsverlag.

Gabriel, Oscar W./van Deth, Jan W. (1995): Political interest. In: van Deth, Jan W./Scarbrough, Elinor (eds.): The Impact of Values. Oxford: Oxford University Press, 390–411.

Hadjar, Andreas/Becker, Rolf (2006): Bildungsexpansion und Wandel des politischen Interesses in Westdeutschland zwischen 1980 und 2002. Politische Vierteljahresschrift 47: 12–34.
Hox, Joop (2002): Multilevel Analysis. Techniques and Applications. Mahwah, NJ: Erlbaum.
Inglehart, Ronald (1990): Culture Shift in Advanced Industrial Society. Princeton, NJ: Princeton University Press.
Kaase, Max/Marsh, Alan (1979): Political action: A theoretical perspective. In: Barnes, Samuel H./Kaase Max et al.: Political Action. Mass Participation in Five Western Democracies. Beverly Hills: Sage, 27–56.
Klingemann, Hans D. (1979): The background of ideological conceptualization. In: Barnes, Samuel H./Kaase Max et al.: Political Action. Mass Participation in Five Western Democracies. Beverly Hills: Sage, 255–277.
Langer, Wolfgang (2004): Mehrebenenanalyse. Eine Einführung für Forschung und Praxis. Wiesbaden: VS Verlag für Sozialwissenschaften.
Lazarsfeld, Paul F./Berelson, Bernard/Gaudet, Hazel (1948): The People's Choice: How the Voter Makes up His Mind in a Presidential Campaign. New York: Columbia University Press.
Lupia, Arthur/McCubbins, Mathew D. (1998): The Democratic Dilemma. Can Citizens Learn What They Need to Know? Cambridge: Cambridge University Press.
Milbrath, Lester W./Goel, M.L. (1977): Political Participation: How and Why Do People Get Involved in Politics? Chicago: Rand McNally.
Miller, Warren E./Shanks, Merrill J. (1996): The New American Voter. Cambridge, MA: Harvard University Press.
Pattie, Charles/Seyd, Patrick/Whiteley, Paul (2004): Citizenship in Britain. Values, Participation and Democracy. Cambridge: Cambridge University Press.
Sigel, Roberta S./Hoskin, Marilyn B. (1981): The Political Involvement of Adolescents. New Brunswick NJ: Rutgers University Press.
Topf, Richard (1995): Beyond electoral participation. In: Klingemann, Hans D./Fuchs, Dieter (eds.): Citizens and the State. Oxford: Oxford University Press, 52–91.
Uslaner, Eric M. (2002): The Moral Foundations of Trust. Cambridge: Cambridge University Press.
van den Broek, Andries/Heunks, Felix (1993): Political culture. Patterns of political orientations and behaviour. In: Ester, Peter/Halman, Loek/de Moor, Ruud (eds.), The Individualizing Society. Value Change in Europe and North America. Tilburg: Tilburg University Press, 67–96.
van Deth, Jan W. (1990): Interest in politics. In: Kent Jennings, Myron/van Deth, Jan W. et al.: Continuities in Political Action. A Longitudinal Study of Political Orientations in Three Western Democracies. Berlin: Walter de Gruyter, 275–312.
――― (1991): Politicization and political interest. In: Reif, Karlheinz/Inglehart, Ronald (eds.), Eurobarometer: The Dynamics of European Public Opinion. London: Macmillan, 201–213.
――― (1996): Politisches Interesse und Apathie in Europa. In: König, Thomas/Rieger, Elmar/Schmitt, Hermann (eds.), Das europäische Mehrebenensystem. Frankfurt am Main: Campus, 383–402.
――― (2000): Interesting but Irrelevant. Social Capital and the Saliency of Politics in Western Europe. European Journal of Political Research 37: 115–147.
――― (2001): The Proof of the Pudding: Social Capital, Democracy, and Citizenship. Paper presented at the EURESCO Conference "Social Capital: Interdisciplinary Perspectives", Exeter (United Kingdom).
――― (2003): Measuring social capital: Orthodoxies and continuing controversies. International Journal of Social Research Methodology 6: 79–92.

―――― (2006): Democracy and involvement: The benevolent aspects of social participation. In: Montero, José Ramon/Torcal, Mariano (eds.): Political Disaffection in Contemporary Democracies. London: Routledge, 101–129.
van Deth, Jan W./Elff, Martin (2000): Political Involvement and Apathy in Europe 1973–1998. Mannheim: Mannheimer Zentrum für Europäische Sozialforschung (MZES Working Paper 33).
―――― (2001): Politicisation and Political Interest in Europe: A Multi-level Approach. Mannheim: Mannheimer Zentrum für Europäische Sozialforschung (MZES Working Paper 36).
―――― (2004): Politicisation, economic development and political interest in Europe. European Journal of Political Research 43: 477–508.
Verba, Sidney/Schlozman, Kay Lehmann/Brady, Henry E. (1995): Voice and Equality. Civic Voluntarism in American Politics. Cambridge, Mass.: Harvard University Press.
Zaller, John R. (1992): The Nature and Origins of Mass Opinion. Cambridge: Cambridge University Press.

CHAPTER EIGHT

SOCIAL CAPITAL AND POLITICAL TRUST

Oscar W. Gabriel and Melanie Walter-Rogg[1]

During the last three decades, political trust has become an outstandingly prominent topic of political research in diverse areas such as normative democratic theory, systems and rational choice theories, cognitive psychology, and neo-institutionalism. All these approaches tried to explore the contribution of political trust to the explanation of individual political behavior and to the performance of democratic systems. Political trust has also been a crucial topic of empirical research. Many theorists were concerned with the downward spiral of political trust observed in modern democracies. This trend was primarily attributed to an increasing discrepancy between the citizens' expectations and the outcomes of political decisions, as well as the conduct of public affairs. According to broad empirical evidence gathered over the years, people blamed political actors and institutions for poor performance. Moreover, they felt disaffected by the conduct of public affairs, which was regarded as distant from the citizens and unresponsive to their real needs (for a short summary see Norris 1999).

Recently, analyses of political and social trust were embedded in a somewhat different context, emphasizing the role of trust as an ingredient for a "good society" and "good governance". According to Putnam (1993: 170), social trust is a core component of civic mindedness, needed for "making democracy work". In his view, social trust fosters political trust. Accordingly, a decline of political trust would be caused by a process of social disintegration, particular by a weakening of the "communal spirit". The same rationale would underly the explanation of cross-national variations of political trust.

In spite of the considerably different levels of political trust in contemporary democracies, investigating the sources of peoples' trust in politics is not only a purely academic matter. The respective findings

---

[1] We feel strongly indebted to Martin Sojer for his contribution to the empirical analyses reported in this chapter.

have important political implications. If a performance-related explanation of political trust held true, improving the performance of political institutions and actors would provide solutions for the current crisis of confidence. From a social capital perspective, however, the roots of the crisis would go deeper and indicate a disconnection of citizens from their fellows and their authorities. Finding the most important causes for peoples' relationship towards politics is particularly relevant in a comparison of old and new European democracies. The perspectives of establishing relations of trust between citizens and their governments would strongly differ, depending on what is more strongly emphasized, performance or social capital.

In empirical analyses, levels and changes of political trust are explained by individual characteristics such as the perceived economic situation, satisfaction with government, partisan affiliation, social trust, mass media perception, and ideological dispositions. However, if variables of this kind are taken into account, variations in political trust among modern democracies will not disappear. This leads us to the question of whether and to what degree systemic characteristics contribute to national variations of political trust. An appropriate strategy used for tackling this issue includes taking into account individual as well as contextual antecedents of trust in political institutions and leaders, which is well in line with the logic of the social capital approach (Gabriel et al. 2002: 25–34; Denters et al. 2007: 79–83). This chapter will explore the macro- and micro-level determinants of political trust, with a focus on the role of social capital.

As a starting point of our analysis, we will compare the level and structure of political trust in 21 European societies in 2002/2003. Subsequently, we will give a short summary of the concept of social capital and its basic components and we will derive the basic hypotheses on the antecedents of political trust entailed in the concept of social capital. In order to assess the genuine explanatory power of the latter concept, additional factors emphasized in previous research will need to be taken into consideration. The most important ones are governmental performance and institutional integration, further explored in section two. This section will be followed by the estimation of a micro-level explanatory model, using only social capital variables. Then other relevant individual-level determinants of political trust will be taken into account. Turning to multi-level analyses in section three, we will analyze whether, to what degree and due to which particular variables, the explanatory power of the micro model can be improved, by additionally taking into account contextual variables. Finally, in section four, we will summarize our basic empirical findings, put them in the context of previous research, and discuss the contribution of social capital to peoples' trust in politics.

1. POLITICAL TRUST IN EUROPE

1.1 *Definition*

Starting from the core research in this area, there has never been a simple and straightforward solution to the problem of what specific issues people have in mind when answering questions on trust in politics. Initially, the debate focused on the public's ability to distinguish trust in the political system from trust in authorities. Later, the debate referred to trust in political institutions versus political actors. Subsequently, some researchers analyzed whether trust in political institutions should be understood as a uni- or a multi-dimensional phenomenon. As demonstrated in several empirical studies, citizens do not only distinguish between trust in the system and in the authorities, but also between private and public, regulatory and representative institutions and politicians as separate, but mutually related referents of trust (Listhaug/Wiberg 1995; Gabriel et al. 2002: 177–182; Denters et al. 2007: 67–69).

The European Social Survey contains several items measuring political trust. In this chapter, the focus will be on three factors performing different functions in political life. The first one is the national parliament as a key institution of representative democracy, which plays the decisive role in rule making. The second one, the legal system, represents a set of regulatory institutions, performing the function of rule adjudication. Finally, we include politicians as the representatives of the political system, visible to the public, and who contribute to all stages of the political process. The wording of the question on trust in these objects was as follows: "Please tell me, on a score of 0–10, how much trust you personally place in each of the institutions I read out. 0 means you do not trust an institution at all, and 10 means you have complete trust. Firstly, (country's) parliament, the legal system, politicians…?"

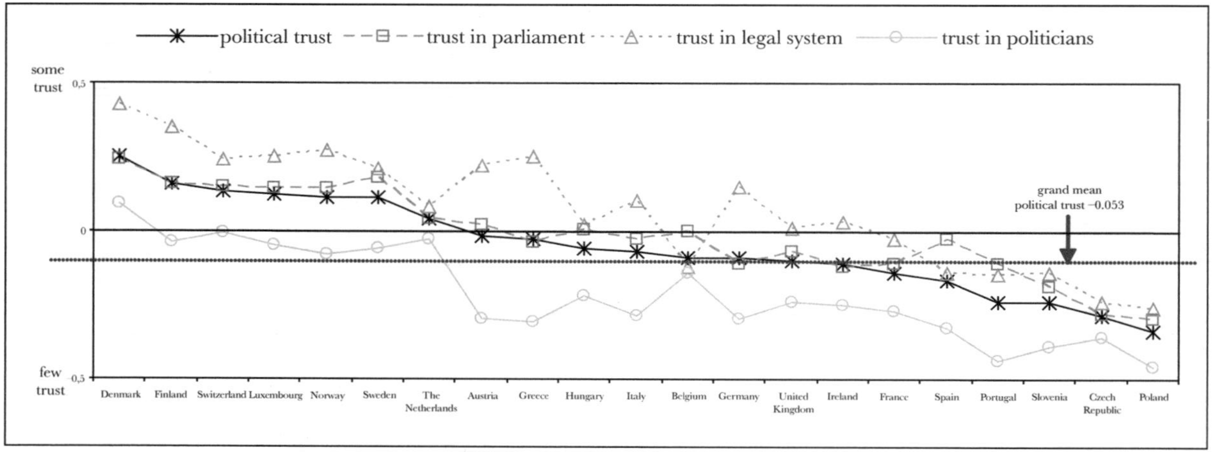

Figure 1: Political Trust in Europe, 2002–2003

Source: ESS Micro Data, Round 1. The values of the trust variables are standardized by transforming the original eleven point scale ranging from 0 to 10 to a new range from −1 (no trust) to +1 (complete trust). Due to a lack of values under −0.5 respectively above 0.5 the presented scale reaches only from −0.5 (few trust) to 0.5 (some trust). The countries are ranked by the index variable "political trust".

1.2 *Trust in the parliament, the legal system and for politicians*

According to the data in Figure 1, Europeans differentiate in their responses when they are asked about their trust in the parliament, the legal system or in politicians. In line with other empirical studies, citizens trust their countries' parliament more than their political representatives do. However, the legal system is by far the most broadly trusted by the European publics (Gabriel et al. 2002: 183–204; Denters et al. 2007: 69–71). This finding holds true for almost all countries under observation here. Only Belgium and Portugal deviate from the general pattern, where people place more trust in the parliament than in the legal system. As the grand mean reported in Figure 1 shows, a balance of trust and non-trust in political institutions is typical for the European public as a whole, with a slight preponderance of positive evaluations of the legal system and an even slighter negative tendency regarding judgments of the parliament. Politicians are the only political object held in low esteem by citizens.

The European average reported before, masks the strong differences between the particular national publics. Regarding the prevalence of trust over non-trust, Denmark is the only country where citizens declare trust rather than non-trust in all three political objects. In all remaining nations, politicians are distrusted by a majority of the respondents, while political institutions are evaluated differently. In the remaining Nordic countries, the Netherlands, Luxembourg, Switzerland, Austria and Hungary, political institutions are rather more trusted than not. Italians, Germans, the English and the Irish show feelings of trust in the legal system, but not in the national parliament and in politicians. Finally, each of the three political objects is facing non-trusting rather than trusting attitudes in seven European countries, all of them belonging to post-communist or predominantly catholic societies. As a summary, politicians do not enjoy a good standing, while the legal system is trusted in most European countries. In comparison, trust in the national parliament is most controversial. Even if the hierarchy of trusted objects can be found in all countries under observation here, this result is accompanied with large differences at the national levels regarding trust in all three objects.

In this chapter, we are interested in generalized political trust, i.e. an attitude encompassing the three sub-dimensions analyzed before. Regarding this attitude, Denmark stands out again. Trust is also widespread in the other Nordic countries, Switzerland and Luxembourg. In opposition, we find three of the four post-communist societies (Slovenia, the Czech Republic and Poland), and two of the three post-authoritarian countries of Southern Europe (Spain and Portugal). Apparently, European publics differ strongly regarding their trust in politics. However so far, we do not have an explanation for why this is the case.

2. Explaining Political Trust

Irrespective of the prominence of trust in social research, a general theory of social and political trust is lacking. So far, two approaches are often used as a basis for empirical research. According to an exchange-based view, positive experience with the performance of actors or institutions or related expectations for the future is the key determinant. An alternative approach, coming close to the concept of social capital, stresses the idea of trust as a community or identity-based orientation. Accordingly, feelings of belonging to the same socio-political community and sharing the same values and norms lead people to trust each other—and politicians as well (Braithwaite 1998; similarly: Chanley et al. 2001; Uslaner 2002).

2.1 *Individual-level Approaches*

2.1.1 *Social Capital*

The idea of social trust as a determinant of political trust is not new in political science. In an early contribution, Cole (1973: 811) traced back political trust to three factors: socioeconomic variables, personality factors, and a sense of political efficacy. Social trust was conceived as one of several factors contributing to political trust. A second approach to the relationship of social to political trust was developed in research on political socialization. Accordingly, young children acquire a positive view of political authorities simply by transferring the positive attitudes to their parents to remote political objects and institutions (Abramson/Inglehart 1970: 419).

Networks and cultural capital

Similar to these research traditions, social trust is conceived as an antecedent of political trust in research on social capital. However, this interrelationship is understood as a product of a nation's collective history rather than of individual personality. According to Putnam, social capital consists of two components; social networks (network capital) and feelings of reciprocity (cultural capital), reinforcing each other and forming a cluster of civic virtues and behaviors, which are elements of or promote a good society and good governance (Putnam 1993: 89–91; van Deth 2004: 295–296, 309–312).

Network capital encompasses membership and activity in voluntary associations such as sports clubs, charitable organizations and parent-teacher associations on the one hand, and informal social activity (helping people outside the own family or friendship networks) on the other. These types of social involvement are assumed to have a beneficial effect on the participating individual and on the society. Being included in social networks provides an opportunity of getting in contact with people beyond the immediate personal environment, of tolerating people with different customs and world views, and for acquiring the skills needed for social co-operation. In general, becoming involved in social networks is an important basis for the development of feelings of reciprocity. Although some organizations and forms of social participation may be more important than others in this respect, the general idea of formal and informal social participation as a training ground for the development of feelings of reciprocity still holds strong (Putnam 2000: 134; similarly: Stolle 2001: 218–231; Uslaner 2002: 125–141). Thus, social networks contribute to social integration and cohesion.

Direct and indirect links
However, we can hardly imagine how social activity, mostly occurring in people's immediate social environment (district, community), could be converted into trust in remote and abstract objects like politicians, the national parliament and the legal system. If this assumption holds true, network capital will primarily have an indirect impact on political trust and will be mediated through feelings of reciprocity. Possibly, the links of network capital to social trust will disappear if feelings of reciprocity are controlled. This expectation is validated by most empirical research conducted so far (Gabriel et al. 2002: 183–197; Zmerli et al. 2007: 51–60; Denters et al. 2007: 75–78).

This leads us to the second component of social capital, cultural capital. In Putnam's view (2000: 134), trust in one's fellow citizen is the "cornerstone" of social capital, but support of norms and values of reciprocity also plays an important role. However, while these norms and values have rarely been investigated empirically so far, considerable efforts have been made to investigate the nature, origin and impact of social trust. As parts of a common cultural syndrome, social and political trust are conceptualized as two sides of the same coin (Newton 1999; Uslaner 2002: 148–159). Moreover, social involvement is seen as an opportunity for developing trust in other people ("thick trust"), which then can be converted into trust in remote political objects ("thin trust").

Although this view is not undisputed (Hardin 1999), several arguments support the generalization hypothesis. As a general individual disposition developed in early childhood, social and political trust will then be upheld later, in adult life. A second argument rests on the view of social trust as part of the citizens' identity. Accordingly, people trust their fellow citizens because they belong to the same social community and share the same values and norms (Braithwaite 1998). If politicians are seen as members of the same community, and political institutions are accepted as representing the values and norms of the respective community, then both politicians and their institutions are included in a benevolent attitude towards one's environment. Nevertheless, as these feelings originate in the immediate social context in which individuals are embedded, they will eventually be extended to "strangers".

Contrary to social trust, the norms and values of reciprocity and their role as antecedents of political trust are poorly understood and even more poorly examined in empirical analyses. Instead of clearly elaborating these concepts and the role they play as elements of cultural capital, Putnam himself presents a series of empirical indicators and manifestations of reciprocity, assuming that they have beneficial social effects (Putnam 1993: 88–89, Putnam 2000: 134–147). In the explanation of political trust, norms and values have played no role so far (Gabriel et al. 2002; Pattie et al. 2004: 29–56; Denters et al. 2007). From a theoretical point of view, we could argue that people supporting norms of solidarity, tolerance and conformity to rules, will also exhibit social and political trust, since all these feelings imply a concern for the common good. However, assuming an indirect link between norms and values of reciprocity on the one hand and social and political trust on the other seems to be more plausible than supposing a direct link. This is well in line with the empirical findings presented so far (Gabriel et al. 2002: 183–197).

As interrelated elements of a broader organizational and cultural pattern, formal and informal social activity, social trust and support of values and norms of reciprocity should all have a positive impact on political trust. However, for the reasons mentioned before, social trust is regarded as, by far, the most important determinant (Newton 1999;

Gabriel et al. 2002). We can then formulate a first hypothesis on the impact of social capital on feelings of political trust.

Hypothesis 1: The stronger an individual's participation in social capital, the more he or she will place trust in politics. All components of social capital should have a positive impact, but social trust should have the strongest positive effect.

2.1.2 *Performance*

The role of social capital cannot reliably be assessed without considering other explanatory concepts. In a previous section of this chapter, performance- or exchange-based views on political trust were introduced as a second broad approach to political trust. The basic idea of this concept is characterized by Braithwaite (1998: 54) as follows: "for the purposes of understanding trust in government, exchange trust norms can be defined as shared beliefs that government and its branches are trustworthy if they act in ways that are predictable, consistent, orderly, and if they deliver on premises in a timely fashion" (see also Chanley et al. 2001: 60–62).

Evaluation of public policies or on the outcomes

The view of trust as an outcome of positive evaluations regarding the performance of political actors and institutions is well-established in research (MacAllister 1999; Miller/Listhaug 1999). Far less clear is what is meant by performance. In attitudinal research, political performance needs to be understood as a positive evaluation of objects, based upon the criteria mentioned in Braithwaite's conceptualization of exchange based trust. Empirical research has focused on the evaluation of public policies or on the outcomes generated for an individual or for the society as a whole. Examples of these kinds of outcomes are citizens' satisfaction with specific policies (welfare provisions, fighting inflation or unemployment, environmental protection) or the perceived distance between people's own stance on issues and the respective policies (Borre/Scarbrough 1995). Specific policy orientations are possibly less important to the generation and maintenance of political trust than an overall positive view of a nation's socioeconomic infrastructure (educational system, health care system) or satisfaction with the performance of the incumbent government or the democratic system in general. However, due to the given data situation, the assessment of a country's or individual's economic situation has been most broadly used as performance-based antecedents of political trust (Miller/Listhaug 1999; MacAllister 1999; Denters et al. 2007).

All attitudes mentioned above are supposed to implicate positively on political trust, and some of the respective assumptions are broadly supported by empirical evidence. With respect to perceived policy distances between citizens and political actors, Borre and Scarbrough (1995: 345) state: "our main hypothesis postulates a negative relationship between policy distance and political support". Miller and Listhaug (1999: 206) introduce a similar hypothesis regarding the interrelationship of government performance to political trust: "the basic thesis we will explore is that failure of government performance may erode confidence in government institutions". Similar views on the impact of economic conditions on political trust can be found in a large number of publications.

Evaluation of political responsiveness
While the attitudes mentioned so far refer primarily to perceived policy performance or distance, trust can also be generated by a positive assessment of more general attributes of political objects. In this case, they are evaluated by using criteria bound to the nature of democratic governance. One of the most important and broadly investigated criteria of democratic performance is (perceived) political responsiveness. In a democracy, politicians are expected to be open to citizens' demands and to consider them when making political decisions; and if they behave in the expected manner, they will be trusted (Chanley et al. 2001; Denters et al. 2007: 71–78). This leads us to a second hypothesis.

Hypothesis 2: The more favorable an individual's evaluation of the performance of political institutions and actors, the more he or she will place trust in politics. Irrespective of the impact of performance evaluations on political trust, social capital effects persist.

Since we are primarily interested in analyzing the role of social capital as a source of political trust, performance-related variables are treated as control variables, but are not analyzed for their own sake. The empirical analysis focuses on the role of social capital variables in the explanation of political trust, but its impact can only be assessed reliably after performance-related attitudes have been controlled.

2.1.3 *Social and Institutional Integration*

While social capital and the assessment of performance can be well-integrated into general theories of trust, this applies less to several other explanatory concepts. However, many of the respective ideas can be subsumed under the concept of institutional and social integration. Party identification is one of the most important linkages between citizens and the political system. As Kaase (1979: 329–332) demonstrated, strong party identifiers show a higher degree of political support than other people do. Another variant of party-related concepts is known as the home-team-hypothesis. Accordingly, political trust depends on an interaction of people's partisan affiliation and the inclusion of the preferred party in the incumbent government. This relationship becomes stronger as the intensity of party identification increases (Denters et al. 2007). Since the indicators of the home-team-hypotheses are highly correlated with one of the performance indicators—satisfaction with the work of the incumbent government—we will not include party-related variables in our empirical analysis.

Some other assumptions can be found in the literature on political trust. There are good reasons to regard cognitive involvement as positively linked to political trust, since these characteristics can both be understood as elements of good citizenship (Almond/Verba 1989; Pattie et al. 2004). However, the hypotheses that increasing knowledge of politics leads to cynical attitudes towards politics and government appears equally plausible. This holds particularly true, if we keep in mind the findings of a negativist trend in mass media reporting about politics, which is the main source of political information for most people (Norris 2000). Religious affiliation, integration in the labor force and family life, are also indicators of institutional integration, possibly fostering political trust. The same applies to indicators such as interpersonal political communication and political participation. Summing up all the assumptions presented, our third hypothesis is as follows.

Hypothesis 3: The stronger people are integrated into social and political life, the more will they place trust in politics.

2.2 *Structural Approaches*

Turning to the contextual determinants of individual political trust raises a fundamental problem of social and political life, namely what kind of society and political regime could foster individual political trust? The contextual variables discussed as possible predictors of political trust in this chapter can be grouped into five different categories.[2] The role of social capital and macroeconomic performance has been already analyzed at the micro-level. Since social capital is seen as a relational (individual) and a systemic (societal) characteristic (Coleman 1988; Gabriel et al. 2002: 25–29), the respective variables should also be included in a macro-level explanatory model. The remaining systemic factors are the following: inclusive political institutions, social development, and cultural homogeneity.

Presumably, living in a democratic regime would be the most important institutional determinant of people's trust in politics, since democracy has a strong impact on people's conditions of life and their overall relationship toward their social and political environment. In the countries under observation here, important systemic properties such as political rights and civil liberties (Norris 1999: 223) are constants. Only the longevity of democratic rule and a missing tradition of communist rule differ among the nations. Democratic experience, as indicated by the longevity of a democratic government, is regarded as promoting political support (MacAllister 1999: 194–195).

Hypothesis 4: The shorter a democratic regime exists, the less people place trust in politics.

In the first analysis of the political culture concept, Almond (1956) pointed to a negative relationship between cultural (religious, ethnic and linguistic) fragmentation, on the one hand, and social and political trust, on the other. Another cultural antecedent of social capital and political trust is Protestantism. The ethos and the horizontal patterns of authority prevailing in Protestant churches are assumed to foster civic values such as individualism, autonomy, and freedom. By contrast, the Catholic, Orthodox and Islamic doctrines provide the normative basis of social hierarchy and corresponding vertical social networks, neither encouraging autonomy nor social and political trust (Putnam 1993, 2000; Uslaner 2002: 87–88). Living in a culturally homogeneous society is then not a sufficient condition for developing trust toward other

---

[2] "History" could be interpreted as a sixth category but it will be left out because of conceptual and measurement problems. Historical developments are, nevertheless mirrored in some other variables such as the longevity of democratic regimes and socioeconomic development.

people and politics. Moreover, Protestantism would need to prevail as the religious denomination. Whether the political impact of religious affiliations has remained as strong in secularized societies as it used to be half a century ago, needs to be questioned.

Hypothesis 5: Political trust will be more widespread in predominantly Protestant, than in culturally heterogeneous or in predominantly non-Protestant, societies.

The strong impact of socioeconomic development on political life is a well established finding in empirical research. According to Lipset (1959) and many others, education, urbanization and prosperity reduce the social tensions and cleavages caused by an unequal access to socioeconomic resources (Uslaner 2002: 181–189).

Hypothesis 6: In socioeconomically higher developed societies, political trust will be more widespread than in less developed societies.

In line with the renewed interest by many political scientists concerning the impact of institutions on political life, some researchers have recently dealt with the role of political institutions as determinants of political trust (Norris 1999). Apart from an uninterrupted tradition of democratic rule, most ideas on this topic concern the idea of inclusive political systems allocating significant allowances to the public to access the power structures of society. According to Norris (1999: 222–226), aherents of those parties who win when they compete for power enjoy extensive political rights and civil liberties. Moreover, being a citizen of a parliamentary, multi-party and federal system is conducive to political trust; and the same is said on a proportional electoral system. The arguments presented in order to support these assumptions are not entirely convincing and in part cannot be applied to our set of countries. The winner-loser hypothesis is already included in the micro-level analysis, the political rights variable lacks sufficient variance, as does presidentialism. The three remaining variables are part of the concept of consensus democracy. In order to conclude the idea of systemic inclusiveness as an antecedent of political trust, we will include some additional constructs mentioned by Lijphart not as parts, but as results of consensus democracy. Our hypothesis on the impact of institutional variables on political trust is as follows.

Hypothesis 7: Political trust will be more widespread in consensus than in majoritarian democracies.

3. Results: Social Capital, Context and Political Trust in Europe

3.1 Micro-level Analysis: Why Do Individuals Place Trust in Politics?

At the beginning of the empirical analyses, we will examine the role of social capital as a determinant of political trust. According to our first hypothesis, all elements of network and cultural capital will contribute to the explanation of political trust. As reported in Table 2, the variance explained by a micro-level model including only indicators of social capital amounts to 16 per cent. However, a complete social capital model cannot be estimated for all 21 countries, since data on organisational affiliation was not available for Switzerland and the Czech Republic. In order to assess whether omitting this variable would diminish the explanatory power of the model, the results of the estimation by a model including these two countries and omitting formalized social participation is also reported in Table 2. As shown by the data, the model estimated for the whole set of countries—not taking into account voluntary associations—explains roughly the same proportion of variance as the original model. Therefore, all subsequently presented results are based on this latter model.

Our first hypothesis is clearly confirmed as social capital—taken as a whole—and has a positive impact on political trust. This is also true for the second assumption, entailed in hypothesis 1. Social trust is by far the most important determinant of political trust, and support of civic norms exerts a moderately positive influence. To the contrary, all forms of social involvement are largely irrelevant as predictors of political trust. Regarding the role of social capital in a broader context, the data in Table 2 provide some clear insights. First and foremost, social capital alone does not provide a good explanation of political trust, since including indicators of political performance leads to a considerable increase of explained variance. If indicators of institutional integration and demographic control variables are added, another three per cent of variance can be reduced (data not shown in Table 2). All performance-related variables bear positively on political trust, but only three of them, satisfaction with democracy, satisfaction with government, and beliefs in the responsiveness of politics, do so in a substantial manner.

Table 2: Determinants of Political Trust in Europe (micro-level estimation)

	Excluding Switzerland & Czech Republic				Including Switzerland & Czech Republic			
	B	Beta	b	Beta	B	Beta	B	Beta
Participation in organized social activities	.13	.04***	.03	.01*	–	–	–	–
Informal participation in social activities	.05	.05***	.01	.01**	.05	.06***	.01	.01***
Helping behavior	−.02	−.03***	−.01	−.01	−.01	−.02***	−.002	−.003
Social trust	.38	.37***	.15	.14***	.39	.37***	.15	.14***
Civic norms	.13	.10***	.07	.05***	.14	.11***	.07	.06***
Responsiveness politicians			.24	.27***			.25	.27***
Satisfaction with democracy			.25	.28***			.25	.28***
Satisfaction with government			.21	.24***			.22	.24***
Constant	−.11		.009		−.11		.007	
Adjusted R^2	.16***		.48***		.17***		.49***	
	33513		31914		36617		34903	

Source: European Social Survey 2002/2003.
Notes: Linear Regression with design weighted pooled data for 21 (19 countries); data weighted by design weight.
Significant for: *** p ≤ .001, ** p ≤ .01, * p ≤ .05.

The effects of all remaining control variables are, in part, statistically insignificant and, in part, negligible because the regression coefficients come close to zero (only the relevant predictors of political trust are shown in Table 2).

What can be inferred from the data presented so far? Social capital does not become irrelevant as an antecedent of political trust, even if powerful additional predictors are taken into account. However, this statement needs to be qualified. Only social trust remains a substantially important, genuine determinant of political trust in a model encompassing the assessment of political performance. The relationship between the support of civic virtues and political trust does not disappear, but becomes considerably weaker after the inclusion of performance-related variables in the model. Again, network capital is not a determinant of political trust. Irrespective of the contribution of cultural capital, and particularly social trust to the generation of political trust, an exchange-based explanation seems to be far more adequate. To put it in the terms of Braithwaite (1998) political trust can be interpreted as a mix of community and exchanged-based orientations to politics. Identification with the social community contributes to political trust, but when deciding whether to trust or not to trust politics, citizens will rather ask political leaders, "what have you lately done for me?"

How do our findings relate to previous comparative research? Compared to the country-by-country analyses of Gabriel et al. (2002), who used a similar explanatory model but a different set of countries and different operationalizations of the social capital model, the amount of explained variance is clearly higher. The two studies arrive at the same conclusion regarding the important role of social trust and the irrelevance of all manifestations of network capital, in the explanation of political trust. The main difference between the studies refers to the role of civic virtues, which were not particularly relevant predictors in the study of Gabriel et al., but show at least a modest impact on political trust in our analysis. Probably, the deviations of the two comparative studies are mainly due to the quality of the database, which is clearly better in many respects in the case of the ESS than in the previously used survey. To summarize our findings presented so far: In line with our hypotheses, cultural, but not network capital, matters in the explanation of political trust (see also: Denters et al. 2007).

3.2 The Multi-Level Explanatory Model: Individual Political Trust in Europe in Context

After discovering which individual factors are conducive to political trust, we will now examine the contribution of the macro setting to the explanation of individual trust in politics. The multi-level model is estimated for the 21 countries. Taking into account 19 micro- and 19 macro-level variables, the model does not meet the ideal of parsimony. Moreover, many of the 19 contextual factors were highly correlated to each other thus causing biased estimates. Since no a priori considerations would justify the exclusion of some variables for purely theoretical reasons, we firstly estimated a model including all 38 predictors and then dropped all predictors lacking statistical significance or causing problems of multicollinearity. Thus, we eventually obtained a parsimonious multi-level model including four micro- and two macro-level variables.

Following the logic of a multi-level analysis, we will present the results in several consecutive steps. Firstly, the so-called empty model was estimated (see Table 3). It does not contain any substantive information on the included micro- and macro-level independent variables, but uses the observed grand mean reported in Figure 1 as an estimate of the intercept. This score indicates an almost even balance of trust and non-trust among all individuals surveyed in all countries under observation. As the intra-class-correlation (ICC) shows, 13 per cent of the observed variance of political trust can be attributed to, unspecified, systemic differences between the 21 countries (see Table 3).

Compositional effects
However, this value needs to be interpreted carefully because of the role of compositional effects. In other words, what first might appear as a genuine contextual effect can turn out as a mere aggregation of individual effects. This applies to our case, since several independent variables within the 21 nations have an impact on the dependent individual-level variable. After having included the relevant individual-level explanatory variables (level–1 only), the composition effects mentioned before disappear. The remaining systemic effect of four per cent can now be interpreted as genuine contextual influence on the dependent micro-level variable. The level–1 model presupposes an inclusion of the relevant micro-level variables (equation not presented).

All independent micro-level variables are now included in the model. If they all assume the value of 0, the estimated score of political trust is roughly similar to the estimation of the unconditional model (−.051). The effects of all four micro-level variables shown in Table 3 are statistically significant and substantially meaningful. Compared to the micro-level model presented in Table 2, social trust remains an important predictor of political trust, even if performance-related attitudes are controlled. The coefficient of the civic virtues variable is no longer statistically significant. Moreover, the most important determinants of people's trust in politics are still satisfaction with democracy, satisfaction with government and perceived responsiveness of politicians, in this sequence. Social trust is the weakest of the four micro-level predictors, but the size of the coefficient comes close to that of perceived responsiveness. The explanatory power of this model is high with around 46 per cent of variance attributable to the micro-level variables. So far, the results of the multi-level model are highly consistent with the micro-level model in Table 2. Hypotheses 1 and 2 are still supported by our empirical findings.

The influence of systemic characteristics
The random intercept model estimates the constant of the micro-level regression equation by taking into account relevant systemic characteristics of the nations as the level–2 units. In general, adding contextual factors to the model does not improve the explanatory power. The intercept deviates only slightly from the model exclusively containing individual-level variables. The same applies to the explained variance, which increases by less than one percentage point. Only two of the macro-level predictors, mean civic norms and longevity of democracy, turn out as unbiased and statistically significant estimates. Nevertheless, in the latter case, the effect parameter is weak and does not indicate a substantial influence, irrespective of statistical significance.

Estimations of cross-level interactions do not change the general results presented so far. In line with a failure to improve the explained variance substantially, only a very small number of statistically significant, though weak slope effects, were detected. However, the direction of the effects conformed to our expectations. Individual social trust is more easily transformed into political trust in high-trust rather than in low-trust societies and when party systems are broadly differentiated. Thus, a climate of interpersonal trust makes it easier for individuals to extend their feelings of trust to their fellow citizens, and then to political institutions and actors. The transfer of satisfaction with the government into political trust is enhanced in societies characterized by economic growth. Finally, satisfaction with democracy contributes significantly to political trust in societies in which income inequality is small (data not presented in Table 3).

In view of these results, the general conclusions regarding the role of contextual factors regarding the explanation of individual trust in politics is obvious. Firstly, the differing levels of political trust reported in Figure 1 can almost completely be attributed to compositional, but not to true contextual effects. Since the Polish are more dissatisfied with democracy and governments, less convinced of the responsiveness of politicians and, most interestingly in our context, have less trust in their fellow citizens than the Danes and the Swiss, they also exhibit less trust in politics. Therefore, almost all hypotheses concerning the role of contextual factors for the explanation of individual political trust need to be rejected if individual characteristics are known. This applies without any qualification to cultural, socioeconomic, macro-economic and institutional variables (hypotheses 5 to 8). No single variable derived from these approaches proved to have had an impact

Table 3: Determinants of Political Trust in Europe (Micro- and Macro-Level)

Fixed effects			Empty Model B	Standard error	Individual-Level only B	Standard Error	Random Intercept only B	Standard Error
Level 1	Constant							
		Level 2	−,0531	,0344	−,0516**	,0139	−,0575***	,0116
		Constant					,4051***	,1051
		Mean Civic Norms					,0010*	,0004
		Years of democracy						
	Social trust				,1719***	,0046	,1738***	,0100
	Satisfaction with government				,2347***	,0044	,2379***	,0161
	Satisfaction with democracy				,2361***	,0044	,2323***	,0093
	Responsiveness of politicians				,1903***	,0035	,1875***	,0058

Random effects	Variance components	Standard deviation	Variance components	Standard deviation	Variance components	Standard deviation
σ² (Individual-Level)	,0248		,0922	,3037	,0911	,3018
T00 (Context-Level)		,1573	,0040	,0634	,0028	,0525
Deviance	39279		16605		16282	
Parameters	2		2		16	
Interclass Correlation (ICC)	0,1341		,0417		,0293	
Maddala-R²	—		,4647		,4695	
Proportion of explained variance at level 1	—		,4229		,4299	
Proportion of explained variance at level 2	—		,8380		,8889	

Notes: Multi-level Analysis (HLM 6), individual-level variables grand mean centered, restricted likelihood estimation method, missing values deleted when running analysis, N=36278.
Significant for: *** $p \leq .001$, ** $p \leq .01$, * $p \leq .05$.
In order to illustrate the contextual effects, we just need the level-2 part of the equation: Y = G00 + G01*(MEANCIVICNORMS) + G02*(YEARSOFDEMOCRACY) + [...].
Data for all countries and for Poland: years of democracy: grand mean = 66; Poland = 37; mean civic norms: grand mean = .3982; Poland = .4157.
If the constant is −.0575 for the grand mean of all predictors, the deviation of the grand mean is counted by the equation: coefficient * value of deviation.
Y = −,0575 + ,4051 * (,4157 − .3982) + ,0010 * (37−66) + [...].
Y = −0.0794 + [...].

on political trust. Poles are not less trusting in politics than the Danes and Swiss, because they are living in a post-communist society or they belong to the Catholic church or their country ranks lower on the Human Development Index. It is mainly the difference in social and political outlooks of the respective publics that matters when explaining political trust. Considering the weakness of the theoretical arguments used in the presentation of the contextual variables, these results do not come as a surprise.

More surprisingly, the assumptions of the role of the durability and quality of democratic regimes in generating political trust are also not supported by empirical evidence. None of the respective indicators are substantially meaningful predictors of political trust. The effect parameters of absence of a communist past and lack of graft and corruption were statistically insignificant, and the only significant parameter estimate, which was obtained for years of democracy, has no substantial meaning since the size of the coefficient comes close to zero (see Table 3).

Finally, we have a look at the role played by systemic social capital, which is in the focus of our interest at the macro-level. With one exception, none of the macro-level indicators of social capital impinges on individual political trust. The only substantially meaningful macro-determinant of political trust, the average level of civic norms of a country, is a social capital variable.

As a summary, the results of the empirical analyses presented so far, lead to the following conclusions.

(1) Political trust depends on social capital, particularly on social trust and to a lesser degree on support of civic virtues. However performance-related variables are more meaningful to the creation and maintaining of political trust than is social capital. Thus, trust in politics can be interpreted as community and exchange-based feelings, but the instrumental base of political trust is stronger than the communal one.
(2) Since political trust can be well explained by a micro-level model including indicators of community and exchange-based orientations, taking additionally into account characteristics of the respondents' national surroundings does not improve the explanatory power of the model.
(3) Almost all the differences in the average level of political trust among the nations included in our analysis, can be attributed to composi-

tional effects, but not to truly contextual variables. Aggregated civic norms are the only exception, but they do not contribute strongly to the reduction of variance.

Due to a lack of comparable studies, our findings cannot be evaluated against other empirical evidence on the relative contribution of individual and contextual determinants of political trust. Denters et al. (2007: 79–84) included contextual factors in an OLS estimation of political trust, but since they used a different method of statistical analyses, the results of that study cannot be compared directly to this one. Freitag and Bühlmann (2005) conducted a multi-level analysis using similar independent variables and discovered that some socio-economic and socio-cultural variables were important. However, the dependent variable was social, not political trust and the sample of countries used was far more heterogeneous than in this chapter. In a study of individual and systemic determinants of trust in American cities, Rahn und Rudolph (2005) found a stronger impact of macro-level characteristics than we did, nevertheless individual factors were more relevant in explaining individual-level variance in political trust. However, cities may play a different role as a context of individual attitudes and behaviors than nation states.

4. Conclusion and Discussion

At the beginning of this chapter, we raised the question of what leads people to trust political actors and institutions. While some observers traced political trust to expectations of favorable political outcomes (exchange-based trust), others conceived political trust as a by-product of people's shared identities (communal-based trust). The social capital approach fits into this second line of reasoning. Accordingly, trust in politics derives primarily from social trust, the internalization of civic norms (cultural capital), as well as formal and informal social activity (network capital). These latter characteristics are conceptualized in the literature on social capital as systemic (macro-level) and relational (individual-level) social capital.

As analyses of political trust presented so far show, exchange-based and community-based explanations do not exclude each other. If the two concepts are examined simultaneously, trust seems to rest on instrumental rather than on identity-based considerations. However, most empirical studies included only micro-level variables. Even if the amount of variance explained by using this kind of estimation models appears as sufficiently high, a large part of variance remains unexplained, leaving room for possible influences of contextual factors. Multi-level explanations aiming to detect the relevance of macro-level variables on individual attitudes and behaviors have become increasingly important over the last two decades for several reasons. First and foremost, variations at the systemic level have strongly increased in Europe in the aftermath of communism in Middle and Eastern Europe. Moreover, the data situation has considerably improved since the institutionalization of truly cross-national surveys, which made available data that was lacking so far. Finally, the statistical methods needed to disentangle individual and systemic influences on individual attitudes and behaviors have become more sophisticated.

The purpose of this chapter was a twofold one. Firstly, we attempted to test a micro-level explanatory model detecting the sources of political trust in European societies. The focus was on social capital as a determinant of political trust, but alternative approaches were also taken into account. The results of the micro-level analyses are quite clear in several regards. An integrated model of estimation, which includes performance- and community-related attitudes provides a good explanation of political trust. Almost half of the variance in political trust among the European publics can be attributed to positive evaluations of institutional performance and trust in one's fellow citizens. Community-based orientations promote political trust, but performance-related attitudes are even more important in this respect. Contrary to the assumption of the theory of social capital, voluntary social activity of any kind does not have a direct impact on political trust. However, as some empirical analyses show, social activity contributes indirectly to trust in politicians and political institutions by strengthening social trust.

In view of the high proportion of variance of political trust, which can be explained by a micro-level estimation model, we should not have too optimistic expectations regarding the improvement of the explanatory model by including macro-level variables. Not surprisingly, taking into account the contextual setting of European societies did not contribute to a better understanding of political trust. Individual factors clearly outweigh systemic properties as determinants of political trust. With regard to the ideal of parsimonious explanatory models, restricting the analysis of political trust to the micro-level seems to be an obvious conclusion that can be drawn from our results, but there are also theoretical arguments that are relevant when utilizing characteristics of the political system as predictors of individual political trust.

Most of the theoretical arguments used to justify the inclusion of specific macro characteristics in the analysis of political trust are not convincing. Why should people living under presidential systems generally be more distrusting than those under parliamentary ones? The respective arguments presented by Norris (1999: 223–225) do not refer to general structural characteristics of presidentialism, but to particular situations such as executive-legislative deadlock or temporal rigidity. Those can occur in presidential systems, but this is not necessarily the case. Incidentally, federalism, which is proposed by Norris to be conducive to political trust, may produce similar constellations of deadlock and rigidity as presidentialism. Finally, as broad empirical evidence demonstrates, trust does strongly fluctuate over time in presidential (Citrin/Luks 2001 for the United States) as well as in parliamentary systems (Holmberg 1999 for Sweden; Gabriel 2005: 502–514) for Germany, which disproves the assumption of an impact of government structure on political trust. Similar objections can be found regarding the role of consensus democracy. Consensus democracy was invented as an institutional arrangement aimed at limiting the disruptive consequences of social distrust prevailing in culturally fragmented societies. At least originally, consensus democracy might have been negatively related to political trust. Whether or not introducing institutions of consensus democracy promotes social trust among the members of various subcultures, and whether this carries over to political objects depends less on the mere existence of a consensus democracy than on its performance.

Even according to the assumptions of neo-institutionalism, institutions do not matter unless they are mediated by individual perceptions. The same can be said about other structural characteristics such as human development, years of democracy and macroeconomic performance, more or less. If unemployment, for example, is not perceived as a problem by individuals and not assessed as salient for their own lives or for the society as a whole, it will hardly impinge on people's attitudes or behavior. Such considerations may apply even more strongly to objects that are more remote from individuals' daily lives. As Coleman (1990) convincingly demonstrated, characteristics of the macro environment always need to be transmitted into individually defined situations in order to become meaningful for an individual's attitudes or behavior. Thus, if perceptions of the functional and structural quality of a society and a state (good performance, responsiveness) are measured at the individual-level, a good deal of systemic influence is already covered.

Moreover, the question needs to be asked whether units such as a nation or society, as a whole, are the appropriate units for multi-level analysis. According to Huckfeldt and Sprague (2006: 4–22), environmental influence should not be equated to contextual influence "that arises due to social interaction within an environment" (Huckfeldt/Sprague 2006: 10). While it seems reasonable to assume that interacting with other people in one's neighborhood, community or voluntary association, may directly implicate on an individual's attitudes and behavior, such an assumption is far less well-grounded in the case of abstract and remote objects and situations. As Rahn and Rudolph (2005) showed, an analysis of the influence of the local community context on political trust of American citizens produced far more convincing macro-level results than ours. With respect to the closeness of the respective contexts to the citizens, this is not at all surprising. Other contexts may be more suitable in multi-level explanations regarding most political attitudes and behavior than nations and societies. Regarding the concept of social capital, structural characteristics of the voluntary associations to which citizens belong to or the density of the voluntary sector of a community would be interesting contexts to be investigated more deeply.

A final word should be said about the selection of nations. Although democratic Europe has become more multi-faceted after the breakdown of communism, European countries are nevertheless similar to each other if compared to other regions in the world. This implies that many systemic attributes that might be important in the explanation of trust, particularly civil liberties, human development or income inequality, do not show sufficient variation in order to account for different levels of trust. Freitag and Bühlmann's (2005) findings on systemic determinants of social trust support this assumption. It should be considered, however, that for those nations ranking low on civil liberties, human development and equal income distribution, we cannot be too confident in the results of opinion surveys.

As a summary of our analysis, we can thus state that if we are interested in finding out why Polish people place far less trust in politics than the Danes and the Swiss, we should primarily turn to individual factors such as satisfaction with the performance of political leaders and the system in general, feelings of responsiveness, and social trust. Systemic characteristics do not contribute much to a better understanding of why people place trust in politics, and the impact of the people's immediate social context, has not yet been adequately investigated.

REFERENCES

Abramson, Paul/Inglehart, Ronald (1970): The Development of Systemic Support in Four Western Democracies. *Comparative Political Studies* 2: 419–442.
Almond, Gabriel A. (1956): Comparative Political Systems. *Journal of Politics* 18: 391–409.
Almond, Gabriel A./Verba, Sidney (1989): The Civic Culture. Political Attitudes and Democracy in Five Nations. Reprint. Boston: Little, Brown and Company.
Armingeon, Klaus (2002): The Effects of Negotiation Democracy. A Comparative Analysis. *European Journal of Political Research* 41: 81–105.
Armingeon, Klaus/Leimgruber, Philipp/Beyeler, Michelle/Menegale, Sarah (2004): Comparative Political Data Set 1960–2002, Institute of Political Science, University of Berne (CPDS I).
Bandelow, Nils (2005): Konsensdemokratische Elemente im Baltikum ("executive party dimension" bzw. "joint decision dimension"). In: http://www.nilsbandelow.de/kd05fo12.pdf.
Barrett, David B. (1982): World Christian Encyclopedia. A Comparative Study of Churches and Religions in the Modern World Ad 1900–2000. Oxford/New York. Oxford University Press.
Borre, Ole/Scarbrough, Elinor (Eds.) (1995): The Scope if Government. Beliefs in Government. Vol. 3. Oxford: Oxford University Press.
Braithwaite, Valerie (1998): Communal and Exchange Trust Norms: Their Value Base and Relevance to Institutional Trust. In: Braithwaite, Valerie/Levi, Margaret (Eds.): Trust and Governance. New York: Russell Sage, 46–74.
Chanley, Virginia A./Rudolph, Thomas J./Rahn, Wendy M. (2001): Public Trust in Government in the Reagan Years and Beyond. In: Hibbing, John R./Theiss-Morse, Elisabeth (Eds.): What is it About Government that Americans Dislike? Cambridge: Cambridge University Press, 9–27.
Citrin, Jack/Luks, Samantha (2001): Political Trust Revisited: Déjà Vu All Over Again? In: Hibbing, John R./Theiss-Morse, Elisabeth (Eds.): What is it About Government that Americans Dislike? Cambridge: Cambridge University Press, 59–81.
Cole, Richard L. (1973): Toward a Model of Political Trust: A Causal Analysis. *American Journal of Political Science* 17: 809–817.
Coleman, James (1988): Social Capital in the Creation of Human Capital. *American Journal of Sociology* 94: 95–120.
——— (1990): Foundations of Social Theory. Cambridge, Mass.: Belknap Press.
Denters, Bas/Gabriel, Oscar W./Torcal, Mariano (2007): Political Confidence in Representative Democracies: Socio-cultural vs. Political Explanations. In: van Deth, Jan W./Montero, José Ramón/Westholm, Anders (Eds.): Citizenship and Involvement in European Democracies. London/New York: Routledge, 66–87.
Freitag, Markus/Bühlmann, Marc (2005): Politische Institutionen und die Entwicklung generalisierten Vertrauens. Ein internationaler Vergleich. *Politische Vierteljahresschrift* 46: 575–601.
Gabriel, Oscar W. (2005): Politische Einstellungen und politische Kultur. In: Gabriel, Oscar W./Holtmann, Everhard (Eds.): Handbuch Politisches System der Bundesrepublik Deutschland. 3. völlig überarbeitete und erweiterte Auflage. München/Wien: Oldenbourg, 457–522.

Gabriel, Oscar W./Kunz, Volker/Rossteutscher, Sigrid/van Deth, Jan (2002): Sozialkapital und Demokratie. Zivilgesellschaftliche Ressourcen im internationalen Vergleich. Wien: Wiener Universitätsverlag.
Hardin, Russell (1999): Do We Want Trust in Government? In: Warren, Mark E. (Eds.): Democracy and Trust. Cambridge, MA: University Press, 22–41.
Holmberg, Sören (1999): Down and Down We Go: Political Trust in Sweden. In: Norris, Pippa (Ed.): Critical Citizens. Global Support for Democratic Governance. Oxford: Oxford University Press, 103–122.
Huckfeldt, Robert/Sprague, John (2006): Citizens, Politics, and Social Communication. Information and Influence in an Election Campaign. Cambridge: Cambridge University Press.
Ismayr, Wolfgang (2002): Die politischen Systeme Osteuropas. Opladen: Leske + Budrich.
Kaase, Max (1979): Legitimitätskrise in westlichen demokratischen Industriegesellschaften: Mythos oder Realität? In: Klages, Helmut/Kmieciak, Peter (Eds.): Wertwandel und gesellschaftlicher Wandel. Frankfurt/New York: Campus-Verlag, 328–350.
Kaufmann, Daniel/Kraay, Aart/Zoido-Lobatón, Pablo (1999): Governance Matters. World Bank Working Paper #2196. In: www.worldbank.org/research/growth/corrupt_data.htm.
Laakso, Markku/Taagepera, Rein (1979): Effective Number of Parties: A Measure with Application to West Europe. *Comparative Political Studies* 12: 3–27.
Lijphart, Arend (1999): Patterns of Democracy: Government Form and Performance in Thirty-Six Countries. New Haven: Yale University Press.
Lipset, Seymour M. (1959): Political Man: the Social Bases of Politics. London: Heinemann.
Listhaug, Ola/Wiberg, Matti (1995): Confidence in Political and Private Institutions. In: Klingemann, Hans Dieter/Fuchs, Dieter (Eds.): Citizen and the State. Beliefs in Government. Vol. 1. Oxford: Oxford University Press, 299–321.
McAllister, Ian (1999): The Economic Performance of Governments. In: Norris, Pippa (Ed.) 1999: Critical Citizens. Global Support for Democratic Governance. Oxford: Oxford University Press, 188–203.
Miller, Arthur H./Listhaug, Ola (1999): Political Performance and Political Trust. In: Norris, Pippa (Ed.) 1999: Critical Citizens. Global Support for Democratic Governance. Oxford: Oxford University Press, 204–216.
Newton, Kenneth (1999): Social and Political Trust in Established Democracies. In: Norris, Pippa (Ed.): Critical Citizens. Global Support for Democratic Governance. Oxford: Oxford University Press, 169–187.
Norris, Pippa (Ed.) (1999): Critical Citizens. Global Support for Democratic Governance. Oxford: Oxford University Press.
––––––– (2000): The Impact of Television on Civic Malaise. In: Pharr, Susan J./Putnam, Robert D. (Eds.): Disaffected Democracies. What's Troubling the Trilateral Countries. Princeton, N.J.: Princeton University Press, 231–251.
Pattie, Charles/Seyd, Patrick/Whiteley, Paul (2004): Citizenship in Britain. Values, Participation and Democracy. Cambridge: Cambridge University Press.
Putnam, Robert D. (1993): Making Democracy Work. Civic Traditions in Modern Italy. Princeton, NJ: Princeton University Press.
––––––– (2000): Bowling Alone. The Collapse and Revival of American Community. New York: Simon and Schuster.
Rahn, Wendy M./Rudolph, Thomas (2005): A Tale of Political Trust in American Cities. *Public Opinion Quarterly* 69: 530–560.
Stolle, Dietlind (2001): Clubs and Congregations: The Benefits of Joining an Association. In: Cook, Karen (Ed.): Trust in Society. New York: Russell Sage, 202–244.
Uslaner, Eric (2002): The Moral Foundations of Trust. Cambridge: Cambridge University Press.

van Deth, Jan W. (2004): Soziale Partizipation. In: van Deth, Jan W. (Ed.): Deutschland in Europa. Die Ergebnisse des European Social Survey 2002–2003. Wiesbaden: VS Verlag für Sozialwissenschaften, 295–315.
von Barrata, Mario (2002): Der Fischer Almanach. Frankfurt: Fischer.
Zmerli, Sonja/Newton, Kenneth/Montero, José Ramón (2007): Trust in People, Confidence in Political Institutions, and Satisfaction with Democracy, In: van Deth, Jan W./ Montero, José Ramón/Westholm, Anders (Eds.): Citizenship and Involvement in European Democracies. London/New York: Routledge, 35–65.

APPENDIX

Table 4: Description of ESS-Micro-Dataset

Variables	Comments
Political Trust	Additive index of the items: Trust in (country's) parliament (B7), Trust in the legal system (B8) and Trust in politicians (B10). Resulting index recoded to -1 (no trust) to 1 (complete trust).
Social Capital at the micro-level	
Formal participation in social activities	Participation or voluntary work in any of 12 organizations (E1–E12): recoded to 0 (no participation/voluntary work) to 1 (participation/voluntary work in all 12 organizations).
Informal participation in social activities	Informal participation in social activities: Proportion of respondents assessing themselves as more active than average people, recoded to 0 (much less than most), 0.25, 0.5, 0.75, 1 (much more than most).
Interpersonal trust	Interpersonal trust: Additive index of the items: Most people can be trusted (A8), Most people are fair (A9), Most people are helpful (A10). Resulting Index recoded to -1 (no trust) to 1 (complete trust).
Helping behavior	Proportion of respondents helping other people at least once a week (E20). Recoded to -1 (never) to 1 (every day).
Civic norms	Additive index of the items: Importance of supporting the worse (E22), Importance of forming an independent opinion (E25), Importance to be active in voluntary organizations (E 26), Importance to be active in politics (E27). Resulting index recoded to -1 (extremely unimportant) to 1 (extremely important).
Performance-related micro variables	
System performance	Satisfaction with economic system (B30), government (B31), democracy (B32), education system (B33) and health system (B34). Recoded to -1 (extremely dissatisfied) to 1 (extremely satisfied).

Table 4 (cont.)

Political responsiveness of politicians	Additive index of the items: Politicians in general care what people like you think (B5), Politicians are just interested in getting people's votes rather than in people's opinions. Recoded to −1 (no responsiveness) to +1 (complete responsiveness).

Control micro variables

Political involvement	Additive index of the items: Political Interest (B1). Recoded to: (no interest) to 1 (strong interest), Internal efficacy (additive index of the items B2-B4 recoded to −1 "no competence" to +1 "strong competence" and divided by the number of items included), and Importance of politics compared to other things in life (E16 subtracted from the values of an additive index of the items E13 to E19, recoded to a range of −1 "not at all important" to +1 "very important" and divided by the number of items included). Resulting index recoded to −1 (very weak) to 1 (very strong).
Frequency of political discussion	Discuss politics and current affairs (E21). Recoded to −1 (never) to 1 (regularly).
Strength of party identification	Feeling closer to a particular political party (B25c). Recoded to: 0 (no party identification) to 1 (strong party identification).
Political ideology	Placement on a scale, where 0 means left and 10 means right (B28). Recoded to −1 (left) to 1 (right).
Education	Highest level of education (F6). Recoded to 1 (lowest), 2 (middle), 3 (highest).
Age	Year born (F3). Recoded to 6 age classes.
Income	Household's total net income (F30). Recoded to income quartiles.
Media consumption	Additive index of the standardized items: Frequency of watching news about politics on TV (A2) and Frequency of reading news about politics in the newspaper (A6). Resulting index recoded to: 0 (no consumption) to 1 (daily consumption).

Source: ESS Micro Data 2002–2003.
Notes: Question wordings can be found on the ESS website: www.europeansocialscience.org.

Table 5: Description of ESS-Macro-Dataset (21 countries)

Variable	Comments	Mean	Stdv.	Range
Political Institutions:				
YEARS OF DEMOCRACY	Years of democratic regime since 1919	66,10	24,11	72
DCVEST	Post-communist democracies vs. established democracies; 0: Post-communist democracies: East Germany, Czech Republic, Hungary, Slovenia, Poland; Post-authoritarian and totalitarian: West Germany, Spain, Portugal, Greece, Germany; 1: Established democracies: Austria, Belgium, Denmark, Finland, France, Ireland, Italy, Luxembourg, The Netherlands, Norway, Sweden, Switzerland, United Kingdom	–	–	2
ENOP	Effective number of parties in parliament according to Laakso/Taagepera (1979) indicating the fractionalization of the party-system. The ENOP can be used as proxy for the degree of horizontal power-sharing 'consociationalism' (cf. Armingeon 2002). Mean value from 1992 to 2002. Source: Armingeon et al. 2004.	4,64	1,80	8,12
CORRUPTION	Lack of graft and corruption. The index ranges from –2,5 to 2,5. High values stand for good governance, lower values stand for bad governance. Source: Kaufmann et al. 1999	1,55	0,69	2,07
CONSENSUS	Consensus vs. majoritarian democratic systems. 0: majoritarian democracy (France, UK, Greece); 1: one dimension consensus democracy (Czech Republic, Denmark, Finland, Hungary, Ireland, Italy, Luxembourg, Norway, Poland, Portugal, Spain, Sweden); 2: consensus democracy (Austria, Belgium, Germany, Netherlands, Slovenia, Switzerland); classification according to Lijphart (1999), Ismayr (2002) and Bandelow (2005).	–	–	2
TURN	Voter turnout in each national election (parliamentary election), mean value of elections held from 1992 to 2002. Source: Armingeon et al. 2004.	72,65	12,56	48,10
WMNPAR	Percentage of women in parliaments for 2002; data are weighted according to the month of election. Note: In bicameral systems, data is taken for the lower house only. Source: Armingeon et al. 2004.	22,87	10,78	36,33

Table 5 (*cont.*)

Economic and Human Development:		Mean	Stdv.	Range
HDI	Human development index (HDI) 2002. The HDI is a summary measure of human development. It measures the average achievements in a country in three basic dimensions of human development; a long and healthy life, as measured by life expectancy at birth; knowledge, as measured by the adult literacy rate and the combined primary, secondary and tertiary gross enrolment ratio; a decent standard of living, as measured by GDP per capita (PPP US$); Source: UNDP 2003: Human Development Report 2003. In: http://hdr.undp.org/reports/global/2003/faq.html#21	0,92	0,03	0,11
GDPPCEXR	GDP (gross domestic product) per capita 2004, current prices, in $. The total output of goods and services for final use produced by an economy, by both residents and non-residents, regardless of the allocation to domestic and foreign claims. It does not include deductions for depreciations of physical capital or depletion and degradations of natural resources; PPP (purchasing power parity): A rate of exchange that accounts for price differences across countries, allowing international comparisons of real output and incomes. Source: IMF 2005: World Economic Outlook 2005. In: www.imf.org/external/pubs/ft/weo/2005/02/data/index.htm.	32371,09	15869,17	63392,5
GROWTH	GDP per capita annual growth rate 1990–99. Least squares annual growth rate, calculated from constant price GDP per capita in local currency units. Source: Armigeon et al. 2004.	2,09	1,37	6,20
INCOMEGINI	The Gini-index, as used in this paper, measures the degree of income inequality in a society. 0 stands for perfect equality and 1 stands for perfect inequality. The values are taken from the OECD Social, Employment and Migration Working Paper No. 22. Gini coefficients of income concentration in 27 OECD countries have been calculated for the most recent year. "Most recent year" refers to the year 2000 for all countries; 2001 for Germany, Luxembourg and Switzerland; and 2002 for the Czech Republic. In the case of Belgium and Spain, the data refer to 1995. Source: www.oecd.org/dataoecd/48/9/34483698.pdf	0,29	0,04	0,14

Table 5 (cont.)

UNEMPLO	Harmonized unemployment rate, mean value 1998–2005. Calculated from EUROSTAT DATA BASE (epp.eurostat.cec.eu.int/portal/) and IMF 2005: World Economic Outlook. In: www.imf.org/external/pubs/ft/weo/2005/02/data/index.htm	7,05	3,45	14,03

Cultural fragmentation:		Mean	Stdv.	Range
ETHNHOMO	Ethnic homogeneity index ranges from 0 to 1 and is calculated from the seven largest ethnic groups. The index is the sum of the squared population fractions. High values indicate ethnic homogeneity; lower values indicate ethnic heterogeneity. Values calculated for the most recent year from von Barrata 2002.	0,82	0,18	0,60
RELHOMO	Religious homogeneity index (ranges from 0 to 1) calculated from the seven largest religious groups. The index is the sum of the squared religious fractions. High values indicate religious homogeneity; lower values indicate religious heterogeneity. Source: United States Naval Academy Genocide and Politicide Model Data (Phase III: 1955–1999). In: www.cidcm.umd.edu/inscr/genocide.	0,75	0,23	0,58
PROTPER	Percentage of Protestants in the mid 1970s, values calculated from Barrett 1982.	0,27	0,36	0,10

Social Capital:		Mean	Stdv.	Range
FORMALPART (without Switzerland Czech Republic)	Formal participation in social activities, country based mean value. Recoded to 0 (no participation/voluntary work) to 1 (participation/voluntary work in all 12 organizations). Source: ESS, Wave 1, 2002–2003.	0,05	0,02	0,06
INFORMALPART (without Switzerland Czech Republic)	Informal participation in social activities, country based mean value. Recoded to 0 (much less than most), 0.25, 0.5, 0.75, 1 (much more than most). Source: ESS, Wave 1, 2002–2003.	0,43	0,04	0,14
INTERTRUST	Interpersonal trust, country based mean value. Recoded to −1 (no trust) to 1 (complete trust). Source: ESS, Wave 1, 2002–2003.	0,01	0,19	0,68

Table 5 (cont.)

HELPBEHAVIOR (without Switzerland & Czech Republic)	Helping behavior, country based mean value. Recoded to −1 (never) to 1 (every day). Source: ESS, Wave 1, 2002–2003.	−0,12	0,17	0,59
CIVICNORMS	Civic norms and virtues, country based mean value. Recoded to −1 (extremely unimportant) to 1 (extremely important). Source: ESS, Wave 1, 2002–2003.	0,40	0,09	0,33

CHAPTER NINE

EXPLAINING LEVEL AND EQUALITY OF POLITICAL PARTICIPATION
THE ROLE OF SOCIAL CAPITAL, SOCIOECONOMIC MODERNITY, AND POLITICAL INSTITUTIONS

Edeltraud Roller and Tatjana Rudi[1]

In a democracy, participation of citizens in the political process is essential, and this participation should be equal among citizens (Dahl 1989). The most basic form of political participation is voting. By voting, the people select their representatives who authoritatively decide on collective matters. Through activities beyond voting such as contacting politicians or attending demonstrations, citizens communicate information about their preferences to political authorities and put pressure on them to act accordingly to their interests. Participation should be as equal as possible because an equal consideration of preferences and interests is a basic principle of democracy. If participation is unequal and biased in favor of citizens with higher socioeconomic resources, as previous studies suggest, this will lead "to a distortion of the...preferences of citizens as they are communicated into the political process", and this might result in policy making in favor of privileged citizens (Verba 2003: 663). Due to its significance, low levels of participation as well as high levels of socioeconomic inequality of participation are interpreted as symptoms of a crisis of democracy.

The prominence of and interest in political participation is responsible for the fact that participation research started very early and is one of the most-developed fields in political science. It carries a large stock of well-founded and well-proven theories. These theories attempt to explain political participation either at the individual-level or at the system-level. The Civic Voluntarism Model (CVM), the most famous and well-developed individual-level theory introduced by Verba, Schlozman, and Brady (1995), explains political participation through individual resources such as education, political engagement such as

---

[1] The authors greatly acknowledge the statistical advice of Markus Klein.

political interest, and personal networks such as voluntary organizations. System-level theories like modernization theory and institutionalist theory stress either national socioeconomic resources (e.g. wealth, education) or political institutions (e.g. electoral and governmental systems) as determinants of political participation. Beyond these single theories, several overarching theoretical models have been formulated integrating both types of theories by conceptualizing system-level characteristics as the context of individual political participation (Barnes, Kaase et al. 1979: 43; Norris 2002: 20). Such comprehensive, multi-level models explain political participation, for example, through resources and motivation at the individual-level, whereas the context consists of mobilizing agencies, societal modernization, and the structure of the state.

While theoretical political participation research is well-developed and encompasses multi-level models, empirical research clearly lags behind. It collapses into two strands. On the one hand, individual-level theories are examined on the basis of national and comparative population surveys (Verba, Nie, and Kim 1978; Barnes, Kaase et al. 1979; Parry, Moyser, and Day 1992; Verba et al. 1995; Roller and Wessels 1996; Wessels 2002; Pattie, Seyd, and Whiteley 2004; Gabriel 2004). On the other hand, the influence of system-level characteristics on national levels of political participation is studied using aggregate-data (Franklin 2004; Norris 2002; Roller and Wessels 1996). Both research designs suffer from drawbacks. The main drawback of survey research has been described as the atomization of citizens by disregarding the context of political participation. Aggregate-data analysis, otherwise, suffers from an ecological fallacy if system-level relationships were explained by individual-level mechanisms. Consequently, theory testing currently stays incomplete. It remains an open question whether system-level theories contribute to the explanation of individual political participation or whether individual-level theories are sufficient. For an adequate testing of comprehensive, multi-level models of political participation, research designs are required to include individual-level as well as system-level determinants of political participation *and* at the same time, to take into account that these predictors are located at different levels of the political system. Multi-level analysis is the most appropriate method that can fulfill these criteria (Steenbergen and Jones 2002; Klein 2002).

In this paper, we will conduct such a multi-level analysis of political participation for European countries. We will analyze two forms of political participation: *voting* as the most basic form of political participation and *activities beyond voting* covering conventional activities such as contacting politicians and unconventional activities like attending demonstrations (Verba, Nie, and Kim 1978; Barnes, Kaase et al. 1979; Topf 1995a, 1995b).[2] Theoretical and empirical reasons can be used to explain this differentiation. Voting has been described as "unique among political acts" (Verba et al. 1995: 360). It is the simplest, regularized and institutionalized mode of participation conveying only low information about the citizen's preferences and interests to the representatives (Verba et al. 1995: 48). Activities beyond voting are more intensive, time-consuming, and less institutionalized. They are, above all, issue-specific forms of political participation involving high or at least mixed information for the addressees of political action. Due to its issue-specificity, activities beyond voting are more episodic and irregular and they mobilize different groups of people. Finally, previous studies have shown that socioeconomic inequality is higher in those activities beyond voting, compared with voting (Kaase 1981; Lijphart 1999).

In the following, we will speak of electoral and non-electoral participation instead of voting and activities beyond voting, in order to simplify matters. This might involve a partial misrepresentation because the modes of political participation beyond voting, such as contacting politicians or attending demonstrations, can take place within the context of elections.

For specification of the multi-level model, we rely on the most prominent and well-developed theories of political participation. This includes the CVM as an individual-level theory on the one hand, and modernization theory and institutionalist theory as system-level theories, on the other. Additionally, we take into account the concept of social capital, as suggested by Robert Putnam (1993). This is due to the fact that it has been established as a further theory of political participation (Gabriel et al. 2002; Kaase 1999; Pattie, Seyd, and Whiteley 2004) that is applicable on both levels. Conceptually, social capital operates on the individual-level as a relational resource and on the aggregate-level as system capital (Esser 2000; Gabriel et al. 2002). By applying the social capital concept to political participation, we will test whether it displays an independent explanatory power, as the advocates of social capital theory assert.

---

[2] The analysis is limited to legal modes of political participation. It is not only that illegal modes of participation, such as unofficial strikes or occupation of buildings, appear rarely; empirically it has been demonstrated that this mode of participation behaves differently (Fuchs 1991; Roller and Wessels 1996).

A distinctive feature of our analysis is that we do not only study whether this multi-level model is successful in explaining the level of political participation, i.e. if someone takes part in politics. Additionally, we analyze the socioeconomic inequality of political participation, i.e. whether participation is biased in favor of citizens with higher socioeconomic resources. We ask whether this multi-level model can also explain the cross-national differences in equality of political participation in Europe. More specifically, we are going to examine the following questions.

(1) How successful are individual-level theories in explaining electoral and non-electoral participation in Europe? Do further differences between nations exist, and if they do, which country factors are responsible for these differences? Are national differences simply the result of composition effects, i.e. the effect of different national population structures, or are system-level factors—social (system) capital, socioeconomic modernization, or political institutions—responsible for these differences? References to composition effects, which is nothing more than an explanation of country differences with the distribution of individual characteristics (e.g. education), has been very popular in comparative participation research (Barnes, Kaase et al. 1979), but the exact size of this effect has not yet been determined neither for electoral nor for non-electoral participation.

(2) Is socioeconomic inequality higher for non-electoral participation compared with electoral participation? Do European countries show the same degree of inequality of political participation or do they differ? If they do differ, could these different conversion rates of socioeconomic resources into political participation be explained by contextual factors, in particular by social (system) capital, socioeconomic modernization, or political institutions? To our knowledge, Verba, Nie, and Kim, in their classic seven-nation study *Participation and Equality* (1978), have been the first and only scholars that tried to explain national degrees of socioeconomic inequality of political participation. However, their analyses fell short due to the lack of sophisticated statistical methods and a simple theoretical model testable.

By applying the same multi-level model to electoral as well as non-electoral participation, we can describe commonalities and differences regarding these fundamental modes of participation. Moreover, to our knowledge, it is the first time that the question of whether the same system-level factors can explain cross-national differences in the level as well as in the equality of electoral and non-electoral participation is analyzed. In technical terms, it is the first time that the same system-level factors are applied to explain the *intercept* of individual-level regression analyses of electoral and non-electoral participation (question 1), as well as the *slope* of socioeconomic resources on electoral and non-electoral participation (question 2).

The paper is organized as follows. The first section focuses on individual-level models of political participation. It combines determinants specified by the classic CVM with factors described by social capital theory. The second section is devoted to the contextual factors (socioeconomic modernization, political institutions and social system capital) and the specification of a multi-level model of political participation. The aim of both sections is to state hypotheses that explain the level as well as the socioeconomic inequality of electoral and non-electoral participation. The individual-level and multi-level empirical analyses are presented in the third section. The paper concludes with a summary and a discussion of the empirical results.

The empirical analysis is based on nineteen European countries, sixteen Western and three Central and Eastern European countries, included in the first wave of the *European Social Survey* (ESS) conducted in 2002/03. It covers Austria, Belgium, Denmark, Finland, France, Germany, Greece, Hungary, Ireland, Italy, Luxembourg, the Netherlands, Norway, Poland, Portugal, Slovenia, Spain, Sweden, and the United Kingdom. Switzerland and the Czech Republic could not be included in the analysis due to missing data. The empirical analysis is limited to eligible respondents (18 years and older, nationality).

1. Individual-level Model of Political Participation

The individual-level model of political participation combines the CVM developed by Verba et al. (1995) with the concept of social capital by Putnam (1993). The former is the most-developed traditional approach to political participation, whilst the latter is a rather new approach to explain political participation.

According to the CVM, political participation can be explained by three factors: resources, political engagement, and networks of recruitment. Firstly, resources refer to time, money and civic skills such as communication and organizational abilities. While time is a precondition for political participation, money is required for some forms of participation (contribution to campaigns), and civic skills allow time and money to be used effectively. Resources represent the *capacity* dimension of political participation (Verba et al. 1995: 3, 15–16, 304). Secondly, political or psychological engagement refers to predispositions such as political interest, political efficacy, political information, and partisanship (or strength of party identification). Psychological engagement works through *motivation* to take part in politics (Verba et al. 1995: 3, 334, 345). Thirdly, networks of recruitment *mobilize* citizens to participate. Requests for political activity mainly take place on the job and in voluntary associations (Verba et al. 1995: 3, 369).

The CVM is an extension of the classic standard socioeconomic status (SES) model of political activity (Verba and Nie 1972) with levels of education, income, and occupation as the main factors. This standard model proves to be empirically powerful, it shows that people "who are advantaged in socioeconomic terms...are more likely to be politically active" (Verba et al. 1995: 19). Its major drawback has been its theoretical weakness. According to the authors themselves, the later CVM "provides a richer theoretical interpretation of the SES model by specifying in detail how socioeconomic position is linked to political activity" (Verba et al. 1995: 19).

Apparently, education and occupation, the main components of the socioeconomic standard model, which are vital for the question of socioeconomic inequality of political participation, are missing in the described CVM. Verba et al. (1995: 367) argue that socioeconomic attributes such as educational attainment and occupation work especially through time, money, and civic skills. They understand time, money, and civic skills as general resources that are derived from the socioeconomic position of citizens. Consequently, education and occupation can be inserted as resource dimensions into the CVM.

Social capital theory puts forward similar and supplementary individual-level characteristics in explaining political participation. According to Putnam's often-cited definition (1993: 167), social capital "refers to features of social organization, such as trust, norms, and networks that can improve the efficiency of society by facilitating coordinated action." Consequently, political participation can be explained by three factors: by one structural dimension, namely networks, and by attitudinal or cultural dimensions, namely trust and norms. *Networks* refer to a subset of social relations that are characterized by regular interactions. They include engagement in formal or voluntary organizations, informal networks like families and friends, as well as networks at the workplace. What they all have in common is that they mobilize for political participation. *Social trust*, defined as trust in other people, is assumed to be a stable attitude. Thus, it is independent from specific situations and persons and it is acquired during socialization. According to the social capital concept, social trust facilitates social cooperation by reducing transaction costs. Hence, it can be suggested that social trust promotes political participation. *Norms*, in general, refer to rules of behavior. The norm of reciprocity, for example, implies that an individual is willing to do another individual a favor, without expecting an immediate return. This norm of reciprocity, very prominent in Putnam's concept (1993), is difficult to apply to political participation. Political norms, such as being active in politics and in public, discussed under the notion of norms of citizenship (van Deth 2007; Rossteutscher 2004), are used instead.

There is an overlap between the social capital concept and the CVM. Networks, on the one hand, are clearly part of both models. Political norms, on the other hand, are also included in both models but with different emphasis. While they are prominent in social capital theory, they are only mentioned as one political engagement variable in the CVM (Verba et al. 1995: 272) and play no significant role. Social trust is the decisive component of the social capital concept when explaining political participation. As far as the question is concerned, whether social capital is able to contribute independently to the explanation of political participation, social trust—sometimes described as the core of the social capital concept (Paldam and Svendsen 2000; Whiteley 2000)—is essential. Additionally, we ascribe political norms to social capital theory, because of its peripheral role in the CVM. Finally, socioeconomic resources and political engagement as determinants of political participation are original contributions from the CVM.

By combining both individual-level theories of political participation, we obtain an individual-level model of political participation with five factors: socioeconomic resources, political engagement, personal networks, political norms, and social trust (see second part of Figure 1). Similar to the CVM, this integrated model claims to be a general model in so far as it is applicable to all modes of political participation; though the importance of single factors might vary with the mode of participation at hand. Socioeconomic resources are the factor that we are most interested in; its effect on political participation indicates the degree of socioeconomic inequality of political participation. Based on previous research, we expect to find a higher effect of socioeconomic resources in the case of non-electoral participation compared to electoral participation. However, we will proceed further by testing whether these effects (technically, slopes) vary across nations and whether social (system) capital, socioeconomic modernization, and political institutions are of relevance here.

2. Multi-level Model of Political Participation

System-level factors constitute the context of individual political participation. Before we describe the three relevant theories regarding this level—the theories of socioeconomic modernization, political institutions, and social (system) capital—and combine them with the individual-level model to become a multi-level model of political participation, we first have to discuss the concept of context.

According to basic concepts of contextual analysis (Huckfeld and Sprague 1993), two different contexts of political participation can be separated: the *individual* organizational context, which refers to effects that arise due to social interaction within an environment, and the *national* political and socioeconomic context, which refers to factors beyond the individual. In earlier work, we have defined the former as the close context and the latter as the wide context of political participation (Roller and Wessels 1996: 92). Applying this analytical distinction to the various theories of political participation, we can see that the CVM as well as the (individual) social capital concept, have adopted the close context by including the network component with its mobilizing effect. Logically, this raises the question of whether the individual-level model described in the last section is rather a multi-level model, integrating individual and contextual elements, than a one-dimensional model. Nevertheless, there is a clear-cut answer to this question. The CVM and the described social capital theory are individual-level theories because they conceptualize the close context as personal networks of the citizens, or—in other words—as individual relational characteristics. Hence, the individual-level model includes two different kinds of individual characteristics: relational and non-relational ones.

Socioeconomic modernization, political institutions, and social (system) capital constitute the national or wider context of political participation. In the following, we will discuss these three components and their effects on political participation. First and foremost, these theories identify factors conducive to the level of political participation (technically, the intercept). These factors, however, can be used as well for the explanation of socioeconomic equality of political participation (technically, the slope) because, as Lijphart (1997) suggested, equality of participation increases with the level of political participation.

The relationship between *socioeconomic modernization* and participation is a long-standing topic in political science. It is an essential component in the theories of Lipset (1981), Deutsch (1961), Bell (1974) and others. According to these theories, high levels of socioeconomic development promote not only the institutionalization of democracies, but at the same time, the use of various forms of political participation. The socioeconomic variables and the mechanisms described by these theories are multifaceted. Generally, the socioeconomic resources of wealth and education are regarded as the most relevant variables for political participation (Norris 2002). Conceptually, they can be interpreted as system-level equivalents of individual socioeconomic resources addressed in the CVM.

Theoretically, the role of *political institutions* regarding political participation is defined by the opportunity structures that enable or limit the possibilities for citizens to engage in politics. Authors have suggested different types of political institutions influencing political participation. They can be classified into two groups: specific institutions relevant for specific modes of participation, and general institutional settings relevant for all modes of political participation. The first category can only be applied to electoral participation because non-electoral participation includes various modes of action. Different characteristics of electoral systems have been suggested as the relevant institutional context, above all compulsory voting and the proportionality of electoral systems (Franklin 2004; Lijphart 1997; Norris 2002). Why compulsory voting should increase the level and equality of voting practices is simple and self-evident. The effect of proportional compared to majoritarian electoral systems, however, is much more indirect. Generally, it is assumed that, regarding proportional electoral systems, the lack of "wasted votes" stimulates citizens to cast their ballot (Norris 2002: 64–66). Hence, the level and equality of voting should increase with the proportionality of the electoral system.

While electoral systems constitute a specific participatory institution, the governmental system characterizes the general institutional setting of a country. As far as the governmental system is concerned, the type of democracy (Lijphart 1999), whether it be a majoritarian or a consensus democracy, is *the* institutional dimension thought to influence political participation. Majoritarian and consensus democracy differ with respect to the distribution of power. While majoritarian democracies, like the Westminster model, concentrate power, consensus democracies like the system implemented in Switzerland, distribute power. It was Lijphart (1999) who claimed that consensus democracies are superior to majoritarian democracies as far as democratic quality is concerned. He coined the phrase of "kinder and gentler qualities" of consensus democracies and studied voter turnout as one dimension of democratic quality. He explained the higher turnout level of consensus democracies by referring to the general aim of these democracies, more specifically, he assumed that the aim "to include as many people as possible" has mobilizing effects (Lijphart 1999: 2). In principle, this argument can be generalized to all activities beyond voting. Finally, although Lijphart studied only turnout levels he argued that this result is also relevant regarding the equality of participation because high turnout levels indicate equality of participation.

Empirically, Lijphart (1999) differentiates between two types of consensus democracies: consensus democracy with respect to the executive-parties dimension and the federalist-unitary dimension. While the first dimension refers to the diffusion of power *within* institutions, such as parliaments and governments (joint-responsibility or joint-power dimension), the second dimension refers to the diffusion of power *between* institutions, such as bicameralism or federalism (divided-responsibility or divided-power dimension). According to his empirical analysis, only the first dimension revealed a clear relationship with voting turnout. Theoretically, however, his argument for better democratic quality refers to the second dimension as well.

To conclude, three political institutions are suggested to be relevant for political participation. It is assumed that the level and equality of electoral and non-electoral participation is higher in consensus democracies. In the case of electoral participation, the specific institutions of compulsory voting and proportional electoral systems are added. Hence, political scientists will strongly agree that the power-distributing institutions of consensus democracies and proportional electoral systems, promote the level and equality of political participation.

Social capital theory rests upon the assumption that different forms of social capital, social trust, norms, and personal networks, do not only constitute individual or relational resources of citizens that facilitate the achievement of goals. Social capital also operates at the aggregate-level in the form of system capital. As a system characteristic, defined by the national levels of social trust, norms and networks, it constitutes a type of collective good. Societies with high levels of social capital

```
┌─────────────────────────────────────────┐
│  Socioeconomic modernization            │
├─────────────────────────────────────────┤
│  Compulsory voting*/Proportional        │
│  electoral system*                      │
│  Consensus democracy                    │
├─────────────────────────────────────────┤
│  Social (system) capital                │
└─────────────────────────────────────────┘
- - - - - - - - - - - - - - - - - - - - - -
┌─────────────────────────────────────────┐
│  Socioeconomic resources                │
├─────────────────────────────────────────┤
│  Political engagement                   │
├─────────────────────────────────────────┤
│  Personal networks                      │         ┌──────────────────────┐
├─────────────────────────────────────────┤  ───►   │ Electoral and        │
│  Political norms                        │         │ non-electoral        │
├─────────────────────────────────────────┤         │ participation        │
│  Social trust                           │         └──────────────────────┘
└─────────────────────────────────────────┘
```

*Electoral participation only.

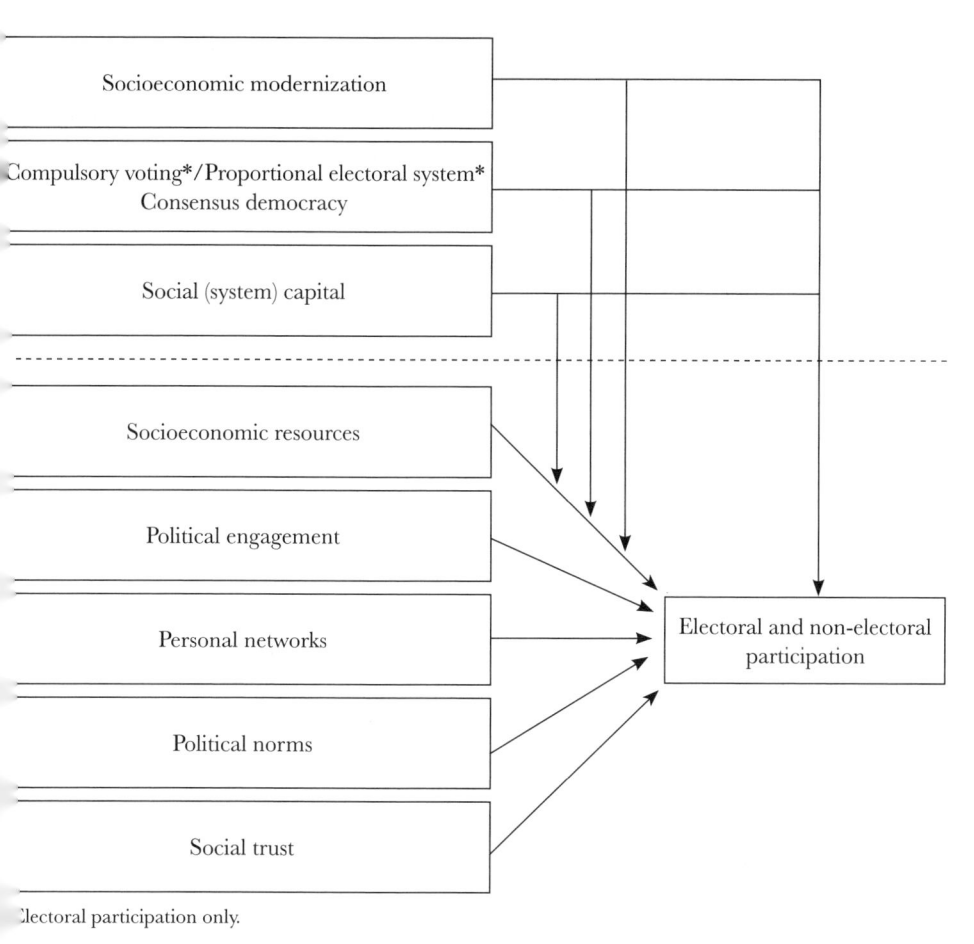

Figure 1: Multi-level model of political participation

are characterized by consistently lower transaction costs compared to societies with low levels of social capital. Applying this logic to political participation, lower transaction costs might help increase the level of political participation and furthermore, it might help citizens with low levels of socioeconomic resources to overcome these shortfalls, thereby promoting socioeconomic equality.

Figure 1 presents the multi-level model of political participation that we will test empirically. The individual-level factors are in the lower half of the graph and the system-level factors are in the upper half. On the system-level, socioeconomic modernization, consensus democracy, and social (system) capital are introduced as factors that explain the cross-national differences in the levels of electoral and non-electoral participation. In the case of electoral participation, the two institutional mechanisms of electoral systems—compulsory voting and proportional electoral systems—are added. It is assumed that these five contextual factors are not only responsible for cross-national differences regarding levels of participation (intercept), but that they also explain varying conversion rates of socioeconomic resources into political participation (slope). More specifically, high levels of socioeconomic modernization, consensus democracy, and social (system) capital, as well as compulsory voting and proportional electoral systems in the case of electoral participation, are assigned to be capable to compensate for low individual-level resources, i.e. to reduce the individual-level effect of socioeconomic resources on political participation.

3. Empirical Analysis

The empirical analysis begins with the measurement and distribution of the two dependent variables: electoral and non-electoral participation. Subsequently, the individual-level and then the multi-level models of political participation are estimated. The presentation of each model begins with a description of the measurement of the respective independent variables.

Voting or electoral participation is measured by asking whether citizens voted in the last national (parliamentary) election or not. Non-electoral participation covers four modes of political participation: contacting a politician, government, or local government official; working in a political party or an action group; signing a petition; and taking part in a lawful public demonstration (for a detailed documentation, see Table A1 in the Appendix). The respondents were asked for every mode whether they have done this activity during the last 12 months. Applying the conceptual distinction suggested by *Political Action* (Barnes, Kaase et al. 1979), the first two modes represent conventional forms of political participation while the other two represent forms of unconventional participation. Regarding the dependent variables, two issues have to be discussed: the dimensionality, and the construction of the index of non-electoral participation.

There is clear empirical evidence that voting, and the four modes beyond voting, constitute two separate dimensions. Firstly, a pooled exploratory factor analysis (with equal weighting of the national samples) compromising all five modes of participation, extracts one factor, but the factor loading of voting is rather low (0.24). Secondly, in a confirmatory factor analysis, the differentiation between the two factors can be validated. The conventional forms of political participation (contacting politicians, party work) show also distinct loadings on the voting factor, however with 0.40 and 0.30, they are relatively low. The blurring of the difference between conventional and unconventional political participation is an already well-known fact, documented by previous research (Fuchs 1991).

The index of non-electoral participation is based on a dichotomous variable measuring whether respondents did not take part in any of the four modes or whether they took part in at least one of the four modes of participation. The idea of this construction is to get some control over the "episodic and irregular form" (Brady 1999: 764) of the modes of participation beyond voting. An alternative summary index, often used in participation research (Verba et al. 1995: 761), is much more sensitive to situation-specific variations. Based on this dichotomized index, we do not explain the number of non-electoral modes of participation undertaken by the respondents during the last 12 months (summary index), but rather whether non-electoral participation is practiced at all. A further, technical advantage of this index is the fact that the same statistical method, logistic regression, can be applied to explain electoral as well as non-electoral participation. Thus, the statistical models for the two participatory dimensions can be compared directly.

The distributions of electoral and non-electoral participation rates present rather different patterns (Figure 2). Firstly, the dimensions differ with respect to the national levels. Voting as the easiest, regularized and standardized mode of participation, is practiced on average by a clear majority of 84 percent of European citizens. Denmark shows the highest voting turnout covering almost all citizens (95 %), and Poland indicates the lowest turnout rate (67 %).[3] By contrast, the

---

[3] The validity of the voting information conducted by the *European Social Survey* is rather high. The correlation between survey data and objective turnout rates amounts to 0.91 (Pearson's r). With the exception of Belgium and Luxembourg, two countries with compulsory voting, the survey data reveal a higher turnout rate. The well-known bias of population samples towards political interested respondents and the desirability of the question could explain this pattern. Objective turnout rates refer to the last national parliamentary election; calculated on the basis of election data collected by the research unit "Democracy: Structure, Performance, Challenges" of the Wissenschaftszentrum Berlin für Sozialforschung (WZB).

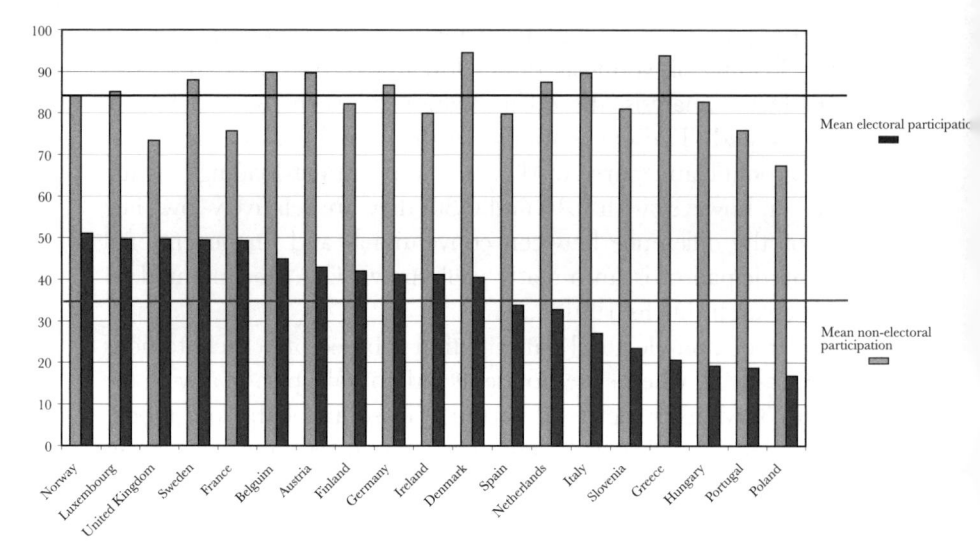

Figure 2: National levels of electoral and non-electoral participation in Europe 2002/03 (in %)

more intensive, time-consuming, and less institutionalized forms of non-electoral participation are practiced by slightly more than a third, namely 37 percent of European citizens. In this case, Norway displays the highest rate with a narrow majority (51 %) practicing non-electoral forms of participation. Poland indicates the lowest rate with only 17 percent. Within the non-electoral forms, signing a petition is the most popular and easiest mode (practiced by 24 % of European citizens), followed by contacting politicians (17 %), taking part in demonstrations (8 %), and, finally, by working in a party or an action group (5 %) [data not presented]. Secondly, the variation between countries is clearly higher for non-electoral compared to electoral participation (measures of variance score 146 for non-electoral and 51 for electoral participation; data not presented).

Thirdly, both participation dimensions differ with respect to the ranking of the countries, similarities in the ranking are rather low. Regarding non-electoral participation, it is striking that the new democracies of Central and Eastern Europe (Slovenia, Hungary, and Poland) as well as Southern European countries (Spain, Italy, Greece, and Portugal) show rates below average, whilst in the case of voting two of these countries, Italy and Greece, belong to the group with above-average turnout rates. This is a first sign that different system-level factors are relevant regarding electoral and non-electoral participation. In the case of non-electoral participation the level of socioeconomic modernization is an obvious factor, while in the case of electoral participation compulsory voting suggests itself because Greece has implemented such a system.

3.1 Individual-level Analysis

As far as the components of the CVM are concerned, *socioeconomic resources* can only be measured by the highest level of education achieved (for a detailed documentation, see Table A1). Due to significant missing data in some countries, income as the second most important socio-economic resource cannot be incorporated into the model. *Political engagement* is differentiated into three concepts: party attachment, political interest, and political efficacy. We focus on measures of internal efficacy (or subjective political competence) such as evaluations of personal skills needed to understand politics or take an active role in a group involved with political issues.[4] Finally, *personal networks* are measured by an index including membership in ten voluntary organizations. These organizations cover a broad range of social, cultural, religious, professional, humanitarian, and environmental organizations (and exclude political parties, due to its close relationship to political participation). As in the case of non-electoral participation, a dichotomous index is constructed. It separates respondents with no membership in any of these organizations, from those who are members of at least one of these ten organizations. We begin with the premise that it is not the number of individual organizational memberships that matter for mobilization but rather whether any organizational memberships exist.

The remaining variables of social capital theory, political norms and social trust, are measured by means indices. The index of *political norms* is based on the importance of different forms of political participation and engagement (vote in elections, active in voluntary organizations, active in politics), law abidingness (always obey laws and regulations), solidarity (support people worse off), and political autonomy (form independent opinions). The index of *social trust* includes evaluations of

---

[4] We do not take into account external political efficacy measures (evaluations of politicians, for example, whether they take care about what the people think). External political efficacy—or system responsiveness—involves evaluations of the political actors and the political system and by that it is rather a measure of political support than of individual political engagement.

Table 1: Individual-level model of electoral and non-electoral participation[a]

	Electoral participation		Non-electoral participation	
	Unstandardized logit coefficient	Standardized logit coefficient	Unstandardized logit coefficient	Standardized logit coefficient
Education	0.03**	0.12	0.18***	0.57
	(0.01)		(0.01)	
Party attachment	0.28***	1.13	0.11***	0.34
	(0.01)		(0.01)	
Political interest	0.36***	0.88	0.27***	0.51
	(0.03)		(0.02)	
Internal political efficacy	0.09***	0.22	0.29***	0.55
	(0.03)		(0.02)	
Personal networks	0.33***	0.44	0.76***	0.78
	(0.04)		(0.03)	
Political norms	0.24***	0.94	0.02*	0.06
	(0.01)		(0.01)	
Social trust	0.02*	0.11	0.02***	0.08
	(0.01)		(0.01)	
Constant	−1.74***		−3.40***	
	(0.08)		(0.07)	
Nagelkerke R^2	0.15		0.18	
N	31424		32253	

*** $p \leq 0.001$; ** $p \leq 0.01$; * $p \leq 0.05$
a Pooled logistic regression with equalizing of weighted national samples; robust standard errors brackets.

three different aspects: most people can be trusted, most people try to be fair, and most of the people are helpful.[5] All indicators are coded in the same manner; low values indicate low levels and high values indicate high levels regarding the respective characteristic (e.g. low and high levels of political interest).

The results of the pooled logistic regression analyses for electoral and non-electoral participation are displayed in Table 1. To begin with, the results demonstrate that the individual-level model combining the CVM with the social capital concept is in fact a general model that is applicable to both, electoral and non-electoral participation. In both cases, all of the suggested factors show significant regression coefficients, and the models can explain 15 percent (electoral participation) or 18 percent

---

[5] We focus on social trust and exclude political trust because it is rather a component of political support than a form of social capital (Fuchs, Gabriel, and Völkl 2002).

(non-electoral participation) of the variance. The actual strength of these single factors, however, varies with the type of political participation. In the case of electoral participation, the effects of party attachment, political interest, and political norms are more important, while in the case of non-electoral participation, the effects of education, internal political efficacy, and personal networks are stronger. This pattern coincides with the different attributes of electoral and non-electoral forms of political participation described in the introduction: Voting is about the selection of parties, hence it is promoted by party attachment; it is not issue-specific and thus calls for general political interest; it constitutes the basic form of political participation and is, therefore, supported by political norms. In contrast, non-electoral participation is an irregular, non-standardized, costly and difficult mode of political participation. It, therefore, deserves more socioeconomic resources, internal political efficacy, and personal networks.

According to the empirical results, social capital theory contributes to the explanation of political participation. The structural component of social capital, namely networks, is the most important factor. This factor, however, is already included in the CVM. As far as the two additional cultural forms of social capital are concerned, only political norms have a considerable effect. However, its effect is limited to electoral participation. Finally, the effect of social trust, the core variable of social capital theory, is rather low for electoral and non-electoral participation (for similar British results, see Pattie et al. 2004: 195). Thus, social trust does not play *the* significant role in explaining political participation, as could have been expected of social capital theory. Nevertheless, the components of social capital might operate as a system-level factor.

Before we present the results of the multi-level analysis, we have to take a closer look at the individual-level effect of education, i.e. the socioeconomic inequality of political participation. We are interested in two questions; is socioeconomic inequality higher for non-electoral compared to electoral participation, and do the European countries have the same degree of socioeconomic inequality of political participation? Firstly, the expectation that socioeconomic inequality is higher in non-electoral participation seems to be confirmed by the data. According to the pooled logistic regressions (cf. Table 1), there is almost no effect of education on electoral participation ($b = 0.03$), whilst a remarkable effect exists for non-electoral participation ($b = 0.18$). The country-level regression analyses (Table 2; columns "unstandardized logit coefficient"), however, demonstrate that this is not a universal pattern occurring in

Table 2: Equality of electoral and non-electoral participation and explained variance of the individual-level models

	Electoral participation Effect of education			Non-electoral participation Effect of education		
	Unstandardized logit coefficient[a]	Change in probablities[b]	Nagelkerke R^2	Unstandardized logit coefficient[a]	Change in probablities[b]	Nagelkerke R^2
Austria	0.12	0.04	0.25	0.21***	0.30	0.20
Belgium	0.08	0.04	0.08	0.24***	0.34	0.17
Denmark	0.07	0.01	0.16	0.22***	0.30	0.09
Finland	0.09	0.06	0.18	0.23***	0.32	0.15
France	−0.14**	−0.14	0.19	0.15***	0.22	0.18
Germany	0.47***	0.19	0.27	0.22***	0.26	0.12
Greece	−0.25***	−0.09	0.07	0.07	0.06	0.16
Hungary	0.22***	0.14	0.20	0.15**	0.12	0.19
Ireland	0.06	0.05	0.12	0.15***	0.21	0.13
Italy	0.23	0.08	0.14	0.23***	0.26	0.29
Luxembourg	0.16	0.10	0.08	0.14**	0.20	0.15
Netherlands	0.13*	0.06	0.21	0.19***	0.24	0.14
Norway	0.20**	0.14	0.19	0.20***	0.29	0.11
Poland	0.10**	0.12	0.14	0.18***	0.13	0.24
Portugal	0.003	0.003	0.20	0.11	0.08	0.33
Slovenia	0.17**	0.12	0.14	0.10	0.08	0.18
Spain	−0.15**	−0.13	0.18	0.29***	0.38	0.27
Sweden	0.09	0.04	0.19	0.08**	0.12	0.13
United Kingdom	−0.01	−0.01	0.23	0.17***	0.26	0.13
All countries	0.03**	0.02	0.15	0.18***	0.24	0.18

*** $p \leq 0.001$; ** $p \leq 0.01$; * $p \leq 0.05$
a Unstandardized logit coefficient measuring the effect of education on political participation, controlling for other factors (see Table 1).
b Discrete change in the probabilities of political participation when education changes from the minimum to the maximum level, holding all other factors constant at their mean.

all European countries, but rather a dominant pattern. There are four countries—Germany, Hungary, Luxembourg, and Slovenia—where socioeconomic inequality is higher for electoral participation. Secondly, as far as socioeconomic inequality of both forms of participation is concerned, the country-level analyses illustrate big differences between the national samples. In the case of electoral participation, there are six countries demonstrating significant positive effects of education (Germany, Hungary, the Netherlands, Norway, Poland, and Slovenia) and ten countries without any significant effect (Austria, Belgium, Denmark, Finland, Ireland, Italy, Luxembourg, Portugal, Sweden, and the United Kingdom). Additionally, in three countries education has significant negative effects (France, Greece, and Spain) indicating inequality in favor of less educated citizens. This reverse type of inequality is well-documented and well-known (Topf 1995a; Lijphart 1997). In the case of non-electoral participation, all national regression coefficients are positive, indicating only the expected form of inequality in favor of the higher educated. Although, the conversion rates of education clearly differ between the countries, ranging between 0.07 in Greece to 0.29 in Spain. Remarkably, there are altogether three countries (Greece, Portugal, and Slovenia) without any significant levels of socioeconomic inequality. Consequently, socioeconomic inequality of non-electoral participation is the dominant but not the universal pattern in Europe.

What do these measures of socioeconomic inequality mean in practice? Because the unstandardized logit coefficients are not easy to interpret, Table 2 includes the change in probabilities, as an additional coefficient. It measures the change in the probabilities of political participation when one moves from the minimum to the maximum level of education, holding all other factors constant at their mean. For example, in the case of non-electoral participation, the Austrian value of 0.30 is due to the difference between the probability of non-electoral participation of respondents with the highest level of education achieved (second stage of tertiary education) and the probability of respondents with the lowest level achieved (not completed, primary education): 0.56–0.26. Based on this compact coefficient, the difference between the lowest and the highest level of education regarding non-electoral participation, totals 0.24 points in all European countries, while it is almost non-existent (0.02) in the case of electoral participation. Both coefficients measure differences between educational groups, controlling for all other factors of the CVM and social capital theory. Thus, the coefficients do not indicate the absolute level of inequality between different educational groups, but they measure the pure effect of socioeconomic resources.

To summarize, European nations are characterized by different degrees of socioeconomic inequality of electoral and non-electoral participation. Unlike the level of political participation, no system-level factors suggest themselves to explain these differences. Even in the new democracies of Central and Eastern Europe, unequal participation does exist.

3.2 Multi-level Analysis

In order to measure the three system-level factors, we introduce eight indicators (for a detailed documentation and distribution, see Table A2).

(1) *Socioeconomic modernization* is measured by the Human Development Index (UNDP 2004). This composite index incorporates GDP per capita, educational attainment and life expectancy at birth. It is broader than GDP and measures "three basic capabilities" that allow people to participate in social and political life.

(2a) Originally, Lijphart (1999) developed two measures—the executives-parties and the federal-unitary index—to measure the two dimensions of *consensus and majoritarian democracy*. Since data for the new democracies of Central and Eastern Europe are missing and, more importantly, empirical analyses have demonstrated that Lijphart's executives-parties index is of dubious quality, we draw instead on alternative constitutional and partisan veto player indices, which have proved to be rather good measures in a study on *The Performance of Democracies* (Roller 2005). Lijphart's federal-unitary dimension, referring to a diffusion of power between institutions, is measured by a parsimonious index labeled the minimal governmental index (Fuchs 2000). This constitutional veto-player index takes into account three institutions: bicameralism, federalism, and presidentialism. Low scores indicate high diffusion of power. Lijphart's executive-parties dimension, referring to the diffusion of power within institutions, is measured by the effective number of parliamentary parties (Taagepera 1997; Laakso and Taagepera 1979), a simple partisan veto player index.

(2b) Established indices are used to measure the two institutional mechanisms of the *electoral system*. The degree of proportionality of electoral systems is measured on the basis of the index of disproportionality, proposed by Gallagher (1991), calculating for elections the vote-seat share differences for each party. Low scores indicate high proportionality. The compulsory voting system is assigned to a country, only if it is enforced either strictly or weakly (IDEA 2006).

(3) The measures of *social (system) capital* rely on aggregated means of the individual-level variables. We take into account all three forms of social capital: personal networks, political norms, and social trust.

All indicators are coded in the same way. Low values indicate low levels and high values indicate high levels of the respective characteristics. There are two exceptions. In the case of the minimal governmental index and the index of electoral disproportionality, low levels indicate dispersion of power and high levels point to concentration of power. As far as the timeframe of the non-constant system-level indices is concerned, the indices effective number of parliamentary parties and electoral disproportionality consider only the last two national parliamentary elections before the fieldwork of the *European Social Survey* (2001 at latest). Former elections have been too unsettled in the new democracies of Central and Eastern Europe. The Human Development Index data refer to the year 2002.

The results of multi-level logistic regressions of electoral and non-electoral participation are displayed in Tables 3 and 4.[6] We examine the explanation of the level of both forms of political participation, and then move on to the question of the socioeconomic inequality of these forms.

We start with the *level* of electoral participation (Table 3). The estimation of the "empty model" is the first step of the statistical analysis. Its aim is to check whether there exists any substantial cross-national variance. According to the Intra-Class Correlation Coefficient (ICC),[7] the share of cross-national variance on the total variance amounts to 8.36 percent. This value is not very high, but it is considerable and worth examining which system-level factors account for this difference. The aim of the next "individual model with random intercept" is to see whether the cross-national differences are caused by composition effects, i.e. the distribution of individual-level factors. This model includes all the independent variables of the individual-level model of participation that we have already examined using simple logistic regression (cf. Table 1), but in addition, it allows the constant to vary (random intercept). The drop of the ICC from 8.36 percent (empty model) to 8.10 percent (individual model with random intercept) is rather small, which means that almost the entire share of cross-national variance on the total variance is not caused by composition effects but rather

---

[6] For estimation full maximum-likelihood with Laplace-approximation has been used as algorithm. The results refer to the population-average model with robust standard errors (for a similar model see Klein 2005).

[7] In the case of logistic multi-level analysis ICC is computed as follows: ICC = $u_0/(u_0 + \pi^2/3)$ (Guo and Zhao 2000).

Table 3: Individual and contextual determinants of electoral participation

	Empty model	Individual model with random intercept	Intercept as outcome model	Random slope model for education	Slope as outcome model for education
Fixed effects					
Constant	1.63***	1.92***	1.94***	1.91***	1.92***
	(0.12)	(0.11)	(0.10)	(0.09)	(0.09)
Compulsory voting			0.76* [0.76]	0.75*	0.69*
			(0.33)	(0.28)	(0.26)
Electoral disproportionality					−0.02
					(0.01)
Education		0.05	0.05 [0.21]	0.08**	0.08**
		(0.03)	(0.03)	(0.03)	(0.02)
Education * Electoral disproportionality					−0.01***
					(0.002)
Party attachment		0.27***	0.27*** [1.09]	0.26***	0.26***
		(0.02)	(0.02)	(0.02)	(0.02)
Political interest		0.44***	0.44*** [1.06]	0.44***	0.44***
		(0.04)	(0.04)	(0.04)	(0.04)
Internal political efficacy		0.05*	0.05* [0.12]	0.05*	0.05*
		(0.03)	(0.03)	(0.03)	(0.03)
Personal networks		0.31***	0.31*** [0.41]	0.31***	0.31***
		(0.04)	(0.04)	(0.04)	(0.04)
Political norms		0.24***	0.25*** [0.97]	0.25**	0.25***
		(0.03)	(0.03)	(0.03)	(0.03)
Social trust		0.05***	0.05*** [0.27]	0.05***	0.05***
		(0.01)	(0.01)	(0.01)	(0.01)
Random effects					
Variance constant u_0	0.30***	0.29***	0.20***	0.20***	0.19***
	(0.003)	(0.003)	(0.003)	(0.003)	(0.002)
Education slope u_1				0.023***	0.017***
				(0.0009)	(0.0007)
Model fit					
Deviance	84474.29	81579.95	815731.64	81485.63	81481.45
Parameter	2	9	10	12	14
Intra-class correlation coefficient (ICC)	8.36%	8.10%	5.73%		

*** p ≤ 0.001; ** p ≤ 0.01; * p ≤ 0.05
N = 31384 (93 %); multi-level logistic regression; unstandardized logit coefficients with robust standard errors brackets and standardized logit coefficients in squared brackets (all independent variables are grand mean centered population-average model; full-maximum-likelihood estimation with Laplace-approximation).

Table 4: Individual and contextual determinants of non-electoral participation

	Empty model	Individual model with random intercept	Intercept as outcome model	Random slope model for education	Slope as outcome model for education
Fixed effects					
Constant	−0.55***	−0.61***	−0.63***	−0.63***	−0.64***
	(0.12)	(0.11)	(0.08)	(0.08)	(0.07)
Human Development Index			11.94*** [0.75]	11.94***	11.85***
			(1.61)	(1.61)	(1.88)
Minimal governmental index					−0.08
					(0.07)
Education		0.16***	0.18*** [0.57]	0.18***	0.17***
		(0.02)	(0.01)	(0.01)	(0.01)
Education * Minimal governmental index					−0.03*
					(0.01)
Party attachment		0.11***	0.11*** [0.34]	0.11***	0.11***
		(0.02)	(0.02)	(0.02)	(0.02)
Political interest		0.27***	0.27*** [0.50]	0.27***	0.27***
		(0.02)	(0.02)	(0.02)	(0.02)
Internal political efficacy		0.34***	0.35*** [0.66]	0.35***	0.35***
		(0.03)*	(0.03)	(0.03)	(0.03)
Personal networks		0.57***	0.58*** [0.59]	0.58***	0.58***
		(0.07)	(0.07)	(0.07)	(0.07)
Political norms		0.05***	0.05*** [0.15]	0.05***	0.05***
		(0.01)	(0.01)	(0.01)	(0.01)
Social trust		−0.01	−0.01 [−0.04]	−0.01	−0.01
		(0.01)	(0.01)	(0.01)	(0.01)
Random effects					
Variance constant u_0	0.30***	0.22***	0.11***	0.11***	0.10***
	(0.003)	(0.003)	(0.002)	(0.002)	(0.002)
Education slope u_1				0.003***	0.002***
				(0.0003)	(0.0002)
Model fit					
Deviance	97116.16	93348.29	93317.93	93317.93	93308.85
Parameter	2	9	12	12	14
Intra-class correlation coefficient (ICC)	8.36%	6.27%	3.24%		

* p ≤ 0.001; ** p ≤ 0.01; * p ≤ 0.05
N = 31384 (93 %); multi-level logistic regression; unstandardized logit coefficients with robust standard errors in brackets and standardized logit coefficients in squared brackets (all independent variables are grand mean centered; population-average model; full-maximum-likelihood estimation with Laplace-approximation).

by other factors. In a third step, we tried to explain the remaining cross-national variance by including all the eight system-level factors, one after the other, described above. Compulsory voting is the only variable showing a significant effect. The effect of this variable is documented in the "intercept as outcome model". As suggested, countries with a compulsory voting system show higher voting turnouts. This result confirms Lijphart (1997: 10), who stated "compulsory voting is the only institutional mechanism...that can assure high turnout virtually by itself". By including this system-level variable, the ICC clearly decreases from 8.10 to 5.73 percent, which means that 2.4 percentage points of the share of cross-national variance on the total variance can be explained by this institutional mechanism. The major part of this variance, however, cannot be explained by the variables derived from the three system-level theories.

The picture is rather different regarding the level of non-electoral participation (Table 4). The first "empty model" reveals also 8.4 percent as the share of cross-national variance on the total variance of non-electoral participation. However, the second "individual model with random intercept" that includes the same set of individual-level factors, results in a decline of the ICC to 6.3 percent, which means that 2.1 percentage points of the share of cross-national variance can be explained by composition effects, i.e. the distribution of individual-level variables such as education, membership in voluntary organizations etc. Unlike electoral participation, the cross-national variation of non-electoral participation is caused, to a certain extent, by different compositions of the population. From the eight system-level factors that we adopted to explain the remaining country differences, only one factor evolves with a significant positive effect; according to the "intercept as outcome model" it is the Human Development Index. As expected, national differences in non-electoral participation can be explained by the national level of socioeconomic modernity. The inclusion of this factor is rather successful; 3 percentage points of the share of cross-national variance can be explained, and only 3.2 percent of the cross-national variance, remains unexplained.

If we put together the results of both forms of political participation, we have to state firstly that the share of country-level variance is indeed not very high. Secondly, out of the three system-level theories studied, only the variables of the social capital concept are unsuccessful, whereas the theories of socioeconomic modernization and political institutions are relevant. Hence, social capital theory displays no additional explanatory power even on the system-level. Political institutions, on the one hand, explain national levels of electoral participation, but they do not matter in the case of non-electoral participation. Socioeconomic modernization, on the other hand, is a rather potent factor in explaining national levels of non-electoral participation, but it cannot explain national levels of electoral participation. The situation is similar to the individual-level explanation, where socioeconomic resources, measured by education, are much more important in the case of non-electoral participation. Thus, we can conclude that socioeconomic resources on the individual-level as well as on the system-level are decisive for non-electoral participation, while they are of minor importance for electoral participation. This mixed pattern is further evidence regarding the fundamental difference between these two modes of political participation.

After analyzing the level of political participation, we move on to the explanation of the socioeconomic *inequality* of political participation. The pattern is rather complicated as far as electoral participation is concerned. While, in the pooled logistic regression, education displays a low but still significant impact on electoral participation (cf. Table 1), education is not significant any longer in the multi-level "intercept as outcome model" (cf. Table 3). If one allows, however, for a systematic variation of the effect of education (slope) in the fourth "random slope model for education", the variance coefficient for the slope of education reveals to be significant, and the slope itself becomes significant. Hence, this random slope model for education represents the adequate modeling of the effect of education. The variance coefficient reveals that the effect of education on electoral participation varies systematically between the national samples. Since we are interested in explaining the variance of the education slope, we introduce in a next step, one after the other, all suggested eight system-level variables. The final "slope as outcome model for education" displays only one system-level factor that has been successful, namely electoral disproportionality. By including this factor, the variance of the education slope could be reduced from 0.023 to 0.017. However, it is still significant. Hence, there are other factors, which are responsible for the variance of this slope that we could not identify yet. While we have found with electoral disproportionality at least one institutional mechanism that can explain the differences in socioeconomic inequality of electoral participation, the main problem is that this institutional mechanism does not work as expected. According to the suggested hypothesis, we have expected a lower conversion rate of education into participation i.e. higher socioeconomic equality with decreasing levels of electoral disproportionality. Empirically, the sign of the regression coefficient is negative and that means, taking the coding of electoral disproportionality into account (cf. Table A2), that socioeconomic equality of electoral participation is increasing with electoral disproportionality (or with concentration of power).

The situation is similar in the case of non-electoral participation (cf. Table 4). The "random slope model for education" also shows significant cross-country variation in the effect of education (education slope). In trying to explain this variation, it is only the minimal governmental index, illustrated in the "slope as outcome model for education", that reduces the variance of the education slope significantly from 0.003 to 0.002. The minimal governmental index, neither, shows the expected effect. The sign of the regression coefficient is negative which again means—keeping in mind the coding of the minimal governmental index (cf. Table A2)—that socioeconomic equality of non-electoral participation is increasing with majoritarian democracy (or with the concentration of power).

In summarizing the results from the multi-level analysis of the socioeconomic inequality of electoral and non-electoral participation, we can state that it is apparently the political-institutionalist theory that is of explanatory relevance. Neither social capital theory nor modernization theory are of any importance for this vital democratic standard. On a general level, the empirical results are rather plausible and in line with the mainstream thinking of political science. The direction of the effect, however, contradicts the common hypothesis suggested by Lijphart and others; dispersion of power, regarding either the electoral system or the institutional setting of democracy in general, does not increase socioeconomic equality of participation. It is rather the other way round; majoritarian electoral systems and majoritarian democracies seem to have an inequality-reducing effect. A detailed analysis yields that no outliers are responsible for this pattern.

4. Conclusion

The level and socioeconomic equality of political participation are often used as standards to gauge the quality and prospects of democracy in a country. In this paper, we have tried to overcome a drawback of participation research by testing a comprehensive multi-level model of political participation, including individual-level as well as system-level determinants by means of a multi-level analysis. Besides the traditional theories of political participation, we have been interested particularly in the explanatory power of social capital suggested to operate at both levels. The analysis tried to explain the level and socioeconomic inequality of two fundamental forms of political participation: voting and the activities beyond voting.

The empirical analysis clearly demonstrates that individual-level models are rather successful in explaining the levels of political participation, while the importance of system-level or contextual factors are rather limited. The share of cross-national variance on the total variance, measured by the Intra-Class Correlation Coefficient (ICC), reaches about 8 percent. This figure is not very high if we keep in mind the rule of thumb that multi-level analysis, in any case, would be worth being employed if the ICC exceeds 10 percent. In the case of non-electoral participation, the effect of contextual factors is further reduced to about 6 percent because the multi-level analysis discovered significant composition effects. This means that the distribution of individual-level variables is responsible for a clear fraction of the cross-national variance. These composition effects mainly refer to education, political interest, internal political efficacy, and personal networks as the results of the individual-level model suggest. Since these variables are closely related to the national level of socioeconomic modernization, it can be suggested that only the national level of non-electoral participation in Europe will increase as a consequence of further modernization processes. This is especially true for the Southern European as well as the Central and Eastern European countries in our sample.

The individual-level model of political participation integrates the CVM by Verba et al. (1995)—the most prominent individual-level model of political participation—with the social capital concept of Putnam (1993). The empirical results are rather disappointing for social capital theory. The core variable, social trust, displays either no significant or very low effects, and political norms are only relevant for electoral participation. Personal networks are rather important determinants of political participation but this factor presents no conceptual innovation, since it is already included in the CVM. Consequently, without any great loss of explanatory power, one could set aside the social capital concept for explaining individual political participation. The CVM still proves to be a very successful individual-level model of political participation. It seems to be a universal model of political participation that is not only valid for the United States but also for Western as well as Central and Eastern European democracies.

Furthermore, social capital theory presents no additional explanatory power on the system-level. None of the three social system capital indicators displays significant effects. To summarize, social capital theory evolves no additional "rainmaker" quality as far as political participation in Europe is concerned.

Regarding the system-level factors, only socioeconomic modernization theory and political-institutionalist theory, offer significant determinants. Their effect, however, varies with the mode of political participation (electoral vs. non-electoral) and the explanandum (level vs. socioeconomic inequality of political participation) at hand. In the case of *levels of electoral participation*, national differences can be explained by one institutional factor: the compulsory voting system. This empirical result confirms the expectation of Lijphart (1997), who, in his presidential address to the *American Political Science Association* in 1996, suggested and discussed this institution as a mechanism to increase turnout rates. Additionally, he recommended compulsory voting as an institutional mechanism to increase socioeconomic equality of voting. Although our multi-level analysis could not detect any effect of this institution on equality of electoral participation there are some hints that compulsory voting goes along with socioeconomic equality. The three countries in our sample with strict or weakly enforced compulsory voting systems—Belgium, Greece, and Luxembourg (cf. Table A2)—not only show above-average turnout rates (cf. Figure 2) but also no significant effects (Belgium, Luxembourg) or significant negative effects of education (Greece), indicating inequality in favor of underprivileged voters (cf. Table 2). These results suggest constitutional engineering through the introduction of compulsory voting systems. From a normative point of view, however, this is a questionable proposition because it contradicts individual freedom, another basic value of democracy (Lijphart 1999; Verba 2003).

In the case of the *levels of non-electoral participation*, we cannot detect any effect of the institutional variables. These levels instead depend on socioeconomic modernization. The results of our analysis support the various theories about the political effects of socioeconomic modernization. We add some further empirical evidence to prior research (Roller and Wessels 1996; Norris 2002) by demonstrating the effect of socioeconomic modernization on the basis of a multi-level analysis with an individual dependent variable, and not on the basis of the common aggregate-data analysis. Additionally, the multi-level model identifies two separate impacts of socioeconomic modernization. It works directly via the composition effect, i.e. by increasing individual resources it encourages citizens to participate in politics beyond voting. It also works as an aggregate factor, i.e. the general level of socioeconomic modernization facilitates non-electoral participation. Both mechanisms come into play with increasing levels of socioeconomic modernization.

Finally, regarding the *socioeconomic inequality of electoral and non-electoral participation*, the empirical analysis indeed detected higher rates of socioeconomic inequality of non-electoral participation compared with electoral participation (although this pattern is seen in a majority, but not all, European countries) and varying degrees of political inequality between European countries. As far as the explanation of these national differences regarding the degree of socioeconomic inequality is concerned, multi-level analysis reveals that only institutionalist theory is successful. Socioeconomic inequality in electoral participation can be explained by the electoral system and socioeconomic inequality in non-electoral participation by the type of democracy. This is further evidence that "institutions matter". The problem, however, lies in the fact that the electoral system and the general institutional setting do not function in the suggested way. According to the hitherto consent in political science, power-distributing institutions such as proportional electoral systems and consensus democracies promote equality of political participation while power-concentrating systems such as majoritarian electoral systems and majoritarian democracies increase inequality. Empirically, however, we have detected the reverse pattern; majoritarian electoral systems and majoritarian democracies go along with increasing socioeconomic equality of political participation. Furthermore, studies will have to show whether this pattern is limited to the specific sample of countries studied or whether it is a general pattern that calls for new theories and explanations. Possible starting points for such explanations could be that power-concentrating institutions motivate political participation by facilitating the identification of the addressees of political action and by promising to be more effective. At the moment, we can only conclude that the common hypothesis regarding the equalizing effect of power-distributing institutions is not valid for the specific sample of countries at hand.

To conclude, national differences in levels and socioeconomic equality of political participation can be primarily explained with the type of national political institutions. Only as far as the level of non-electoral participation is concerned, socioeconomic modernization matters. Political institutions play a significant role in explaining political participation, even if their effects do not always comply with common wisdom.

REFERENCES

Barnes, Samuel H./Kaase, Max et al. (1979): *Political Action: Mass Participation in Five Western Democracies*, Beverly Hills, Cal.: Sage.
Bell, Daniel (1974): *The Coming of Post-industrial Society. A Venture in Social Forecasting*, New York: Basic Books.
Brady, Henry E. (1999): "Political Participation". In: John P. Robinson/Phillip P. Shaver/Lawrence S. Wrightsman (eds.), *Measures of Political Attitudes. Volume 2 of Measures of Social Psychological Attitudes*, San Diego et al.: Academic Press, 737–801.
Dahl, Robert A. (1989): *Democracy and Its Critics*, New Haven/London: Yale University Press.
Deth, Jan W. van (2007): "Norms of Citizenship". In: Russell J. Dalton/Hans-Dieter Klingemann (eds.), *The Oxford Handbook of Political Behaviour*, Oxford: Oxford University Press (in print).
Deutsch, Karl W. (1961): "Social Mobilization and Political Development". *American Political Science Review* 55: 493–514.
Esser, Hartmut (2000): *Soziologie. Spezielle Grundlagen. Band 4: Opportunitäten und Restriktionen*, Frankfurt a. M.: Campus.
Franklin, Mark (2004): *Voter Turnout and the Dynamics of Electoral Competition in Established Democracies since 1945*, Cambridge: Cambridge University Press.
Fuchs, Dieter (1991): "The Normalization of the Unconventional. New Forms of Political Action and New Social Movements". In: Gerd Meyer/Franciszek Ryszka (eds.), *Political Participation and Democracy in Poland and West Germany*, Warschau: Osrodek Badan Spolecznych, 148–169.
——— (2000): „Typen und Indizes demokratischer Regime. Eine Analyse des Präsidentialismus- und des Veto-Spieler-Ansatzes". In: Hans-Joachim Lauth/Gert Pickel/Christian Welzel (eds.), *Empirische Demokratiemessung*, Opladen: Westdeutscher Verlag 2000, 27–48.
Fuchs, Dieter/Gabriel, Oscar W./Völkl, Kerstin (2002): „Vertrauen in politische Institutionen und politische Unterstützung". *Österreichische Zeitschrift für Politikwissenschaft* 4: 427–450.
Gabriel, Oscar W. (2004): „Politische Partizipation". In: Jan W. van Deth (eds.), *Deutschland in Europa. Ergebnisse des European Social Survey 2002–2003*, Wiesbaden: VS Verlag für Sozialwissenschaften, 318–338.
Gabriel, Oscar W./Kunz, Volker/Roßteutscher, Sigrid/van Deth, Jan W. (2002): *Soziales Kapital und Demokratie. Zivilgesellschaftliche Ressourcen im Vergleich*, Wien: Facultas.
Gallagher, Michael (1991): "Proportionality, Disproportionality and Electoral Systems". *Electoral Studies* 10: 33–51.
Guo, Guang/Zhao, Hongxin (2000): "Multilevel Modeling for Binary Data". *Annual Review of Sociology* 26: 441–462.
Huckfeld, Robert/Sprague, John (1993): "Citizens, Contexts, and Politics". In: Ada W. Finifter (ed.), *Political Science. The State of the Discipline II*, Washington: American Political Science Association, 281–303.
IDEA—International Institute for Democracy and Electoral Assistance (2006): "Compulsory Voting" (http://www.idea.int/vt/compulsory_voting.cfm; 10/19/2006).
Kaase, Max (1981): „Politische Beteiligung und politische Ungleichheit—Betrachtungen zu einem Paradoxon". In: Lothar Albertin/Werner Link (eds.), *Politische Parteien*

auf dem Weg zur parlamentarischen Demokratie in Deutschland, Düsseldorf: Droste, 363–377.
—— (1999): "Interpersonal Trust, Political Trust and Non-Institutionalized Political Participation in Western Europe". *West European Politics* 22: 1–21.
Klein, Markus (2002): Einführung in die Mehrebenenanalyse, PolitikON (http://www.politikon.org).
—— (2005): „Die Entwicklung der Beteiligungsbereitschaft bei Bundestagswahlen. Eine Mehrebenenanalyse auf der Grundlage der Politbarometer-Trenderhebungen der Jahre 1977 bis 2002". *Kölner Zeitschrift für Soziologie und Sozialpsychologie* 57: 494–522.
Laakso, Markku/Taagepera, Rein (1979): "'Effective' Number of Parties: A Measure with Application to West Europe". *Comparative Political Studies* 12: 3–27.
Lijphart, Arend (1997): "Unequal Participation: Democracy's Unresolved Dilemma. Presidential Address, American Political Science Association, 1996". *American Political Science Review* 91: 1–14.
—— (1999): *Patterns of Democracy. Government Forms and Performance in Thirty-Six Countries*, New Haven/London: Yale University Press.
Lipset, Seymour Martin (1981): *Political Man. The Social Bases of Politics*, Baltimore, Maryland: The Johns Hopkins University Press (expanded edition, 1st edition 1959).
Norris, Pippa (2002): *Democratic Phoenix: Reinventing Political Activism*, Cambridge: Cambridge University Press.
Paldam, Martin/Svendsen, Gert Tinggard (2000): "An Essay on Social Capital: Looking for the Fire Behind the Smoke". *European Journal of Political Economy* 16: 339–366.
Parry, Geraint/Moyser, George/Day, Neil (1992): *Political Participation and Democracy in Britain*, Cambridge University Press.
Pattie, Charles/Seyd, Patrick/Whiteley, Paul (2004): *Citizenship in Britain. Values, Participation and Democracy*, Cambridge: Cambridge University Press.
Putnam, Robert D. with Robert Leonardi/Nanetti, Raffaella Y. (1993): *Making Democracy Work: Civic Traditions in Modern Italy*, Princeton, N.J.: Princeton University Press.
Roller, Edeltraud (2005): *The Performance of Democracies: Political Institutions and Public Policy*, Oxford: Oxford University Press.
Roller, Edeltraud/Wessels, Bernhard (1996): "Contexts of Political Protest in Western Democracies: Political Organizations and Modernity". In: Frederick D. Weil (ed.), *Research on Democracy and Society, Volume 3*, Connecticut/London, England: JAI Press, 91–134.
Rossteutscher, Sigrid (2004): „Die Rückkehr der Tugend?". In: Jan W. van Deth (eds.), *Deutschland in Europa. Ergebnisse des European Social Survey 2002–2003*, Wiesbaden: VS Verlag für Sozialwissenschaften, 175–200.
Steenbergen, Marco R./Jones, Bradford S. (2002): "Modeling Multilevel Data Structures". *American Journal of Political Science* 46: 218–237.
Taagepera, Rein (1997): "Effective Number of Parties for Incomplete Data". *Electoral Studies* 16: 145–151.
Topf, Richard (1995a): "Electoral Participation": In: Hans Dieter Klingemann/Dieter Fuchs (eds.), *Citizens and the State*, Oxford: Oxford University Press, 27–51.
—— (1995b): "Beyond Electoral Participation". In: Hans Dieter Klingemann/Dieter Fuchs (eds.), *Citizens and the State*, Oxford: Oxford University Press, 52–91.
UNDP-United Nations Development Programme (2004): *Human Development Report 2004*, New York: Oxford University Press.
UNESCO (1999): *World Social Science Report 1999*, Paris: UNESCO.
Verba, Sidney (2003): "Would the Dream of Political Equality Turn Out to Be a Nightmare?" *Perspectives on Politics* 1: 663–679.
Verba, Sidney/Nie, Norman H. (1972): *Participation in America. Political Democracy and Social Equality*, New York: Harper & Row.

Verba, Sidney/Nie, Norman H/Kim, Jae-on (1978): *Participation and Political Equality. A Seven-Nation Comparison*, Cambridge: Cambridge University Press.
Verba, Sidney/Lehman Schlozman, Kay/Brady, Henry E. (1995): *Voice and Equality: Civic Voluntarism in American Politics*, Cambridge: Harvard University Press.
Whiteley, Paul F. (2000): "Economic Growth and Social Capital". *Political Studies* 48: 443–466.
Wessels, Bernhard (2002): "Wählen und politische Ungleichheit: Der Einfluss von individuellen Ressourcen und politischem Angebot". In: Dieter Fuchs/Edeltraud Roller/Bernhard Wessels (eds.), *Bürger und Demokratie in Ost und West*, Wiesbaden: Westdeutscher Verlag, 145–168.

Appendix

Table A1: Individual-level indicators

Electoral participation	Voted in last national parliamentary election: 0 = no, 1 = yes
Non-electoral participation	Index covering participation in four activities during the last 12 month: contacting a politician, government or local government official; working in a political party or action group; signing a petition; taking part in a lawful public demonstration. 0 = not taking part in any activity, 1 = taking part in at least one of these four activities
Socioeconomic resources (education)	Highest level of education achieved: 0 = not completed, primary education, 1 = primary or first stage of basic, 2 = lower secondary or second stage of basic, 3 = upper secondary, 4 = post secondary, non-tertiary, 5 = first stage of tertiary, 6 = second stage of tertiary
Party attachment	Is there a particular political party you feel closer to than all the other parties? 0 = no, 1 = yes
Political interest	How interested would you say you are in politics? 1 = not at all interested, 2 = hardly interested, 3 = quite interested, 4 = very interested
Internal political efficacy	Means index summarizing three aspects: politics too complicated understand; could take an active role in a group involved with political issues; how difficult or easy do you find it to make your mind up about political issues. 1 = low internal efficacy...5 = high internal efficacy
Personal networks	Index including membership in ten voluntary organizations: sports club, cultural organization, trade union, professional organization, consumer organization, humanitarian organization, environmental organization, religious organization, science organization, and social club. 0 = no membership, 1 = membership in one of these ten organizations at least
Political norms	Means index summarizing the importance of six characteristics for being a good citizen: support people worse off; vote in elections; always obey laws and regulations; form independent opinion; to be active involuntary organizations; to be active in politics. 0 = extremely unimportant...10 = extremely important
Social trust	Means index including three different aspects of social trust: most people can be trusted; most people try to be fair; most of the time people helpful. 0 = low social trust...10 = high social trust

Table A2: Distribution of system-level indicators

	Human Development Index	Type of democracy		Electoral system		Aggregated mean of ...		
		Minimal govern- mental index	Effective number of parties	Electoral dispropor- tionality	Compul- sory voting	personal networks	political norms	social trust
Austria	0.934	4	3.45	2.39	0	0.74	6.93	5.32
Belgium	0.942	4	8.54	3.67	1	0.71	6.21	4.97
Denmark	0.932	6	4.60	0.65	0	0.93	7.39	6.86
Finland	0.935	5	5.01	2.59	0	0.76	7.11	6.33
France	0.932	4	3.20	21.38	0	0.48	6.57	4.84
Germany	0.925	2	2.91	3.32	0	0.71	6.74	5.11
Greece	0.902	6	2.29	8.46	1	0.23	7.55	3.40
Hungary	0.848	6	3.64	9.02	0	0.24	6.70	4.25
Ireland	0.936	5	3.25	5.20	0	0.67	6.95	5.81
Italy	0.920	4	5.92	12.20	0	0.34	7.05	4.39
Luxembourg	0.933	5	4.12	4.29	1	0.82	7.33	5.12
Netherlands	0.942	5	5.12	1.75	0	0.84	6.76	5.73
Norway	0.956	6	4.86	3.46	0	0.82	7.28	6.58
Poland	0.850	3	3.28	8.77	0	0.17	7.18	3.73
Portugal	0.897	5	2.55	4.75	0	0.25	7.20	4.41
Slovenia	0.895	5	5.19	5.02	0	0.50	6.89	4.25
Spain	0.922	4	2.60	6.47	0	0.36	6.38	4.83
Sweden	0.946	6	3.90	1.73	0	0.91	7.01	6.27
United Kingdom	0.936	5	2.15	17.36	0	0.70	6.54	5.35
Mean	0.920	4.74	4.03	6.45	(0.16)	0.59	6.94	5.13
Standard deviation	0.03	1.10	1.54	5.47	(0.37)	0.25	0.36	0.96

Sources: Minimal governmental index (Fuchs 2000) including bicameralism, federalism, and presidentialism ranging from 0 = dispersion of power...6 = concentration of power; Effective number of parliamentary parties (Taagepera 1997; Laakso and Taagepera 1979) and electoral disproportionality (Gallagher 1991) both calculated for the last two national parliamentary elections (2001 at latest) on the basis of election data collected by the research unit "Democracy: Structures, Performance, Challenges" of the Wissenschaftszentrum Berlin für Sozialforschung (WZB); Compulsory voting strict or weak enforced (IDEA 2006); Aggregated mean of personal networks/political norms/social trust calculated on the basis of ESS (see individual-level variables in Table A1); Human Development Index 2002 combining GDP per capita (PPP US$), education (adult literacy rate and combined gross enrolment ratio in primary, secondary, and tertiary level), and life expectancy at birth with high numbers indicating high level of human development (UNDP 2004).

CHAPTER TEN

THE CIVIC SOCIETY AS A SCHOOL OF LABOR RELATIONS? SOCIAL CAPITAL AND EMPOWERMENT AT THE WORKPLACE

Heiner Meulemann

Social capital can be defined as the sum of social relations in which a person is embedded, beyond intimate living arrangements. There are three types of such social relations. The first comprises *non-intimate, face-to-face relations*, namely kinship, neighborhood, and friendship; the second comprises relations between members of *associations of civic society* such as clubs, local chapters, local citizen groups; and the third refers to relations within *large-scale social organizations* such as firms, public administrations, interest organizations, political parties and churches (Warren 2001: 56–59). As the associations of civic society bridge, on the one hand, intimate and non-intimate face-to-face relations, that are, the two pillars of private life, and on the other hand, large scale social organizations, they contribute to the social integration of society at large. Civic society associations provide avenues *from private life to organized social life*, and the social capital acquired by a person in civic society is useful for acting within and contributing to public life. The larger a society's intermediate sphere of associations, the better the prospects of its social integration. Therefore, social capital, accumulated within civic society associations, has been extensively studied in comparative perspectives by social scientists (Anheier/Salamon 2001, Curtis/Baer/Grabb 2001, Gabriel et al. 2002, Schofer/Fourcade-Gourinchas 2001).

As these studies assume, involvement in the civic society is a model for political action and it strengthens a democracy. Yet it could be, as well, a model to articulate interests within labor relations and to strengthen a market economy. If the civic society is a school of democracy, it may also be a school of labor relations. To be sure, there are differences between political action and the articulation of interests in labor relations. Partners in political action are, in principle, on equal footing, whilst employers have more means of survival in the case of conflict, than employees do. Consequentially, political action endeavors, in principle, toward the common good of the polity, as well as to personal interests, whilst employees aim to improve their lot, thereby improving the common interest of their industry and the economy.

Yet, these differences refer to the distinct constitutions of the polity and the economy, and cannot conceivably affect the process of how persons transfer their learning experiences between life domains. Involvement in associations of the private life, as opposed to large-scale organizations of politics, labor, and religion, may foster the capabilities to act in these very organizations. Being a youth trainer in a football club may not only help to raise one's purpose vis-à-vis the representatives of the local community, but also vis-à-vis the management of one's firm. In both cases, capabilities are needed to get along with people, to develop and to advocate new ideas, to assert one self, to lead others and to get their approval. In both cases, these capabilities may result in a better realization of one's interests. In both cases, successful public action may also contribute to the common good, although this effect is indirect in the case of labor relations. The better workers feel at their workplace, the better their product can be. The following research tests this *labor relations version* of the *transfer hypothesis: The more someone is involved in private associations the more he or she will attain empowerment at the workplace.*

That civic involvement transforms into empowerment at the workplace, is a bold hypothesis. Qualifications and workplace characteristics may have a more immediate impact on the level of persons, and institutions and opportunity structures may determine mean empowerment on the level of countries. Therefore, the hypothesis is examined, controlling for personal conditions, and in several countries, with differing labor relations. In section 1, the research design—samples, hypotheses and measurements of empowerment and its determinants at the level of persons and countries—will be introduced. In section 2, results are presented for the level of persons, and in section 3, for both the level of persons and countries.

1. Design of Research

1.1 *Samples*

Samples are taken from the European Social Survey 2002, which comprises 22 countries. Since Eastern and Western parts of Germany are treated separately, the total number is 23 countries. As empowerment at the workplace refers to the dependent *employed population only*—self-employed people empower themselves and unemployed people have no workplace to be empowered at—this population had to be selected.

Respondents were asked: "Are you currently employed, self-employed or not in paid work?" In the total sample of 42,359 respondents, 0.7% refused to answer this question. While of those who responded, 44.7% specified "employed", 9.1% specified "self-employed", and 46.2% specified "not in paid work". Only employed respondents (18,779) were asked questions about their current working situation. The following analyses are restricted to this group. However, selectivity, according to employment, varied greatly between countries, from 24.7% in Greece, to 62.0% in Norway, reflecting the different levels of employment, particularly of female participation rates and the differences in entry and exit processes from the labor market across Europe. In order to represent each country equally, the samples of employed persons were weighted to equal size, given the total sample size.

Furthermore, several countries had data limitations. Questions regarding civic involvement were not carried out in Switzerland and in the Czech Republic, the occupational status was not asked in France, and important aggregate variables were not available for Israel. Therefore, the multivariate analysis could be applied to a reduced set of 19 countries, with 15,336 un-weighted cases, ordered according to their location in Western or Eastern Europe, (and within that according to the alphabetical order of the labels used in the ESS): Austria (A), Belgium (B), Denmark (DK), Spain (E), Finland (FIN), Greece (GR), Ireland (IRL), Italy (IT), Luxembourg (L), Norway (N), the Netherlands (NL), Portugal (P), Sweden (S), the United Kingdom (UK), West-Germany (D-W), East-Germany (D-E), Hungary (H), Poland (PL), Slovenia (SLO).

1.2 *Dependent Variable*

Empowerment at the workplace can be defined as the range of discretion a worker has, in order to make decisions about his or her work. It refers to the *social relations* between an employer and an employee, or more specifically, to the balance of influence between them. Influence is one of four aspects of the social, as against the substantive, side of this relation—the three others being trust, commitment and communication (Lowe/Schellenberg 2001: 31–32). While trust, commitment and communication can be one-sided, they are inherently geared toward becoming mutual and are not antagonistic. One-sided trust or commitment is dissatisfying for the side unreciprocated to, one-sided communication is inefficient for both sides, and neither of these mismatches stems from conflict. Yet, attempts to influence the other will call upon counter-active efforts. It is inherently antagonistic, even in a relationship with a co-operative intention, such as the one between employer and employee. Although both parts need to co-operate, one side has more power over the other, being in a system with less buyers than sellers of labor, thereby the buyer less strongly depends on signing a work contract (Offe/Wiesenthal 1980). The antagonism between both sides can be cushioned by the participation of the weaker side in the decision processes constructed under the sovereignty of the stronger side. In this way, the efficiency and the quality of the working conditions may increase, at the same time. The more empowered workers are, the more they will be capable of working in a more autonomous way. The improvement of their lot will also encourage the development of their industry.

Empowerment was measured by an inventory of five questions and by a single item. The inventory was phrased as follows: "I am going to read out a list of things about your working life. Using this card, please say how much the management at your work allows you: to be *flexible* in your working hours, to *decide* how your own daily work is organized, to influence your work *environment*, to influence decisions about the general *direction* of your work, to *change* your work tasks if you wish to?" For each of these questions, there were 11 response options, ranging from "0: I have no influence" to "10: I have complete control"; options in between were numbered and not named. The single question was: "To what extent can you *organize* your own work; to a large extent, to some extent, very little, or not at all?" In order to give these four response options a weight comparable to the 11 options of the inventory, it has been recoded to approximately span the value range of the inventory (the lowest response received value 1, the second, value 4, the third, value 6 and the highest, value 9).

These six items can be ordered according to a core-periphery model of the workplace. It proceeds from the *daily routine* to the *general regime*, from the way *bits and pieces* of work are split up and arranged sequentially, to the way *work as a whole* is fitted into the division of labor within the shop. The worker may have more or less *leeway* in the way work is organized, with respect to time and according to substance. Furthermore, the worker may have more or less *impact* on decisions of how the work is to be fitted into the frame of the firm. Thus, *flexible, decision,*

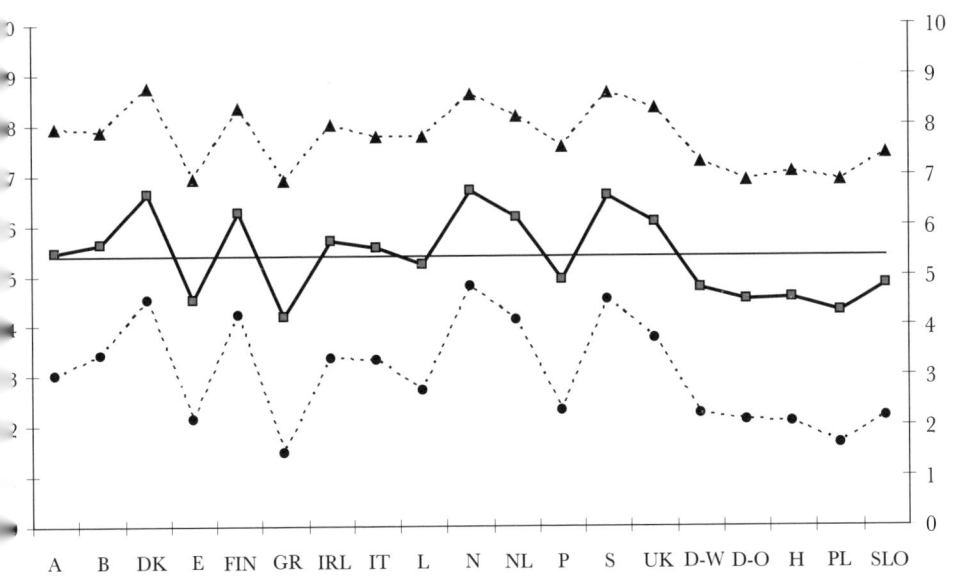

Figure 1: Mean empowerment, one standard deviation above and below the means

and *organize* refer to the *daily routine* of work, either in the dimension of time or of substance. *Environment, direction,* and *change* refer to the *general regime* of work.

This dimensional structure was investigated with exploratory and confirmatory factor analyses. Exploratory factor analyses (with orthogonal rotation) of the total sample, yielded a first factor with an eigenvalue of 3.72, followed by a second factor with an eigenvalue of 0.61. A single factor, then, takes over the variance of almost four of the six variables. Confirmatory factor analyses with LISREL 7.62, were applied, to test whether two factors fit better than a single factor. They did not, as they yielded an extremely high factor correlation of about $r = .90$, which identifies the two factors (Meulemann 2006). Therefore, an additive index was constructed with the six variables using all available information: if one or more variable had missing values it was constructed using the remaining five or less variables. The range of the index is the same as that of the inventory variables.

The mean empowerment in all countries is 5.39 with a standard deviation of 2.49. Figure 1 shows, for each country, the means, together with the range of one standard deviation above and below the means and provides the overall mean for comparison. One can highlight three groups of countries. Empowerment is *high* in the four Scandinavian countries, and in the Netherlands; is *medium* in Austria, Belgium, Ireland, Italy, and Luxemburg; and is *low* in Spain, Greece, Portugal, the two parts of Germany and all the East European countries. Empowerment is high in countries with a "social-democratic regime", while it is medium or low in countries with a "traditional-corporatist regime" (Janoski 1998: 23), and in the former Eastern bloc. The range between the highest (Norway, 6.69) and the lowest (Poland, 4.28) country stretches over almost a standard deviation of the total sample.

1.3 Hypotheses and measurements: Level of persons

Civic involvement

Involvement in, altogether 11 kinds of associations, has been asked with the following question: "For each of the voluntary associations I will now mention, please use this card to tell me whether any of these things apply to you now or in the last 12 months, and, if so, which. (Card)—A member of such an organization.—Participated in an activity arranged by such an organization.—Donated money to such an organization.—Done voluntary (unpaid) work for such an organization." Of these four forms of involvement, membership and participation have been combined under the term *belonging*, and donation of money and voluntary work have been combined under the term *engagement*, for each kind of association. As the assumed transfer runs from the private to the professional domain, belonging and engagement in any of the five *private* associations—sports clubs, consumer associations, scientific/educational/teachers' associations, social clubs, and cultural associations—is considered (Meulemann, chapter 3 in this volume). Thus, there are two variables: *private-belonging* and *private-engagement*. Both should, according to the transfer hypothesis, increase empowerment at the workplace.

Individual and collective strategies as choices for the worker

If workers strive for empowerment at the workplace, they have one of two basic choices they can undertake. On the one hand, the worker may use capabilities of self-assertion in order to put through improvements at the workplace even against the will of the management. That is, the worker may be more or less able to empower him or herself. On the other hand, the worker may use institutional avenues to attain empowerment. Workers may attain empowerment via *individual or collective strategies*.

Whoever has the more human capital or bargaining power vis-à-vis the employer is ready to achieve a high level of discretion at work by themselves; whoever has less individual capabilities will advance their interests via the collective route, by becoming a member of a union, getting active at the workplace, and showing solidarity with co-workers. Individual strategies resort to personal *qualities*, while collective strategies depend on *decisions* to collaborate with others.

The qualities that individual strategies rest upon become effective either within the workplace or beyond the firm. Accordingly, individual strategies can be subdivided into *firm-specific* and *personal* human capital of the worker.

Individual strategy: Firm-specific human capital
The firm-specific human capital is embodied in the relations of the worker to the firm. It is largely lost once the worker leaves the firm. Two of its facets are considered here: the worker's position in the firm and the worker's attachment to the firm.

The *worker's position in the firm* is, given the qualifications and motivation of the employee, determined by the employer. It can be analyzed in a social and a substantive perspective. Analyzed from a social perspective, every collaborative work process must be planned in advance, and carried through according to this plan, so that it inevitably comprises *authority relations*. Apart from the highest and lowest levels of the hierarchy ladder, every worker is supervised by others and supervises others, and the level of discretion increases through climbing the hierarchy ladder. Analyzed from a substantive point, every collaborative product is produced collectively, but the more demanding the production task is, the less a non-specialist is able to interfere and the greater is the range of discretion open to the specialist. *Therefore, the higher a person is situated in the hierarchy of supervision within a firm and the higher the quality of his or her work, the more empowerment he or she is likely to attain at the workplace.*

The worker's position in the firm was measured in the social dimension by his or her authority and in the substantive dimension by the quality of the work completed. The *authority* can be gauged by the number of co-workers supervised, which was ascertained by the following question: "In your main job, do you have any responsibility for supervising the work of other employees?" If yes, "how many people are you responsible for?" Responses were divided into five groups: 0, 1–4, 5–9, 10–19, 20+ treated as a metric variable of *people supervised*. The *quality of the work* was measured by the occupational status. Answers to the open question: "What is the title or name of your main job?", were coded according to ISCO and transformed into Treiman *prestige scores* (Leiulfsrud/Bison/Jensberg 2005).

The *worker's attachment to the firm* reflects, in principle, given the opportunities within the firm, his or her choice. Such employment choices are working full or part-time and having an unlimited or limited labor contract. Long-term tenure and full-time jobs will provide the worker with more firm-specific knowledge that cannot easily be replaced by other or new workers. Internal labor market models (Doeringer/Piore 1971) and efficiency wage models (Samuelson/Nordhaus 2005: 702–703) of economics predict similarly more favorable working conditions for tenured workers. Whoever works full-time and with a long-term career prospect has a stronger interest in improving work conditions and organizing collectively, than someone who holds a job with a partial or temporary status. Therefore, *the more someone is strongly attached to the firm the more empowerment he or she is likely to attain at the workplace.*

The worker's attachment to the firm was measured by the effective working hours: "Regardless of your basic or contracted hours, how many hours do you *normally* work in your main job, including any paid or unpaid overtime?" Responses were divided into five groups: 20, 21–35, 36–45, 46–50, 51+ treated as metric variable of *working hours*.[1]

Individual strategy: Personal human capital
In contrast to the firm-specific human capital, the personal human capital belongs to the worker. Either it is "owned" by the worker, as a qualification, or it stems from the relation of the worker to institutions other than the firm.

Qualifications are acquired continuously in the process of self-assertion in the public life, and they are certified piecemeal by educational institutions geared to develop these qualifications. The capability to get along with others accumulates with everyday experiences, such that a feeling of self-efficacy is developed; and it is, in general, one of the outcomes of education. Efficacy and education are general resources useful to act successfully in specific social arenas—to talk to an audi-

---

[1] Whether the work contract is unlimited, has been ascertained for all countries except Hungary. In order not to lose one more of the few East European countries, we dropped the variable. Inserting a dummy variable for unlimited work contracts into the regression in Table 2 further below and omitting Hungary from the sample, resulted in a moderately high positive standardized effect of Beta = .056.

ence and to hold ones standpoint in politics, to gratify children for their accomplishments and to help them find the right friends during child rearing, or to arrange duties at work and to negotiate with co-workers at the workplace. Both kinds of capital widen the range of feasible actions within life domains; they result in a type of self-empowerment. Even in an unkind environment, opportunities may arise if one is eager to locate them and inventive enough to seize them. *Therefore, the stronger the self-efficacy that has been developed and the higher the educational degree that has been attained, the more empowerment he or she should have at the work place.*

Unfortunately, efficacy has not been measured with regard to the work sphere, only with regard to politics. However, as in European democracies political efficacy is understood as a precondition of public action in general, it can be taken as an indicator of efficacy in work relations as well. It was measured by the following three questions: "How often does it seem that you cannot really understand what is going on in politics due to its complexity; never, seldom, occasionally, regularly, frequently?", "Do you think that you could take an active role in a group involved with political issues; definitely not, probably not, not sure either way, probably, definitely." "How difficult or easy do you find it to make your mind up about political issues; very difficult, difficult, neither difficult nor easy, easy, very easy." They have been combined into an additive index of *political efficacy*, with the range of 1 to 5.

The highest educational degree attained was ascertained by questions specific to each country. Country-specific codes were transformed into the seven educational levels according to the ESCED code common to all European nations, treated as a metric variable of *education*.

Institutions beyond the firm are the labor relations system and the economy at large, where job opportunities are available for the worker to leave the firm or to establish their own business. Whilst the worker is at the firm, these opportunities constitute his or her *exit options*. These options are dependent on the fact that the worker has qualifications that are appealing to other firms and that alternative jobs are available on the market without major transaction costs. If the worker can highlight these options outside the firm vis-à-vis the current employer, he or she can bargain for more empowerment through the threat of exit. *Therefore, the more exit options a worker has, the more empowerment he or she is likely to attain within the current firm.*

The worker may exit the current firm either to join another firm or to establish his or her own firm. Accordingly, exit options were ascertained by two questions: "How difficult or easy would it be for you to get a similar or better job with another employer?...and to start your own business?", for which the same response options as for the empowerment questions were applied. Both questions were combined into an index of *exit options*. Furthermore, employees who have a partner also employed, have another form of an exit option, and a dummy variable of *partner employed* was constructed.

Collective strategy
Although production processes largely affect how the work is divided, there remain options for negotiations between management and labor on how work is organized in terms of time, workload, demand, stress, and variability. Trade unions or workplace representatives, such as work councilors, are geared to handle these negotiations on behalf of the workers. *Therefore, workers should be more empowered in a workplace where a trade union is present than in a workplace where no collective organization is available.* Moreover, if workers themselves are members of a trade union and participate in its activities, they should be more capable to advance their interests than those without such a collective engagement. *Therefore, workers belonging to a trade union should be more empowered in a workplace than workers without such collective organizational ties.*

The presence of a trade union at the workplace has been ascertained by the question: "Is there a trade union or a similar organization at your workplace?", with yes coded as a dummy variable of *trade union at work place*. The membership has been ascertained in the inventory on civic involvement mentioned above. Belonging to any of two *professional associations*—trade unions and business/professional/farmers associations—was coded as a dummy variable of *professional-belonging*.

Workplace
Independent from the choice between individual or collective strategies, *conditions of the workplace* may restrict or widen the range of options at the workplace. They are allocated regarding the goals and the techniques of the production of the firm.

Firstly, the more people that work together in a firm, the stronger the bureaucratic regulation of the workplace and the less the impact a single worker will have on the functioning of the environment—with everything else being equal. *Therefore, the size of the workplace should decrease empowerment.* It was ascertained by the following question: "Including yourself, about how many people are employed at your workplace;

under 10, 10–24, 25–99, 100–499, or 500 or more?", treated as a metric variable of *firm size*.

Secondly, the function of the firm shapes, to a large degree, the kind of work employed there, and this influences the management-labor relations. It is analyzed in three dimensions. (1) If *services* are produced or if the work consists of the handling of symbols, that is, of data or texts, there is more leeway for arrangements between workers and within the tasks for each worker. While in industrial production firms hierarchical management-labor relations empower only those at higher levels in the hierarchy, workers in service jobs, particularly amongst the professions, are more autonomous in their work organizations. (2) In the *public sector*, with its bureaucratic regulation, the individual strategy is difficult to enact. (3) In the *exposed sector*, that is, sectors with marketable goods or services that are subject to international competition, workers will more likely be under tight control by the management. *Therefore, (1) workers in service firms should have more empowerment than in non-service firms, (2) workers in the public sector should have less than in the private sector, and (3) workers in the exposed sector less than in the non-exposed sectors.*

The sector of the firm was ascertained by answers to the open question: "What does the firm/organization you work for mainly make or do?", which were coded into 95 codes. We recoded sectors with high public employment or high state regulation as *public* (public administration, education, health and social services; transport sector; public utilities); and sectors that are under strong international competition, including manufacturing (but not construction) and finance (but not retail) as *exposed*.[2] Furthermore, classes 2 to 6 of the Esping-Anderson 10 classes' scheme based on ISCO-codes by Leiulfsrud/Bison/Jensberg (2005), were recoded as *service*. These three dummy variables overlap. *Public* correlates r = −0.55 with *exposed* and r = .41 with Service; *exposed* and *service* correlate r = −.22.

Finally, gender (dummy for *male*) and *age* in years were controlled. With respect to empowerment at the work place, age has at least three understandings. Negatively, it may be understood as decreasing exit options; positively, it may indicate increasing work experience, which may be used to attain empowerment, through the accumulation of

---

[2] For Hungary, this variable was not available. Instead, the sector has been coded as *public* if it was a service sector, and as *exposed* if it was not.

entitlements regarding work conditions that are granted by certain age limits implemented by social policy regulations.

1.4 Hypotheses and measurements: Level of countries

Mean differences

The section of the social constitution of a country, which regulates labor relations, can be called the *labor relation system* (Ebbinghaus/Visser 2000). It can be understood in two dimensions. Relations are established either between *collectivities*—state, trade unions, and employer associations—or between *individuals*—employer and employee. In both cases, *normative* rules or *factual* opportunity structures may be more or less favorable to the unions. Looking at collectivities, rules that widen the range of workers covered by the bargaining process and a high degree of organization and public support, may favor unions. Looking at individuals, rules that favor employment and restrict dismissal, and a labor market situation with high employment and many secure work contracts, may favor unions.

From this, the *union efficiency hypothesis* results: *the more collective or individual labor relations of a country favor normatively, or strengthen factually, the unions, the higher the mean empowerment.* It predicts a positive effect of a labor relation system favoring unions on mean empowerment.

Slope differences

Just as workers may substitute individual and collective strategies in their personal endeavour to secure empowerment, the personal endeavor of either sort may be substituted by the collective action of workers' representations. The labor relation system provides a rule set and a power structure, which may exonerate workers from the personal endeavor to attain empowerment at the workplace. If the labor relation system provides ample avenues to foster empowerment and if unions are successful in their processes, workers are much less dependent on their own initiative. Instead, they can rely on bargaining institutions. This substitution should hold, in particular, for individual strategies. The more the labor relation system grants opportunities to attain and maintain empowerment, the less the workers are driven to use their firm-specific or personal human capital, that is, their power within the firm and their exit options outside the firm.

From this, the *substitution hypothesis* results: *the more the labor relation system of a country favors unions, the less important individual strategies become for*

Table 1: Variables of the labor relation system

	Normative	Factual
Collective	Bargaining Coverage	**Mean Union Membership**
		Union Presence at Work Place
Individual	Employment Protection Legislation	Percent Temporary Work Contracts
		Income Inequality

the worker in order to attain empowerment. It predicts a negative cross-level interaction effect between a labor relation system favorable to the unions and the persons' individual strategies to attain empowerment.

Classification and selection

Six variables of the labor relation system were taken partly from an updated version of the data presented in Ebbinghaus/Visser (2000), and partly from the ESS. Their position in the two above dimensions is given in Table 1, their values, intercorrelations and sources are given in the appendix.[3]

If empowerment was regressed on these variables, only *mean union membership* and *percentage temporary work contracts* showed steeper slopes (4.29, 2.94) and R^2 values beyond .20 (.64, .57). Moreover, *mean union membership* and *percent temporary work contracts* correlated strongly (r = .77). Therefore, only *mean union membership* could be taken as an indicator of a labor relations system favorable to empowerment at the workplace.[4]

2. Results: Level of persons

In order to compare the impact of civic engagement with the more immediate personal factors of empowerment at the workplace, three regressions have been computed: on civic involvement, on this and personal factors, and on these and control variables additionally. The results are presented in Table 2.

---

[3] I am grateful to Bernhard Ebbinghaus for providing the data and calculating regressions and correlations on the country level, given in this section and in the appendix.

[4] Other inventories did not provide data for the complete ESS countries. Kenworthy (2000) covers only 11 countries. As far as these countries are concerned, the indicators overlap with mean union membership. Tangian (2005) provides indicators mainly for subjective assessments of the work situation and the EU-15 countries only.

Table 2: Regression of Empowerment at the Work Place on Civic Involvement, Work Involvement and Socio-demographic Control Variables: Employees of 19 European countries, weighted to be equal

Variables (categories)	M	SD	Civic Involv B	+ Person B	+ Contrl B	− not sign. B	Beta
Intercept			4.812	2.772	2.003	1.827	
Civic Involvement							
Private-Belonging	.56		.971	.382	.383	.398	.077
Private-Engagement	.22		.500	.244	.245	.233	.041
Firm-Specific Human Capital							
People Supervised (5)	.66	1.14		.452	.434	.434	.201
Prestige (b for 10 scores)	42.2	13.6		.305	.282	.280	.156
Working Hours (5)	2.99	1.01		−.108	−.076		−.031
Personal Human Capital							
Political Efficacy (5)	2.83	0.87		.125	.126	.120	.042
Education (7)	3.32	1.40		.077	.097	.094	.055
Exit Option (11)	3.50	2.56		.261	.275	.275	.285
Partner employed	.53				.166	.160	.034
Collective Strategy							
Trade Union at Workplace	.59			(−.074)	(−.099)		(−.027)
Professional-Belonging	.44			.238	.182	*.119*	.037
Workplace							
Firm size (5)	2.81	1.63		−.178	−.170	−.190	−.094
Service	.42			.191	.168	.132	.034
Public	.39			(−.072)	*−.158*		−.03
Exposed	.33			(.091)	(.060)		(.01
Control Variables							
Male	.52				−.177	−.176	−.036
Age (b for 10 years)	39.8	11.5			.185	.179	.08
R²			.057	.269	.278	.278	

Valid n = 15336, 81,7% of the unweighted total sample. Weighted to equal number of employee every country Coefficients not significant at 0.01% level in italics, coefficients not significant at 0.1% level in brackets. Dummy variables: no standard deviation.

As the *first regression* shows, belonging to and engagement in private associations together increase empowerment at the workplace, one and a half scale points. However, when, in the *second regression*, work characteristics are included, this effect is reduced to a half scale point. Of the more immediate personal factors, individual strategies take the lion's share of the impact of the effect on empowerment, while collective strategies and the workplace context are negligible. Of the individual strategies, furthermore, the firm-specific human capital has the strongest impact—in particular the worker's position in the firm: *people supervised* and *prestige*. Of the variables pertaining to personal human capital, *exit option* only has a stronger impact. Of the work context, *firm size* has a rather strong negative impact. This picture does not change if, in the *third regression, gender* and *age* are controlled. Men depict themselves as less empowered than women. Age increases empowerment. Of the three meanings of age, only the two positive ones fit: age means either increasing work experience or the accumulation of entitlements.

The *standardized* coefficients of the *third* regression given in the last column allow the comparison between the variables independently of their measurement scales. The strongest predictor of empowerment is the *exit option*, it is followed by the two indicators of the worker' position in the firm. According to this rank order, then, empowerment at the work place is the payoff from the worker's position in the firm and his or her alternatives outside the firm. It is by and large independent of the attachment of the worker to the firm, the collective strategy, and the work context. Empowerment depends on qualities of the worker inside and outside the firm—it results only weakly from collective action and mirrors only dimly the context of work. On the level of persons, individual strategies clearly overcome collective ones as a means to empowerment at the workplace.

If one overlooks the three models, the *transfer hypothesis* is confirmed. It retains its impact on empowerment at the workplace even if more immediate personal factors are controlled for. Furthermore, its effects are stronger than many effects of the more immediate personal factors. In particular, belonging to and engagement in private associations has more impact than belonging to trade unions or professional associations. In line with our reasoning in the introduction, the articulation of one's interest in the *private realm* is more easily transformed into empowerment at the workplace than in the *public realm* of large-scale social organizations of work. Paradoxically, the more distant route is the more effective one. Obviously, longer distances are needed in order to acquire the general capacities of self-assertion, which are useful in many arenas, while focusing on the very arena of interest narrows down the opportunities to learn the general capacities. Longer distances provide more challenges to generalize. Therefore, qualifications of goal-directed civic action are more easily acquired in the foreign than in the domestic arena, and the foreign experience is more successful at home than in the domestic arena.

As for the other hypotheses, they are almost always confirmed, yet there are two unexpected negative effects: *working hours* and *trade union at workplace* decrease, rather than increase empowerment. These two variables will not be included in the person-level regression of the following multilevel analysis—together with the two variables, which had no significant effects: *public* and *exposed*. For purposes of comparison with the following multi-level analyses, raw regression coefficients of a fourth regression with the remaining predictors are given in the second last column. There are only marginal differences between this and the third regression.

3. Results: Level of Persons and Countries

The multi-level regressions of empowerment on person and country variables are presented in Table 3;[5] in contrast to the regressions of Table 2, the person-level variables are now centered around the grand mean so that the intercept is the value for a person with the total sample mean on each predictor variable, that is, for the "average European".

The so-called empty model (Snijders/Bosker 1999: 45–47) *in the first column*, which estimates how much variance is due to persons and to countries without predictors on either level, serves as a base line. As its Intra-Class-Correlation—the quotient of the country-level variance over the sum of the person and country-level variance (Snijders/Bosker 1999: 16–21)—shows, 11% of the total variance is due to country differences, just more than the conventional limit of 10% to make the multi-level-analysis of country means worthwhile.

The so-called random intercept model (Snijders/Bosker 1999: 38–41) *in the second column* differs from the models in Table 2, by introducing an error term for each country. It estimates how much variance remains on the person and on the country-level after controlling for the person variables and examines whether country can be ignored as a predictor. As the comparison of the variance components show and the corresponding R^2-values—computed as variance reduction relative to the

---

[5] HLM2 6.0 was used for computation (Raudenbush et al. 2004).

empty model (Hox 2002: 63–71)—state explicitly, the person variables reduce the error variance on the person-level strongly. However, they even more strongly reduce the error variance of the countries—in other words, much of the country differences, more than half, are due to the different composition of the country populations. Ignoring countries is a misspecification: countries differ not only—as the empty model has shown—according to the mean of the dependent variable but also according to the mean of the independent variables, the effects of which are erroneously attributed to persons. *At least some* independent variables have a low dispersion within countries and different means between countries. To find out *which*, the regression coefficients must be compared between the person level and the country level, that is, between the second last column of Table 2 and the random intercept model in Table 3. Indeed, four regression coefficients change: *service* and *male*, *professional-belonging* and *private-belonging*. Thus, while the interpretations of the effects of the remaining coefficients can be upheld, the effects of these four have to be discussed.

The coefficients of *service* and *male* are reduced so that they lose significance but they do not switch signs. The reduction points to country level correlations no longer attributed to persons once the country means are controlled for. Thus, countries with a higher proportion of workplaces in the service sector have a higher mean empowerment independently of the fact that within countries, employees in service industries have better opportunities for empowerment than other employees. Similarly, countries with a larger share of women in the work force have a higher mean of empowerment independently of the fact that within countries women are better off at the workplace than men. In both cases, taking the corresponding country level effect into account weakens the person level effect.

Professional-belonging has a positive regression coefficient when countries are not controlled (.119), and a negative regression coefficient when countries are controlled (−.203). The positive impact of belonging to a trade union does not represent a transfer of belonging into empowerment on the level of the worker, but results from the fact that countries with a high percentage of belonging have a high mean empowerment. Between 19 countries, there is an impressive regression coefficient (significant below the 0,1% level) of *mean* empowerment on *the percentage* belonging of 2.89. Between 15,536 workers the regression

Table 3: Multi-Level-Regression of Empowerment on Person and Country Variables: Raw Coefficients

Variables (Categories)	Empty	Random Intercept	Intercept Outcome	Intercept+ 2 Slopes	Intercept+ 1 Slope
Intercept					
Mean Intercept	5.233	5.406	5.472	5.509	5.512
Union Membership mean			.019***	.019***	.019***
Civic Involvement					
Private-Belonging		.242	.240	.227	.233
Private-Engagement		.207	.205	.203	.203
Firm-Specific Human Capital					
People Supervised (5)		.445	.445	.456	.445
P Superv * UM mean (*100)				−.298*	
Prestige (*10)		.282	.284	.283	.283
Individual Strategy: Personal Human Capital					
Political Efficacy (5)		.143	.143	.144	.143
Education (7)		.139	.137	.132	.134
Exit Option (11)		.213	.213	.216	.217
Exit Option * UM mean				−.174*	−.198*
Partner Employed		.124	.123	.126	.124
Collective Strategy					
Professional-Belonging		−.203	−.210	−.207	−.205
Workplace					
Firm size (5)		−.191	−.191	−.192	−.189
Sector: Service		(.064)	(.065)	(.063)	(.063)
Control Variables					
Male		(−.125)	(−.125)	(−.128)	(−.128)
Age (b for 10 years)		.160	.160	.160	.160
Variance Components					
Person-Level	5.047	3.809	3.810	3.774	3.784
Country-Level: Intercepts	.616	.285	.129	.111	.114
Slope1: P Supervised (*100)				.689	
Slope2: Exit Option (*100)				.331	.332
Intercept*Slope1-Correlation				−.760	
Intercept*Slope2-Correlation				−.383	−.416
Slope1*Slope2-Correlation				−.187	
Intra-Class-Correlation	.1094	.0696	0.033		
R^2 Persons		.245	.245	.252	.250
R^2 Countries		.538	.791	.819	.815
Deviance	69411	60383	60380	60295	6031
Df (Deviance)		2	2	2	7
N of persons	15333			14429	

Valid n = 15336, 81,7% of the unweighted total sample. Weighted to equal number of employe every country. RML estimation. All independent variables grand mean centered.—Significance Le *Person-level coefficients:* italics = not significant at 0,01% level, in bracket = not significant at 0,1% le *Country-level coefficients*: *** p < .001, ** p > .01, *p > .05. *Variance components*: all coefficients signifi at 0,01% level.

coefficient of empowerment on belonging to professional associations alone is .686 (which is comparable to the effects in the first regression of Table 2 and is highly significant). Within countries of roughly 800 respondents, however, the regression coefficients are smaller and even negative; the mean of the 19 within country regression coefficients is .169 with a range from −.382 to .943 and a standard deviation of .231. Clearly, ignoring countries misrepresents the person level relationship The genuinely person level effect of belonging on empowerment is—contrary to our hypothesis—not positive, but negative. It is tempting to interpret this result by changing the causal perspective. Maybe, those who do not experience empowerment at their workplace resort to membership in professional associations.

Private-belonging has a strong positive regression coefficient when countries are not controlled (.398), and a weak positive regression coefficient when countries are controlled (.242). Here, the same logic applies—but within the range of positive coefficients only. Between countries, there is a strong regression coefficient of mean empowerment on the percentage belonging of 2.69. Between workers, the regression coefficient of empowerment on belonging to private associations alone is 1.109. Within countries, however, the mean of the 19 within country regression coefficient is .797 with a range from .350 to 1.838 and a standard deviation of .338. Ignoring countries does not misrepresent the sign of person-level relationship, but it overestimates its strength. The genuine impact of a person's belonging is smaller as it seemed to be, but still positive and significant—as expected.

Taking countries into account, then, does not disconfirm, but rather reinforces the transfer hypothesis. In comparison to belonging to professional associations, belonging to private associations still has a stronger impact on empowerment at the workplace.

In the random intercept model, there remains still a highly significant variance of the intercept over countries; also, the Intra-Class-Correlation is still substantive. Therefore, it is worthwhile to test the *union efficiency hypothesis* in a so-called intercept as outcome model (Snijders/Bosker 1999: 73). It predicts the intercept by *mean union membership*, which has a mean of 36.5% over all 19 countries, and ranges from 14.6% in Portugal to 84.4% in Denmark with a standard deviation of 22.2% (see appendix). The results presented *in the third column* confirm the union efficiency hypothesis. The coefficient for mean union membership of .019 is highly significant: A country 25 percentage points above the grand mean has a predicted intercept of 5.472 + 0.019*25 = 5.947;

the mean for this country is heightened half a point on the 11 point scale of empowerment. On the country level, then, *mean union membership* has a fairly strong positive effect on empowerment, while within countries membership in professional associations goes together with low empowerment. Where professional organizations are strong, they are able to establish normative rules and to create a power balance in favor of higher empowerment at the workplace. Nevertheless, irrespective of how strong professional organizations are at the country level, it is the less privileged who seek support of professional organization in order to improve their workplace conditions.

Just as the union efficiency hypothesis presupposes that intercepts vary significantly over countries, the *substitution hypothesis* presupposes that slopes of individual strategy variables vary significantly over countries. To examine this, so-called random slope models (Snijders/Bosker 1999: 67–72) were applied to those individual strategy variables with the greatest standard regression coefficients (see Table 2), namely *people supervised* and *exit option*. The results are not presented in the table but they showed that both slopes indeed vary significantly.

Therefore, it is worthwhile to test the substitution hypothesis with a so-called slope as outcome model (Snijders/Bosker 1999: 62–80), which predicts the slopes of *people supervised* and *exit option* by *mean union membership*. It is presented *in the fourth column*. In comparison with a model with two random slopes, it reduces the slope variances by 30.2% for *people supervised* and by 25.0% for *exit option*. Moreover, the substitution hypothesis is confirmed. The predicted negative cross-level interaction effects are significant at a level below 5% and quite strong. If *mean union membership* is high, employees are less inclined to resort to the two individual strategies. In a country 25 percentage points above the mean, the slope for *people supervised* is .456 + (−.00298*25) = .382; and for *exit option* .216 + (−.00174*25) = .172. In other words, the frame of collective empowerment granted by trade unions obliterates individual strategies to attain empowerment.

In this model, however, the slope for *people supervised* correlates strongly negatively (r = −.760) with the intercept although all independent variables have been grand mean centered to prevent this (Snijders/Bosker 1999: 68–72). The indicators for our two country level hypotheses, union efficiency and substitution, strongly overlap. In order to examine them more independently, a model without the interaction effect between *people supervised* and *mean union membership* is presented *in the fifth column*. It reduces the variance of the random slope by 31.8%. It fares only slightly less well than the model with two interactions, according to R^2-values and the deviance, and it uses less degrees of freedom. It has a stronger and more significant interaction effect: in a country 25 percentage points above the mean, the slope for exit option is .217 + (−.00198*25) = .167.

In none of the three models with country level predictors, person level regression coefficients differ from the random intercept model without country level predictors. Thus, the hypotheses are confirmed for the remaining person level variables. In particular, the transfer hypothesis stands firm: civic involvement in private associations has a stronger *positive* impact on empowerment at the workplace than involvement in professional associations, even if more immediate person level determinants are controlled for and the differences between countries in labor relation systems are taken account of.

4. Conclusion

Many political scientists have suggested a transfer from civic engagement to political action and, ultimately, the stability of democracy (e.g. Norris 2002: 153–167). We have examined the transfer from civic engagement to empowerment at the workplace and, ultimately, the legitimacy of the market economy. As it has turned out, civic engagement does indeed increase empowerment at the workplace—net of the effects of the worker's human capital and workplace and the country's labor relation system. The transfer is not strong, as was to be expected taking its distance into account. However, it is stronger than the short distance transfer within the work sphere. Possibly, a transfer requires *some* distance in order to elicit the generalizations needed to make experiences fruitful in foreign surroundings.

Beyond the effects of civic engagement, we have examined the efficiency of different strategies to obtain empowerment at the workplace. The individual strategy relies on personal qualities, the collective strategy on the person's decision to participate in associations geared to improve empowerment; moreover, the successes of the collective strategy are reflected in a country's labor relation system, which grants more or less empowerment collectively. The individual and the collective strategy may substitute each other and we have looked at this substitution on two levels.

On the level of persons, only the individual strategy—firm-specific and personal human capital—is productive, while the collective strategy—membership in professional organizations—is counter-productive. The former have a strong positive, the latter has a *negative* effect on empowerment at the workplace. In line with our reasoning in the introduction, involvement in private arenas is more easily transformed into empowerment at the workplace than belonging to interest groups acting within large-scale social organizations. Possibly, persons choose the collective strategy not in order to attain empowerment, but because they could not attain empowerment via the individual strategy.

On the level of countries, labor relations favorable to unions—as measured by mean membership—heightened mean empowerment so that unions are effective in furthering empowerment. However, there was also a substitution of the collective strategy of unions and the individual strategy of workers. The more unions grant a legal and political frame in favor of empowerment the less the workers apply, or need, individual strategies.

In sum, the picture is somewhat ambivalent. On the person level, workers must and do rely on their personal qualities in order to attain empowerment, and resort to collective avenues only if personal qualities have failed. On the country level, unions are the more successful to grant empowerment the more powerful they are in the labor relation system, that is, the better they have organized their constituency. One may ask how a collective strategy of unions towards empowerment at the workplace can be sustained if personal union membership does not keep its promises. How shall unions fight for labor conditions if the employee's calculus does not motivate towards participation? How shall unions act if their very success on the country-level thwarts their endeavors to recruit members from their basis?

References

Anheier, Helmut K./Salamon, Lester M. (2001): Volunteering in cross-national perspective: Initial comparisons. *Civil society Working Paper 10. Available from the Center for Civil Society Studies at the Institute for Policy Studies at the Johns Hopkins University.*
Curtis, James E./Baer, Douglas E./Grabb, Edward G. (2001): Nations of Joiners: Explaining Voluntary Association Membership in Democratic Societies. *American Sociological Review* 66: 783–805.

Doeringer, Peter B./Piore, Michael J. (1971): Internal Labour Markets and Manpower Analysis. Lexington, MA: D.C. Heath.
Ebbinghaus, Bernhard/Visser, Jelle (2000): Trade Unions in Western Europe since 1945. London: Macmillan.
Gabriel, Oscar W./Kunz, Volker/Roßteutscher, Sigrid/van Deth, Jan W. (2002): Sozialkapital und Demokratie. Zivilgesellschaftliche Ressourcen im Vergleich. Wien: WUV-Universitätsverlag.
Hox, Joop (2002): Multilevel Analysis. Techniques and Applications. Mahwah, NJ: Erlbaum.
Janoski, Thomas (1998): Citizenship and civil society. A framework of rights and obligations in liberal, traditional, and social democratic regimes. Cambridge: Cambridge University Press.
Kenworthy, Lane (2000): Quantitative Indicators of Corporatism: A Survey and Assessment. Max-Planck-Institut für Gesellschaftsforschung. MPIfG Discussion Paper 00/4.
Leiulfsrud, Hakon/Bison, Ivano/Jensberg, Heidi (2005): Social Class in Europe. www.europeansocialsurvey.org.
Lowe, G./Schellenberg, G. (2001): What's a good job? The importance of Employment Relationships, Canadian Policy Research Network. Ottawa: Renouf Publishing Company. www.cprn.com/en/doc.cfm?doc=50.
Meulemann, Heiner (2006): Empowerment the work place—An analysis of a measurement instrument used in the European Social Survey 2002. Paper prepared for the session on the quality of measure of the ESS at the EAM conference in Budapest July 2006.
Offe, Claus/Wiesenthal, Helmut (1980): Two Logics of Collective Action: Theoretical Notes on Social Class and Organizational Form. *Political Power and Social Theory* 1: 67–115.
Norris, Pippa (2002): Democratic Phoenix: Reinventing Political Activism. Cambridge, UK: Cambridge University Press.
Raudenbush, Stephen W./Bryk, Anthony S./Cheong, Yuk Fai/Congdon, Richard T. (2004): HLM 6: Hierarchical and Nonlinear Modeling. Lincolnwood, Ill.: Scientific Software International.
Samuleson, Paul A./Nordhaus, Willian D. (2005): Economics. Eighteenth Edition. Boston: etc.: Mac Graw Hill.
Schofer, Evan/Fourcade-Gourinchas, Marion (2001): The structural Contexts of Civic Engagement: Voluntary Association Membership in Comparative Perspective. *American Sociological Review* 66: 806–828.
Snijders, Tom/Bosker, Roel (1999): Multilevel Analysis. London etc.: Sage.
Tangian, Andranik S. (2005): Ein zusammengesetzter Indikator der Arbeitsbedingungen in der EU-15 für Politik-Monitoring und analytische Zwecke. WSI in der Hans-Böckler Stiftung, Düsseldorf: Diskussionspapier Nr. 135.
Warren, Mark E. (2001): Democracy and Association. Princeton University Press: Princeton—Oxford.

Appendix: Variables of the Labor Relation System

	Country	Collective Regulation			Individual Regulation		
		A1 Coverage	A2 UM	A3 WRKPL	B1 EPL Sum	B2 WRKCTR	B3 Q5/1 Income
AT	Austria	98	32.5	59.3	2.15	10.1	4.0
BE	Belgium	90	43.7	65.8	2.50	11.7	4.0
CH	Switzerland	40	22.0	42.4	1.60	10.6	4.1
CZ	Czech Republic	25	30.0	43.5	1.94	22.4	3.4
DE	Germany	67	20.7	49.9	2.47	11.6	4.3
DK	Denmark	83	84.4	67.0	1.83	14.4	3.6
ES	Spain	81	14.7	41.2	3.07	26.1	5.1
FI	Finland	67	74.8	81.0	2.12	17.1	3.6
FR	France	90	10.8	65.2	2.89	17.0	3.8
GB	United Kingdom	36	28.2	47.2	1.04	12.9	5.3
GR	Greece	70	19.6	43.4	2.90	19.2	6.6
HU	Hungary	34	17.3	42.8	1.75	11.4	3.3
IE	Ireland	66	37.0	52.8	1.32	18.8	5.1
IL	Israel		23.4	38.9		26.8	
IT	Italy	90	22.9	66.0	2.44	11.0	4.8
LU	Luxembourg	58	41.0	58.8	2.50	9.4	4.0
NL	Netherlands	88	29.6	64.7	2.27	14.1	4.0
NO	Norway	62	57.7	77.9	2.61	12.3	3.8
PL	Poland	40	14.7	43.6	2.14	26.8	5.0
PT	Portugal	87	14.6	34.4	3.52	18.2	7.4
SE	Sweden	90	77.1	85.8	2.62	13.5	3.3
SI	Slovenia	99	42.4	72.2	1.84	16.3	3.1
D-E	Germany East	55	20.1	45.9	2.5	15.0	4.3
D-W	Germany West	70	21.1	52.0	2.5	9.9	4.3

Correlation	Coverage	UM	WRKPL	EPL Sum	WRKCTR	Q5/Q1 Income
Coverage		0.2154	0.4974	0.4876	−0.1545	0.02
UM	0.2312		0.7650	−0.1820	−0.2516	−0.4⁞
WRKPL	0.5087	0.7707		0.0016	−0.3627	−0.6⁞
EPL Sum	0.4713	−0.1907	−0.0111		0.1973	0.3⁞
WRKCTR	−0.1500	−0.2456	−0.3539	0.1950		0.3⁞
Q5/Q1 Income	0.0259	−0.4763	−0.5927	0.3757	0.3343	

Upper part: with Germany; lower part: with separate data for West and East Germany.

Notes:
A1) Bargaining Coverage
% Employees covered by collective agreements; Greece, Italy: estimated.
Sources: OECD, Employment Outlook, Paris: OECD, 2004 (http://www.oecd.org); Traxler, Franz (2002), "Collective bargaining coverage and extension procedures", EIROnline: TN0212102S (http://www.eurofound.europa.eu/eiro/).

A2) UM
Current member of trade union or similar organization in % of all dependent employed or unemployed. Source: ESS1 Variable F28—MBTRU (Switzerland, Czech Republic: union density rate, EIROnline).

A3) WRKPL
Working in workplace with trade union presence (% employees). Source: ESS 2002.

B1) Employment Protection Legislation (EPL) Summary Index
Employment protection legislation Index (Summary of regular, temporary and collective dismissal rules); Luxembourg: EPL assumed to be same as Belgium; Slovenia estimated as average of Czech Republic and Hungary.
Source: OECD Employment Outlook, Paris: 2004 (http://www.oecd.org).

CONCLUSION

CHAPTER ELEVEN

THE EUROPEAN SOCIAL SURVEY—RETROSPECT
AND PROSPECT

Max Kaase

After seven years of preparation, the European Social Survey (ESS) went into the field in 21 European countries and in Israel, for the first time in 2002. The ESS is special in many ways, but mostly in the way that it is financed jointly by national research councils, which pay for the national surveys in the respective countries, the European Commission, which pays for the Central Coordinating Team, and the European Science Foundation (ESF), which pays for the cost of the meetings of the ESS' Scientific Advisory Board (SAB). This combination is truly unique, but with one pitfall; an issue of which I will elaborate upon shortly.

There is no question that the ESS initially would not have been possible without the interaction of many dedicated individuals and institutions in the ESF, which embraces, as members, national research councils, academies and similar organizations (such as the Max Planck Society) across Europe. It is not an overstatement to regard the ESF as the independent voice of science in Europe. Prepared by the ESF Standing Committee for the Social Sciences (SCSS) since 1995, the 1999 ESF publication "The European Social Survey (ESS)—a research instrument for the social sciences in Europe" paved the way for decisions to be taken in the various governing bodies of ESF to seek financial and scholarly support for the ESS from its member organizations. Considering that for Round 1 of the survey 22 countries decided to go along, is a success story in its own right alone.

The blueprint document had made it clear right from the beginning that the concept of the ESS would be realized only if it could develop into a longitudinal study to be conducted every second year for an extended period. Given the logic of how the national research councils and the European Commission operate, it has to be recognized that the element of longitudinality is a continuous challenge both for the ESS funders and for the parties involved in running the survey. What is equally remarkable, though, is the fact that it was also possible to convince the Directorate Research of the European Commission to get involved in the funding of the survey, an important facilitating condition for the participating ESF member organizations. It is therefore absolutely astonishing that at the time of writing of this chapter (early 2007), Round 3 of the survey (2006) had just come out of the field, and preparations for Round 4 were already going ahead.

A little stocktaking will show that by 2006, 32 countries had participated in the ESS at least once, and 17 of those in all three rounds. However, these figures highlight problems especially in the way the national surveys are funded. Despite a lot of effort by the ESF, it just cannot be taken for granted that all national research councils find themselves in a position to continuously grant funding. In order to improve this situation, the ESF, in the fall of 2006, implemented a *Memorandum of Understanding* among member organizations to ascertain ongoing funding for the national ESS surveys. The outcome of this initiative, though, is still not yet clear, and it is obvious that the variability in the participation of countries in the various ESS rounds will, in the long run, create a major problem for the ESS, which at this point in time is regarded by many scholars in terms of content, method, documentation, as well as easy data access, to be the best comparative survey to date. By now, the ESS has about 12,000 registered users from all parts of the world, from academia to business and administration, and about 6000 people who have downloaded the data from the first two rounds of the survey. (For detailed analyses on the basic concepts, challenges, and problems, as well as various substantive findings regarding the ESS see Jowell, Roberts, Fitzgerald and Eva (2007).)

1. THE LOGIC OF COMPARATIVE SURVEY RESEARCH

Already in 1950, Paul F. Lazarsfeld was concerned about the obligations of survey researchers for historians in light of the fact that surveys might, in the long run, become a new invaluable source of information for social science research. At that time, this seemed an immensely insightful, but not a very pertinent consideration given the fact that quantitative survey research was just being established. However, since the early sixties, Lazarsfeld's concern has made an impact with the establishment of data archives first in the USA, then in Europe and then in other parts of the world, and now one can rather speak of an abundance than a scarcity of survey data.

For comparative politics, the new methodology of survey research made its way into the comparative analysis of socio-political attitudes and behaviors, first with Almond and Verba's seminal *Civic Culture Study* (1963), followed by Verba, Nie and Kim's *Participation and Political Equality* (1978) and Barnes, Kaase and others' *Political Action* (1979. However, it was the book by Adam Przeworski and Henry Teune *The Logic of Comparative Social Inquiry* (1970), one of the very few comparative East-West survey studies of the time (The International Study of Values in Politics), that provided researchers with important theoretical underpinnings for the conduct of comparative research.

Przeworski and Teune developed the distinction between the "most similar" and the "most different" systems design, a guiding light in comparative social research still today. The logic of the most similar systems design is to compare countries, which are similar on many accounts, but different in some systemic macro properties, in order to assess the explanatory impact of such macro variables and to replace the proper names of countries by a value on one or more systemic variables. By contrast, the logic of the most different systems design is to compare countries, which vastly differ in macro properties, in order to test whether certain regularities in micro relationships would pertain despite large differences in macro variables.

Given the fact that the ESS covers only European countries, which share many properties of history and culture, one can deduce that the micro-macro analyses of this survey follow the logic of the most similar systems design. This type of analysis requires a substantial number of macro units (countries in the ESS case), and enough variation in theoretically pertinent properties of those macro units in order to make a micro-macro analysis meaningful, which aims at identifying an impact of systemic properties on individual attitudes and behaviors. To do just this has been a core interest in the preceding chapters of this book. Przeworski and Teune (1970, p. 46) have described this approach very succinctly. "In general, when a relationship between two variables is found to be the same across social systems, the number of systemic characteristics operating on the dependent variable is reduced. The systems factors, however, are not completely eliminated from explanation. If and only if initial variation of the dependent variable disappears when independent variables are adjusted in each system can systemic factors be completely disregarded. But, if at some stage of analysis systems do yield a gain in prediction, systemic factors must be considered."

For quite some time, micro-macro analyses had not found their way into the social sciences. This, however, has changed, not least because of the increasing availability of suitable data and an emerging agreement on the way to statistically conduct such analyses. It is a great asset that the chapters of this book systematically, in theory and in practice, approach the micro-macro problem and, in line with the above quotation, look at the amount of variance that exists after independent variables on the micro level have been permitted to explain all the variation between countries in the sample. Since, in line with the logic of the most similar systems design, the countries included are all European (except Israel, which is consequently eliminated from all the analyses), it therefore cannot come as a surprise that indeed a lot of the overall variation can be accounted for by micro variables. Still, there is enough variation left to justify the study of systemic factors; a core interest in micro-macro analysis. This has already been pointed out in the above-mentioned 1999 ESS blueprint as a major reason for getting the project off the ground (ESF, 1999: p. 15).

2. Origins and Consequences of Social Capital in Europe

All the chapters in this edited volume build on data from the first Round, in 2002, of the ESS and concentrate on a theoretical concept, which has become very much en vogue in the social sciences—social capital. As Meulemann points out in his introduction, some chapters in part one look at the determinants of social capital, while the chapters in part two look at the role social capital plays, either on the micro or on the macro level, for explaining certain individual attitudes and behaviors. These are worthwhile efforts indeed, as they systematically analyze social capital in the context of a broad spectrum of democratically organized societies.

Most chapters rightfully refer to the seminal work by Robert Putnam (1993) "Making Democracy Work" and his conceptualization of social capital, which introduced the idea into the international scholarly debate. This concept has undoubtedly made major inroads into political science and sociology, as well as regarding reflections on the future of democracy. After the 1993 publication, the major thrust of follow-up analyses by Putnam and many others has come from secondary analyses of existing data sets and has, as of now, not resulted in agreed-upon operationalizations of social capital for empirical research, a fact that contributes very much to the ambiguity in many of the findings. Fortunately, the ESS includes a set of indicators, which can and have been used in various chapters to measure the concept.

"Despite its widespread attention, the concept of social capital is far from clear." (Halman and Luijkx, 2006: p. 65). The chapters in this book can clearly corroborate this assessment; social capital is operationalized not in a uniform way although this is probably too much to expect for an edited volume despite its common database. The core element shared in almost all analyses is social trust, which is part of the cultural elements of social capital, next to its structural component, associational integration. What makes these analyses especially interesting is the fact that they put indicators of social capital in competition with a broad set of other variables, "classical" variables, in an effort to explain variations in the various dependent variables under scrutiny in this book.

There is no point in repeating details of the various analyses. Rather, comments will be restricted to two general observations. Firstly, as was mentioned before, the amount of variation not explained by micro variables is not very high—around 10 percent on average. This, given the research design, cannot come as a surprise. However, what is worthwhile pointing out is that of the macro variables used in the various chapters, only a handful turned out to be of relevance. There can be many reasons for this outcome. If one looks at the chapters by Schmitt-Beck and by Roller and Rudi, on can detect the payoff of good macro reasoning. Thus, there is no reason for macro despair; in the future, as more micro-macro analyses can be conducted because of the availability of the appropriate data, surely many interesting research findings will emerge, pushing socio-political analysis into new, promising directions.

Secondly, social capital neither as a micro nor as a macro concept and neither as a dependent nor as an independent variable seems to fare well in competition with other, more established sets of variables. This finding should inject a new thrust into the ongoing discussion on the role of social capital in modern democracies. Moreover, as an extra benefit for political scientists, the finding by Roller and Rudi in their analysis of political participation in Europe, must be highlighted—that majoritarian electoral systems and majoritarian democracy seem to enhance political equality—a finding not at all in line with common political science wisdom.

3. Where Will the ESS Go?

As information on publications originating from the ESS is slowly coming in, it is already visible that the ESS will have an important impact on the state of the art of comparative survey research. The ESS is a multidimensional project indeed, with a lot of emphasis not only on the substantive data collected, but also on methodological innovations in the field. The options for multilevel analyses are exploited very well in this volume, and there is surely more to come in the future, as theorizing, especially regarding micro-macro level interactions, will further develop.

The ESS does not only have a large set of core questions repeated in every round, but also offers the option of competitive biddings from the European social science community for two modules of about 15 minutes each on varying topics in each round. It remains to be seen to what extent these options will also lead to innovative publications in these fields and will stimulate further research; this was another core interest when the ESS was planned.

Among those who have registered as users or have downloaded the data, one finds a large number of students at various levels: undergraduates, graduates and PhD students. This points not only to the future possible research impact of the project, but also to the option that the ESS will become an important teaching device in the social sciences. It is in the spirit of this consideration that the Norwegian Data Archive (NSD) not only perfectly documents the data and makes them ready for easy access, but has also developed, with EDUNET, a device based on ESS data meant to help in teaching comparative survey research.

In the future, apart from the problem of funding already discussed, two major challenges lie ahead. The first is a challenge for researchers. With a survey covering more than twenty countries, each researcher will have to design his or her special way, embedded in good theory, of how to deal with such a large number of countries. Certainly, in line with the Przeworski and Teune logic, the proper names of countries have to be replaced in data analysis by theoretically meaningful concepts; just to compare country marginals and describe the differences and the sameness between countries will not suffice. However, the situation will become vastly more complicated and challenging as more and more rounds of the ESS will become available, permitting not only structural, but also dynamic analyses.

The second problem relates to the mode of data collection. Up to this point, the Central Coordinating Team (CCT) and the Scientific Advisory Board (SAB) have stuck with their initial decision to rely exclusively on face-to-face personal interviewing. However, as telephone interviewing becomes even more widespread than it is today, completion rates for probability samples decline and sampling frames become ever more complicated through the spread of cellular phones and internet telephoning. The ESS will, in the not too distant future, have to confront the problem of whether to continue with its face-to-face interviewing approach, or to move on to mixed-mode interviewing (the CCT is already running such experiments), or whether it will even have to consider, some years from now, to move on to internet interviewing. These are not only technical matters, but such decisions will also be highly relevant for one major concern of the ESS, the longitudinal study of socio-political attitudes and behaviors, which has to be based on the equivalence of methods and measurements.

References

Almond, Gabriel A./Verba, Sidney (1963): The Civic Culture: Political Attitudes and Democracy in Five Nations, Princeton: Princeton University Press.
Barnes, Samuel H./Kaase, Max et al. (1979): Political Action: Mass Participation in Five Western Democracies, Beverly Hills: Sage Publications.
European Science Foundation (1999): The European Social Survey (ESS)—a research instrument for the social sciences in Europe, Strasbourg: European Science Foundation.
Jowell, Roger/Roberts, Caroline/Fitzgerald, Rory/Eva, Gillian (eds.) (2007): Measuring Attitudes Cross-Nationally: Lessons from the European Social Survey, London: Sage Publications.
Halman, Lock/Luijkx; Ruud (2006): Social capital in contemporary Europe: evidence from the European Social Survey. Portuguese Journal of Social Science 5: 65–89.
Lazarsfeld; Paul F. (1950): The Obligations of the 1050 Pollster to the 1984 Historian. The Public Opinion Quarterly 14: 617–638.
Przeworski, Adam/Teune, Henry (1970): The Logic of Collective Social Inquiry, New York. John Wiley.
Putnam, Robert D. (1993): Making Democracy Work: Civic Traditions in Modern Italy, Princeton: Princeton University Press.
Verba, Sidney/Nie, Norman H./Kim, Jae-On (1978): Participation and Political Equality, Cambridge: Cambridge University Press.

INDEX OF NAMES

Abramson, 224
Adam, 4 n. 3
Ajzen, 82
Allport, 129
Almond, 103, 118, 137 n. 4, 141 n. 6, 143, 144, 161, 191, 216, 229–230, 315
Altman, 42, 49
Andreß, 1 n. 1
Anheier, 8, 74, 285
Armingeon, 147 n. 9, 150, 247
Arnold, 165
Arts, 24 n. 15, 31 n. 21, 42, 45, 47, 68
Axelrod, 5, 10

Badescu, 104, 112
Baer, 47, 74, 81, 84, 86–87, 92 n. 9, 94 n. 10, 285
Bandelow, 119, 247
Banfield, 41
Barnes, 252–254, 262, 315
Barrata, 121
Barrett, 87 n. 6, 122, 249
Beck, 41
Becker, 6 n. 5, 200, 217
Beckers, 1 n. 1, 49, 50, 73 n. 1, 81–82, 83 n. 5, 101
Bell, 259
Belsley, 60 n. 5
Bengtson, 41
Bennett, 193 n. 4, 196, 216
Berelson, 191, 196, 216–217
Beyeler, 247
Bian, 42, 48
Billiet, 82
Bison, 292, 295
Boix, 120
Bollen, 54
Books, 167
Bornschier, 10 n. 8, 13, 15 n. 12, 25 n. 16, 105
Borre, 227–228
Bosker, 32, 34, 56, 127, 148, 148 n. 10, 300, 303–304
Bovenberg, 3
Bowlby, 41
Brady, 200, 218, 251, 263

Braithwaite, 103, 224, 226–227, 234
Brehm, 106, 110–111, 114, 120, 164–165, 173–174
Bryk, 91 n. 8
Bühlmann, 21 n. 13, 81–82, 84, 105, 108, 114–115, 117–120, 123, 126–128, 165, 239, 242
Bullen, 42
Burt, 6

Campbell, 196, 216
Careja, 147 n. 9, 150
Castells, 135
Chanley, 224, 227–228
Citrin, 241
Clay, 43
Cole, 224
Coleman, 103, 161, 167, 192 n. 2, 216, 230, 241
Congdon, 91 n. 8
Conover, 136 n. 3, 137, 137 n. 4, 141, 145
Cook, 104
Cortell, 43
Crewe, 136 n. 3, 137, 137 n. 4, 141, 145
Cullen, 42
Curtis, 47, 74, 81, 84, 86–87, 92 n. 9, 94 n. 10, 285

Dahl, 159, 251
Dalton, 196, 216
Davis, 51, 91 n. 7
Day, 252
de Graaf, 49, 51
de Hart, 165
de Leeuw, 56
Dekker, 3, 23 n. 14, 29 n. 19, 165
Delhey, 104, 108, 110, 112, 114, 121
Delli Carpini, 161–162, 194, 216
Denters, 13, 18, 35, 137 n. 4, 138, 142–146, 220–221, 223, 225–226, 228–229, 234, 239
Deutsch, 259
Dobbelaere, 96
Doeringer, 292
Durkheim, 13, 16

Eastis, 112
Ebbinghaus, 296–297, 297 n. 3
Elff, 193 n. 3, 195–197, 200, 206 n. 9, 208–209, 218
Eliasoph, 47–48
Erikson, 55 n. 4, 129
Erlinghagen, 76 n. 4
Esping-Andersen, 45, 53, 120
Esser, 6 n. 5, 7, 7 n. 6, 12, 192 n. 2, 211, 216, 253
Ester, 24 n. 15, 29 n. 19
European Commission, 313
European Science Foundation (ESF), 313
Eva, 314
Evans, 118, 126

Field, 4, 4 n. 3
Fine, 4 n. 3
Fishbein, 82
Fitzgerald, 314
Flap, 44, 50
Fourcade-Gourinchas, 74, 76 n. 4, 80–82, 84, 86–87, 285, 307
Frank, 21 n. 13
Franklin, 252, 259
Freitag, 21 n. 13, 42, 81–82, 84, 104–105, 108, 110–112, 114–115, 117–120, 123, 126–128, 142, 145–147, 165, 173, 239, 242
Friedman, 143
Fuchs, 253 n. 2, 263, 266 n. 5, 270, 283
Fukuyama, 41–42, 110–111, 122

Gabriel, 3, 8, 11 n. 9, 22, 34, 74, 78, 81, 104–109, 111–113, 115, 118–121, 128, 137 n. 4, 138, 142–146, 162, 164–165, 169–170, 173, 193 n. 4, 196, 201, 216–217, 220–221, 223, 225–230, 234, 239, 241, 252–253, 266 n. 5, 285
Gallagher, 270, 283
Galston, 136
Gambetta, 103
Gelissen, 35 n. 24, 42, 45, 49–51, 53, 68
Gerbner, 163
Glaeser, 106
Goel, 200, 217
Goldstein, 56
Goldthorpe, 55 n. 4
Goss, 76 n. 4
Gouldner, 11 n. 10

Grabb, 47, 74, 81, 84, 86–87, 92 n. 9, 94 n. 10, 285
Graeff, 73 n. 1
Gunsteren, 135
Guo, 271 n. 7
Gwartney, 86

Hadjar, 200, 217
Hall, 43
Halman, 12 n. 11, 35 n. 24, 47, 80–81, 83 n. 5, 84, 87, 90, 317
Halpern, 4 n. 3, 6 n. 5, 10, 11 n. 9, 12 n. 11, 41
Hardin, 103–104, 226
Harty, 43
Heitmeyer, 47
Heunks, 196, 217
Hochschild, 47
Holmberg, 241
Hooghe, 2 n. 2, 11 n. 10, 12 n. 11, 23 n. 14, 41, 165, 167, 173
Hoskin, 193 n. 4, 217
Howard, 136 n. 2, 145
Hox, 27, 123–124, 160, 179, 198, 217, 301
Huckfeld, 242, 258
Humphreys, 176

Iannaccone, 87 n. 6
IDEA, 270, 283
Inglehart, 54, 81, 98 n. 11, 105, 110, 115, 117, 122–123, 126–128, 161, 196, 217, 224
Ingram, 43
Isin, 135
Ismayr, 119, 247

Jagodzinski, 96
Janoski, 76 n. 4, 92 n. 9, 290
Janssen, 41, 50–51
Jarren, 184
Jennings, 137 n. 4
Jensberg, 292, 295
Jones, 58, 252
Jowell, 314

Kaase, 196, 217, 229, 252–254, 262, 313, 315
Kaufmann, 120, 247
Keefer, 11, 47, 121–122
Keele, 106
Keeter, 194, 216
Kenworthy, 297 n. 4
Kepplinger, 159

INDEX OF NAMES

Kim, 252–254, 315
Kiyonari, 10
Klein, 252, 271 n. 6
Klingemann, 172, 196, 217
Knack, 11, 47, 121–122
Komter, 44, 46, 50
Kraay, 247
Krasner, 43
Kreft, 56
Kreuter, 76 n. 4
Kumlin, 118–120
Kunz, 83, 104–106, 108, 110–111, 113–115, 117, 117 n. 5, 122–123, 128, 220–221, 223, 225–227, 230, 234
Kymlicka, 135–136, 138 n. 5, 143–145

Laakso, 247, 270
Lam, 84, 90
Landry, 41
Lane, 161
Langer, 31, 193 n. 3, 209, 217
Lawson, 86
Lazarsfeld, 194, 216, 217, 314
Lecours, 43
Lee, 165–166
Leimgruber, 247
Leiulfsrud, 292, 295
Leonardi, 144
Letki, 118, 126
Levi, 42
Lijphart, 119, 146, 147 n. 9, 150–151, 231, 247, 253, 259–260, 270, 274, 278
Lim, 42
Lima, 29 n. 19
Lin, 4, 4 nn. 3–4, 7 n. 6, 42, 45, 47
Lipset, 231, 259
List, 76 n. 4
Listhaug, 221, 227–28
Lowe, 287
Luhmann, 16
Luijkx, 12 n. 11, 35 n. 24, 317
Luke, 160
Luks, 241
Lupia, 194, 217

Maas, 123
MacAllister, 227–228, 230
Maloney, 145
Mangen, 41
Marbach, 73 n. 1
Mars, 42, 49

Marsh, 196, 217
Maslow, 45–46
McCubbins, 194, 217
Mead, 82
Menegale, 247
Meulemann, 11, 13, 15–18, 22–23, 35, 73, 81–82, 83 n. 5, 101, 289–290, 316
Milbrath, 200, 217
Miller, 196, 216–217, 227–228
Mishler, 142, 145–146
Misztal, 103
Moerbeek, 42
Montero, 3, 4, 104, 225
Moy, 165
Moyser, 252
Muffels, 3
Muller, 118
Musick, 81, 83–84

Nanetti, 144
Neller, 1 n. 1, 13, 17–18, 24, 34–35, 112
Newton, 4, 4 n. 4, 12, 12 n. 11, 25 n. 16, 104, 108–110, 112, 114, 121, 173, 225–226
Nie, 252–254, 256, 315
Niemi, 137 n. 4
Nisbet, 45
Nordhaus, 307
Norman, 135–136, 138 n. 5
Norris, 81, 91 n. 7, 98 n. 11, 164–165, 169, 177, 219, 229–231, 241, 252, 259, 278, 305
North, 43
Norwegian Data Archive (NSD), 318
Novo, 29 n. 19

Offe, 104, 119, 288
Olson, 6
Onyx, 42
Ostrom, 104

Paldam, 4, 4 n. 3, 10, 12, 106, 257
Parboteeah, 42
Parry, 252
Parsons, 7, 74
Pattie, 200, 217, 226, 229, 252–253, 267
Paxton, 4, 11 n. 9, 12, 74, 87
Pericles, 191
Peters, 135
Petersen, 43
Pettersson, 12 n. 11, 80, 81, 83 n. 5, 84, 87, 90

Pfetsch, 166, 175
Pierre, 135
Piore, 292
Poortinga, 35 n. 24
Portacarero, 55 n. 4
Portes, 4, 4 n. 3, 11
Posner, 120
Prior, 138
Prysby, 167
Przeworski, 23, 33, 315, 318
Putnam, 4, 6 n. 5, 12, 23 n. 14, 41–42, 50–51, 76 n. 4, 101, 103, 109–113, 117, 121–123, 126, 144, 159–164, 166–168, 173, 176, 183–184, 219, 225–226, 230, 253, 255–257, 277, 316

Rae, 121
Rahn, 106, 110–111, 114, 120, 164–165, 173–174, 224, 227–228, 239, 242
Raudenbush, 91 n. 8
Reitsma, 81, 84, 90
Rhodes, 135
Roberts, 147 n. 9, 150
Robinson, 161
Rochon, 112
Roller, 22, 35, 252, 253 n. 2, 258, 270, 278, 317
Roncevis, 4 n. 3
Rory, 314
Rosar, 160, 179
Rose, 48–49, 137 n. 4, 142, 145–146, 177
Roßteutscher, 113, 137 n. 4, 138, 141 n. 6, 143, 220–221, 223, 225–227, 230, 234, 257
Rothstein, 108, 113–114, 118–120, 126
Rudi, 22, 35, 317
Rudolph, 224, 227–228, 239, 242
Ruiter, 51

Salamon, 8, 74, 76 n. 4, 87, 285
Sassen, 135
Scammell, 159
Scarbrough, 227–228
Scharpf, 43
Scheepers, 1 n. 1, 41–42, 45, 49–51, 68–69
Schellenberg, 287
Schlozman, 200, 218, 251
Schmitt-Beck, 16, 18, 105 n. 2, 112, 201, 317
Schmitz, 73 n. 1

Schneider, 165
Schofer, 74, 76 n. 4, 80–82, 84, 86–87, 285
Schulz, 174–175
Schwartz, 80
SCP, 53
Searing, 136 n. 3, 137, 137 n. 4, 141, 145
Seligman, 122
Seligson, 118
Seyd, 200, 217, 226, 229, 252–253
Shah, 164–165, 173–174
Shanks, 196, 217
Shils, 7, 74, 101
Sigel, 193 n. 4, 217
Skocpol, 42
Smidt, 81
Smith, 145
Snijders, 32, 34, 56, 127, 148, 148 n. 10, 300, 303–304
Sokolowski, 76 n. 4, 87
Sprague, 242, 258
Stahlberg, 137 n. 4
Steenbergen, 58, 252
Stewart, 138
Stoker, 145
Stolle, 2 n. 2, 11 n. 10, 12 n. 11, 23 n. 14, 41, 74, 108–109, 112–115, 118, 119, 121, 126, 129, 225
Svendsen, 257
Szreter, 42
Sztompka, 104, 122

Taagepera, 247, 270, 283
Tangian, 297 n. 4
Tarrow, 42
te Grotenhuis, 1 n. 1, 42, 45, 49–51, 68–69
Teune, 23, 33, 315, 318
Tocqueville, 45, 112, 161, 163–164, 166
Topf, 196, 217, 253
Torcal, 3, 4, 137 n. 4, 138, 142–146, 220–221, 223, 225–226, 228–229, 234, 239
Turner, 135
Tyler, 103

UNDP, 270, 283
Uslaner, 3, 6 n. 5, 10, 11 n. 9, 23 n. 14, 37, 42, 104, 110, 112, 115, 117, 120, 122, 126–127, 129, 165–166, 173–174, 201, 217, 224–226, 230–231

van den Broek, 3, 196, 217
van der Kolk, 13, 18, 35
van der Meer, 1 n. 1, 2 n. 2, 6 n. 5,
   17–18, 20, 31, 35, 42, 45, 50, 69
van Deth, 1 n. 1, 3, 4, 4 n. 4, 8, 12,
   12 n. 11, 20–22, 34–35, 74, 76 n. 4,
   103, 106, 169, 191, 192 n. 2, 193,
   193 nn. 3–4, 195–197, 200–202, 206
   n. 9, 208–209, 216–218, 220–221,
   223, 225–227, 230, 234, 257
van Kersbergen, 135
van Oorschot, 42, 45, 47, 68
van Waarden, 135
Verba, 103, 109, 118, 137 n. 4,
   141 n. 6, 143, 144, 161, 191, 200,
   216, 218, 229, 251–257, 263, 277,
   315
Vinken, 29 n. 19
Visser, 296–297
Volken, 10 n. 8, 13, 15 n. 12, 25 n. 16
Völkl, 266 n. 5
Vollebergh, 44, 46, 50
Voltmer, 172
von Barrata, 249

Walker, 104
Walsh, 138
Walter-Rogg, 11 n. 9, 22, 34
Warren, 6 n. 5, 74, 74 n. 2, 104,
   285
Weale, 138
Weber, 5, 6 n. 5, 13
Welkenhuysen-Gybels, 82
Wellman, 21 n. 13
Wessels, 76 n. 4, 252, 253 n. 2, 258,
   278
Whiteley, 29 n. 19, 200, 217, 226, 229,
   253, 257
Whitely, 12 n. 11, 252
Wiberg, 221
Wiesenthal, 288
Wilson, 76 n. 4, 81, 83–84

Yang, 7 n. 6, 10 n. 7

Zaller, 193 n. 4, 218
Zhao, 271 n. 7
Zmerli, 104, 225
Zoido-Lobatón, 247

INDEX OF SUBJECTS

achievement, 80
age, 109, 191, 200–201, 210
altruism, 80
analysis of variance, 27
association, 122, 127
association, civic, 8, 144, 147–149, 153
association, type of, 112, 117
association, voluntary, 162–165, 167–168, 170–171, 193, 201, 207, 209–211, 225
associational integration, 317
authority relations, 291

belonging, 77, 290, 294
benefits, 42, 44, 47–48
benevolence, 80

catholizism, 122
church attendance, 200, 205, 211, 214
church membership, 144, 154
civic mindedness, 219
civic norms and values, 201–202, 205, 207
civic rights, 135
civic society, 285
civic virtue and behavior, 225
civil liberties, 118
civil rights, 48, 54, 63, 66, 69–70
civil society, 2, 73–74, 78, 85, 99–100
cleavage, cultural, 121
climate of trust, 5, 10
cognitive involvement, 229
collective actors, 16
communal spirit, 219
community size, 113
compensation, 21
constitution, 1
contextual antecedents, 220
cooperation, 103
corruptability, 121
corruption, 48–49, 54, 63–64, 66, 69
cosmopolitanism, 111
crisis of confidence, 220
cross-level interaction, 19
crowding out thesis, 44–46, 63, 68
cultivation, 163
cultural approach, 42

data archives, 314
democracy, 43, 49, 51–52, 54, 63–64, 69, 118, 144–147, 151–152, 191, 200, 203, 251
democracy, consensus, 231, 259
democracy, majoritarian, 232, 259, 276
democracy, new, 177, 180–181
democracy, satisfaction with, 114
density of social relations, 9
discrimination, 114, 119
discussion of intimate matters, 51, 53, 56, 68
duration of residence, 113
dynamic analyses, 318

economic development, 47, 54, 63–64, 67, 69–70, 193, 204, 206–208, 210, 212–213, 215, 218
economy, 114
education, 109, 116, 127, 143, 147–149, 153–155, 191, 200–201, 205, 207–208, 211, 213–214
effectiveness, 121, 128
efficacy, 191, 200, 202–203, 205–206, 210, 210, n. 10, 214–215
efficiency, 119
electoral system, 259, 275
employer-employee relation, 287
employment, 145
engagement, 77, 290
engagement, political, 256
entertainment, 159–160, 164–167, 171–172, 175–177, 181, 183
equality, political, 251, 254, 257, 259–260, 262, 267, 269, 275, 278–279
equivalence of methods and measurements, 319
exit option, 293
exposed sector, 295

fairness, 120
family, 44, 49–50, 69
feelings of reciprocity, 225

GDP, 146, 150, 152–153
gender, 109, 191, 200–201, 214

generational, 143–144, 148, 153
good governance, 120, 123–124, 126, 128
government final consumption, 209
government receipts, 209

happiness, 110
hedonism, 80
help provision, 45, 50–51, 53, 56, 60, 63–70
home-team-hypothesis, 229
human capital, 84, 291, 292

ideological dispositions, 220
impartiality, 119–120
inclusiveness, 119, 128
income, 45, 54, 64, 83, 109, 200, 202
incorruptibility, 120
institutional approaches, 118
institutional integration, 220
institutional setting, 118, 126
institutionalism, 42–43, 67
institutions, political, 119, 251, 259–260, 274, 278–279
interdependency, 8
intimate relations, 6
involvement, associational, 112

justness, 120

labour relation system, 296, 305, 308
liberalism, 111
life satisfaction, 173–174, 179, 181

management-labor relations, 295
market economy, 305
media consumption, 199, 201–202, 207–208, 211, 214
media malaise, 160–162, 183
media, 111
membership, 112, 116–117, 127
minority, 114
mode of data collection, 319
modernization, socioeconomic, 251, 259, 274, 277–278
morality, 110

national research councils, 313
neighborhoods, 155
networks, 5, 8, 256, 260, 267
networks, social, 103, 113, 161–162, 166–167, 169–170

newspapers, 159–161, 163–166, 168, 172, 176–181, 183–184, 201–203
norms, political, 257, 260, 267

obligations, 135, 137–138, 144
opportunity structure, 13, 17, 20, 85–86, 92, 94–95, 99, 286, 296
organization, 4

participation, non-electoral, 252, 263, 266, 274, 278
participation, political, 251–252, 254
partisan affiliation, 220
party identification, 229
person-centered approaches, 116, 127
perturbation analysis, 60 n. 5
political efficacy, 224, 293
political responsiveness, 228
political setting, 118
political socialization, 224
political support, 229
politicization, 192, 205, 208–212, 214, 216
post-communism, 122, 124
postmaterialism, 115
press, 159–160, 166, 168, 176, 183–185
prestige, 292
professional status, 109
protestantism, 111, 122, 124, 127
public sector, 295
public security, 114, 119
public television, 166, 175–177, 180–181, 184–185

random sampling, 9
reciprocity, norms of, 103, 110, 161–163, 165–167, 169–170
reinforcement, 20
religion, 116, 122, 124
religiosity, 81
religious question, 76
resources, 109–120
resources, socioeconomic, 251, 256–257, 259
rights, political, 118

safe refuge thesis, 47–48, 68–69
saliency of politics, 194, 197, 201, 205, 212, 214
satisfaction, 110, 123, 199–200
self-determination, 76
self-enhancement, 80
self-transcendence, 80

service sector, 295
social context, 226
social differentiation, 16, 73
social disintegration, 219
social inequality, 120, 123–124, 126, 128
social integration, 229
social meetings, 50–51, 56, 60, 63–70
social network, 224
social order, 13, 17, 77, 85, 92, 94–95, 99
social participation, 225
social security, 44–46, 50, 53, 63, 66, 68–69
socialization, 115, 128, 143–145, 154
society-centered approaches, 116, 127
socio-cultural factors, 191
socio-demographic factors, 199, 201–202
socio-economic development, 121
socio-economic security thesis, 45–47, 69
solidarity, 41, 50, 53
state intervention, 193, 204–206, 208–211, 213, 215
state, 135–138, 145–146, 155
stimulation, 80
subjective norm, 82
subjective political interest, 194, 197, 200, 211

success, 109, 123
supervision, 291
systemic properties, 315

television, 80, 159–168, 171–172, 174–177, 179–181, 183–185, 201
trust, 82
trust, interpersonal, 142
trust, political, 114, 116, 118, 123, 126–128, 219, 221
trust, social, 103, 124, 127–129, 161–167, 169–171, 201, 207, 215, 219, 257, 260, 267, 317

union, 294, 296
urbanization, 113

validity of norms, 5, 11
voting, 251–252, 259, 263, 266, 271, 278
voting, compulsory, 259, 274, 278

welfare state, 118–120
well-being, 110, 116, 123, 126–128
workforce, 208
working hours, 292